Java EE 7:
The Big Picture

About the Author

Dr. Danny Coward is a Principal Architect at Oracle. Coward has been a contributor to all editions of the Java platform from Java ME to Java EE, and he founded the JavaFX project. A member of the first Java EE platform team at Sun Microsystems, he led the definition of a number of versions of the Java Servlet API and most recently led the definition of the Java WebSocket API for Java EE 7. He served as an executive member of the Java Community Process for several years, guiding the evolution of the expert groups that create new APIs for the Java platform in partnership with developers across a large number of companies and industry organizations. Dr. Coward holds a doctorate in Number Theory from the University of Oxford.

About the Technical Editor

John Yeary is a Principal Software Engineer on Epiphany CRM Marketing at Infor Global Solutions. John is a Java evangelist who has been working with Java since 1995. He is a technical blogger with a focus on Java Enterprise Edition technology, NetBeans, and GlassFish. John is currently the President of the Greenville Java Users Group (GreenJUG), as well as its founder. He is an instructor, mentor, and a prolific open source contributor.

John graduated from Maine Maritime Academy with a B.Sc. in Marine Engineering with a concentration in mathematics. He is a Merchant Marine officer, and has a number of licenses and certifications. When he is not doing Java and F/OSS projects, he likes to hike, sail, travel, and spend time with his family. John is also a Cubmaster in the Boy Scouts of America (BSA) Pack 833, Unit Commissioner, and Southbounder District Chairman for Activities and Civic Service in the Blue Ridge Council of the BSA.

Oracle Press™

Java EE 7:
The Big Picture

Dr. Danny Coward

New York   Chicago   San Francisco
Athens   London   Madrid   Mexico City
Milan   New Delhi   Singapore   Sydney   Toronto

Cataloging-in-Publication Data is on file with the Library of Congress

1234567890   DOC/DOC   10987654

ISBN   978-0-07-183734-7
MHID   0-07-183734-5

Sponsoring Editor Brandi Shailer	**Technical Editor** John Yeary	**Production Supervisor** George Anderson
Editorial Supervisor Patty Mon	**Copy Editor** Kristina Youso	**Composition** Cenveo Publisher Services
Project Manager Shruti Awasthi, Cenveo® Publisher Services	**Proofreader** Lisa McCoy	**Illustration** Cenveo Publisher Services
Acquisitions Coordinator Amanda Russell	**Indexer** James Minkin	**Art Director, Cover** Jeff Weeks

This book is dedicated to David, Olive, Matthew, Bill, Jared, and Alex.

Contents at a Glance

vii

PART IV
The Java EE Toolbox: Java EE Environment

Contents

PART II
The Brain of Java EE: The Middle Tier

PART III

The Collective Memory: The Information Tier

PART IV
The Java EE Toolbox: Java EE Environment

Introduction

As a relatively new employee of Sun Microsystems, in 1998 I found myself a member of a fledgling team called the Enterprise Java group. This was the heyday of interest in Java technology: APIs were being created for Java at a breakneck pace. Even the announcement of the creation of a new API for Java was headline news in the computing press, as though in the computing world it was only a matter of time before every idea, construct, and program would be expressed as a Java technology. Ideally, each technology would have a "J" in front of the name, as though each were part of a crowd of surfers barely ahead of the crest of a wave that was engulfing the programming world. Whether or not it made any business sense, developers declared they would convert programs, written in dull, corporate, unhip languages into Java, as if simply by doing so, they would automatically become better.

Complete with my Java Ring, an early wearable computer with 6KB of RAM and a JVM with the all-important coffee cup logo on it, I soon discovered that I was to work on a piece of software that would run Enterprise JavaBeans. At the time, this was considered a kind of server-side answer to the JavaBeans component model intended to be able to embed GUI components in IDEs, but suspected by some to be a new higher level of abstraction that would make object-oriented programming look like assembly language. For a year, distinguished engineer Vlada Matena had worked with Sun's key partners and competitors to create a server-side component that could run in a cosseted environment called a container within an application server, and rely on the container to abstract away some of the tricky and vendor-specific mechanisms for programming security, transactions, and thread management. The server-side component was called, of course, the EJB: Enterprise JavaBean. The new component model promised to revolutionize the world of enterprise middleware.

And what a dull and slow-moving world it was in the eyes of the web developer, whose often-renegade approach called for any tool to be picked up and used to great effect, whose rapid development cycles made the enterprise developers' eyes water. And who, furthermore, was starting to take a great interest in a technology that had been developed as part of the standard Java platform: Java servlets. The standard technique for processing information dynamically on a website at the time was CGI programming. Unfortunately for the web developer, CGI programs were rooted in the C programming language. The Java Servlet API offered a more interesting, more functional, and more fashionable approach to creating dynamic web sites that could process user input and requests and serve back interesting, context-based content tailored to the user. The servlet model allowed the creation of HTML pages within a Java component. This made for great flexibility, but for the web developer, well-versed in the nuances of HTML programming, led to lines and lines of HTML code trapped within Java statements, editable only within Java IDE rather than with the HTML editing tools with which they were already familiar. Already, other groups at Sun were starting to experiment with APIs that would allow a Java servlet–emitting HTML to be turned "inside out" so that the HTML code was outside the Java code instead of the other way around in a Java servlet. This, of course, led to the creation of JavaServer Pages, which provided a syntax and runtime environment in which Java code could be embedded within an HTML page directly. Thus, the power of the Java platform was brought directly into HTML pages, and into the hands of the renegade web developer. Dynamic content creation no longer needed to be the preserve of the nerd in the corner, limited to CGI bin scripts; instead, web developers had a doorway to the rich new world of the Java platform that they could open anywhere they needed in their web pages.

When it was proposed that these two technologies, the buttoned-up Enterprise JavaBeans and renegade Java servlets, should be brought together into one platform, suffice it to say that, given the vastly differing sensibilities of the enterprise and web developers at the time, many words (a good deal of which were quite heated) were exchanged in the meeting rooms and corridors of the JavaSoft building in Cupertino in the heart of Silicon Valley. But that was in fact what our group did, releasing after a very intense year and a half's work, the 1.0 version of the Java EE platform in December 1999 in New York.

Since that first release, the platform has become the foundation of server-side development for much of the corporate world, being adopted by and improved by industry heavyweights such as IBM and Oracle. My own contributions to the platform continued after the first release by leading various versions of the Java servlet specification, up to most recently leading the definition of the new Java WebSocket API for the most recent version of the platform. Over the course of the last 15 years, the Java EE platform has added a great number of features and adapted to a changing world of standards and technologies, some of which I was involved in and some of which I was not.

What this has meant is that the Java EE platform is far more relevant and useful as a computing platform today than it was 15 years ago. But it also bears the weight of a platform that has evolved as developers have been using it. It means that there is frequently more than one way to solve a problem in the platform, and there are several areas of functionality in the platform that have been superseded by superior frameworks and APIs that do the same jobs better and more easily.

In part because of this legacy and in part because of the sheer range of functionality encompassed in the platform, approaching the Java EE platform for the first time can be a daunting prospect. The reason I wrote this book was because I wanted to create something that cuts through the complexity of the platform, with all its myriad features and choices, by exploring as straightforwardly as possible the most important aspects of the platform. The task of producing an exhaustive survey of every feature of the platform I have left to other authors. In reading this book, you will understand the key component models and APIs that the platform has to offer, with enough context and some encouragement to explore the more specialized and less frequently used aspects of each component and API. I have chosen straightforward sample code in the chapters in a way that both illustrates how to use specific features of the platform, and that also indicates the class of real-world applications for which the features are intended to be used. I have also chosen sample applications to which the book returns chapter after chapter, to illustrate with a known application how an API or component model or technique can be applied naturally to improve or add functionality to an application.

Chapter 1: The Big Picture

This introductory chapter immediately presents a simple end-to-end Java EE application, running from the web tier through the Enterprise Bean and data tiers to introduce in overview form the whole Java EE platform at once.

Thereafter, the book is divided into four parts.

Part I: The Mouthpiece of Java EE: The Web Tier

This part covers the web technologies in the Java EE platform.

Chapter 2: Java Servlets and Web Applications: Foundations of the Web Tier

Here we introduce the Java servlet component model and API. This chapter is both an exploration of how to create a Java servlet application, and also an introduction to the fundamental ideas and objects of the Java web container, used by the other web technologies in the Java EE platform.

Chapter 3: Dynamic Web Pages: JSP

Chapter 3 explores JavaServer Pages (JSPs), starting with the idea of a JSP as an inside-out servlet, and examining tag libraries and JSP Expression Language, converting the main application encountered in Chapter 2 into a JSP application.

Chapter 4: Assembling Dynamic Web Pages: JavaServer Faces

In this chapter, we look at JavaServer Faces, which build on many of the ideas and mechanisms in both the Java servlet and JSP model, providing a syntax for quickly creating modular web applications with a high degree of separation between application logic and presentation code.

Chapter 5: Web Sites for Non-browsers: JAX-RS

Focusing on the RESTful web service APIs, JAX-RS, Chapter 5 explores the primary technology in the Java EE platform for exposing web application data and logic out to non-browser clients such as rich clients and other web applications.

Chapter 6: Adding Sparkle: Java WebSockets

One of the most recent additions to the Java EE web tier is the Java WebSocket API, introduced in Java EE version 7. Chapter 6 looks in some detail at how to create Java WebSocket endpoints, thereby allowing web applications to push application data at will to interested browser and non-browser clients.

Chapter 7: Securing Web Applications

This chapter looks in detail at the mechanisms available to the Java EE developer to secure a web application, using the built-in declarative model as well as the programming APIs in the web container controlling access to web components and resources.

Chapter 8: The Self-Contained Web Site: Java EE Web Applications

Here we look at how web applications are packaged and at some more advanced features of web applications such as servlet filters, web listeners, and asynchronous servlet execution.

Part II: The Brain of Java EE: The Middle Tier

Part II of the book covers Enterprise Beans, the essential component and container model of the middle tier of the Java EE platform.

Chapter 9: The Fundamentals of Enterprise Beans

In Chapter 9, we look at the most important features of the Enterprise Bean model; the different types of Enterprise Beans; their lifecycle; and how they are packaged, published, and located.

Chapter 10: Advanced Thinking with Enterprise Beans

With this grounding in Enterprise Beans, in Chapter 10, we explore more of the features of the model, such as concurrency, transactions, and the Timer Service.

Part III: The Collective Memory: The Information Tier

In Part III, the book turns to the data tier of the Java EE platform, which holds all the important data a Java application needs to use and store away.

Chapter 11: Classic Memories: JDBC

Starting with an examination of the Java Database Connectivity APIs, Chapter 11 looks at how to store and retrieve Java EE application data in a relational database and how best to manage the SQL code needed for such operations.

Chapter 12: Modern Memories: The Java Persistence API

Chapter 12 looks at the more streamlined approach offered by the Java Persistence API. I have included both modes of interacting with relational data from the Java EE platform, since JDBC is well established and SQL is a relatively well-known and well-understood language, while the Java Persistence API is the more modern and simpler approach.

Part IV: The Java EE Toolbox: The Java EE Environment

In the last part of the book, we look at some aspects of the Java EE platform that cut across more than one or even all the tiers of the platform.

Chapter 13: The Big Picture Revisited: Java EE Applications

Chapter 13 looks at the overall architecture of a Java EE application: its packaging format. With a small diversion into the Java EE application client, the chapter also looks at some well-known objects and services available to Java EE application components.

Chapter 14: Deconstructing Components: Java EE Contexts and Dependency Injection

In Chapter 14, we look at the powerful Context and Dependency Injection (CDI) framework, which offers a variety of techniques for modularizing a Java EE application into more reusable components called CDI beans.

Chapter 15: Java EE Security

We return to the topic of security in Chapter 15, looking at how to secure the Enterprise Bean layer of a Java EE application, and how the security models of the Enterprise Bean and web layers that Chapter 7 presented relate to each other.

Chapter 16: Many Hands Make Light Work: Java EE Concurrency

Finally, in Chapter 16, we look at another very recent addition to the Java EE platform: the Java Concurrency API. Focusing on how the API can support parallel execution of large, computer-intensive tasks, we see how this API can lead to useful performance gains in certain types of Java EE applications.

The most difficult thing about writing this book was deciding what to leave out. I hope you become a better Java EE programmer as a result of reading this book: I certainly became a better one by writing it.

Intended Audience

This book is suitable for developers new to the Java EE platform and with some familiarity with the Java EE platform alike. Readers need only have some prior knowledge of the Java language and some of the core standard APIs.

Retrieving the Examples

All the code and other files used in this book can be downloaded from the Oracle Press web site at www.OraclePressBooks.com. The files are contained in a zip file. Once you've downloaded the zip file, you need to extract its contents.

CHAPTER

1

The Big Picture

A familiar form in the realm of musical composition is that of theme and variations. A theme encapsulates a musical idea; the variations add to the basic structure that the theme establishes, adding new musical ideas, flourishes, and stylistic enhancements often yielding a more elaborate and complex result. The variations never alter the underlying theme on which they build. If you know the theme, you can always discern it in the variations; in the theme, you may see the possibilities for all the variations to come.

In the same way, this first chapter of *Java EE 7: The Big Picture* establishes a fundamental application that embodies all the core concepts of the Java Platform, Enterprise Edition (Java EE) platform. As you progress through the book and increase your understanding of the capabilities of the Java EE platform, you will see that every application you write will contain the core concepts established in this chapter. Every application that you write will be a variation of the basic application that this chapter introduces.

With the Java EE platform, you can develop and run a huge range of interesting applications. While powerful and flexible, the platform is also complicated. It has evolved over 15 years, adding numerous technologies, packages, classes, and methods. To the new and seasoned developer alike, the list of capabilities can be daunting and the collection of technologies intimidating. In particular, the Java EE platform contains technologies that, for some purposes, can perform the same or similar function.

This chapter examines an application that is familiar to most readers: HelloWorld.

Java EE Architecture

Before we dive into the application, we will start with a diagram of the Java EE platform, as shown in Figure 1-1.

In the diagram, we see that the large box, labeled Java EE, represents the Java EE platform. This refers to the runtime environment provided by a Java EE application server. All the Java EE code you write as a developer runs in this environment. A common term for this environment is the Java EE container, the word *container* derived from the idea that the environment envelops your application code. In technical terms, the concept of the container is a powerful one: in enveloping application code, the container can mediate or intercept calls to and from the application code, and insert other kinds of logic that qualify and modify the calls to and from the application code. A good example, which we shall see throughout the book, is the security services that the Java EE container provides: the Java EE container can enforce security rules on the application that is running, for example, a rule such as "only allow access from Mary and Ian to my application." The Java EE server container is itself made up of two other containers: the web container and the Enterprise JavaBeans (EJB) container. The web container is the part of the Java EE environment devoted to running the web components in a Java EE application: the web pages, Java servlets, and other Java EE web components that can interact with clients connecting to the Java EE application with standard web protocols. The EJB container is the part of the Java EE environment that is devoted to running the application logic part of the Java EE application. Enterprise JavaBeans are Java classes that contain and manipulate the core data structures of the Java EE application. Finally, the database tier of the Java EE platform holds all application data that the Java EE application needs to exist longer than the scope of a single session of the application, or simply between different steps in the application that are separated in time.

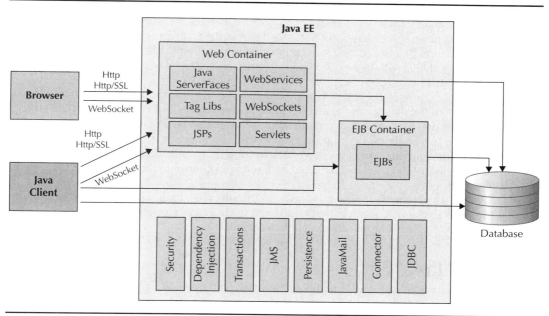

FIGURE 1-1. *Architecture of the Java EE platform*

The Java EE platform supports a wide variety of protocols that clients may use to interact with a Java EE application that it is running, the main client types being the browser client, which connects to the Java EE application using standard web protocols such as HTTP and WebSockets. Many Java EE applications have non-Java clients, perhaps a Java desktop application, or another Java EE application running on a different application server. This other client type can connect to a Java EE application running on the Java EE application server using standard web protocols, in addition to TCP-based protocols such as Remote Method Invocation (RMI).

The final part of the diagram is the boxes contained within the Java EE container box. These other boxes represent a variety of services that a Java EE application may choose to use. The security service enables a Java EE application to restrict access to its functions to only a certain set of known users. The dependency injection service enables a Java EE application to delegate the lifecycle management and discovery of some of its core components. The transaction service enables Java EE applications to define collections of methods that modify application data in such a way that either all the methods must complete successfully, or the whole set of method executions is rolled back as though nothing has ever happened. The Java Message Service (JMS) exposes a Java EE application to the ability to reliably send messages to other servers in the deployment environment of the Java EE application server. The Persistence service in the Java EE platform enables application data in the form of a Java object to be synchronized with its equivalent form in the tables of a relational database. The JavaMail service enables a Java EE application to send email, particularly useful in the kind of application that takes some action initiated by and on behalf of a user, and which needs to notify the user at some later time of the outcome of the action. The Java EE platform's main extensibility point comes with the Java EE Connector Architecture (JCA), which provides a framework into which a new service that is not a standard part of the Java EE platform may be added and that can then, in turn, be utilized by a Java application running in the platform. Finally, the Java Database Connectivity (JDBC) API supports traditional storage and retrieval of Java EE application data in a relational database using the SQL query language.

Some of these services and APIs will already be familiar to you. If others are not, then a key takeaway from the diagram is the architectural concept of the Java EE container, the web container, and the EJB container's ability to provide these services to a Java EE application. Sometimes, this requires the Java EE developer to use an API to utilize the service, but many times, by means of metadata, for example, a configuration XML file or a Java annotation embedded within the code, these services may be used and adjusted with minimal change to the basic application logic of the application.

Before we get too deep into this survey of the specific capabilities of the Java EE platform, let us turn now to the Java application that we will study in this chapter, and the one that forms a template for all Java EE applications: HelloWorld.

Hello Java EE

Many presentations, tutorials, and books devoted to technology begin with the example of the HelloWorld application. One reason is that the application is invariably a simple one. Another is that it is possible to copy this kind of application and use it as a starting point for building your own, because it already contains the basic setup tasks of any application. But more importantly, the HelloWorld example, if designed properly, connects all the major points of the technology that applications of the technology need to work together.

Running Hello Java EE

The Java EE HelloWorld application is a simple Java EE application. Let's examine what it does. When you first access the application, you access a Java servlet component that is part of the application from your browser, and you will see something like what is shown in Figure 1-2. When you enter a message, you will see what is shown in Figure 1-3, and when you press the Enter button, you will see the page change to the image shown in Figure 1-4.

This application is built with two Java servlets in the web tier. Java servlets are the foundation of all the web component technologies in the Java EE platform. A solid understanding of the Java servlet model and Java servlet API in Java EE is fundamental to understanding all the other web components in the platform. In this HelloJava EE application, the `DisplayServlet` Java servlet is responsible for rendering the web page you see from the browser in the application, for creating the HTML elements that make up the web page, and for displaying the message that the Java EE application is holding for you. The second Java servlet, the `WriteServlet`, is responsible for processing the message that is input to the application when you press the Enter button in the web page. The `WriteServlet`, in turn, passes the message it receives to an Enterprise Bean component, called `ModelEJB`. This processes the message and formulates a Java object from the `Message` class that is part of the application. The `ModelEJB` uses the Java Persistence API (JPA) to store this message object in the database for later retrieval. The `ModelEJB` performs this retrieval on behalf of the `DisplayServlet` we first met when the servlet needs to create the web page to display in the browser. In this way, the circle is completed.

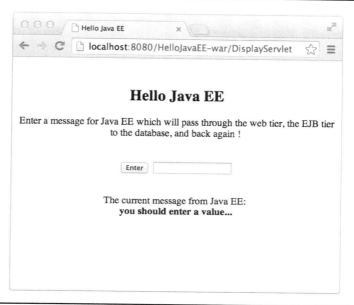

FIGURE 1-2. *Hello Java EE first page*

FIGURE 1-3. *Hello Java EE with unsent message*

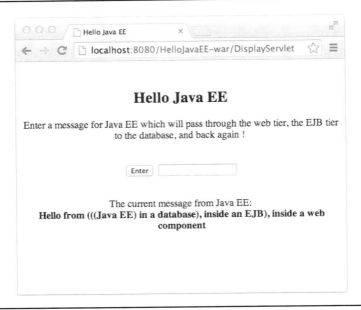

FIGURE 1-4. *Hello Java EE message received*

Inside Hello Java EE

Before we look at the code in the application (don't worry, it is not complicated), let's take a look at how the different pieces of the Hello Java EE application are arranged and what their primary functions are, as shown in Figure 1-5.

The role of the browser client in this application is to render the HTML content that the Java EE application creates for it, and also to send a message typed in by the user to the text field on the web page. The role of the web components, the DisplayServlet and WriteServlet servlets, is to create the HTML content for the browser and to direct the incoming user message to the correct portion of the application that can handle the message processing logic. In this application, the message processing logic is handled by the ModelEJB, which in turn manages the storage and retrieval of the user message to the database.

Let us look at the code that is first executed when you press the Enter button on the web page. The browser formulates an HTTP POST request and sends it to the Java EE server, to a URL that will look something like this: http://localhost:8080/HelloJavaEE-war/WriteServlet (depending on the hostname your Java EE server is using: here, the Java EE server is deployed to the local machine and uses the hostname localhost).

We shall see that the WriteServlet is mapped to the URI /WriteServlet, and because of this fact, the Java EE server routes the HTTP POST request to the WriteServlet.

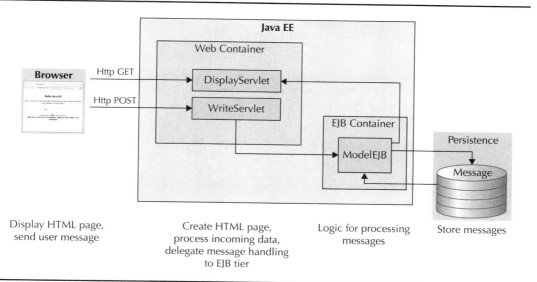

Display HTML page,
send user message

Create HTML page,
process incoming data,
delegate message handling
to EJB tier

Logic for processing
messages

Store messages

FIGURE 1-5. *The Hello Java EE application*

Listing: *The WriteServlet in the Hello Java EE application*

```
import java.io.IOException;
import javaeems.chapter1.model.MessageException;
import javaeems.chapter1.model.ModelEJB;
import javax.ejb.EJB;
import javax.servlet.ServletException;
import javax.servlet.annotation.WebServlet;
import javax.servlet.http.HttpServlet;
import javax.servlet.http.HttpServletRequest;
import javax.servlet.http.HttpServletResponse;


@WebServlet(name = "WriteServlet", urlPatterns = {"/WriteServlet"})
public class WriteServlet extends HttpServlet {
    @EJB
    private ModelEJB ModelEJB;
    private static String PUT_MESSAGE = "put_message";


    @Override
    protected void doPost(HttpServletRequest request,
                          HttpServletResponse response)
            throws ServletException, IOException {
```

```
            String message = request.getParameter(PUT_MESSAGE);
            if ("".equals(message)) {
                ModelEJB.deleteMessage();
            } else {
                try {
                    ModelEJB.putUserMessage(message);
                } catch (MessageException nme) {
                    throw new ServletException(nme);
                }
            }
            response.sendRedirect("./DisplayServlet");
        }

    }
```

   If you are entirely new to Java EE, one of the first things you will notice is that there is no constructor. As we progress through the sample, you will find that there is no application code that instantiates this `DisplayServlet`. In fact, this is true of most all Java EE components that you will write: one of the functions that the Java EE containers perform is that of managing the lifecycle of components. In particular, the web container manages the lifecycle of Java servlet components for you, so you can focus on the application logic instead. You do not need to understand every detail of this code at this point in the book, but you should note the key elements of this web servlet. First, the following annotation defines its position in the URI space of the Java EE server:

```
@WebServlet(name = "WriteServlet", urlPatterns = {"/WriteServlet"})
```

   This is how this web component receives all the HTTP requests that end in /WriteServlet. Second, this web component intercepts HTTP POST requests, which we know because it has a doPost() method, a method it overrides because it is a servlet of the HttpServlet class in the Java EE API. When this method is called, we can see that from the `HttpRequest` object, we can pull out the post parameters the web page sent, and thus pull out the user message. When this is done, the `doPost()` method asks the `ModelEJB` to delete the current message it manages if the user message is blank, or, if the user message is not blank, to accept the user message for processing. Once these tasks are performed, the work of the `WriteServlet` is done. We next turn our attention to the `ModelEJB`.

   The `ModelEJB` is an Enterprise Bean. Don't be daunted by that definition, it is mostly just the kind of Plain Old Java Object (POJO) you have created many times over.

Listing: *The ModelEJB in the Hello Java EE application*

```
import java.io.UnsupportedEncodingException;
import java.net.URLDecoder;
import java.util.List;
import javax.ejb.*;
import javax.persistence.EntityManager;
import javax.persistence.EntityManagerFactory;
import javax.persistence.PersistenceUnit;
```

```
@Stateful
public class ModelEJB {
    @PersistenceUnit
   private EntityManagerFactory emf;

    public void putUserMessage(String messageString) throws MessageException {
        this.deleteMessage();
        try {
            String decodedMessage = URLDecoder.decode(messageString, "UTF-8");
            Message message = new Message("1", "(" +
                        messageString + ")" + " in a database");
            EntityManager em = emf.createEntityManager();
            em.persist(message);
        } catch (UnsupportedEncodingException uee ) {
            throw new MessageException("something odd
                        about that message..." + messageString);
        }
    }

    public String getStoredMessage() throws MessageException {
        EntityManager em = emf.createEntityManager();
        List messages = em.createNamedQuery("findMessages").getResultList();
        if (messages.size() > 0) {
            Message message = (Message) messages.get(0);
            return "(" + message.getMessageString() + "), inside an EJB";
        } else {
            throw new MessageException("There was nothing in
                                            the database.");
        }
    }

    public void deleteMessage() {
        EntityManager em = emf.createEntityManager();
        em.createNamedQuery("deleteMessages").executeUpdate();
    }

}
```

What makes this Java class an Enterprise Bean is the annotation

```
@Stateful
```

that occurs immediately prior to the class declaration. You will quickly become familiar with the use of this kind of statement in Java EE programming: Java EE defines many standard Java annotations that make the task of creating Java EE components easier than always hand coding or hand configuring them. The `@Stateful` annotation declares this class as a particular kind of Enterprise Bean: a Stateful session bean. This means that the Enterprise Bean container that will run this Enterprise Bean will create one instance of the bean for each client that talks to it. You will learn about the lifecycle and scope of Enterprise Beans in much more detail; for now, it is sufficient to know that an instance of this Enterprise Bean exists when either the `DisplayServlet` or

`WriteServlet` needs to call it. And in that regard, you can see that this Enterprise Bean can manage a user-provided message: storing it to the database with the `putUserMessage()` method, clearing the stored message with the `deleteMessage()` method, and retrieving the message held in the database with the `getStoredMessage()` method.

You will also notice in the implementation of the `putUserMessage()` that the message string that the `WriteServlet` passes into this Enterprise Bean is converted into an instance of the `Message` class. The `Message` class, although it mostly looks like a normal class, is actually a very special class that has been annotated with Java annotations in such a way that it can very easily be persisted and managed within a database, which is precisely what this application needs to do with the message provided by the user in the web page. You will notice, for example, that if you close the browser window to the application and then reload the page, the last message you stored in the application is still there. You will also notice that if you stop and restart the Java EE server and return to the application that the same message is still displayed. This is because the user message is persisted in the database using the Java Persistence API and the `Message` class. Let's examine the code for the `Message` class.

Listing: *The Message class in the Hello Java EE application*

```java
import java.io.Serializable;
import javax.persistence.Column;
import javax.persistence.Entity;
import javax.persistence.Id;
import javax.persistence.NamedQueries;
import javax.persistence.NamedQuery;
import javax.persistence.Table;

@Entity
@Table(name = "MESSAGE")
@NamedQueries({
    @NamedQuery(
        name="findMessages",
        query="select m from Message m"
    ),
    @NamedQuery(
        name="deleteMessages",
        query="delete from Message"
    )
}
)
public class Message implements Serializable {
    @Id
    @Column(name = "ID")
    private String id;

    @Column(name = "MESSAGE")
    private String messageString;

    public Message() {
    }
```

```
public Message(String id, String messageString) {
    this.id = id;
    this.messageString = messageString;
}

public String getId() {
    return this.id;
}

public String getMessageString() {
    return this.messageString;
}

}
```

The first thing to notice about this class is that, at its core, it represents a data object that has an ID and a message. The less familiar part of this class may be the use of the annotations at the class level, beginning with

```
@Entity
```

which identifies this class to Java EE as a class that the application will need to be stored in a database, and the annotation

```
@Table (name = "MESSAGE")
```

which identifies the name, MESSAGE, of the database table into which Java EE will store instances of the Message class and the annotation.

Listing: *The @NamedQueries annotation from the Hello Java EE application*

```
@NamedQueries({
    @NamedQuery(
        name="findMessages",
        query="select m from Message m"
    ),
    @NamedQuery(
        name="deleteMessages",
        query="delete from Message"
    )
}
)
```

that defines a list of the two SQL queries that will be used to retrieve instances of the Message class from the database and to remove all instances of the Message class from the database. From these annotations, we can see that we have a POJO with the special ability to be persisted in a database, and carrying the exact database instructions to do so.

Now returning to the code of the ModelEJB, we can see in the implementation of the methods that causing this storage, retrieval, and deletion of the Message objects from the database is a matter of executing the queries that the Message class carries in the @NamedQuery annotations.

One note before we complete the journey of the message from user to browser to web component to Enterprise Bean to database and back again: let's notice how the `ModelEJB` references an instance of the `EntityManagerFactory`, which it uses to obtain an `EntityManager` instance in order to carry out commands to store and retrieve the following message:

```
public class ModelEJB {
    @PersistenceUnit
    private EntityManagerFactory emf;
```

You will not find any code in this application that ever initializes this instance variable, yet the `ModelEJB` makes calls to it. Similar to how the Java EE containers manage the lifecycle of Java components such as the Java servlets and Enterprise Beans that they are running, the Java EE containers can initialize certain variables while the component is coming to life, provided they are specially marked with Java annotations, in this case, the `@PersistenceUnit` annotation. This process of initializing variables is called *injection*, and is a pattern and technique that you will see used in many places in the Java EE platform. Returning for a moment to the `WriteServlet`, you might deduce that the same process of injection is used to initialize the instance variable holding the reference to the `ModelEJB` that the `WriteServlet` needs to store the user message it received from the browser.

```
public class WriteServlet extends HttpServlet {
    @EJB
    private ModelEJB ModelEJB;
```

This time, the instance variable is annotated with the Java annotation `@EJB`, which indicates to the Java EE web container that this Java servlet wants the value of this instance variable to be initialized to reference a suitable instance of the `ModelEJB`.

The final piece of code in this application is the `DisplayServlet`, which queries the `ModelEJB` for the stored message and creates the HTML that forms the web page that is shown to the user. It uses the same technique of injection to request the initialization of its reference to a suitable instance of the `ModelEJB`, as you can see immediately after the class declaration:

Listing: *The `DisplayServlet` in the Hello Java EE application*

```
import java.io.IOException;
import java.io.PrintWriter;
import javaeems.chapter1.model.MessageException;
import javaeems.chapter1.model.ModelEJB;
import javax.ejb.EJB;
import javax.servlet.ServletException;
import javax.servlet.annotation.WebServlet;
import javax.servlet.http.HttpServlet;
import javax.servlet.http.HttpServletRequest;
import javax.servlet.http.HttpServletResponse;

@WebServlet(name = "DisplayServlet", urlPatterns = {"/DisplayServlet"})
public class DisplayServlet extends HttpServlet {
    @EJB
    private ModelEJB modelEJB;
```

```
    @Override
    protected void doGet(HttpServletRequest request, HttpServletResponse response)
            throws ServletException, IOException {
        response.setContentType("text/html;charset=UTF-8");
        PrintWriter out = response.getWriter();
        try {
            out.println("<html>");
            out.println("<head>");
            out.println("<title>Hello Java EE</title>");
            out.println("</head>");
            out.println("<body>");
            out.println("<br>");
            out.println("<div align='center'>");
            out.println("<h2>Hello Java EE</h2>");
            out.println("Enter a message for Java EE which will pass
                through the web tier, the EJB tier to the database,
                                            and back again !");
            out.println("<br><br><br>");

            out.println("<form action='./WriteServlet' method='POST'>");
            out.println("<input type='submit' value='Enter'>");
            out.println("<input type='text' name='put_message'> ");
            out.println("</form>");
            out.println("<br>");
            String displayMessage;
            try {
                String storedMessage = modelEJB.getStoredMessage();
                displayMessage = "Hello from (" + storedMessage + "),
                                        inside a web component";
            } catch (MessageException nme) {
                displayMessage = "you should enter a value...";
            }
            out.println("The current message from Java EE: <br><b>"
                                        + displayMessage + "</b>");
            out.println("</div>");
            out.println("</body>");
            out.println("</html>");
        } finally {
            out.close();
        }
    }
}
```

Recalling the `WriteServlet` code at the start of this exposition of the Hello Java EE application, the `DisplayServlet` subclasses the Java EE API class `javax.servlet.http.HttpServlet` and uses the `@WebServlet` annotation to declare its place in the URI namespace of the application as /DisplayServlet. It, too, contains a single method, but this time, instead of a `doPost()` method for handling any HTTP POST requests, it has a `doGet()` method so that it will intercept any HTTP GET requests. Inside the implementation of the `doGet()` method, you will see that it is mainly writing out the HTML code for the web page, line by line; for example:

```
out.println("<html>");
...
out.println("</html>");
```

with only an interlude in the middle, where it uses its reference to the `ModelEJB` to obtain the current value of the message stored in the database by the Enterprise Bean and to insert it into the HTML page it is producing.

Listing: *Excerpt from the `DisplayServlet` in the Hello Java EE application*

```
String displayMessage;
try {
    String storedMessage = modelEJB.getStoredMessage();
    displayMessage = "Hello from (" + storedMessage + "),
                                inside a web component";
} catch (MessageException nme) {
    displayMessage = "you should enter a value...";
}
out.println("The current message from Java EE: <br><b>"
                        + displayMessage + "</b>");
```

When the `doGet()` method of the `DisplayServlet` completes, the round trip of the user message is complete: the user message is displayed in the web page, with some helpful additions to explain where it has been on its journey.

Hello to the Major Elements of Java EE

In examining the code for this application, we have also taken a brief tour of the main elements of the Java EE platform. The application is a classic, three-tier application, with a web layer that provides the user interaction point, displaying information and consuming user input, with an Enterprise Bean tier for processing the application logic of the application, and with a data tier for storing application data. The application is made up of two Java servlets, Java servlets being the fundamental type of web components in the Java EE platform on which all other web components are based. One of the Java servlets, the `WriteServlet`, is responsible for processing the incoming message and passing it to the Enterprise Bean tier for further processing. The other Java servlet, the `DisplayServlet`, is responsible for generating the HTML page that you see when you access the application, containing the button that sends the user message into the Java EE application, and containing the last user message that was sent. You saw the `ModelEJB` that processes the incoming message and manages its storage and retrieval in the database. Finally, you saw the `Message` class, which is a special kind of Java class that is a Java Persistence entity, meaning it can be stored and retrieved easily in the database. You didn't have to write any initialization code to instantiate any of the Java EE components, and you didn't have to connect any of the Java EE components together: both those functions were managed for you by the underlying Java EE container.

The Many Variations of Java EE Applications

The Hello Java EE application may seem a reductive application, and one that you may never wish to write yourself. However, as a three-tier Java EE application that interacts with a user through a client interface, processes incoming information, and stores and retrieves application data in a database, it captures the essence of almost every Java EE application. Most of the Java EE applications you will write will have this basic structure in common with the Hello Java EE application. Every Java EE application that you write can be viewed as a variation on this archetype. Let's take a look at some of the most common variations, many of which are further examined later in the book.

Many Flavors of Web Interface

We've already seen the cornerstone of the web interface model for Java EE: the Java servlet. Java servlets are very powerful and flexible and make a great foundation for web applications. Their original purpose was to be, on one hand, a replacement for CGI programming, and, on the other, a kind of all-purpose server-side component model for handling any request/response style network protocol, not just HTTP. But powerful as Java servlets are, their inconvenience for serious web programming may already be obvious from the application we have seen. The basic model of generating HTML content by embedding the HTML inside Java code is too cumbersome an approach for experienced web developers. Imagine creating a complicated web page using a Java servlet, with custom formatting and look-and-feel, and then imagine how many lines of Java code you would have to edit to give the page a makeover. Experienced web developers are accustomed to treating HTML pages in a very fluid manner, without the heavyweight machinery of compilation and a new syntax (Java) required by the Java servlet model. Therefore, Java EE offers a superior web component model to generate dynamic web content for browsers of all kinds: JavaServer Pages (JSP) and JavaServer Faces (JSF).

The first variation on the basic Java servlet theme is to introduce the first alternative web component to Java servlets: JavaServer Pages. JSPs can be thought of as "inside-out Java servlets." Instead of the programming model being a matter of embedding HTML content within Java statements, JSP code looks pretty much like HTML content, but with Java code embedded within it. This makes the task of creating interesting web pages that connect to all the relevant application data in the rest of the Java EE environment an endeavor that is much closer to that of the traditional HTML developer.

JSPs can be further enhanced by taking any snippets of Java code that are embedded within them, and that may be used in several other JSPs, and turning them into a kind of reusable Java component called a JSP tag library. From web page analytic components to HTML table rendering components, JSP tag libraries are a powerful organizing technology, and they enhance the reusability of the user interface logic held within a JSP page.

Using JSPs with tag libraries is a very convenient alternative to the Java servlet model. Yet fundamentally, JavaServer Pages are Java servlets: the Java EE server compiles JSPs dynamically into servlets at runtime. Thus, Java servlets form the underpinnings of this second kind of web component in the Java platform.

We are familiar with many different kinds of web applications on the Internet. A common variant of the user interaction model of our Hello Java EE application provides a much more complicated interaction flow than simple entry of one piece of data and the display of said data. Some web applications, such as airline booking sites or college course registration web sites, need to guide the user through several pages, each of which gathers information, including validation steps, and flows based on previous information the user has entered. Many web sites combine such flows with presentation of complex information, such as shopping catalogs, which are taxonomies of media content. For these kinds of applications, building such flows, display elements, and validations is complicated.

JavaServer Faces is the second type of web component that provides a higher-level framework, including prebuilt user interface components such as lists, buttons, and tables, together with the ability to validate input and define user interaction flows. JavaServer Faces, like JSPs, are based on

Java servlets, so a solid understanding of Java servlets is also essential to learning the JavaServer Faces framework.

One need look only at the proliferation of rich client applications that run on smartphones to interact efficiently with our favorite online shopping, television, and social networking sites to see that not all web applications have browser clients. In addition to their publicly facing functions exposed as HTML web pages, these sites expose their functions to nonbrowser clients using web services. The Java EE platform contains a variety of web components that can handle and respond to incoming web service calls. Known as Java Web Service components, these components are to both Simple Object Access Protocol (SOAP) and to Representational State Transfer (REST) web services what Java servlets, JSPs, and JavaServer Faces are to HTML content. Like JSPs, JSF components, and Java servlets, these components are another flavor of Java component that can respond to an HTTP request with an HTTP response.

The HTTP client/server model underpinning web applications is best suited to an interaction style where a server can give out information only when a client requests it. But many server applications contain interesting information that is changing more often than its clients are requesting it. And many clients of such web applications do not wish to have to keep asking for updates, not knowing whether new information is available. The range of such applications is wide, from social networking applications that broadcast the status of your friends, including their location or even the latest pictures of their lunch, financial applications that track current market conditions, and group gaming sites that maintain the state of a shared game. These applications need a way to broadcast information to interested clients. While there are many techniques that can be employed to simulate this kind of server push of information, such as variations on a central theme of intermitted polling, they are complicated and inefficient. The final type of web component in the Java EE platform gives a server component the ability to send data out to interested clients and is called the Java WebSocket.

The web layer of a Java EE application of some sophistication may be a mix of any or all of these web components, depending on the nature of the application.

Many Kinds of Application Logic

Turning our attention to the EJB layer, our Hello Java EE application contained one very simple Enterprise Bean: a stateful session bean. Such Enterprise Beans are instantiated by the EJB container each time a new client wishes to use it. This is especially useful in the kind of application that needs to hold its application state for each of its connected clients, for example, if the application needs to model a shopping cart, or to hold the currently entered data values as the user works through the process of entering information for purchasing insurance online. Other kinds of Enterprise Beans can be created in the Java EE platform, such as stateless session beans, whose ephemeral nature means they are brought into existence each time they are called. This makes this kind of Enterprise Bean perform very well in large-scale systems, because these beans are instantiated only when needed and can easily be instantiated on a node in a cluster that has spare capacity, without worrying about replicating any client state between calls. Singleton session beans are ideal for representing an application state that is common to all connected clients of the application, because singleton session beans are instantiated only once in the Java EE application that contains them. Modeling a news feed viewable by all logged-in users, or a high score table, are variations on the model used in our archetype HelloJava EE application that singleton session beans are made for. Finally, for applications that implement many long-running activities, such as backing up large amounts of data, handling a complicated purchase order, or analyzing demographic information over large datasets, message-driven beans offer a programming model wherein instead of making method invocations, tasks are initiated by sending a message, with task completion occurring asynchronously with the sending of another message.

Of course, it is worth noting at this point that for a variety of reasons, a large class of Java EE applications does not use any Enterprise Beans at all. The web application model is quite capable of interfacing directly with the data tier and can manage its own application data model. In this process, such Java EE applications must have as part of their design some of the thread safety, object lifecycle management, and other services that Enterprise Beans enjoy with little development effort. Despite these challenges, the variant of Java EE application that uses only the web and data tiers of the platform is a perfectly valid and quite popular form.

Different Ways to Store Application Data

The data layer of the Hello Java EE application was created and managed using the Java Persistence API. This API offers a high-level framework with which applications can perform object-relational mapping. In other words, data objects that you want to model in your application can easily be translated into equivalent data tables in a relational database, which can be a shortcut to designing relational schemas and the various queries needed to store and retrieve the data. But for those developers very comfortable with SQL and the design of relational database tables, Java EE offers the alternative and more traditional Java Database Connectivity API. Instead of modeling data objects that reflect a relational table in the database counterpart, the JDBC API models connections to the relational database and the execution of SQL statements to store, manage, and retrieve that data.

In the database where they store their data, most Java EE applications have data management tasks to perform that are much more complicated than the simple, atomic read, write, and delete operations you have seen in the Hello Java EE application. Even making a transfer of money between two bank accounts involves two separate transactions: deducting the transfer amount from one account while adding the transfer amount to another. In case of something going wrong in the middle of these operations, it is essential that the whole transaction either complete fully or not complete at all (though some of us wish money could magically appear from nowhere into our bank accounts). For these wide classes of applications, the Java Transaction API allows multiple activities to be grouped into a single atomic action that either succeeds, meaning each member of the atomic action succeeds, or fails, in which case the individual activities that completed before the failure are reversed, in which case the overall effect is as though nothing had happened.

Interfacing with Other Systems

Many Java EE applications need to extend outside of the Java EE environment to interface with other systems deployed in the network, and three technologies in the platform cater to this outgrowth of the class of Java EE applications. The first we have already touched on: many Java EE applications interface with other systems such as analytics servers, purchasing systems, and order management servers and equivalent systems using the Java web services APIs. While not providing a framework of reliable messaging, this allows for loosely coupled interactions, where systems evolve and add functionality separately from their peers without disrupting a working system. Other Java EE application variants need a kind of reliable asynchronous message exchange mechanism such as is provided by the Java Message Service, perhaps to fulfill a complex order from a central Java EE application, which needs to initiate various activities such as performing a financial purchase transaction, ordering a part number, or requesting a delivery scheme in order to complete its work. Finally, for custom enterprise systems that present a more complicated interface into applications that use them, the all-purpose extensibility mechanism that is the Java

EE Connector Architecture enables a class of Java EE applications that uses it to rely on arbitrary external information systems.

Modularity

The fundamental three-tier approach of the Java EE platform inherently divides Java EE applications into the three corresponding areas: presentation in the web tier, application logic in the Enterprise Bean tier, and persistent application data in the data tier. However, the dependency injection framework allows for the separation of a wide variety of application functions into separate Java classes, and whose instances; lifecycles can be managed by the Java EE container rather than the application. This design pattern can dramatically increase the modularity of Java EE applications. This general-purpose model we have already seen to great effect in the Hello Java EE application, wherein by means of Java EE dependency injection, we can reference Enterprise Beans easily from web components, and persistence services easily from Enterprise Beans. We thus have an easy way to perform this kind of core application plumbing, as well as being able to inject other services into Java EE applications, such as auditing, customer security checks, and arbitrary application components, without changing core application code at all.

Ways to Secure Java EE Applications

Last but certainly not least, the Java EE security model focuses on the tasks of restricting access to Java EE applications only to certain known users and to a certain range of protocols. Using a mix of Java annotations, static configuration, and runtime API calls, Java EE applications can be adapted to a wide range of security policies. These range from requiring access from browsers only with encrypted connections, to being able to specify fine-grained access models that can express role-based access control to individual or groups of web components, to runtime security checks and identity propagation throughout the tiers of the Java EE platform. The security service is a core building block of the server.

Packaging and Deploying the Hello Java EE Application

With this tour of the range of variants you can build from the core Hello Java EE application in mind, let us return to examining how to develop, package, and deploy the application.

The Hello Java EE application, as we have seen, consists of web components and an Enterprise Bean and data code. The vehicle for deploying the web components in a Java EE application is a file called the Web ARchive file (WAR). The WAR format is a kind of ZIP file, with a predefined structure consisting of a root directory to hold any textual web pages such as HTML pages, JSP, or JSF files. Additionally, this file type has a special /WEB-INF directory under which any Java class files they need, such as Java servlets, are held, in addition to other configuration information, as we will explore further in later chapters. For example, in the case of our Hello Java EE application, the archive entries of the WAR file that contains them are as follows:

```
/META-INF
        /MANIFEST.MF
/WEB-INF
        /classes
                /javaeems
```

```
/chapter1
        /web
            /DisplayServlet.class
            /WriteServlet.class
```

You can choose your own nomenclature for WAR files. In this example, the file is called `HelloJavaEE-war.war`.

Moving to the application's next tier, the application code residing in the Enterprise Bean is packaged in a similar but different kind of archive called an Enterprise Bean JAR. The Enterprise Bean JAR uses the /META-INF directory to store configuration information about the Enterprise Beans it contains, together with the class files that the beans use at the root level of the archive. Since the ModelEJB in the Hello Java EE application uses the Java Persistence API, a special file called the persistence.xml is held in the /META-INF directory. We will not worry too much about the contents of this file at this point, but will simply note that it is needed to ensure that the ModelEJB can access the database through the Java Persistence layer. And so we see that the structure of the Enterprise Bean JAR file is as follows:

```
/META-INF
        /MANIFEST.MF
        /persistence.xml
/javaeems
        /chapter1/
            /model
                    /ModelEJB.class
                    /Message.class
                    /MessageException.class
```

Again, the name of the Enterprise Bean file is important only to those people who are going to need to know what it is: it has no significance to how the application works. In this application, the filename is `HelloJavaEE-jar.jar`.

These relatively straightforward WAR and Enterprise Bean JAR file structures do have variations: some Java EE applications need more configuration information. This information is contained in special configuration files called *deployment descriptor* files, which are co-packaged in the archives in the /WEB-INF directory of the WAR file and the /META-INF directory of the Enterprise Bean JAR file. Some Java EE applications co-package JAR files containing library classes and resources, as we shall see in later chapters. But the structure of the Hello Java EE WAR and JAR files is, like the application itself, the archive theme upon which these variations are built.

The final step, which allows the Hello Java EE application to be packaged into one single, self-contained file, is to package these two archives into a third kind of ZIP file called the Enterprise ARchive or EAR file. This, too, may carry extra configuration information for more sophisticated applications, in which case this configuration information would be held in the /META-INF directory of the WAR file. Otherwise, the EAR file simply contains the web WAR and Enterprise Bean JAR files, yielding an archive structure like this:

```
/META-INF
        /MANIFEST.MF
/HelloJavaEE-jar.jar
/HelloJavaEE-war.war
```

called `HelloJavaEE.ear`. Figure 1-6 shows a diagram of the logical structure of this file.

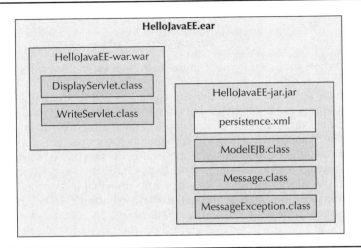

FIGURE 1-6. *Hello Java EE EAR file*

Once a Java EE application has been packaged into this form, it can be deployed to any Java EE server. The Hello Java EE application in this form contains all the configuration information needed to deploy it.

Java EE Platform and Implementations

Aside from the breadth and depth of the features and services available in the Java EE platform, the great strength of the platform is that it has many different implementations. What this means is that there are several application servers that support all the application API calls, component models, configuration semantics, security model, database model, and so on that are part of the definition of the platform.

This does not mean that all Java EE application servers are the same: far from it. There are compact application servers that run Java EE applications with a minimal footprint, with fast, nimble startup times, and with the ability to run on computers with limited computing power. There are Java EE application servers that run Java EE applications in a multi–Java Virtual Machine (JVM) environment, that can service requests from thousands of clients, that can recover from failures of the underlying software and hardware in the environment without the Java EE applications it runs even noticing any disruption. Some Java application servers offer straightforward, basic tools for deploying and managing applications and for administering the server. Other Java EE applications offer sophisticated suites of tools for managing applications and analytics, and monitoring many dimensions of the performance of the running server. But they can all run the same Java EE application in the same way.

Guide to the Rest of the Book

In this chapter, you have examined the most fundamental aspects of the Java EE platform. In musical terms, you have explored in detail the theme that is the basis and that will be the source of variations for all the Java EE applications you write. Imagining that the Java EE platform were a factory, you have been on a quick tour of all the important areas of the factory, understanding how the major elements of the platform are laid out and how they interrelate in the context of a simple application. You have peeked through the glass at some of the secondary areas of the factories, paused at open doors into other areas such as other types of web components for different clients, and other Enterprise Bean models for other application lifecycle needs, but not yet gone in.

The rest of the book explores, variation by variation, open door by open door, the other dimensions of the Java EE platform that this chapter has outlined. As you progress through the chapters, you will learn about the expansive and diverse range of Java EE applications that you can imagine and write yourself.

We will start by entering the domain of the Java EE web container.

PART
I

The Mouthpiece of Java EE: The Web Tier

CHAPTER
2

Java Servlets and Web
Applications: Foundations
of the Web Tier

J ava servlets support the creation of a wide range of dynamic web content. From online catalogs, to chat applications, to stock trading sites, to complex portals, Java servlets can do almost anything that you can do with HTTP and a markup language.

Since their introduction in 1997 as a primary development model for dynamic web content, however, Java servlets are used less and less widely today. Consequently, you may be wondering why Java servlets have not been relegated to a later chapter, which could be skimmed over in favor of discussion of the more modern web components in the Java EE platform.

In fact, Java servlets are by far the most widely used Java web component, although today they are usually used indirectly. Since they were introduced, they have been followed and superseded by a variety of Java web components and web languages with Java underpinnings. From the web technologies that are part of the Java EE platform, including JSPs, tag libraries, JavaServer Faces, Java API for RESTful Web Services (JAX-RS), and WebSocket endpoints, to implementations of popular scripting languages such as PHP, to web frameworks such as Struts and Spring, the Java servlet model, and the Java Servlet API that supports it, form the foundation of most Java-based web technologies.

In this chapter, we will look at the basic Java servlet component model and lifecycle. By gradually adding features to an online photo album application written exclusively with Java servlets, we will explore all the features of the Java servlet model and the Java Servlet API.

The reason we start our journey into the Java EE web container with Java servlets, aside from the fact that they are both interesting and useful, is that understanding them is the key to understanding all the web components in the Java EE platform.

The HTTP Protocol

Once you are familiar with the Java Servlet API, you will see that in addition to constituting an API and component model for programming server-side Java components for HTTP interactions, it also can be extended to other Internet protocols on the server side that share the same basic interaction model as HTTP. While there are extensions to the Java Servlet API for other protocols, most notably, for the File Transfer Protocol (FTP) and for the Session Initiation Protocol (SIP), such extensions are not a part of the Java EE platform, and therefore, the Java Servlet API remains an API for HTTP.

We start this examination of the Java Servlet API with an overview of the main elements of the HTTP protocol.

Inside the HTTP Protocol

HTTP is a client-server TCP-based protocol whose interaction model is a synchronous request-response. This means that an HTTP client formulates an HTTP request, sends it to the server, and awaits a response. The server, in turn, receives the HTTP request from the client, examines it, and accordingly formulates a response. The server sends this response back to the client, who reads the information out of the response, and the interaction is complete. Figure 2-1 shows a diagram of this basic interaction model, using an example of an HTTP web server that is running a photo sharing application, and a browser acting as an HTTP client accessing the photo pages.

On the HTTP web server, each web component that is able to respond to an HTTP request has an address that identifies it in the space of web components on that server. The address is a

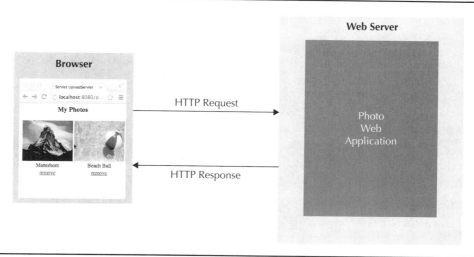

FIGURE 2-1.   *Browser interaction with web application using HTTP*

uniform resource identifier (URI), relative to the hostname of the web server. If the web server has a hostname of

`photoserver.com`

and the web component on the server has an address of

`/myphotos.html`

then the HTTP client can access the web component using the URL

`http://photoserver.com/myphotos.html`

Let's take a look at the structure of the HTTP request and HTTP response involved in this kind of interaction. Both request and response messages share a common structure: each consists of a section containing information that describes what kind of data the message is carrying. This information comes in the form of key-value pairs called HTTP headers. Additionally, the message contains a section that contains the data the message is carrying. For example, many of the HTTP responses we experience in our daily lives contain web page information. In this case, the HTTP response objects carrying the content to a web page to our browser have a special header with value `content-type` and value `text/html` to denote that they carry HTML text, and the response objects data is a string consisting of the HTML code that makes up the web page being transmitted. Let us look at this type of common example in Figure 2-2.

 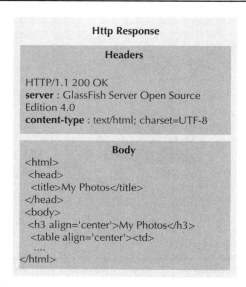

FIGURE 2-2. *Example HTTP request and HTTP response*

In this example, we can see a diagrammatic form of the kind of HTTP requests and responses a browser might send to the photo application.

HTTP requests always contain a signifier called an HTTP method and a request URI that identify for the server the type of request and the address of the web component on the web server it would like to access. The HTTP methods are `GET`, `HEAD`, `POST`, `PUT`, `DELETE`, `TRACE`, `OPTIONS`, `CONNECT`, and `PATCH`. Most commonly in web programming, you see only two of those methods in use:

- ■ `GET` Used when the request is seeking information from the server, typically without sending any accompanying information in the request body, for example, when requesting the content of the web page `/myphotos.html`, as in the diagram.

- ■ `POST` Used when the request is carrying some information in the body that accompanies the request. A very common example of this occurs when you upload a file to a web site; in this case, the browser formulates the HTTP request. We will see an example of this shortly.

In the example, the `host` header carries the hostname of the web server to which the client is sending the request, and the `accept` header contains a listing of MIME types that describe the kinds of response body information the client will be able to deal with and the response the server will send back. The `user-agent` header identifies the HTTP client, in this case, the Mozilla browser, and finally the `accept-encoding` and `accept-language` headers are used to inform the server what kind of language formats the client will be able to accept in a response.

When the server formulates an HTTP response, it always includes an HTTP status code and a three-digit number signifying what kind of response it is making, together with a message string identifier. Most of the time, the status code is as the example shows: a 200 OK status code that is used to say that the server has processed the request normally and is making its response in the way it expects to. Many other status codes indicate a range of situations. Some common ones we have all seen are 404 Not Found, indicating that the server has no web component at that address the client. 401 Not Authorized indicates that the web component is accessible only to certain authenticated clients and not the requesting client, and 500 Internal Error indicates that the server has encountered an error on its side processing the incoming request. The server header is used, analogously to the `user-agent` header, to name the web server software, in this example, the GlassFish server. The `content-type` header is used to describe what kind of data is held in the body of the HTTP response; in the example, the data held is HTML.

Because HTTP is so widely used, many mechanisms have been built on top of this basic interaction model. It is possible to use the headers to cause clients to be redirected to other web responses to keep HTTP connections open after the HTTP responses have been received, and even to emulate asynchronous messaging wherein web servers are able to send out information and updates, such as changing stock quote information, or chat messages, unsolicited with an HTTP request by interested clients. It is beyond the scope of this book to examine all such mechanisms, but we will encounter them from time to time, and will describe them briefly when we need to in order to understand the capabilities of the Java EE platform.

Introducing Java Servlets

Now that we are grounded in the fundamental aspects of the HTTP protocol, we can turn our attention to the Java servlet.

A Java servlet is a Java object that processes the server side of HTTP interactions.

What a Java Servlet Does

Let us suppose for a moment that the web component in our example was a Java servlet. In such a case, we would be able to see the primary functions of the Java servlet. In Figure 2-3, this Java servlet is called a `PhotoServlet` and is running in the web container of a Java EE server.

The diagram shows the main tasks of the photo servlet: looking at the request header to discover that the client would like HTML content to be returned, gathering photo data to send back, and formulating the response by assigning the correct header to describe the HTML web page containing photos it will send back.

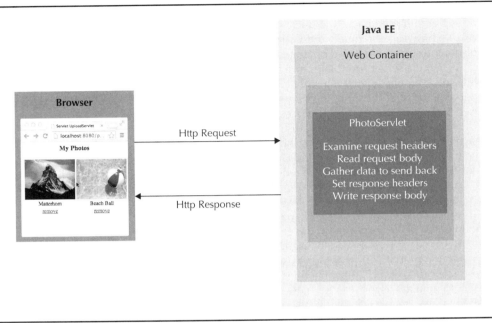

FIGURE 2-3. *Main tasks performed by a Java servlet*

Together, these tasks are a special case of the general tasks all Java servlets undertake:

- **Examine request headers** The servlet ascertains what kind of information the client is requesting and how it would like to receive it.

- **Read request body** This step further qualifies the request, or gathers further information accompanying the request, for example, for a POST request carrying an uploaded photo or document. This step may not always apply if the client request does not carry a payload of information in the request body, which is the case for many HTTP GET requests.

- **Gather data to send back** The power of the Java servlet model is that it brings together the HTTP request into the Java EE environment in which the Java servlet can access other Java EE components or a database or other external systems to gather up dynamically application data that it will use to formulate the response.

- **Set response headers** Java servlets then fill out the response headers in order to describe to the client what kind of information is held in the payload of the response it is returning.

- **Write response body** Finally, the response body is written by the servlet and transmitted, after the HTTP response headers, back to the calling client, and the Java servlet's work is done until the next request comes in.

How to Create a Java Servlet

Creating a Java servlet is straightforward: first you subclass the Java Servlet API class:

```
javax.servlet.http.HttpServlet
```

The Java Servlet API contains two other very important classes:

```
javax.servlet.http.HttpServletRequest
javax.servlet.http.HttpServletResponse
```

that model incoming HTTP requests and outgoing HTTP responses, respectively. The heart of a Java servlet is implementing the request/response interaction we have been looking at. In order to do that in a servlet, you simply override one of the following methods of the `HttpServlet` superclass, depending on what kind of HTTP requests you wish to process with your method, or more specifically, the HTTP requests of which HTTP method you wish to process.

HttpServlet method	Purpose

`public void service(HttpServletRequest req,`
`        HttpServletResponse res)`
`    throws ServletException, IOException`
	Handle all HTTP requests

`protected void doget(HttpServletRequest req,`
`        HttpServletResponse res)`
`    throws ServletException, IOException`
	Handle only HTTP GET requests

`protected void doHead(HttpServletRequest req,`
`        HttpServletResponse res)`
`    throws ServletException, IOException`
	Handle only HTTP HEAD requests

`protected void doOptions(HttpServletRequest req,`
`        HttpServletResponse res)`
`    throws ServletException, IOException`
	Handle only HTTP OPTIONS requests

`protected void doPost(HttpServletRequest req,`
`        HttpServletResponse res)`
`    throws ServletException, IOException`
	Handle only HTTP POST requests

`protected void doPut(HttpServletRequest req,`
`        HttpServletResponse res)`
`    throws ServletException, IOException`
	Handle only HTTP PUT requests

`protected void doTrace(HttpServletRequest req,`
`        HttpServletResponse res)`
`    throws ServleTexception, IOException`
	Handle only HTTP TRACE requests

If you only ever learn one method of the `HttpServlet` class, it is the `service()` method: it will handle all HTTP requests! In reality, much of the time you will be implementing either the `doGet()` or the `doPost()` methods because they are the most common forms of HTTP requests in web applications.

The `HttpServletRequest` object contains a variety of methods for reading HTTP request headers and for reading the HTTP request body content, if there is any. The key methods are

```
public Enumeration getHeaderNames()
public String getHeader(String name)
```

and

```
public InputStream getInputStream()
public Reader getReader()
```

Similarly, the `HttpServletResponse` object contains a variety of methods for setting HTTP response headers and for writing HTTP response body content. The key methods are

```
public void setHeader(String name, String value)
```

and

```
public OutputStream getOutputStream()
public Writer getWriter()
```

Now we can fit together these pieces of the Java Servlet API into a picture that shows how they fit together to form a functioning Java Servlet, as shown in Figure 2-4.

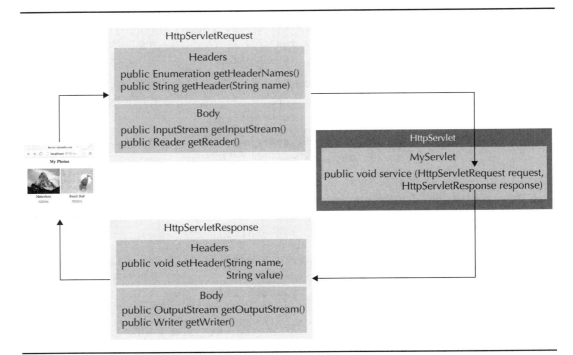

FIGURE 2-4. *Java servlet API classes in action*

Finally, we are now in a position to show the skeleton code for how most every Java servlet you will ever write will look, using the key APIs and the five-step task list common to all Java servlets:

```java
import java.io.*;
import java.util.*;
import javax.servlet.ServletException;
import javax.servlet.annotation.WebServlet;
import javax.servlet.http.HttpServlet;
import javax.servlet.http.HttpServletRequest;
import javax.servlet.http.HttpServletResponse;

@WebServlet(name = "TemplateServlet",
        urlPatterns = {"/TemplateServletURI"})
public class TemplateServlet extends HttpServlet {

 @Override
 protected void service(HttpServletRequest request,
                        HttpServletResponse response)
                  throws ServletException, IOException {

  for (Enumeration e = request.getHeaderNames();
                          e.hasMoreElements(); ) {
   String nextRequestHeaderName = (String) e.nextElement();
   String nextRequestHeaderValue =
         request.getHeader(nextRequestHeaderName);
     // 1. Examine request headers
  }

  // 2. Read request body
  InputStream is = request.getInputStream();
  // or
  Reader reader = request.getReader();

  // 3. Gather data to send back

  // 4. Set response headers
  response.setHeader(myResponseHeaderName,
              myResponseHeaderValue);

  // 5. Write response body
  PrintWriter writer = response.getWriter();
  // or
  OutputStream output = response.getOutputStream();

 }
}
```

Publishing a Java Servlet to the Web Container

One final thing to notice before we get our hands on a real Java servlet is the annotation

```
@WebServlet(name = "TemplateServlet",
        urlPatterns = {"/TemplateServletURI"})
```

This annotation defines how this Java servlet will be deployed. In particular, in the case of this pseudo-servlet, its logical name is `TemplateServlet`, only coincidentally the same as the class name, and it will be published for clients using `/TemplateServletURI` as the partial URI. Each web application residing on a Java EE server also has a partial URI called the context path of the web application. The complete path a client uses to access a servlet that declares a partial URI in this way is

```
http://<hostname:port>/<context-path>/<url-pattern>
```

where `hostname` is the hostname of the Java EE server, `context-path` is a partial URI for the web application containing the servlet, and `url-pattern` is the partial URI of the servlet.

Example Java Servlet Application: Photo Application

Now that we have examined the basic structure and functions of a Java servlet, we have enough knowledge to write the photo application. This web application allows users to upload photos to a web page, which provides a simple thumbnail display of all the user's uploaded photos, the ability to see any of the photos in full size, and the ability to remove photos from the album.

In Figure 2-5, we can see a browser view of this web application in which a user has uploaded two photographs to the album. By pressing the `Choose File` button, selecting a photo file, and clicking upload, the user can upload more photos to the album. By clicking on the photo, the user can see the photo full size, and by clicking the remove link, the user can remove the relevant photo from the album.

This web application is composed of three servlets, the `DisplayAlbumServlet`, the `DisplayPhotoServlet`, and the `RemovePhotoServlet`, as shown in Figure 2-6. Additionally, the `PhotoAlbum` class holds all the photo information that these three Java servlets access. We shall see once we have looked through the application that these three Java servlets are like the Three Wise Monkeys known in fairy tales.

Let's tackle the easiest of the three servlets first: the `DisplayPhotoServlet`. Figure 2-7 displays its output, showing the tallest mountain in Europe.

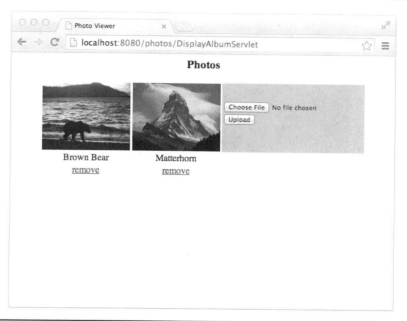

FIGURE 2-5. *Viewing a photo album*

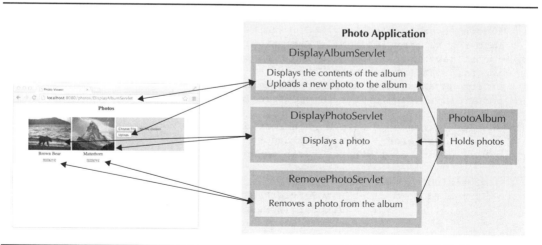

FIGURE 2-6. *Java servlet anatomy of the photo application*

FIGURE 2-7. *Viewing a single photo*

Here is the code:

```java
import java.io.*;
import javax.servlet.ServletContext;
import javax.servlet.ServletException;
import javax.servlet.annotation.WebServlet;
import javax.servlet.http.HttpServlet;
import javax.servlet.http.HttpServletRequest;
import javax.servlet.http.HttpServletResponse;

@WebServlet(name = "DisplayPhotoServlet",
        urlPatterns = {"/DisplayPhotoServlet"})
public class DisplayPhotoServlet extends HttpServlet {

  @Override
  protected void doGet(HttpServletRequest request,
                       HttpServletResponse response)
                       throws ServletException, IOException {
```

```
      String indexString = request.getParameter("photo");
      int index = (new Integer(indexString.trim())).intValue();
      response.setContentType("image/jpeg");
      OutputStream out = response.getOutputStream();
      try {
        ServletContext myServletContext =
          request.getServletContext();
        PhotoAlbum pa = PhotoAlbum.getPhotoAlbum(myServletContext);
        byte[] bytes = pa.getPhotoData(index);
        for (int i = 0; i < bytes.length; i++) {
          out.write( bytes[i]);
        }
      } finally {
        out.close();
      }
    }

}
```

The first thing to notice is that the servlet is mapped to the URI `/DisplayPhotoServlet`, which means that it is accessed by the client at the URI

`http://<hostname:port>/photos/DisplayPhotoServlet`

because `photos` is the context path of the containing web application.

Next we can see that this servlet overrides the `doGet()` method of the `HttpServlet` API class from which it inherits. This means that this servlet only handles HTTP `GET` requests; any other HTTP requests to its URI originating from other HTTP methods, for example, `POST` or `DELETE`, are never passed to this servlet by the Java EE web container. Inside the `doGet()` method, we notice that the first thing this servlet does is to parse out the parameters in the query string in the request URI. As we will observe later, this servlet always expects a query string, with `photo` as a parameter name and an integer as a value; for example:

`http://<hostname:port>/photos/DisplayPhotoServlet?photo=3`

The `doGet()` method parses out the value of the photo parameter that was passed in and sets the content type of the response to be image/jpg because it will be sending back image data to the client. Then it obtains a reference to the response's `OutputStream`, which is where it will write the image data. Notice that the servlet next obtains a reference to an object of type `javax` `.servlet.ServletContext`. The `ServletContext` of a web application is an object that represents to all the servlets inside the web application the web container in which it runs. It is a very important object that we will examine further. For now, we will simply note that the `DisplayPhotoServlet` obtains a reference to the photo album by passing in the `ServletContext` to the `PhotoAlbum` class. Then it obtains the image data from the `PhotoAlbum` instance and writes it to the response, closing the stream when all of the image data has been written.

We look next to the `DisplayAlbumServlet`. It is this servlet that both displays the main page of the web application (the photo album) and also handles the upload of a new photo. Let's start by looking at its basic structure:

```java
import java.io.*;
import javax.servlet.ServletException;
import javax.servlet.ServletContext;
import javax.servlet.annotation.MultipartConfig;
import javax.servlet.annotation.WebServlet;
import javax.servlet.http.HttpServlet;
import javax.servlet.http.HttpServletRequest;
import javax.servlet.http.HttpServletResponse;
import javax.servlet.http.Part;

@WebServlet(name = "DisplayAlbumServlet",
            urlPatterns = {"/DisplayAlbumServlet"})
@MultipartConfig()
public class DisplayAlbumServlet extends HttpServlet {

  @Override
  protected void doGet(HttpServletRequest request,
                       HttpServletResponse response)
                             throws ServletException, IOException {
    handleRequest(request, response);
  }


  @Override
  protected void doPost(HttpServletRequest request,
                        HttpServletResponse response)
                              throws ServletException, IOException {
    handleRequest(request, response);
  }

  protected void handleRequest(HttpServletRequest request,
      HttpServletResponse response)
                                  throws ServletException, IOException {
    ServletContext servletContext = request.getServletContext();
    PhotoAlbum pa = PhotoAlbum.getPhotoAlbum(servletContext);
    if (request.getContentType() != null &&
          request.getContentType().startsWith("multipart/form-data")) {
      this.uploadPhoto(request, pa);
    }
    response.setContentType("text/html;charset=UTF-8");
    PrintWriter writer = response.getWriter();
    try {
      writer.write("<html>");
      writer.write("<head>");
      writer.write("<title>Photo Viewer</title>");
      writer.write("</head>");
      writer.write("<body>");
```

```java
        writer.write("<h3 align='center'>Photos</h3>");
        this.displayAlbum(pa, "", writer);
        writer.println("</body>");
        writer.println("</html>");
    } finally {
        writer.close();
    }
}

private void uploadPhoto(HttpServletRequest request,
                         PhotoAlbum pa) throws IOException, ServletException {
    ByteArrayOutputStream baos = new ByteArrayOutputStream();
    String filename = null;
    for (Part p: request.getParts()) {
        this.copyBytes(p.getInputStream(), baos);
        filename = p.getSubmittedFileName();
    }
    if (!"".equals(filename)) {
        String photoName = filename.substring(0, filename.lastIndexOf("."));
        pa.addPhoto(photoName, baos.toByteArray());
    }
}

private void displayAlbum(PhotoAlbum pa,
                          String label,
                          PrintWriter writer) {
    writer.write("<h3 align='center'>" + label + "</h3>");
    writer.write("<table align='center'>");
    for (int j = 0; j < pa.getPhotoCount(); j++) {
        writer.write("<td>");
        writer.write("<a href='./DisplayPhotoServlet?photo=" + j + "'>");
        writer.write("<img src='./DisplayPhotoServlet?photo=" +
                        j + "' alt='photo' height='120' width='150'> ");
        writer.write("</a>");
        writer.write("</td>");
    }

    writer.write("<td bgcolor='#cccccc' width='120' height='120'>");
    writer.write("<form align='left' action='DisplayAlbumServlet'
                        method='post' enctype='multipart/form-data'>");
    writer.write("<input value='Choose' name='myFile' type='file'
                                        accept='image/jpeg'><br>");
    writer.write("<input value='Upload' type='submit\'><br>");
    writer.write("</form>");
    writer.write("</td>");
    writer.write("</tr>");

    writer.write("<tr>");
    for (int j = 0; j < pa.getPhotoCount(); j++) {
        writer.write("<td align='center'>");
        writer.write(pa.getPhotoName(j));
```

```
      writer.write("</td>");
    }
  writer.write("</tr>");

  writer.write("<tr>");
  for (int j = 0; j < pa.getPhotoCount(); j++) {
    writer.write("<td align='center'>");
    writer.write("<a href='RemovePhotoServlet?photo=" + j +
                                       "'>remove</a>");
    writer.write("</td>");
  }
  writer.write("</tr>");
  writer.write("</table>");
}

private void copyBytes(InputStream is, OutputStream os)
                                  throws IOException {
  int i;
  while ( (i=is.read()) != -1) {
    os.write(i);
  }
  is.close();
  os.close();
}

}
```

We can see immediately from the @WebServlet declaration that this servlet is available at

```
http://<hostname:port>/photos/DisplayAlbumServlet
```

Additionally, because it overrides both the doGet() and doPost() methods, it will respond to HTTP GET and HTTP POST requests. The GET requests will be requests to display only the album, and the POST requests will be requests from the client to upload a file and display the updated album. Now both of these intercepting methods delegate to the handleRequest() method, so let us look at this implementation. The first thing the method does is check whether the content type of the request is

```
multipart/form-data
```

If so, then the method ascertains that there is photo information to upload. This is delegated to the uploadPhoto() method. Since this method always returns a response containing the HTML code displaying the photo album, it sets the content-type of the response to text/html. In contrast with the DisplayPhotoServlet that writes binary image data to its response by using the java.io.OutputStream, this servlet will write textual HTML output to its response. Therefore, it obtains a reference to the Writer object from the HttpServletResponse. Then it proceeds to start writing the HTML code for the web page. The meat of the HTML it writes to the response is the code for displaying the table that forms the display of the photo album and the grey panel that allows for the upload of a new photo. This code is held in the implementation of the `displayAlbum()` method. Once the album has been written, the `handleRequest()` method has finished writing the HTML document, closing the final `<html>` tag and closing the output. Let us look at the method for writing the HTML code to display the album:

```java
private void displayAlbum(PhotoAlbum pa,
                          String label,
                          PrintWriter writer) {
  writer.write("<h3 align='center'>" + label + "</h3>");
  writer.write("<table align='center'>");
  for (int j = 0; j < pa.getPhotoCount(); j++) {
    writer.write("<td>");
    writer.write("<a href='./DisplayPhotoServlet?photo=" + j + "'>");
    writer.write("<img src='./DisplayPhotoServlet?photo=" + j +
                     "' alt='photo' height='120' width='150'> ");
    writer.write("</a>");
    writer.write("</td>");
  }

  writer.write("<td bgcolor='#cccccc' width='120' height='120'>");
  writer.write("<form align='left' action='DisplayAlbumServlet'
                   method='post' enctype='multipart/form-data'>");
  writer.write("<input value='Choose' name='myFile' type='file'
                              accept='image/jpeg'><br>");
  writer.write("<input value='Upload' type='submit\'><br>");
  writer.write("</form>");
  writer.write("</td>");
  writer.write("</tr>");

  writer.write("<tr>");
  for (int j = 0; j < pa.getPhotoCount(); j++) {
    writer.write("<td align='center'>");
    writer.write(pa.getPhotoName(j));
    writer.write("</td>");
  }
  writer.write("</tr>");

  writer.write("<tr>");
  for (int j = 0; j < pa.getPhotoCount(); j++) {
    writer.write("<td align='center'>");
    writer.write("<a href='RemovePhotoServlet?photo=" + j +
                                      "'>remove</a>");
    writer.write("</td>");
  }
  writer.write("</tr>");
  writer.write("</table>");
}
```

This method is writing the HTML code for the table, iterating over the items in the `PhotoAlbum`, embedding within the table cells the anchor and image tags that use the relative URI

`/DisplayPhotoServlet?photo={n}`

both as a source for the image thumbnail and as a hyperlink, so that when the user clicks on the image, it invokes the `DisplayPhotoServlet` to display the full image. The final row of the table inserts a hyperlink to the `RemovePhotoServlet`, generating the same query string used by the `DisplayPhotoServlet` to identify which photo is to be removed from the album.

Before we look at photo removal, we will finish examining the `DisplayAlbumServlet` by looking at the method that uploads the photo data:

```java
private void uploadPhoto(HttpServletRequest request,
            PhotoAlbum pa)
            throws IOException, ServletException {
  ByteArrayOutputStream baos = new ByteArrayOutputStream();
  String filename = null;
  for (Part p: request.getParts()) {
    this.copyBytes(p.getInputStream(), baos);
    filename = p.getSubmittedFileName();
    }
  String photoName = filename.substring(0, filename.lastIndexOf("."));
  pa.addPhoto(photoName, baos.toByteArray());
}


private void copyBytes(InputStream is,
        OutputStream os) throws IOException {
  int i;
  while ( (i=is.read()) != -1) {
    os.write(i);
  }
  is.close();
  os.close();
}
```

Larger chunks of data uploaded as multipart data over HTTP will likely arrive in a number of parts. This is dependent on a number of factors, including the client, the size of the file, the network, and the Java EE server. However many parts the photo arrives in, by iterating over the `javax.servlet.http.Part` objects, this method obtains all the photo data from the `HttpServletRequest` object by means of its `InputStream`, collecting it in a byte array, retrieving the filename chosen by the user, and inserting the photo and its name into the photo album.

We have almost finished our tour of the photo application. Let's jump right to the `RemovePhotoServlet`, whose job it is to remove photos from the album on demand:

```java
import java.io.IOException;
import javax.servlet.ServletException;
import javax.servlet.annotation.WebServlet;
import javax.servlet.http.HttpServlet;
import javax.servlet.http.HttpServletRequest;
import javax.servlet.http.HttpServletResponse;


@WebServlet(name = "RemovePhotoServlet",
    urlPatterns = {"/RemovePhotoServlet"})
public class RemovePhotoServlet extends HttpServlet {
```

```
@Override
protected void doGet(HttpServletRequest request,
                     HttpServletResponse response)
                throws ServletException, IOException {
   String indexString = request.getParameter("photo");
   int index = (new Integer(indexString.trim())).intValue();
   PhotoAlbum pa = PhotoAlbum.getPhotoAlbum(request.getServletContext());
   pa.removePhoto(index);
   RequestDispatcher rd =
          request.getRequestDispatcher("DisplayAlbumServlet");
   rd.forward(request, response);
}

}
```

Thanks to its @WebServlet annotation, this servlet is available to the client at

```
http://<hostname:port>/photos/RemovePhotoServlet
```

and since it overrides only the doGet() method of the API class HttpServlet, it responds only to HTTP GET calls, which is precisely the kind of HTTP request that is generated when the user presses on a hyperlink, such as the Remove link under any of the photos in the album.

Similar to the DisplayPhotoServlet, this servlet is expecting a query string of the form

```
?photo={some number}
```

from which it extracts the index of the photo to be deleted from the PhotoAlbum. Once it removes the photo in question, the servlet obtains a reference to a Java Servlet API class called the RequestDispatcher, using the relative URI of the DisplayAlbumServlet. The RequestDispatcher object returned acts as a wrapper on other web components in the same web application, in this case, the DisplayAlbumServlet. By calling the forward() method, the RemovePhotoServlet is delegating the creation of the HTTP response to the DisplayAlbumServlet, which proceeds by displaying the remaining photos in the newly reduced photo album.

Finally, the PhotoAlbum itself is a relatively straightforward store of byte data representing the photos along with a name for each:

```
import java.util.*;
import javax.servlet.ServletContext;

public class PhotoAlbum {
  public static String ATTRIBUTE_NAME = "Photo_Album";
  private List<byte[]> photoDataList = new ArrayList<byte[]>();
  private List<String> names = new ArrayList<String>();


  public static PhotoAlbum getPhotoAlbum(ServletContext servletContext) {
    if (servletContext.getAttribute(ATTRIBUTE_NAME) == null) {
      PhotoAlbum pa = new PhotoAlbum();
      servletContext.setAttribute(ATTRIBUTE_NAME, pa);
    }
```

```
    return (PhotoAlbum) servletContext.getAttribute(ATTRIBUTE_NAME);
  }

  public synchronized void addPhoto(String name, byte[] bytes) {
    this.photoDataList.add(bytes);
    this.names.add(name);
  }

  public synchronized byte[] getPhotoData(int i) {
    return (byte[]) photoDataList.get(i);
  }

  public synchronized String getPhotoName(int i) {
    return (String) names.get(i);
  }

  public synchronized int getPhotoCount() {
    return photoDataList.size();
  }

  public synchronized void removePhoto(int i) {
    photoDataList.remove(i);
    names.remove(i);
  }
}
```

Notice the implementation of the getPhotoAlbum() method, which takes an instance of the ServletContext as a parameter. You'll remember that the ServletContext object is an object global to the web application representing the web container hosting the web application. One of its many features is that it holds an object map of key-value pairs into which web applications may store and retrieve application objects using the method calls

```
public void setAttribute(String name, Object value)
public Object getAttribute(String name);
public Enumeration<String> get AttributeNames()
```

It is here that the instance of the PhotoAlbum that all three servlets reference lives: as an attribute on the instance of the ServletContext associated with the photo application. In this way, all three servlets are always using the same photo album. Notice that all the methods that read or write photos to the PhotoAlbum are synchronized: we will return to the reason for this later in the chapter.

Now we can explain the riddle of how the fable of the Three Wise Monkeys applies to this example application: since the RemovePhotoServlet never produces output, it speaks no evil. Since the DisplayPhotoServlet does not expect any request data, it hears no evil, and because readers of this book will upload only pretty pictures, the DisplayAlbumServlet sees no evil.

Understanding the Java Servlet API

Now that we have looked at an example of a web application made of Java servlets of different varieties, we are in a position to more formally examine the Java Servlet API.

The `javax.servlet.http.HttpServlet` Class

The `HttpServlet` class is the central class of the Java Servlet API and of most of the web components in the Java EE platform, whether they are directly aware of it or not. We have seen that the way to create any Java servlet is to subclass `HttpServlet` and override one or more of the doXXX() methods, where XXX corresponds to the HTTP method of the kind of HTTP request you wish your servlet to intercept. Let's step back for a moment and look at the lifecycle of a Java servlet.

At some point after the Java servlet is deployed to the Java EE server, and before the first HTTP request comes in that it has to handle, the Java EE web container creates an instance of the Java servlet class in preparation for handling the first HTTP request. When the Java servlet instance has been created, the web container makes a call to its

```
public void init(ServletConfig config) throws ServletException
```

method. The `init()` method may be overridden in the servlet in order to perform any type of expensive operation that needs to complete before the servlet is able to respond to requests, for example, opening a database connection. The web container passes a `ServletConfig` object into the `init()` method. The `ServletConfig` object gives the servlet a view into the configuration information of the servlet. If the `init()` method throws a `ServletException` or does not complete in a timely manner, as determined by the web container, the web container interprets this situation as meaning that something has gone wrong while the servlet is setting itself up and does not allow it to come into service.

Once the `init()` method completes, the Java servlet is put into service, and at this point waits for incoming HTTP requests. Based on the HTTP method of the HTTP request, one of the doXXX() methods of the servlet will be called.

```
protected void doXXX(HttpServletRequest req,
                     HttpServletResponse resp)
           throws ServletException, IOException
```

Java servlets that wish to handle absolutely any HTTP request, no matter the HTTP method, must implement the `service()` method, which will handle any and all HTTP requests to this servlet, and any doXXX() methods will not be called.

Once the web container decides that it has finished using this instance of the Java servlet, after allowing it to service its last request and before allowing it to be garbage collected, it calls the servlets

```
public void destroy()
```

which gives it the opportunity to clean up or close any expensive resources such as database connections that it opened during its lifetime. Once the `destroy()` method has been called, the servlet instance has served its purpose: the same instance can never be reused. This lifecycle is shown in Figure 2-8.

Number of Instances of Java Servlets

One question that may not always be clear from the lifecycle of a Java servlet instance is: how many instances will the web container create of my servlet? The exact number of instances a web container will use varies. Some containers may use just a single instance of a Java servlet for all the time that the web application that contains it is deployed, with the instance sitting in readiness

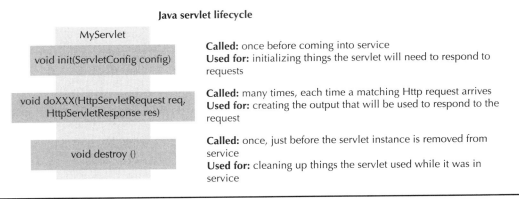

FIGURE 2-8.   *Java servlet lifecycle*

whether or not there are clients sending requests to it or not. Other web containers may instantiate a pool of Java servlet instances to handle requests from large numbers of clients, sometimes running the instances on separate Java Virtual Machines to spread out the processing load. Other web containers may remove servlet instances from use during periods they judge to be quiet in order to save computing resources, bringing up new instances only when a client sends in a new request after such a quiet period. However, whatever the scheme, the servlet developer needs to know the following two things:

- Each Java servlet instance may handle simultaneous requests from multiple clients.
- Each Java servlet may be instantiated multiple times by the web container.

In particular, this means that you need to be careful when you implement the `doXXX()` methods of the servlet that you program with concurrent requests in mind. This is why the `PhotoAlbum` in the example we looked at synchronizes access to its data: it is possible for one client to be adding a photo at the same time that another is removing one.

It also means that you need to be careful when using instance variables in a Java servlet instance: if, for example, you use an instance variable on a servlet to count the number of times it is called over a period of time, it will count the number of times that instance of the Java servlet is called. However, if the web container instantiates more than one instance of the Java servlet, the count on any particular instance of the Java servlet may not be what you expected.

Thus, the servlet developer looks to other places in the Java servlet API to store application state. In our photo application, you will remember that the global instance of the `PhotoAlbum` was not held as an instance variable on any of the Java servlets, but rather as an attribute on the `ServletContext`.

The ServletContext

Each web application has access to a single instance of the `javax.servlet.ServletContext` class. This instance offers the web application its own private view into the web container. The `ServletContext` holds methods that allow a Java servlet to query information about the environment, such as the version of the Java Servlet API it supports. It holds the means to query at runtime other aspects of the web application to which it is associated, for example, the context path of the web application, and the ability to register other web components dynamically during the startup phase of the containing web application. One of its most used features is the simple map of attributes that it holds on behalf of the application. This is a highly useful place to store any application data in a web application that you wish to be global to all the web components and to all clients that access it. Here is the API for manipulating application data on the `ServletContext`:

```
public Object getAttribute(String name)
public Enumeration<String> getAttributeNames()
public void removeAttribute(String name)
public void setAttribute(String name, Object value)
```

If you rerun the photo application from two separate browsers, when you upload a photo in one browser and then refresh the display of the photo application in the other browser, you will notice that both browsers display the same photo album.

What if you wanted each client to upload photos only to their own photo album? As an example, if a second client viewed the web application, rather than seeing all the photos that any client of the web application had uploaded, would they see only the photos they had uploaded?

This brings us to the next object in the Java servlet environment: the `HttpSession`.

The `HttpSession`

The `javax.servlet.http.HttpSession` object is a representation of a series of interactions with a single web application from a single client. If a web application wishes to adapt its behavior for a particular user based on previous knowledge of that user, or based on the user's previous interactions with the web application, then the `HttpSession` is the object to use. Each `HttpSession` object associated with a particular client is available to all Java servlet instances, and it can be obtained each time the client makes a new HTTP request to a servlet by either of the methods

```
public HttpSession getSession()
```

Each `HttpSession` object has a identifier available by the `getId()` call that is unique across all the active sessions in the web container. `HttpSessions` ultimately expire, either by an explicit call to its

```
public void invalidate()
```

method, or because the session times out because the client that the session is representing doesn't make any calls to the web application, defined by a timeout quantity controlled by the methods

```
public int getMaxInactiveInterval()
public void setMaxInactiveInterval(int interval)
```

These methods allow the web container the opportunity to invalidate the sessions once the maximum period of inactivity has been reached. This does not mean that the client has not been accessing other web applications deployed to the web container: like the `ServletContext` instances, `HttpSession` instances cannot cross the boundaries of web applications.

Returning to the question of how to store application states associated with a particular client of a web application, the most commonly used feature of HttpSession is its ability to store arbitrary objects on behalf of web components. The API for this is analogous to that of the ServletContext:

```
public Object getAttribute(String name)
public Enumeration<String> getAttributeNames()
public void removeAttribute(String name)
public void setAttribute(String name, Object value)
```

Let's pause here to take a look at how we would make this switch in our photo application to store photos in a different photo album for each client of the application. Fortunately, it is very simple. First, we would need to change the place where each PhotoAlbum instance is stored from the ServletContext to the HttpSession:

```
public class PhotoAlbum {
  public static String ATTRIBUTE_NAME = "Photo_Album";
  private List<byte[]> photoDataList = new ArrayList<byte[]> ();
  private List<String> names = new ArrayList<String>();

  private PhotoAlbum() {
  }
...
  public static PhotoAlbum getPhotoAlbum(HttpSession session) {
    if (session.getAttribute(ATTRIBUTE_NAME) == null) {
      PhotoAlbum pa = new PhotoAlbum();
      session.setAttribute(ATTRIBUTE_NAME, pa);
    }
    return (PhotoAlbum) session.getAttribute(ATTRIBUTE_NAME);
  }
...
}
```

and then, in the Java servlets that access the PhotoAlbum, pass in the HttpSession instead of the ServletContext:

```
    HttpSession session = request.getSession();
    PhotoAlbum pa = PhotoAlbum.getPhotoAlbum(session);
```

Now when you access this amended photo application from two different browsers, you will notice that uploading photos in separate browsers uploads photos to separate photo albums.

This makes the HttpSession object an invaluable tool when writing websites that have any kind of user personalization, such as websites that remember your name, remember the last page you looked at, maintain a shopping cart as you browse through the site, or need to display any information about you that you have previously given it.

How HttpSessions Are Maintained

In order to maintain HttpSession instances, the web container has to know that a series of requests are all coming from the same user. It would be no use if you spent an hour doing your holiday shopping at an online store, only to find when you came to check out that you had someone else's selections in your shopping cart. How does the web container do it?

The web container has various mechanisms at its disposal. Primarily, web containers depend on HTTP cookies to maintain the `HttpSession`: when a client makes a first request to a web application, the web container inserts a cookie containing a session id into the response. In turn, the client sends a cookie containing the same session ID back each time that it makes a new request. This session exchange inside HTTP cookies allows the web container to determine with which past request a new request is associated. But not all clients support cookies; some users turn off cookies in their browsers, and some HTTP clients are not browsers at all. In such cases, the web container may use a technique to maintain sessions called URL rewriting wherein any links the web application returns to the client have the session id added in as a query string, under the name `JSESSIONID`; for example:

```
JSESSIONID=123456
```

much as the photo application uses the query string to carry the photo index. Finally, for web applications accessed using HTTP over the secure SSL protocol, web containers can use the stateful nature of the underlying SSL protocol to maintain the session.

Whichever technique a web container uses to maintain `HttpSessions`, they are an invaluable tool in web application development.

Java Servlet API Runtime Architecture

We can now draw the architecture of the main classes of the Java Servlet API. In Figure 2-9, we see two browser clients accessing the same `HttpServlet`. There is one `ServletContext` object for the web application containing the servlet. Each client has made multiple HTTP requests to the servlet and received multiple HTTP responses from the servlet in return. Each client's collection of request and response pairs is associated with a unique `HttpSession` object.

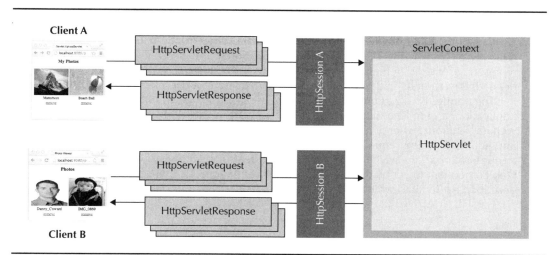

FIGURE 2-9. *Java servlet API object instances, two clients*

The RequestDispatcher

The final API class in our examination of the Java Servlet API is the RequestDispatcher. We already saw the RequestDispatcher in action in the RemovePhotoServlet in our photo application: once the photo was removed, this servlet used the RequestDispatcher to simply forward the request it received to the DisplayAlbumServlet, which treated it just like any HTTP request that had come directly from the client in order to display the newly updated photo album.

RequestDispatcher objects provide a representation of a web resource in a web application, whether it is a web page, Java servlet, or other kind of HTTP web component, and allows the caller to invoke it. In calling a RequestDispatcher object from a Java servlet, you can choose either to *forward the request* to it or *include the response* from it. If you forward the request to it, what you are doing is asking the web resource represented by the RequestDispatcher to write the response for you. This means you must not have already written any of the response yourself, and you must not try to write the response after you have called the RequestDispatcher. This mode is useful when you want another web resource to simply take over the formulation of the response completely. If you use the RequestDispatcher to include the response, then what you are doing is asking the web resource the RequestDispatcher represents to write its response out to the response object you are formulating but may not have completed writing to yourself. This mode is useful when you want another web resource to fill in a gap in the response you are formulating. But similarly to the forward mode, you have to be careful not to trip: in this case, you have to be sure if you are going to continue writing to the response after you have called the RequestDispatcher that the web resource you use the RequestDispatcher to invoke does not close the underlying response. Here are the two methods of the RequestDispatcher:

```
public void forward(ServletRequest request,
                    ServletResponse response)
                        throws ServletException, IOException

public void include(ServletRequest request,
                    ServletResponse response)
                        throws ServletException, IOException
```

You can obtain instances of the RequestDispatcher from the ServletContext in one of two ways: either by the URI path of the web resource in the web application you need it to represent, as we did in the photo application, or by the logical name of the web resource, as defined, for example, in the @WebServlet annotation that decorates the Java servlet class.

The RequestDispatcher can be a very useful class to use to start modularizing a web application, and indeed, it is the cornerstone of many Model-View-Controller frameworks for web applications, wherein a facade "controller" servlet uses the RequestDispatcher to direct and adapt incoming requests to the appropriate "view" web components. But use the RequestDispatcher with care: since the RequestDispatcher is allowing more than one web component to act on the same HttpServletResponse, there are some basic traps, as described earlier, into which it is easy to fall.

Web Applications

We have talked about web applications in an informal way so far: a collection of related web resources and components with a common purpose. The Java Servlet API defines the web application as the collection of web resources and web components that have been collected into the single unit of deployment for the web container: the WAR file.

WAR stands for Web ARchive. It is a zip-based file format that defines a specific structure into which you can put web resources, Java classes, and libraries for Java web components, together with any deployment information the web components need. The term web components here includes, Java servlets, but beyond that, it includes any JSPs, tag libraries, JSF components, web service, or WebSocket components that are part of an application.

File-based web resources such as web pages, stylesheets, image files, JSPs, and JSF files live in the root of the WAR file. The web container uses the directory structure of these entries to map the files to the URI space of the web container. So, for example, if an HTML page is included in a WAR file as `/cars/catalog.xhtml`, and the web application is deployed to the Java EE web container with context root `/car-app`, then the `catalog.xhtml` file will be available to browsers at

`http://mycars.com/car-app/cars/catalog.xhtml`

The WAR file contains a reserved top-level directory name of `WEB-INF/`. This directory is not exposed into the URI space of the web container. In other words, no client of the web container can access this directory as a web resource, nor anything contained within it. Any class files for web components such as Java servlets, web service resources, and WebSockets are packaged into the WAR file under this directory in `/WEB-INF/classes`. If the web application's Java components use any library files, then there is a second name subdirectory of `/WEB-INF` called `/WEB-INF/lib` that will contain any such JAR files.

Finally, WAR files may contain deployment information that accompanies any or all of the web components it holds. This deployment information, held in an XML document called a deployment descriptor located at `/WEB-INF/web.xml` in the WAR file, is a type of configuration information that the web container uses to set up the web application ready for action. We will explore this deployment information shortly, but in fact, we did not need to provide any extra information about how to deploy the Java servlets in our photo application other than that contained within the `@WebServlet` annotation at the class level of each servlet. This may often prove to be the case for Java servlets that you write, but you will need to understand all the possibilities, especially as you expand the repertoire of web components that you create.

We'll summarize the structure of a WAR file with the diagram in Figure 2-10 showing the logical structure, together with an example layout of a fictitious car website.

Deployment Information for Java Servlets

Deployment information for Java servlets may be found in two places! The first place you have already seen is the most convenient: in the class level `@WebServlet` annotation. This holds critical information: the URL mapping that the web container will use to deploy the servlet and

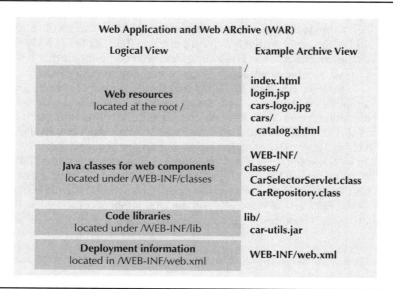

FIGURE 2-10. *WAR file contents and example*

make it available to clients. The second place that may hold deployment information that governs how a Java servlet is brought into service on the Java EE web container is in the deployment descriptor for the web application, or in other words, in the web.xml file in the WAR file holding the Java servlet. For most Java servlets, using the @WebServlet annotation is sufficient, so we will defer a full examination of the web.xml file until Chapter 8. Let's take a look at all the possible configuration options in the @WebServlet annotation in Table 2-1.

Servlet Path Mapping

In our photo application, all we needed was to be able to assign a URI to each Java servlet it contained, relative to the context root of the web application, and rely on the fact that the web container would direct any client requests to that URI to our Java servlet. This may be sufficient for many simple Java servlet applications, but the Java servlet API allows for other modes of mapping servlets into the URI space of the web container.

The Java Servlet API uses the idea of a URL pattern to denote the kind of signifier you can assign to a servlet that the web container will use to route incoming requests to it. As we have seen, a URL pattern can be a relative URI, but it can also come in other forms. A URL pattern can be

- a relative URI

  such as /catalog/albums, /images/display/photo
- a relative URI with wildcard of the form <relative-uri>/*

  such as /catalog/*, /*
- a file extension of the form *.<name>

  such as *.jsp, *.images, *.fruitbaskets

@WebServlet	Purpose	Example
`boolean` `asyncSupported`	Flag to indicate to the container whether this servlet supports the advanced asynchronous operation (see Chapter 8)	`asyncSupported=true`
`String description`	Text description of the servlet, used to display the servlet in tools	`description="A photo display servlet"`
`String displayName`	Text display name of the servlet for showing in tools	`displayName="PhotoComponent"`

`WebInitParam[]`
`initParam`
	An array of key-value pairs that can be retrieved at runtime inside the servlet using `ServletConfig` `.getInitParameter(String name)`	`initParams = {`
		`  @WebInitParam(name="size",`
		`value="large "),`
		`  @WebInitParam(name="frame",`
		`value=" antique")`
		`})`

`String largeIcon`	Relative path to an image in the WAR file used to display the servlet in a tool	`largeIcon="/images/PS_lrg.jpg"`
`String smallIcon`	Relative path to an image in the WAR file used to display the servlet in a tool	`smallIcon="/images/PS_sm.jpg"`
`int loadOnStartup`	Guide to the web container to what order relative to other servlets in the web application to instantiate this servlet	`loadOnStartup=5`
`String name`	Logical name for the Java servlet, used, for example, to create a `RequestDispatcher` to this servlet	`name="PhotoServlet"`
`String[] urlPatterns`	Array of strings used to map the servlet into the URI space of the web container	`urlPatterns="/` `DisplayAlbumServlet"`
`String[] value`	Same as `urlPatterns`, but must not be used at the same time as `urlPatterns`.	`urlPatterns="/` `DisplayAlbumServlet"`

TABLE 2-1. *The @WebServlet annotation*

Each servlet may have one or more URL patterns. So when a request comes into the web container, it must attempt to find the correct servlet to call based on the request URI of the request and the URL patterns of all the servlets in the web application.

As you might imagine, especially in large web applications with many servlets, this can be a complex process. Fortunately, the Java servlet API defines simple rules to help determine which servlet matches a request URI, and in the cases where more than one servlet may match, which one wins out.

First, the web container will look for an *exact match* of the request URI. This means if it finds a Java servlet with a URL pattern that is a relative URI, and the relative URI is the same as the request URI, that servlet will be called.

If no such servlet is found, the web container will look for a servlet that uses a URL pattern that is a *relative URI with wildcard*, where the beginning segment of the relative URI with wildcard matches the beginning segment of the request URI. If more than one such servlet exists with a matching URL pattern under this rule, then the web container selects the servlet with the longest matching relative URI with wildcard.

Finally, if still no servlet is found, the web container checks the end of the request URI for a *filename ending*. If one is found, based on the location of a "." in the last segment of the request URI, then the web container will look for a servlet using a URL pattern with matching *filename ending*. If there is one, it will call it.

Let's look at some examples of this in action. Suppose we have three servlets: `Apple`, `Tree` and `Orange`:

`Apple` uses the url pattern `/orchard/apple`

`Tree` uses the url pattern `/orchard/*`

`Orange` uses the url pattern `*.peel`

Suppose that these three servlets are contained in a web application with context root `/fruits-app`, hosted at `www.fruits.com`:

A request to `http://www.fruits.com/orchard/fruits-app/orchard/apple` will call the `Apple` servlet.

A request to `http://www.fruits.com/orchard/fruits-app/orchard/slippery.peel` will call the `Tree` servlet

A request to `http://www.fruits.com/orchard/fruits-app/orange.peel` will call the `Orange` servlet.

Java Servlets: The Good and the Bad

The Java servlet model is a very open model: it is very flexible and gives a great deal of access to the basic plumbing that forms the basic request and response interaction model of HTTP in the web container. This is both a boon and a curse for developers. As a developer, you are given simultaneous access to the request object and the response object of an HTTP call from the client at the simplest level, from within the handling Java servlet itself, and also from other components. We shall see more of some of these in Chapter 8, and one, the `RequestDispatcher`, we have already seen. Moreover, you are given simultaneous access to requests and responses from all and any clients calling at any one particular moment in time. Even more, the access you have to these interactions encompasses all stages in the lifecycle of the data actually arriving and being transmitted. For example, you can attempt access to request data even before it has all arrived, and you can write to the response even before all the request has arrived. Furthermore, as we shall see in Chapter 8 with servlet filters and listeners, you have enormous flexibility in intercepting interactions from a client in several separate components.

The flip side of this open access to the model is that the API design does not preclude the possibility of abusing the API. It is very easy to attempt to write data to the `HttpServletResponse` object after you have forwarded the request to another web component, resulting in a runtime error. It is possible to attempt to obtain both an `InputStream` and a `Reader` to read the data out of the `HttpServletRequest` object. It is also not easy to determine when the data in an `HttpServletResponse` is actually sent, since the API allows the web container some discretion in buffering the response data. This can be a particular issue if a servlet writes data to the response and then encounters an error: what data has actually been transmitted to the client at the point at which the error occurs?

Programming a Java servlet to be multithreaded puts an extra burden on the Java developer: the servlet API could have been designed so that each Java servlet instance was called by only one thread at a time, which would mean that the developer would not need to worry about concurrent access to data referenced in the servlet.

Perhaps the most common complaint about Java servlets as a component model for building large dynamic websites is that writing HTML code inside Java statements makes for a very heavyweight development model, particularly for web developers used to WYSIWYG HTML editors. It takes some skill to look at a Java servlet that writes a large HTML page and picture how it is going to look, and still more to tweak the look of the web page it generates.

One further complaint about the Java servlet model is that there is little support for the separation of presentation code—for example, the HTML tags making up a web page—from the code that defines the interaction model with the website—for example, the pathways a user traverses as they use the application.

These last two deficiencies in the model led to the development of two of the other web component technologies in the Java EE platform: The first deficiency led to the development
of JavaServer Pages, which attempt to solve the problem of burying markup code inside compiled Java statements. And the second deficiency led to the evolution of a number of Model-View-Controller frameworks for the web container that ultimately led to the development of JavaServer Faces.

Today, the Java Servlet API is the foundation of web technology in Java, mostly due to its relatively low level and open approach to modeling HTTP interactions on the server. While the API allows developers to fall into some traps, with careful use, it is used to build the most popular Java web frameworks in use today.

Summary

In this chapter, you have seen the fundamental building blocks of the Java EE web container: the Java Servlet API. You started out with an overview of the HTTP protocol. Then you looked at the basic functions of a Java servlet for processing the server side of HTTP interactions, examining the form of the `HttpServletRequest` and `HttpServletResponse`. By examining an example application, a photo application, we saw how a web application that allows users to upload photos to an online photo album can be written using three Java servlets, each with different characteristics. This led to a more detailed exposition of the Java Servlet API, the lifecycle of a Java servlet and its threading characteristics, the `ServletContext`, the `HttpSession`, and the `RequestDispatcher`. You saw how Java servlets are packaged into a portable deployment file called a WAR file, and looked at the deployment attributes of a Java servlet as expressed in the `@WebServlet` annotation. You ended the chapter with an exploration of the strengths and weaknesses of the Java Servlet API.

If you spend a lot of time writing dynamic web applications for the Java platform, you will very likely write much of your application using one or more of the other web component technologies other than Java servlets available in Java EE. But as you learn these other component technologies, you will see the echoes of the Java Servlet API that underpins them all. A solid grounding in the Java Servlet API will take you far.

CHAPTER
3

Dynamic Web Pages: JSP

A JavaServer Page (JSP) is a Java servlet turned inside out. In other words, a JSP is equivalent to a servlet in the sense that almost everything you can do in a Java servlet you can also do in a JSP; it is how you do it that is different.

In the last chapter on the Java Servlet API, you learned that a Java servlet is a Java component that analyzes an HTTP request and writes out response content either to an `OutputStream` or to a `Writer`. As you write more Java servlets, you will observe that much of the content that you write to the response object is static, and only a relatively small amount of the code is dynamically generating the data to write to the output. This is particularly true for Java servlets that write HTML content: much of the Java servlet code is of the form

```
out.println(....Java string literal representing a line of HTML code...);
```

The inspiration for JSPs came from the observation that embedding HTML code inside `out.println()` statements not only makes the HTML code difficult to maintain, it is counterintuitive to web developers who are used to editing HTML code directly in an HTML-friendly editor, rather than in a Java text editor or integrated development environment (IDE).

Thus, in JSP programming, instead of the static content of the web component being embedded inside Java code, the dynamic fragments of the JSP are embedded as Java code within the static content, as shown in Figure 3-1.

This feature makes JSPs especially well suited to the creation of web components that contain a great deal of static content that is frequently tweaked and adjusted in a publishing tool, together with small amounts of embedded dynamic content. In other words, JSPs are well suited to creating content for a typical dynamic HTML website. In such sites, many of the pages are static: static layouts; infrequently changing portions of static content that embeds more dynamic generated content, such as breaking news headlines; personalized information such as account names; and dynamically retrieved data such as top news headlines or recent purchases.

The key to understanding JSP technology is understanding what Java environment you have available when you use Java code to embed dynamic content into a JSP, and the relationship between the content language you are using (more often than not HTML, but not always) and the dynamic data you wish to present.

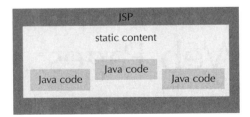 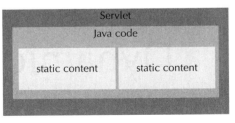

FIGURE 3-1. *JSPs versus Java servlets*

JSP Runtime Architecture

Much becomes clear about the Java environment available in a JSP when you understand what happens to a JavaServer Page when you deploy it to the Java EE web container. After the JSP has been deployed as part of a WAR file to the Java EE web container, and some time before the web container attempts to process the first request to that JSP, the web container reads the JSP you deployed. From that information, it generates the Java code for a Java servlet that fulfills the objectives of the JSP. It compiles the generated Java servlet and invokes it with the request that the client intended for the JSP. In this way, the JSP never really deals with the HTTP request or the response. The HTTP request intended for the JSP is handled in fact by the generated Java servlet that the Java EE web container created for it. This process is shown in Figure 3-2.

This provides a large clue as to which parts of the Java EE web container environment are available to the JSP: it is largely the same environment we have already seen in the Java Servlet API.

The JSP technology at its essence uses syntax to allow Java code to be embedded within static content. The first and most basic form of this syntax is `<% %>`. You can write regular Java code inside the `<% %>` braces and have access to the Java servlet and JSP APIs in such a context. When the Java EE web container comes to create the generated Java servlet that will "implement" the JSP, it takes any static content lines in the JSP and wraps them in an `out.println()` statement. The web container also takes any Java code in the JSP embedded within the `<% %>` braces and writes it directly, in sequence, in the generated Java servlet, as shown in Figure 3-3.

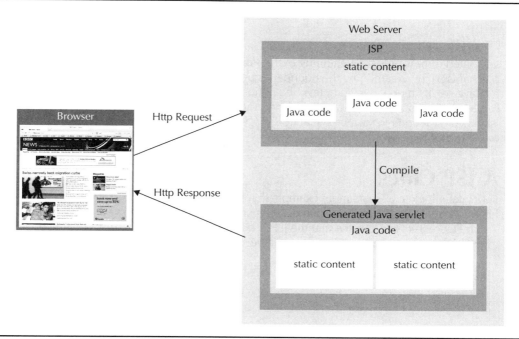

FIGURE 3-2. *Interpreting JSPs in the web container*

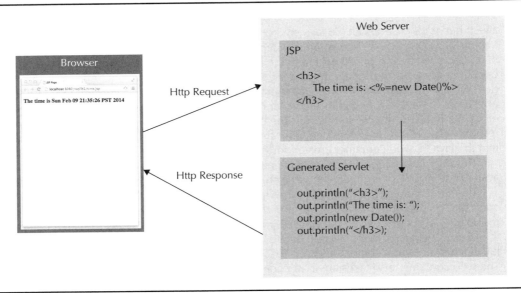

FIGURE 3-3. *Generating the servlet code from a JSP*

In this view of a JSP, the basic syntax for embedded code fragments and their equivalent generated form is only the beginning of the story. JSP provides a rich environment and set of mechanisms for streamlining the boundaries between static and dynamic content built on top of the Java servlet model. Nevertheless, the notion of JSP as being fundamentally the same as a Java servlet, but with a different programming model consisting of a sea of static content containing islands of Java code in various syntactical disguises, is the key to understanding the many aspects of JSP technology.

A JSP Clock

Let's take a look at a very simple example that shows some of the foundations of JSP. Here we have a very simple JSP clock, which displays an HTML page containing the time.

In Figure 3-4, you can see that the JSP is in the page `clock.jsp`. You can already see that much of the page is static: no matter when you load the page in the browser, it will probably say

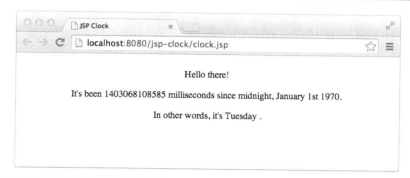

FIGURE 3-4. *JSP clock example*

"Hello there!" every time. But you can also see that the time must be generated dynamically at the time your browser requests the page. Let's take a look at the code:

```
<%@page contentType="text/html" pageEncoding="UTF-8"%>
<%@page import="java.util.Date" %>
<%@page import="java.text.SimpleDateFormat" %>
<!DOCTYPE html>
<html>
    <head>
        <title>JSP Clock</title>
    </head>
    <body>
        <div align='center'>
            <br/>
            Hello there!
            <br/><br/>
            It's been <%=System.currentTimeMillis()%> milliseconds
            since midnight, January 1st 1970.
            <br/><br/>
            In other words, it's
            <%
                Date now = new Date();
                SimpleDateFormat sdf = new SimpleDateFormat("EEEEEEEE");
                String today = sdf.format(now);
                out.println(today.trim());
            %>.
        </div>
    </body>
</html>
```

First, we start by noticing the `<%@page%>` lines at the top of the JSP page. These statements are called JSP directives. The JSP `@page` directive is used to set up properties that are used by the whole of the JSP page. In this example, we have three `@page` directives: the first defines the MIME type and encoding for this HTML page, the second two define that the JSP page is going to use two Java classes: `java.util.Date` and `java.text.SimpleDateFormat`.

Reading beyond the page directives, we encounter the HTML code that we would expect for this page, until we get to the line:

```
It's been <%=System.currentTimeMillis()%> milliseconds
```

The text `<%=System.currentTimeMillis()%>` is called a JSP scriptlet. When we enter it, we leave the world of static HTML code and we rejoin the world of dynamic Java code. There are two kinds of JSP scriptlets

```
<%= java expression %>
```

where `java expression` evaluates to a value. This value is then used when the page is called and the value becomes part of the page output, and

```
<% java expression %>
```

where `java expression` is a collection of Java statements that perform some calculation and take some action. We see the second form in our example page when we come to calculate and display the current day of the week:

```
<%
    Date now = new Date();
    SimpleDateFormat sdf = new SimpleDateFormat("EEEEEEE");
    String today = sdf.format(now);
    out.println(today.trim());
%>
```

Notice that in this Java statement block, the JSP page is relying on the `@page` imports it declared at the top in order for the Java classes `Date` and `SimpleDateFormat` to be resolved. Second, look at the variable `out`. What is it?

In this line of code, `out` refers to the output of the underlying HTTP response that carries the content back to the calling client, and is a type of `java.io.Writer` from the JSP API, specifically, `javax.servlet.jsp.JspWriter`. Notice that this variable has not been declared anywhere else in the JSP: that is because the Java environment within JSP expressions comes preconfigured with a number of objects called implicit objects. Other examples include the `session` variable (the current `HttpSession`) and the `response` variable (the current `HttpServletResponse`).

So the line

```
out.println(today.trim());
```

writes the day string to the response writer, and that is how it appears on the page when loaded in the browser.

More complicated JSPs that make further use of embedded Java code that is in the form of a scriptlet, as we see in this simple example, tend to suffer some of the same maintainability issues that Java servlets can, except in reverse. Ideally, static markup content and dynamic Java content are separated into different files. The JSP techniques and technology for doing this will lead us into the topics of JSP beans, tag libraries, and expression language. But first, we need to more fully understand the core JSP syntax that this simple example has introduced.

JSP Syntax

By convention, JSP files should have the file ending `.jsp`. This identifies to the Java EE web container that it should attempt to interpret the file as a JSP. The URL for a JSP is just like the URL for a regular static content file in a web application. That is, for a JSP file located at

```
/mysite/hello.jsp
```

in a WAR file, the complete URL to the JSP at runtime is

```
http://<hostname:port>/<web-app-context-root>/mysite/hello.jsp
```

It is possible to map a JSP to additional URLs within the web application, but we will leave the more complicated topic of custom URL-mapping in a web application until Chapter 9. For now, it will be sufficient simply to use the URL that is derived from the archive path within the WAR file.

JSP syntax falls into two categories: JSP directives and JSP actions. JSP directives are statements in the JSP syntax that govern properties that are global to the JSP, for example, the MIME type of the content that the JSP will produce, as we saw in the clock example, or to which page the browser should be directed should the JSP encounter an error. JSP actions are statements in the JSP syntax that control some aspect of how a portion of the JSP output is created, such as including the output of another web component within the JSP, or including a property value from a JavaBean in a JSP. Let's start our examination of the syntax with JSP directives.

JSP Directives

JSP directives, which dictate properties global to the JSP, are all of the form

```
<%@ directive_name attribute-1="value-1"...attribute-n="value-n" %>
```

They can appear anywhere in the JSP file, though by convention, they are usually listed at the top of the JSP file. This makes good sense, because their effect is on the whole of the JSP. The three directives are

```
page
```

This directive governs general properties of the JSP, such as characterizing its output, buffering properties, and using imports for Java scriptlets.

```
include
```

This directive allows a JSP to include the content of another file. This can be useful for including, for example, a standard header in your JSP.

```
taglib
```

This directive allows a JSP to declare that it will use special tags from something called a tag library. A tag library is a collection of Java classes that formulate small snippets of markup output, each of which is associated with a markup tag that can be included in a JSP page. We will see tag libraries later in this chapter.

Each JSP directive may appear multiple times with different attributes, so there is a design choice as to whether to use multiple attributes with the same directive name, or whether to list multiple directives, each with one attribute. The type of design choice is really a matter of aesthetics, but developers usually group related attributes together in the same directive and use separate directives for attributes that are not related.

Page Directives: General Properties Global to the JSP

JSP page directives are a collection of instructions to the JSP runtime as to how to process the JSP. There are several different kinds; let's take a look at them one by one.

Attributes Governing JSP Output   Two page directive attributes declare information about the output of a JSP: `contentType` and `pageEncoding`. The `contentType` attribute allows the JSP to declare the MIME type of the content it produces, and the `pageEncoding` allows the JSP to declare the character encoding it uses. These may be listed as separate attributes, or, for brevity, the `pageEncoding` may be combined into the `contentType` attribute. For example

```
<%page contentType"text/html"%>
<%page pageEncoding="utf-8"%>
```

is equivalent to

```
<%page contentType"text/html; utf-8" %>
```

Here are some additional examples of `contentType`:

```
<%page contentType"image/jpeg" %>
<%page contentType" text/plain"%>
```

Attributes Governing Languages Used in JSPs   JSPs use the Java language for scriptlets and JSP Expression Language (JSP EL). Languages other than Java may be used for scriptlets if the underlying implementation supports them. Four page directive attributes govern the use of these languages in a JSP: `language`, `isELIgnored`, `isScriptingEnabled`, and `import`. A JSP may declare the

```
<%page language="java"%>
```

directive to indicate it uses Java in its scriptlets, although this particular value is not usually necessary to declare because Java is always supported in JSPs. If a JSP does not use JSP EL, it may declare it as

```
<%page isELIgnored ="true"%>
```

which can yield some performance gains. The default is that the JSP implementation always looks for uses of JSP EL in the JSP. Finally, a JSP that uses no scriptlets at all may declare it by using the page directive `isScriptingEnabled`.

```
<%page isScriptingEnabled ="false"%>
```

The JSP implementation assumes that every JSP has scriptlets unless it is told otherwise using this directive.

When Java scriptlets are used, they often need to import classes from other Java platform packages, in which case the JSP must declare a page directive using the `import` attribute. The value is a comma-separated list of packages the scriptlet code in the JSP will need. For example,

```
<%page import ="java.util.*, java.text.*"%>
```

which is equivalent to

```
<%page import ="java.util.*"%>
<%page import ="java.text.*"%>
```

Many developers prefer the second style, where the import is split into multiple page directives using the import with a single package, as it more closely mimics the single package per import statement pattern found in the Java language.

JSP scriptlets may use any of the classes in `java.lang`, the Java servlet API, and the JSP Java API, which are located in `javax.servlet` with subpackages, and `javax.servlet.jsp` with subpackages.

Attributes Controlling How the JSP Behaves at Runtime   When the JSP page output is gathered in order to be written into the underlying output stream back to the calling client, there are a number of choices about how the content is written. The implementation may buffer the content, and may wish to choose when to write the buffer to the output. Without using any special page directive, JSP implementations buffer the page output and automatically flush the content to the output when the buffer fills, so these switches are definitely for more advanced developers. They can give useful control to the developer in optimizing JSP performance for particular pages and particular clients. The last two attributes of the JSP page directive are a request to the JSP implementation to control aspects of how the JSP output is buffered: `autoFlush` and `buffer`. The `buffer` attribute defines whether any buffering is used at all and, if so, how large the buffer should be. The second, the `autoFlush` attribute, is a switch that instructs the JSP implementation whether to flush the buffer when it fills or whether to require the JSP to flush the buffer manually. For example

```
<@page autoFlush="false" buffer="8kb"%>
```

instructs the JSP implementation to use a buffer no smaller than 8 kilobytes and not to flush it automatically. Contrastingly,

```
<@page buffer="none"%>
```

instructs the JSP implementation not to use a buffer at all, and

```
<@page buffer="6kb"%>
```

instructs the JSP implementation to use a buffer of size at least 6 kilobytes with automatic flushing of content when the buffer fills.

As for Java servlets, the default threading model for JSPs is that they are expected to handle multiple incoming HTTP requests concurrently. This frequently happens in web applications with more than one client! However, it can be useful to be able to create JSPs that you know will only ever be called by one thread at a time. In such cases, JSP implementations may choose to make any concurrent requests form a line and invoke only the JSP one thread at a time, or it may choose to instantiate multiple instances of the same JSP, each handling only one request at a time. With either approach, the JSP implementation can guarantee that each JSP instance is handling one HTTP request, or thread, at a time. You can use the `isThreadSafe` attribute:

```
<@page isThreadSafe="false"%>
```

to let the JSP implementation know that this JSP needs gentle handling and should be called only one thread at a time.

JSP Error Pages   JSPs may act as error pages for other web components. This is useful if you wish to customize the page that the client sees if a JSP generates an unhandled runtime error. In such cases, the JSP that wishes to act as a nicely formatted error page must use the `isErrorPage` attribute in a page directive:

```
<@page isErrorPage="true"%>
```

and a JSP that wishes the client to be redirected to this error page in the event of an unhandled exception at runtime can indicate the name of the JSP that it wishes to use using the `errorPage` attribute; for example:

```
<@page errorPage="/myerror.jsp"%>
```

Turning Off `HttpSession` Tracking   As we will see when we look at JSP implicit objects shortly, JSP developers can easily get hold of the `HttpSession` from the JSP Java environment available to scriptlets. However, session tracking comes with some overhead, and as an optimization, some JSPs that do not make use of the `HttpSession` can turn off the session tracking mechanism by using the `session` attribute of the page directive, such as

```
<@page session="false"%>
```

By default, that is, without such a directive, the `HttpSession` is always maintained by the JSP implementation. We will see that this is a useful way to share a client-specific application state.

Now that we have toured all the attributes of the `@page` directive, let's summarize what we have learned in the following table.

Page Directive	Purpose	Values	Default
autoFlush	If buffering is used to write JSP content to the output stream, determines whether to flush the buffer when it fills or raise an exception	true or false	true
buffer	Defines the size of the buffer used to write JSP content to the underlying output stream.	None for no buffering or the number of KB, e.g., 8KB	Depends on implementation—typically a few KB

Page Directive	Purpose	Values	Default
`contentType`	Defines the MIME type of the JSP content	MIME type strings	`Text/html`
`errorPage`	Defines whether this JSP can be used as an error page for another JSP	`true` or `false`	`false`
`extends`	Defines a subclass of HttpServlet that the servlet for this JSP will extend	`Mypackage` `.MyServletClass`	`javax.servlet` `.HttpServlet`
`import`	Defines the Java imports for scriptlets in the JSP	Comma-separated list of package names	`java.lang`, the Java servlet, and JSP APIs
`info`	A text description of the JSP used in tools	A string	Empty string
`isELIgnored`	Declares whether JSP Expression Language is can be ignored in this JSP	`true` or `false`	`false`
`isThreadSafe`	Declares whether this JSP is able to receive multiple concurrent requests	`true` or `false`	`true`
`isScriptingEnabled`	Declares whether this JSP uses scriptlets	`true` or `false`	`true`
`language`	The language used in scriptlets in this JSP	TBD	`Java`
`pageEncoding`	The file encoding of the JSP	String representing a charset	
`session`	Declares whether this JSP uses `HttpSessions`	`true` or `false`	`true`

The `include` Directive

The JSP `include` directive allows you to pull in static content into your JSP page. This could be used to add a standard header or footer to your web page, or to insert content at any point. The syntax is simple: the file attribute allows you to define the relative URL of the file you wish to incorporate:

```
<% @include file="myHeader.html"%>
```

The `taglib` Directive

The JSP `taglib` directive allows you to import custom tags that are implemented in one or more Java classes in a JSP tag library. We will examine JSP tag libraries shortly, but for now, you use this directive to specify the descriptor file (ending in `.tld`) that describes all the available tags and the prefix that the JSP will use when it incorporates the tags:

```
<%@ taglib uri="myShoppingTags.tld" prefix="shopping" >
```

Now that we have seen all the JSP directives, our next step is learning the JSP syntax that allows us to generate dynamic content: JSP actions. Before we do that, we need to take a look at a central aspect of the JSP programming model, and one to which several of the JSP actions relate.

Using Java Beans from JSPs

As we mentioned earlier, the heavy use of Java scriptlets within a JSP leads to a code file containing a mix of code in two different languages: one for the static content and one for the dynamic content. On one hand, the central feature of JSPs is to be able to mix those worlds together. On the other hand, as with Java servlets that produce web pages, it leads to code with a poor separation of responsibilities. All aspects of the JSP, whether it be code for presentation, code for data retrieval from a data source, code that checks input values, or code that governs the user's interaction flow with JSPs, are all in one place. Fortunately, JSP includes two central mechanisms to factor out dynamic Java code from static web content more cleanly than the scriptlet syntax allows. Those mechanisms are the use of JavaBeans from JSPs and JSP tag libraries.

A JavaBean is a regular Java class that conforms to a number of conventions that allows it to be a reusable component in a variety of settings. In order for a Java class to be a JavaBean, it must

- Have a zero args constructor
- Use the JavaBean property pattern to expose any data that the class wants client code to use

For example, any data of class `Foo` JavaBean wishes to be retrieved must have a method of the form

```
public Foo getFooPropertyName()
```

where `fooPropertyName` is the name of the property of type `Foo`, and any data of class `Bar` the JavaBean wishes to be stored must be of the form

```
public void setBarPropertyName(Bar bar);
```

where `barPropertyName` is the name of the property of type `Bar`.

To be able to use a JavaBean from within a JSP, you need three pieces of syntax for all JSP actions:

```
<jsp:useBean id="name for bean" class="full y qualified classname of bean">
```

The `id` gives the JavaBean a name you can use elsewhere in the JSP, and `class` tells the JSP implementation the `classname`. Now you are ready to use the JavaBean in a JSP. You can use the JavaBean two ways: either you can retrieve a property from the JavaBean using the

```
<jsp:getProperty name="name for bean" property="property name">
```

action, or you can set a value on the JavaBean by using the

```
<jsp:setProperty name="name for bean" property="property name" value="property value string">
```

Let's take a look at an example. Since one of the goals of using JavaBeans in JSPs is to separate the dynamic Java code from the static web content in a JSP, let's take our clock example and see whether using this technique achieves that goal.

First, we remember that there are two scriptlets in the `clock.jsp`:

```
<%=System.currentTimeMillis()%>
```

and

```
<%
    Date now = new Date();
    SimpleDateFormat sdf = new SimpleDateFormat("EEEEEEEE");
    String today = sdf.format(now);
    out.println(today.trim());
%>
```

First, let's take this code and put it into a JavaBean instead of having it float in scriptlets:

```
import java.text.SimpleDateFormat;
import java.util.Date;

public class ClockBean {

    public long getCurrentTimeSinceEpoch() {
        return System.currentTimeMillis();
    }

    public String getReadableDate() {
        Date now = new Date();
        SimpleDateFormat sdf = new SimpleDateFormat("EEEEEEEE");
        String today = sdf.format(now);
        return today;
    }
}
```

Next, we will replace the scriptlets in the JSP page, yielding:

```
<%@page contentType="text/html" pageEncoding="UTF-8"%>
<!DOCTYPE html>
<html>
    <head>
        <title>JSP Clock</title>
    </head>
    <body>
        <jsp:useBean id="myBean" class="javaeems.chapter3.clockbean.ClockBean"/>
        <div align='center'>
            <br/>
            Hello there!
```

```
            <br/><br/>
            It's been
                <jsp:getProperty name="myBean" property="currentTimeSinceEpoch"/>
            milliseconds since midnight, January 1st 1970.
            <br/><br/>
            In other words, it's <jsp:getProperty name="myBean"
property="readableDate"/>.
        </div>
    </body>
</html>
```

Note that we no longer have any need for the @import directives at the top of the JSP, and we have replaced the scriplets by retrieving the values of the currentTimeSinceEpoch and readableDate properties of the bean we declare under the ID myBean.

We can go a little further and allow the JavaBean to be configurable in terms of how it formats the readable date. Let's add a new property called dateFormat to our bean, use it to display the readable Date, and call it ConfigurableClockBean:

```
import java.text.SimpleDateFormat;
import java.util.Date;

public class ConfigurableClockBean {
    String dateFormat = "EEEEEEEE";

    public long getCurrentTimeSinceEpoch() {
        return System.currentTimeMillis();
    }

    public void setDateFormat(String dateFormat) {
        this.dateFormat = dateFormat;
    }

    public String getReadableDate() {
        Date now = new Date();
        SimpleDateFormat sdf = new SimpleDateFormat(this.dateFormat);
        String today = sdf.format(now);
        return today;

    }
}
```

Now from the JSP, we can choose how we would like the date to be displayed on the page, but setting the property of the bean using the <jsp:setProperty> action:

```
<%@page contentType="text/html" pageEncoding="UTF-8"%>
<!DOCTYPE html>
<html>
    <head>
        <title>JSP Clock</title>
    </head>
    <body>
        <jsp:useBean id="myBean" class="javaeems.chapter3.clockbean.ConfigurableClockBean"/>
        <div align='center'>
        <br/>
```

```
        Hello there!
        <br/><br/>
        It's been
            <jsp:getProperty name="myBean" property="currentTimeSinceEpoch"/>
        milliseconds since midnight, January 1, 1970.
        <br/><br/>
        In other words, it's <jsp:getProperty name="myBean" property="readableDate"/>
        <br/><br/>
        <jsp:setProperty name="myBean" property="dateFormat" value="MMMMMMMMM"/>
        Or in other words, it's the month of <jsp:getProperty name="myBean"
property="readableDate"/>
        in
        <jsp:setProperty name="myBean" property="dateFormat" value="YYYY"/>
        <jsp:getProperty name="myBean" property="readableDate"/>
    </div>
  </body>
</html>
```

This yields the result shown in Figure 3-5.

Have we achieved our goal? Yes, all the dynamic code has been separated from the presentation code. This means that the dynamic code can be separately maintained from the presentation code, perhaps by different developers with different skill sets. You can probably imagine how useful this technique becomes as the complexity of a JSP increases from this rather simple level.

Several other attributes can be used on the three JavaBean-related actions of `<jsp:useBean ...>`, `<jsp:getProperty ...>`, and `<jsp:setProperty ...>`. First, when declaring that the JSP will use a particular JavaBean, the ID attribute is mandatory: the JavaBean must have a name so that the bean can be identified and called from elsewhere in the JSP (for example, from a `<jsp:getProperty ...>` action). The JavaBean instance can be instantiated through two mechanisms: by class name using the class attribute, as we saw in the example, or by passing a bean name, which is interpreted as the name understood by a call to `java.beans.Beans.instantiate()`. Typically, JSPs simply refer to the JavaBean by its fully qualified Java classname, that is, the first mechanism.

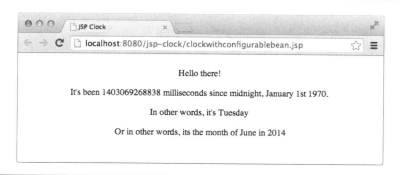

FIGURE 3-5. *JSP clock with JavaBean*

The management of objects by the platform is a recurring feature of many aspects of the Java EE platform. One question that Java EE developers often ask is: what is the scope of an object? When is it created, what is the period in which it can be used, and when is it destroyed? These are good questions for instances of JavaBeans used by JSPs. Without intervention by the developer, JavaBean instances created for a JSP in the cases we are exploring are instantiated at some point before the `<jsp:useBean>` action is encountered in the JSP, and they are valid until all the JSP output has been written to the buffer. In other words, the JSP bean can be used anywhere within the same JSP after its `<jsp:useBean>` declaration, but not outside the JSP. This is called page scope.

Four scopes are available to the JSP developer:

- *Page scope* is the scope that is active within the same JSP.

- *Request scope* is the scope that is active in the context of the same HTTP request. This is similar to page scope, but this scope is still active if the JSP forwards the request to another JSP, or within a JSP that the original JSP has included using the `<jsp:include>` mechanism described later.

- *Session scope* is the scope that is active within the same HTTP session. This may span several interactions from the same client to several JSPs within the same web application from the same client.

- *Application scope* is the scope that is active within the same application. This spans all interactions within the same web application with all its clients.

So, the final optional attribute of the `<jsp:useBean>` declaration is the scope attribute and can take the values page, request, session, or application. If omitted, the default value is page.

When a JavaBean is in a specific scope, it means the JSP implementation will instantiate one instance of the JavaBean for that scope. If your JavaBean is in page scope, each time the JSP is called, a new instance of the JavaBean will be created and will be valid only within that page. If your JavaBean is in request scope, the JSP implementation will instantiate one instance of the JavaBean for each HTTP request, and the instance will be valid within the JSP and any other JSPs that the original JSP forwards to or includes from. If your JavaBean is in session scope, the JSP implementation will create one instance of the JavaBean that will be valid for each active session in the application. If your JavaBean is in application scope, then the JSP implementation will maintain one instance of the JavaBean for the whole lifetime of the application, no matter which client is calling the JSP.

Now that we have learned all the ways to declare a JavaBean, let's look at the variants for getting and setting the JavaBean properties. The syntax

```
<jsp:getProperty name="myBean" property="myBeanProperty" />
```

retrieves the value from the call `getMyBeanProperty()` on the JavaBean, which has been declared in the containing context in this JSP. The JSP implementation uses the string representation of the returned object from the JavaBean. Both name and property are required, and are the only attributes of this JSP action.

The syntax

```
<jsp:setProperty name="myBean" property="myBeanProperty"
                    value="myBeanPropertyValue"/>
```

is the most typical form of the JSP action for setting the value on a JavaBean. The JSP implementation attempts a call to the method `setMyBeanProperty()` on the JavaBean, passing in a parameter based on the value string from the declaration and parameter type of the method. If the parameter method is a `String`, which is the simplest and most straightforward case, the JSP implementation passes in the value string directly. If the parameter type is not a `String`, the JSP implementation makes an attempt to convert the value `String` into an object of the parameter type, looking for a single-argument `String` constructor.

Alternatively, you can set the properties on the JavaBean from the HTTP request properties, that is to say, the key-value pairs passed in through the query string on the HTTP request. In this case, instead of specifying the `value` attribute, you can use the `param` attribute, giving the value as the name of the request property. In such a situation, the JSP implementation parses out the value of the given request parameter as a string and passes that to the setter on the JavaBean. For example, the action

```
<jsp:setProperty name="myColorBean" property="color" param="brush-color"/>
```

in a JSP called `painting.jsp` and invoked with the URL

```
painting.jsp?brush-color=red
```

will cause the JavaBean named `myColorBean`'s `setColor(String colorName)` method to be called with the value "red."

jsp:forward and jsp:include

These JSP actions allow a JSP to forward the HTTP request to another web component (servlet, JSP, static file) and to include the output of another web component into it.

The forwarding action syntax looks like this:

```
<jsp:forward page="relative URL of the web component" />
```

and there are no variants. Just as with Java servlets, once a JSP has forwarded its request to another web component, any content it attempts to write after the forward has been processed is simply ignored.

The including action syntax looks like this:

```
<jsp:include page="relative URL of the web component" flush="true" />
```

where `flush` is an optional attribute that controls whether the content of the JSP using the include's buffer is flushed (that is, all its content written to the client) prior to the include or not. Typically, JSPs want all their content to have been sent before including the output from another JSP in this manner, so this default is `true` if the flush attribute is absent. When the included web component's output has been sent, the remainder of the content on the calling JSP is sent.

When using the `<jsp:include>` action, you can pass request parameters from the calling JSP to the web component being called. This can be achieved using

```
<jsp:param name = "paramName" value = "paramValue">
```

For example, the code

```
<jsp:include page="brush.jsp">
      <jsp:param name="softness" value="very soft">
</jsp:include>
```

passes the request parameter `softness=very soft` to the `brush.jsp`. This is a very useful technique for passing application state between a JSP and a web component it includes.

Finally, be careful not to confuse the `<jsp:include>` action with the `@include` directive we saw earlier. The `<jsp:include>` action is used to include the output of any web component, be it a static web resource such as a web page or image file, or any dynamic web component such as another JSP or Java servlet. The `@include` directive is used to incorporate only static web resources.

jsp:plugin

The `jsp:plugin` action allows you to use a Java applet in a JSP without worrying about how to generate the appropriate client-browser-dependent tags (`<object>` or `<embed>`). Here is the syntax:

```
<jsp:plugin
   type="bean|applet"
   code="objectCode"
   codebase="objectCodebase"
   { align="alignment" }
   { archive="archiveList" }
   { height="height" }
   { hspace="hspace" }
   { jreversion="jreversion" }
   { name="componentName" }
   { vspace="vspace" }
   { width="width" }
   { nspluginurl="url" }
   { iepluginurl="url" } >
   { <jsp:params>
     { <jsp:param name="paramName" value= paramValue" /> }+
   </jsp:params> }
   { <jsp:fallback> arbitrary_text </jsp:fallback> }
</jsp:plugin>
```

Here is an example of the `jsp:plugin` action used for an applet of the Banner class, which uses two parameters, and a text error message:

```
<jsp:plugin
      type="applet"
      codebase="/myapplet"
      code="Banner.class"
      width="100"
      height="25">
   <jsp:param name="highlight" value="true" />
   <jsp:param name="repeat" value="20" />

   <jsp:fallback>
      Error initializing the Banner applet
   </jsp:fallback>

</jsp:plugin>
```

`<jsp:text>`

The `<jsp:text>` action enables you to dynamically include text in a JSP. This is particularly useful when using JSP Expression Language, as we will see later. But you can also use a scriptlet to dynamically generate the text.

The remaining JSP actions allow the developer to dynamically create XML content from a JSP. They are `<jsp:element>`, `<jsp:attribute>`, and `<jsp:body>`. These actions allow you to generate an XML element, its attributes, and its body. Here is an example:

```
<%@page language="java" contentType="text/html"%>
<html>
    <head>
        <title>Generate XML Element</title>
    </head>
    <body>
        <jsp:element name="my-element">
            <jsp:attribute name="my-attribute">
                Here is the value of my-attribute
            </jsp:attribute>
            <jsp:body>
                Here is the body of my-element
            </jsp:body>
        </jsp:element>
    </body>
</html>
```

which generates the following HTML when returned to the client:

```
<html>
    <head>
        <title>Generate XML Element</title>
    </head>
    <body>
        <my-element my-attribute="Here is the value of my-attribute">
            Here is the body of my-element
        </my-element>
    </body>
</html>
```

The Java Environment for JSPs

Now that we have explored the JSP syntax in some detail, it is time we turned our attention to the Java environment available to Java code embedded in a JSP. This will become especially important to understand when we come to the topic that follows, and our second mechanism that helps organize dynamic code and presentation code in JSP applications: tag libraries.

The Java environment in which JSPs can operate can be described in two different ways. The first is to describe the Java objects that the JSP implementation makes available in the form of named variables from a scriptlet. The second approach is to tour the JSP Java API classes. We will start with the first approach, as it leads naturally to the second.

Java objects in the form of named variables that are available in the Java environment for a JSP are called the JSP's implicit objects. They are considered implicit because the JSP doesn't know where they come from; like the next meal to a fortunate child, they simply appear when needed.

We already encountered an implicit object in the clock example: the `java.io.Writer` object with the name `out` that we used to print the formatted date in the scriptlet:

```
<%
    Date now = new Date();
    SimpleDateFormat sdf = new SimpleDateFormat("EEEEEEEE");
    String today = sdf.format(now);
    out.println(today.trim());
%>
```

This object is already familiar because it is based on the Java Servlet API `java.io.Writer` that you can obtain from the `HttpServletResponse` object passed into a Java servlet when servicing a client request.

The following table shows the most frequently used implicit objects available from a JSP.

Implicit Object	Used for
`javax.servlet.ServletContext`	Access to the web container, storing custom attributes
`javax.servlet.ServletConfig`	Access to the configuration information about the servlet backing this JSP
`java.lang.Throwable`	For JSPs that are acting as error pages; the exception gives the developer access to the exception that caused the current error page to be called
`javax.servlet.jsp.JspWriter`	Access to the writer for writing textual context out to the client in the HTTP response body
`HttpServlet`	Access to "this," the instance of the Java servlet backing this JSP
`javax.servlet.jsp.PageContext`	Access to a JSP API object that represents the JSP page and its properties
`javax.servlet.http.HttpServletRequest`	Access to the HTTP request that came from the client
`javax.servlet.http.HttpServletResponse`	Access to the HTTP response for writing content out to the client
`javax.servlet.http.HttpSession`	Access to the current HTTP session for this JSP

A few more implicit objects, all of which can be derived from those in the tables, are available to access cookies, headers, and request parameters. As a Java servlet developer, all of the JSP implicit objects will be very familiar: they are mostly the same objects that are available to you inside a Java servlet's service method. This is no surprise given that a JSP is turned into a Java servlet's service implementation at runtime!

JSP Standard Tags

Standard with the Java EE platform, JSP defines a collection of very useful tags that can be freely used in any JSP. They fall into a handful of categories; JSP standard tags exist for general JSP programming, some of which we are about to explore. Additionally, there are tags for accessing

SQL data, XML and text processing and formatting, and a collection of functions for string manipulation. It is beyond the scope of this book to example all of these tags, known as the JSP Standard Tag Library. However, we will look closely at some of the core tags from that library, since they are the most frequently and widely used ones.

When looking for ways to reduce the amount of embedded code in a JSP file, we frequently encounter Java control statements within the embedded code, statements such as the for loop, and the if-then-else statement. The JSP Standard Tag Library contains tags that allow you to replace those control statements with tags: `<c:forEach>` and `<c:if>`.

`<c:forEach>` has two main variants: one for iterating through a sequence of numbers with a step value, and one for iterating over an array, or Java collection. This is particularly useful when iterating over properties of a JavaBean. For the first variant, the form is

```
<c:forEach var="index name" begin="start index" end="end index" step="step increment">
```

and the `var value` may be used anywhere within the `<c:forEach>` element using `${index name}`, and for the second

```
<c:forEach var="variable name" items="collection name">
```

where the variable may be referenced anywhere inside the `<c:forEach>` loop using `${variable name}`. Let's look at an example.

In this example, we use a JavaBean called `MyWallet`, the code for which is shown here:

```java
import java.util.*;

public class MyWallet {
    String[] coins = {"1¢", "1¢", "5¢", "25¢", "25¢"};
    String[] currency = {"$1", "$1", "$1", "$5", "$10", "$10", "$20"};
    String[] receipts = {"gas - $42.50", "groceries - $35.26", "bookstore - $12.99"};

    public String[] getCoins() {
        return coins;
    }

    public List getNotes() {
        return Arrays.asList(notes);
    }

    public Set getReceipts() {
        return new HashSet(Arrays.asList(receipts));
    }

}
```

You will notice that this example exposes three read-only JavaBeans properties: coins, notes, and receipts of types `Java array`, `java.util.List` and `java.util.Set`: the `<c:forEach>` syntax is the same for each of them. Before we look at a JSP that uses this iteration tag, in order to use any tags from the standard tag library, the JSP has to use the `@taglib` directive to say it is going to:

```
<%@ taglib uri="http://java.sun.com/jsp/jstl/core" prefix="c" %>
```

The uri is the well-known URI for the standard tag library, and is always the same. The prefix may be chosen according to taste, but the conventional prefix for tags in the standard tag library is c. Now let's look at the code:

```
<!DOCTYPE html>
<html>
    <jsp:useBean id="myWallet" class="javaeems.chapter3.beans.MyWallet"/>
    <head>
        <meta http-equiv="Content-Type" content="text/html; charset=UTF-8">
        <title>For each</title>
    </head>
    <body>
        Odd Numbers up to 20:
        <c:forEach var="i" begin="1" end="20" step="2">
            ${i} 
        </c:forEach>
            <p/>
        Coins I have:
        <c:forEach var="coin" items="${myWallet.coins}">
            ${coin} 
        </c:forEach>
            <p/>
        Notes I have:
        <c:forEach var="note" items="${myWallet.notes}">
            ${note} 
        </c:forEach>
            <p/>
        Receipts:
        <c:forEach var="receipt" items="${myWallet.receipts}">
            ${receipt} 
        </c:forEach>
    </body>
</html>
```

Notice that this JSP uses both variants of the `<c:forEach>` tag: iteration through a sequence of numbers, and iteration through a collection, or array. It's useful to know that in the former case, if the step attribute is omitted, the default value is 1. When you execute the JSP page, you will see the output shown in Figure 3-6.

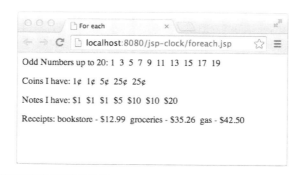

FIGURE 3-6. *JSP example with iteration tags*

The `<c:if>` tag is equally useful, having the general form:

```
<c:if test="condition">
```

where the body of the tag is written to the JSP only if the condition evaluates to be true.

Using dynamically calculated attribute values such as the condition in this pseudo-code, we have focused only on JavaBean properties such as `${myBean.property}`. This type of expression is an example of the JSP Expression Language, which we will be covering shortly. We have many ways to test conditions in the JSP EL, the `==` operator being a very commonly used equality tester. We examine it in the following example, which uses the `<c:if>` tag to test what we should be drinking based on the time of day:

```
<%@page contentType="text/html" pageEncoding="UTF-8"%>
<%@ taglib uri="http://java.sun.com/jsp/jstl/core" prefix="c" %>
<!DOCTYPE html>
<html>
    <head>
        <meta http-equiv="Content-Type" content="text/html; charset=UTF-8">
        <title>If page</title>
    </head>
    <body>
        <jsp:useBean id="myBean" class="javaeems.chapter3.clockbean.ConfigurableClock-
Bean"/>
        <jsp:setProperty name="myBean" property="dateFormat" value="a"></
jsp:setProperty>
        <c:if test="${myBean.readableDate=='PM'}">
            time for tea!
        </c:if>
        <c:if test="${myBean.readableDate=='AM'}">
            time for coffee!
        </c:if>
    </body>
</html>
```

If you evaluate this JSP in the afternoon, you will get the output shown in Figure 3-7, and in the morning you will get the output shown in Figure 3-8.

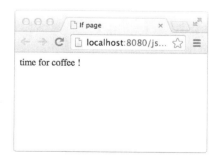

FIGURE 3-7. *JSP example with conditional tag in the afternoon*

FIGURE 3-8. *JSP example with conditional tag in the morning*

Custom Tag Libraries

We touched on some of the standard tags available to the JSP developer. You can also create your own tags in a custom tag library. With technologies that have been around for a while, there is often more than one way of doing the same thing. A key motivation for using JavaBeans from JSPs was to be able to separate Java code from presentation or markup code in a web application, making it easier to focus on one task in one place: always a plus when developing or maintaining code. Tag libraries offer a powerful mechanism for furthering this kind of separation: they allow developers to create new tags that they can use in their JSPs, while providing Java classes that implement the behavior. Let's take a look.

We use three steps to create and use a custom tag.

First, create a Java class that implements the JSP Java API interface `javax.servlet.jsp.tagext.JspTag`

The easiest way to do this is to subclass `javax.servlet.jsp.tagext.SimpleTagSupport` and to override the

```
public void doTag()
```

method. In order to write content out when your tag is used in a JSP, write the content to the HTTP response by calling

```
super.getJspContext().getOut().print(...).
```

Second, you need to tell the JSP container that you have a tag in this Java class and some of its attributes. In order to do this, you create a Tag Library Descriptor (.tld) file. We will see an example of one shortly.

Third, you use the custom tag you created in a JSP file. Using the `<% @taglib ...>` directive:

```
<%@ taglib prefix="prefix name" uri="relative uri of tld file in web app"%>
```

where "prefix name" is the prefix you will use to use the tag: `<prefix:tagname>` in the JSP.

The setup of a custom tag is somewhat complicated. Let's review what we have learned by reaching back to our clock example. We can rewrite the clock example to use custom tags instead of embedded Java code.

We will need two tags, one to display the number of milliseconds since the computing epoch, and another to display the current time in a nice format. Let's take the tag implementations in order. First, a class called `MyTimeSinceEpochTag`:

```java
import java.io.IOException;
import javax.servlet.jsp.JspException;
import javax.servlet.jsp.JspWriter;
import javax.servlet.jsp.tagext.SimpleTagSupport;

public class MyTimeSinceEpochTag extends SimpleTagSupport {
    @Override
    public void doTag() throws JspException, IOException {
        JspWriter out = getJspContext().getOut();
        out.print(System.currentTimeMillis());
    }

}
```

which you can see simply writes the current time in milliseconds to the HTTP response via the JSPWriter it obtains from the `JspContext`, available on the API class `SimpleTagSupport` this class extends.

Our next tag has an attribute, the date format string, for nicely formatting the current time, so is a little more complicated:

```java
import java.io.IOException;
import java.text.SimpleDateFormat;
import java.util.Date;
import javax.servlet.jsp.JspException;
import javax.servlet.jsp.JspWriter;
import javax.servlet.jsp.tagext.SimpleTagSupport;

public class MyDateTag extends SimpleTagSupport {
    private String dateFormat;

    public void setDateFormat(String dateFormat) {
        this.dateFormat = dateFormat;
    }

    public void doTag() throws JspException, IOException {
        JspWriter out = getJspContext().getOut();
        Date now = new Date();
        SimpleDateFormat sdf = new SimpleDateFormat(this.dateFormat);
        String today = sdf.format(now);
        out.println(today);
    }
}
```

We have now completed the first step. Next, we need to declare these tag implementations in the web application using a TLD file:

```xml
<?xml version="1.0" encoding="UTF-8"?>
<taglib version="2.1" xmlns="http://java.sun.com/xml/ns/javaee"
        xmlns:xsi="http://www.w3.org/2001/XMLSchema-instance"
        xsi:schemaLocation="http://java.sun.com/xml/ns/javaee http://java.sun.com/xml/
ns/javaee/web-jsptaglibrary_2_1.xsd">
  <tlib-version>1.0</tlib-version>
  <short-name>My Custom Tags for Chapter 3</short-name>
  <tag>
    <name>time-since-epoch</name>
    <tag-class>javaeems.chapter3.clockbean.MyTimeSinceEpochTag</tag-class>
    <body-content>scriptless</body-content>
  </tag>
  <tag>
    <name>date</name>
    <tag-class>javaeems.chapter3.clockbean.MyDateTag</tag-class>
    <body-content>scriptless</body-content>
    <attribute>
      <name>dateFormat</name>
      <required>true</required>
    </attribute>
  </tag>
</taglib>
```

Once we have identified the versions of the JSP and tag extension APIs, we can give our collection of tags a name that can be used in tools, the `<short-name>`. Then the `<tag>` element, a subelement of `<taglib>` that may occur as many times as you have tags to declare, contains the name of the tag as it will appear in the JSP and the tag class that implements the tag, together with a collection of `<attribute>` subelements that define what bean properties on the tag may be set. In our case, our `<date>` tag, implemented in the `MyDateTag`, has a bean property called `dateFormat` that may be set. For the tag to function property, a value must be set when the tag is used, as we shall see, which explains why this attribute has been marked `<required>`.

Third, we will use the tags in a version of the clock JSP, but with all the Java code replaced with our new custom tags:

```jsp
<%@page contentType="text/html" pageEncoding="UTF-8"%>
<%@ taglib prefix="custom" uri="WEB-INF/my_custom_tags.tld"%>
<!DOCTYPE html>
<html>
    <head>
        <title>JSP Clock</title>
    </head>
    <body>
        <div align='center'>
            <br/>
            Hello there!
            <br/><br/>
            It's been <custom:time-since-epoch/> milliseconds
            since midnight, January 1, 1970
            <br/><br/>
            In other words, it's
```

```
            <custom:date dateFormat="h:mm a, zzzz"/>.
        </div>
    </body>
</html>
```

Notice in particular that the tags are used with the prefix declared in the `@taglib` directive. When this JSP is run, it looks something like what is shown in Figure 3-9.

You should be able to see how simple the JSP code is compared with both the version at the beginning of the chapter with embedded Java code, and even with the version using a JavaBean.

Tag Libraries vs. JavaBeans

We should address the relative merits of customer tag libraries compared with using JavaBeans in a JSP, because they both fulfill the same goal of separating Java code from presentation code in a web application. There is no clear answer as to which is the best, nor clear circumstances as to when to use one technique versus the other. However, a few factors may help you decide which approach to take in a particular setting.

The setup and configuration of a JavaBean called from a JSP is simpler than the setup and configuration for a tag library.

Custom tags allow much greater freedom in choosing names that appear in JSP code. With the JSP/JavaBean model, you are limited to the preset `<jsp:useBean>`, `<jsp:setProperty>`, and `<jsp:getProperty>` tags. For the latter two cases, you can use JSP Expression Language as well, whereas with custom tags, you can choose your own descriptive and more personalized nomenclature.

It is easier to use JSP implicit objects in a custom tag. Thanks to the ease of accessing the JspContext, it is easy to get to the implicit objects such as the `request`, `application`, and `session`. For JavaBeans to be able to use these objects, they must have these objects explicitly set as properties.

Custom tags may have only `page` scope, whereas JavaBeans can be used in any of the four scopes: `page`, `request`, `session`, and `application`. In other words, an instance of a custom tag lives only for one invocation of the JSP page. JavaBeans, on the other hand, have other lives to live.

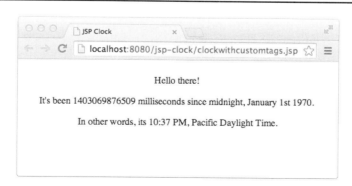

FIGURE 3-9. *JSP clock with custom tag*

Expression Language

Before we can look at a more substantial example of JSPs in action, we need to consider the JSP Expression Language. The JSP Expression Language is a small and powerful syntax that originated as a means to read and process values from JavaBeans components, but now is a general-purpose way to process data in a JSP.

JSP EL expressions are evaluated in JSPs to produce values either

- Anywhere in an element body to produce text content
- In a tag attribute

We already saw this in action when you accessed MyWallet; for example:

```
<c:forEach var="coin" items="${myWallet.coins}">
      ${coin} 
/c:forEach>
```

and you also saw an example of the EL syntax when testing a condition for use in the `<c:if>` standard tag:

```
<c:if test="${myBean.readableDate=='AM'}">
      It's time for tea!
</c:if>
```

We will be returning more to the topic of JSP EL in the JavaServer Faces Chapter 4. For now, we will quickly tour the language and use an example to illustrate its possibilities.

A JSP EL expression is declared in the form

```
${ expression }
```

and can be used in any JSP element body to product text content dynamically, or to produce a tag attribute value dynamically. Here are some examples of JSP EL expressions:

```
A) ${myBean.color}
B) ${true}
C) ${session.maxInactiveInterval / 60 }
```

These expressions illustrate all the key aspects of the language. In order to understand them, let's look at what objects are already available in the language for you to use and how you can manipulate and combine them.

The JSP EL makes available

- Any declared JavaBean, using "." to access properties (example A)
- Any JSP EL literal (example B)
- Any JSP implicit object (example C)

for use within a JSP EL expression.

The JSP EL literals are

Literal Type	Literal Value
Boolean	`true` or `false`
Numbers	Integer and floating-point literals as defined in the Java language
Strings	String literals using either single or double quotes
no value	`Null`

JSP EL can manipulate variables using its language operators. There are operators for arithmetic operations, such as addition and multiplication, and also for logic operators, for example, for equality testing and negation and size comparison. Here is a listing of the logical operators in the JSP EL.

Operator Type

Arithmetic	+, - (binary), *, / and div, % and mod, - (unary)
Relational	`eq` or `==`, for equality `!=` or `ne`, for negation < or `lt`, for less than > or `gt`, for greater than < = or `ge`, for greater than or equal to > = or `le`, so comparisons can be made For comparisons against other values, or against `boolean`, `String`, `int`, or `float` literals.
Empty	Empty Unary operation determining whether the following value is empty or `null`
Conditional	`A ? B : C` Evaluated to B or C depending the value of the `boolean` A

With this short introduction to the language, let's take a look at an example. This example considers a week and makes some evaluations of how it works out, as shown in Figure 3-10.

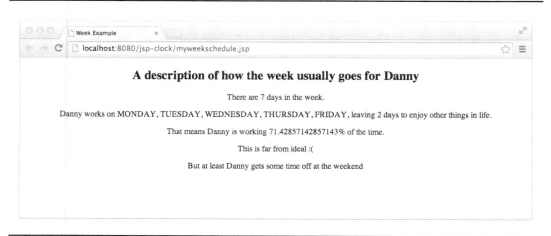

FIGURE 3-10. *JSP week schedule example*

Let's look at the code. It uses the JSP Expression Language to access a bean representing data about a week in time:

```java
import java.util.Arrays;
import java.util.List;


public class MyWeek {
    private String name;

    public enum Day {
        SUNDAY, MONDAY, TUESDAY, WEDNESDAY,
        THURSDAY, FRIDAY, SATURDAY
    }

    public MyWeek() {}

    public void setName(String name) {
        this.name = name;
    }

    public String getName() {
        return this.name;
    }

    public String getDescription() {
        return "A description of how the week usually goes for " + name;
    }
```

```java
    public int getNumberDays() {
        return 7;
    }

    public List<Day> getWorkingDays() {
        return Arrays.asList(Day.MONDAY, Day.TUESDAY, Day.WEDNESDAY, Day.
THURSDAY, Day.FRIDAY);
    }

    public int getNumberWorkingDays() {
        return this.getWorkingDays().size();
    }

    public boolean isWeekendOff() {
        return true;
    }


}
```

Now to the JSP that generates the page.

```jsp
<%@ taglib uri="http://java.sun.com/jsp/jstl/core" prefix="c" %>
<%@page contentType="text/html" pageEncoding="UTF-8"%>

<!DOCTYPE html>
<html>
    <jsp:useBean id="weekBean" class="javaeems.chapter3.beans.MyWeek"/>
    <jsp:setProperty name="weekBean" property="name" value="Danny"></
jsp:setProperty>
    <head>
        <meta http-equiv="Content-Type" content="text/html; charset=UTF-8">
        <title>Week Example</title>
    </head>
    <body><div align='center'>

        <h2>${weekBean.description}</h2>
        There are <jsp:getProperty name="weekBean" property="numberDays"/>
days in the week<p>
        <jsp:getProperty name="weekBean" property="name"/> works on
        <c:forEach var="day" items="${weekBean.workingDays}">
            ${day},
        </c:forEach>
        leaving ${weekBean.numberDays - weekBean.numberWorkingDays} days
to enjoy other things in life.<p>
        <c:set var="numberDaysOff" scope="session" value="${weekBean.number-
Days - weekBean.numberWorkingDays}"/>
        That means ${weekBean.name} is working ${100 * weekBean.numberWorking-
Days / weekBean.numberDays}% of the time.
        <p>
```

```
        <c:if test="${weekBean.numberWorkingDays > (weekBean.numberDays -
weekBean.numberWorkingDays)}" >
            This is far from ideal :(
            <p>
        </c:if>
        <c:if test="${weekBean.weekendOff && !((weekBean.numberDays - week-
Bean.numberWorkingDays) == 0)}" >
            But at least ${weekBean.name} gets some time off at the weekend.
        </c:if>
    </div></body>
</html>
```

Notice that this page uses the standard tag library, using the `<c:forEach>` and `<c:if>` tags. It uses the JavaBean representing the week to fish out how many days are spent working and whose week it represents. It does so using the "." syntax to access properties; for example:

```
${weekBean.description}
```

It also uses the `<jsp:getProperty>` syntax to do this, as in

```
<jsp:getProperty name="weekBean" property="name"/>
```

Which do you prefer?

It uses number literals and arithmetic operations to calculate the percentage of the week spent working:

```
${100 * weekBean.numberWorkingDays / weekBean.numberDays}
```

and uses logical operators to evaluate conditions for the `<c:if>` operator; for example:

```
${weekBean.weekendOff && !((weekBean.numberDays - weekBean.numberWorkingDays) == 0)}
```

Even this simple example shows some of the power of the JSP Expression Language.

JSP Photo Album

The goal of JSPs was originally to turn a servlet inside out for the purposes of extricating lines and lines of static content output from being buried within `out.println()` expressions. The goal of many aspects of the JSP syntax that we have seen has been to further separate the concerns of presentation from dynamic content generation in a JSP, so that each kind of code is easier to manage and evolve.

Let's pull together all that we have learned in this tour of JSPs and apply it to an example we already know: the photo application we examined in Chapter 2. We will take this application and turn two of the key Java servlets it used into JSPs, aiming for a clean separation between the application logic of processing photos and managing the album and the presentation code that renders the album and its photos on screen.

Figure 3-11 shows the photo application with an album containing three photos.

FIGURE 3-11. *Photo album using JSPs*

You can already see that this page is a JSP, the `album.jsp`, instead of the `DisplayAlbumServlet` you saw in Chapter 2. To approach this example application, let's take a look at the `PhotoAlbum` class that holds all the data:

```java
import java.util.*;
import javax.servlet.http.HttpSession;

public class PhotoAlbum {
    public static String ATTRIBUTE_NAME = "Photo_Album";
    private List<byte[]> photoDataList = new ArrayList<byte[]> ();
    private List<String> names = new ArrayList<String>();

    public PhotoAlbum() {
    }

    public void setSession(HttpSession session) {
        session.setAttribute(ATTRIBUTE_NAME, this);
    }

    public List getPhotoNames() {
        return names;
    }

    public void addPhoto(String name, byte[] bytes) {
        this.photoDataList.add(bytes);
        this.names.add(name);
    }
```

```
public byte[] getPhotoData(int i) {
    return (byte[]) photoDataList.get(i);
}

public String getPhotoName(int i) {
    return (String) names.get(i);
}

public int getPhotoCount() {
    return photoDataList.size();
}

public void removePhoto(int i) {
    photoDataList.remove(i);
    names.remove(i);
}

public static PhotoAlbum getPhotoAlbum(HttpSession session) {
    return (PhotoAlbum) session.getAttribute(ATTRIBUTE_NAME);
}
}
```

This class is largely the same as in Chapter 2, except that it now has a public no-argument constructor that allows it to be used as a JavaBean from the JSPs in the application, and also has a new JavaBean property for setting the value of the HttpSession with which this album is associated.

Now let us look at the first JSP that has replaced a Java servlet: this is the JSP that displays a photo, photo.jsp:

```
<%@page import="javaeems.chapter3.photos.beans.PhotoAlbum" %>
<%@page contentType="image/jpeg" %>
<%java.io.OutputStream binaryOut = response.getOutputStream();
    String indexString = request.getParameter("photo");
    int index = (new Integer(indexString.trim())).intValue();
    PhotoAlbum photo = PhotoAlbum.getPhotoAlbum(session);
    byte[] bytes = photo.getPhotoData(index);
    for (int i = 0; i < bytes.length; i++) {
        binaryOut.write(bytes[i]);
    }
%>
```

You will immediately notice that this JSP doesn't look like any other JSP that you have seen so far: that's because it isn't. All the JSPs we have looked at so far have produced HTML content. This one produces only binary content, and it does so in a Java scriptlet: the binary content of the photo, which you can see from the @page directive that defines the MIME type of the output. The JSP uses the request, response, and session JSP implicit objects. It uses the request implicit object to derive the index of the photo that it is to display. It uses the session object to look up which instance of the photo album to use for this client from the PhotoAlbum class, and it uses the response implicit object to get at the binary OutputStream it will use to write the binary JSP data.

So far so good: we have seen scriptlets, implicit objects, @page directives, and binary MIME types in action, but we have not yet used an expression language, standard tags, or custom tags. Let's get to that now.

First, this application uses a custom tag to display each photo in the main page. This tag produces the HTML code that contains the photo image and a link to get a larger view of the photo. In an application, how this HTML code is created is something you may well want to tweak and use in more than one other JSP. By making it a custom tag, you have both separated out its implementation from everything else and made it highly reusable. You saw this tag in operation in the main page of the application.

Let's first take a look at the code for the tag:

```java
import java.io.*;
import javax.servlet.jsp.*;
import javax.servlet.jsp.tagext.SimpleTagSupport;

public class PhotoTag extends SimpleTagSupport {
    private int index;
    private int width;
    private int height;

    public void setIndex(int index) {
        this.index = index;
    }

    public void setWidth(int width) {
        this.width = width;
    }

    public void setHeight(int height) {
        this.height = height;
    }

    @Override
    public void doTag() throws JspException, IOException {
        JspWriter out = getJspContext().getOut();
        out.println("<a href='photo.jsp?photo="+index+"'>");
        out.println("<img src='photo.jsp?photo="+index+"' alt='photo'
height='"+this.height+"' width='"+this.width+"'>");
        out.println("</a>");
    }

}
```

The custom tag has three properties that can be set: the index of the photo in the album, and the display width and height. It overrides the doTag() method of SimpleTagSupport in order to produce the HTML when the tag is called. Looking at the TLD file that declares this class as a custom tag to the JSP implementation:

```xml
<?xml version="1.0" encoding="UTF-8"?>
<taglib version="2.1" xmlns="http://java.sun.com/xml/ns/javaee"
        xmlns:xsi="http://www.w3.org/2001/XMLSchema-instance"
```

```
        xsi:schemaLocation="http://java.sun.com/xml/ns/javaee http://java.sun.
com/xml/ns/javaee/web-jsptaglibrary_2_1.xsd">
  <tlib-version>1.0</tlib-version>
  <jsp-version>2.0</jsp-version>
  <short-name>Example TLD</short-name>
  <tag>
    <name>photo</name>
    <tag-class>javaeeme.chapter3.photos.tags.PhotoTag</tag-class>
    <body-content>scriptless</body-content>
    <attribute>
      <name>index</name>
      <rtexprvalue>true</rtexprvalue>
    </attribute>
    <attribute>
      <name>height</name>
    </attribute>
    <attribute>
      <name>width</name>
      <rtexprvalue>true</rtexprvalue>
    </attribute>
  </tag>
</taglib>
```

We can see that these properties of the class are formally declared as tag attributes, and so can now be called from a JSP with values to suit the situation in which it is called. The <rtexprvalue> element governs whether the attribute value may be a scriptlet or Expression Language expression: in the example, both attributes allow this possibility.

Let's take a look then at the album.jsp, which pulls everything together and displays the photo album:

```
<%@ taglib uri="http://java.sun.com/jsp/jstl/core" prefix="c" %>
<%@ taglib prefix="photo-tags" uri="WEB-INF/mytaglib.tld"%>
<%@page contentType="text/html" pageEncoding="UTF-8"%>
<!DOCTYPE html>
<html>
    <jsp:useBean id="photoAlbum" scope = "session" class="javaeems.chapter3.photos.
beans.PhotoAlbum"/>
    <jsp:setProperty name="photoAlbum" property="session"
                                    value="<%=session%>"/>

    <head>
        <meta http-equiv="Content-Type" content="text/html; charset=UTF-8">
        <title>Photo Viewer</title>
    </head>
    <body>
        <h3 align='center'>Photos</h3>
        <table align='center'>
            <tr>
                <c:forEach var="i" begin="1" end="${photoAlbum.photoCount}">
                    <td align='center'>
                        <photo-tags:photo width='150' height='120'
                                        index='${i-1}'></photo-tags:photo>
                    </td>
```

```
        </c:forEach>
        <td bgcolor='#cccccc' width='120' height='120'>
            <form align='left' action='UploadServlet'
                method='post' enctype='multipart/form-data'>
            <input value='Choose' name='myFile'
                    type='file' accept='image/jpeg'><br>
            <input value='Upload' type='submit'><br>
            </form>
        </td>
    </tr>
    <tr>
        <c:forEach var="item" items="${photoAlbum.photoNames}">
            <td align='center'>
                ${item}
            </td>
        </c:forEach>
    </tr>
    <tr>
        <c:forEach var="i" begin="1" end="${photoAlbum.photoCount}">
            <td align='center'>
                <a href='RemovePhotoServlet?photo=${i-1}'>remove</a>
            </td>
        </c:forEach>
    </tr>
        </table>
    </body>
</html>
```

From the @page directives, you can see that this JSP produces HTML content, uses the custom tag we just looked at, and uses the standard tag library, using the prefixes c and photo-tag, respectively:

```
<%@page contentType="text/html" pageEncoding="UTF-8"%>
<%@ taglib uri="http://java.sun.com/jsp/jstl/core" prefix="c" %>
<%@ taglib prefix="photo-tags" uri="WEB-INF/mytaglib.tld"%>
```

Moving into the HTML code, you can see it uses the PhotoAlbum bean, declaring it to be used in session scope, so that the instance of the PhotoAlbum that is used has the same lifespan as the HttpSession associated with the client requesting the page. You will also notice that this session-scoped bean has its session property set so that the PhotoAlbum instance associated with this HttpSession can be retrieved from other web components at any other time, like the servlets that manage the upload of the photos and the servlet that removes photos from the album:

```
<jsp:useBean id="photoAlbum" scope = "session"
                    class="javaeems.chapter3.photos.beans.PhotoAlbum"/>
<jsp:setProperty name="photoAlbum" property="session"
                    value="${session}"/>
```

In order to display the contents of the photo album, the page uses the <c:forEach> custom tag and the <photo-tags:photo>.
    It uses

```
<c:forEach var="i" begin="1" end="${photoAlbum.photoCount}">
```

to iterate over the photos in the album, accessing properties of the `PhotoAlbum` bean using the "." syntax in a JSP EL expression. And it uses the custom tag

```
<photo-tags:photo width='150' height='120' index='${i-1}'></photo-tags:photo>
```

to render the HTML code for displaying a photo within the table cell used to display the album, passing in the attributes it wishes the tag to use in the context in which this custom tag is called.

This example shows just how far you can go in modularizing web page code using JSPs, JavaBeans, and tag libraries. As your JSP applications get larger and more complicated, you will come to see the virtues of such separations of concerns.

Summary

In this chapter, we started out by thinking of a JSP as a Java servlet that was inside-out. Starting with scriptlets and the style of JSP programing that embeds Java code directly into the page, we moved through all the main areas of the JSP syntax, showing at each stage this idea of teasing out code with the different responsibilities into different components like JavaBeans and tag libraries, an overview of which is shown in Figure 3-12.

This programming paradigm leads to much more manageable and well-organized applications that developers with different skill sets can work on side by side, using JSP Expression Language as both the lubricant and the glue that eases and binds the presentation world with the world of application data and Java code.

This sets us up well for the next chapter: JavaServer Faces, which builds on much of these concepts and much of this syntax to take the production of more complicated web interfaces to a higher level.

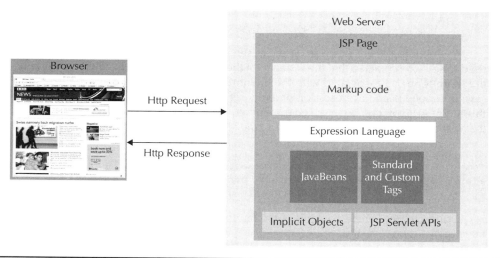

FIGURE 3-12. *The anatomy of a JSP application*

CHAPTER
4

Assembling Dynamic Web
Pages: JavaServer Faces

A JavaServer Faces page is a better version of a JSP.

This, of course, is a simplified way to describe what a JavaServer Faces page is. If you are concerned that all that you learned about JSPs will not be relevant if you choose to use only JavaServer Faces for all your web application development: fear not! JavaServer Faces applies many of the concepts and techniques that JSPs employ, including a variety of both standard and custom tags, to help display content, and many of uses of JavaBeans to integrate pages into the Java environment of the application. But JavaServer Faces takes many of the common tasks that developers build into web applications and provides specific mechanisms, tags, and APIs to help those tasks be built into a web application more easily. In particular, JSF gives you

- **A standard set of commonly used UI components**   Over and above the basic components available in HTML, the JSF UI components, in the form of a set of tags, are prewired into the rest of the JSF programming model. This not only makes it easy to add lists, check boxes, tables, and other such UI components into a web application, it makes them very easy to wire into the application data in the web application.

- **A mechanism for connecting UI state with application state**   JSF provides the means to connect UI components in a web page with the JavaBean data components that hold the application data that the UI components are supposed to represent. It's actually very easy to bind a UI component to a JavaBean, similar to the JSP-to-JavaBean binding, only using simpler syntax. Once the binding is in place, it is easy to elaborate on that binding by the use of separable components. For example, event handlers manage custom events generated in the UI and allow the JavaBean to catch up with what has happened, and validators check the values of data being set from the UI to the JavaBean. Converters adapt the value of a UI component to the value that is set on the JavaBean.

- **Mechanisms for page navigation**   Web applications with more than a handful of web pages have a number of predefined pathways for navigating through the content. The particular paths may depend on the kind of user activity with the web application. Maintaining these pathways in the form of relative links at the point of traversal can get the job done, but usually some kind of overhaul is required to bring the navigation rules into some sort of order. This becomes particularly apparent if you start renaming web pages or trying to add a new pathway or modify an existing one. JSF defines mechanisms for defining all the navigation rules in one place, which makes for a more manageable and adaptable web application.

- **Defines various mechanisms for extensibility**   Like JSPs, JSF components include a model that allows you to define custom UI components for your applications built from Java code. It also includes the means by which you can take a fragment of UI code and reuse it across other web components in the application. JSF also separates the definition of its UI components from the way in which they are rendered. A kind of look-and-feel for web applications, this allows web applications built using JSF to be "skinned" appropriately to the condition in which they are deployed without needing to redesign the application or rework the code.

In this chapter, you learn three different web technologies for building web applications. You may already be wondering why you need to know all three and in which circumstances you might choose to use one technology over another, or which to combine in a web application.

Architecture of a JSF Application

From the application point of view, the easiest way to understand a JSF application is to look at what is in it.

A JSF application is made up of a collection of XHTML pages, Java classes, and JSF metadata. The XHTML pages make up the visual part of the web application, holding the various JSF tags, markup, and scripting content that define the UI elements.

The Java classes in the JSF application define the application data that is housed in the web application, and also mediate the way the application data is bound into the presentation layer of the application. So these Java classes include JavaBeans that hold various parts of the application data, together with Java classes that mediate the data by implementing various types from the JSF APIs, including event handlers, data validators, and data converters.

The JSF metadata defines how the XHTML pages and JavaBeans are treated in the JSF runtime. A mix of Java annotations and XML documents, this metadata defines the scope of the JavaBeans, how many instances are used, and their lifecycles, together with navigation rules, and can be used to control how the UI components are rendered.

These three pieces, XHTML, Java code, and JSF metadata, as shown in Figure 4-1, may look somewhat familiar to any developer that has developed user interfaces before: it is, of course, the JSF version of the well-known Model-View-Controller pattern.

Model-View-Controller

The Model-View-Controller pattern is a widely adopted design pattern used to fit the particular needs of a user interface application. It is used across many different programming languages and platforms. It is used in the Java Swing and JavaFX frameworks, and is the basis of several web application frameworks, including JavaServer Faces.

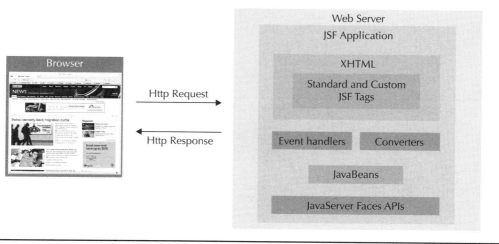

FIGURE 4-1. *Architecture of a JavaServer Faces application*

In simple terms, the task in all user interface applications is how the user can interact with the data model of the application, adding information to it, updating it, and deleting data from it. An often elaborate layer allows the user to do this, and provides the visual means to make the changes while at the same time showing the user an up-to-date view of the data. This layer is separated into the view and controller functions, as shown in Figure 4-2.

The user makes a change to the UI, which is passed to the controller. The controller's job in this design pattern is to interpret the changes to the data model that the user is asking for and transform that request, or series of requests, into a form that can be used to edit the data model. When the model changes, the controller's job is to make sure that the view is informed of the change. The view, in turn, has the task of altering its state in such a way that the display information it presents to the user of the application is consistent with the newly edited state of the data model. Using this kind of separation of concerns, the data model never needs to interpret all the different ways that a user may ask for a change to the data model, because the controller is taking care of that. The data model need never concern itself with how the data model is displayed to the user, because the view is taking care of that.

In other words, the heart of the application is insulated from any changes to how users interact with the data model. New users with new modes of interacting with the application can be added without disrupting the data model. New user interfaces, new means of control, and new ways to filter, order, and present the data model can be added by adding new views and controllers, or adapting the ones that are there.

There are few kinds of applications more prone to multiple users and ever-evolving user interfaces as web applications; this is why JavaServer Faces adopted them. Let's take a look at how by looking at a very simple JSF application.

Hello JavaServer Faces

Let's examine what this application does. When you first run the application, your browser loads the `index.html` page as shown in Figure 4-3.

If you type a different name in the text box and hit return, you should see something like Figure 4-4.

Before we look into the code, let's look at what this application contains. This application, like all JSF applications, is packaged in a WAR file, as shown in Figure 4-5.

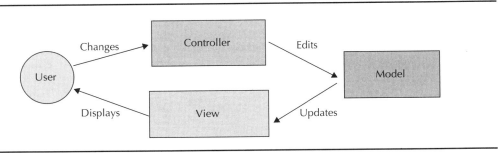

FIGURE 4-2.   *The Model-View-Controller pattern*

FIGURE 4-3. *Hello JavaServer Faces*

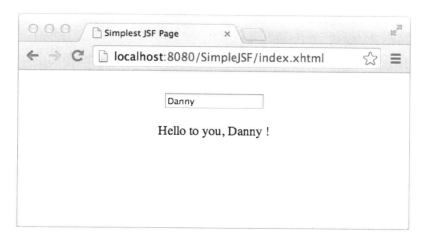

FIGURE 4-4. *Hello Danny*

Simple JSF WAR

/index.xhtml
WEB-INF/
  web.xml
  beans.xml
  classes/
    HelloBean.class

FIGURE 4-5.   *A Simple WAR containing JavaServer Faces*

The code for the application lies in `index.xhtml` and the `HelloBean` class, the `web.xml` containing the configuration information. Let's first take a look at the `HelloBean` class.

Listing: *The `HelloBean` class*

```
import javax.inject.Named;
import javax.enterprise.context.*;

@Named(value = "myHelloBean")
@RequestScoped
public class HelloBean {
  private String name = "dear reader";

  public void setName(String name) {
      this.name = name;
  }

  public String getName() {
      return this.name;
  }
}
```

As you can see, the `HelloBean` class is mostly just a JavaBean with a readable and writeable property called name, which assumes a default value of `dear reader`.

The only things that are not usually found in a regular JavaBean class are the Java annotations that it uses at the class level.

```
@Named(value = "myHelloBean")
@RequestScoped
```

The `@Named` annotation gives this JavaBean a name `myHelloBean` that can be used to refer to it from various contexts, but in particular, from the `index.xhtml` file. The `@RequestScope` annotation is an annotation that makes this JavaBean something called a *managed bean*, a concept that runs throughout the entire Java EE platform. Being a managed bean means that the lifecycle of instances of this class are controlled by the platform. The `@RequestScope` annotation is one of a handful of annotations that define a class to be a managed bean, and this one defines that the Java EE platform will create precisely one instance of this bean whenever it is needed within the context of a single HttpRequest/HttpResponse interaction.

So when is our `HelloBean` needed within the context of an HttpRequest/HttpResponse interaction? Let's look at the `index.xhtml` code to see.

Listing: *The `index.xhtml` page*

```
<?xml version='1.0' encoding='UTF-8' ?>
 <!DOCTYPE html PUBLIC "-//W3C//DTD XHTML 1.0 Transitional//EN"
       "http://www.w3.org/TR/xhtml1/DTD/xhtml1-transitional.dtd">
 <html xmlns=http://www.w3.org/1999/xhtml
       xmlns:h="http://xmlns.jcp.org/jsf/html">
  <head>
    <title>Simplest JSF Page</title>
  <head>
  <body>
    <div align="center">
      <br />
      <h:form>
      <h:inputText value="#{myHelloBean.name}"/>
      </h:form>
      <br />
      Hello to you, #{myHelloBean.name} !
    </div>
  </body>
 </html>
```

First we notice the namespace declaration for the XML document for HTML also using the prefix h for all the JSF tags this page will use. This should be familiar to you, as we used a similar mechanism to declare the sets of tags we would use for JSPs in Chapter 3. The only JSF tags that this page uses are `<h:form>` and `<h:inputText>`, which define the form element and contained text field, respectively. The value of the text field is bound to the value of the name property of the `HelloBean` JavaBean in the element

```
<h:inputText value="#{myHelloBean.name}"/>
```

which uses JSF Expression Language (which is unified with JSP Expression Language except for the use of # instead of $) to refer to the bean and its property. Notice also that the value of the JavaBean is retrieved using the same expression in order to print the value on the page.

The most important thing to notice about this sample is that there is no code that you need to write to bind the value of the text field to the JavaBean property: it is done for you by the `value` attribute. Whenever the value of the text field is changed, the JavaBean property value is accordingly changed and the page refreshed to reflect this.

Finally, the `web.xml` file contains configuration information about the application. We examine the `web.xml` syntax in much more detail in a later chapter. For now, all we need to know is that the `web.xml` file is necessary so that the container knows that this is a JavaServer Faces application.

Listing: *The web.xml configuration file*

```
<?xml version="1.0" encoding="UTF-8"?>
 <web-app version="3.1" xmlns="http://xmlns.jcp.org/xml/ns/javaee"
             xmlns:xsi="http://www.w3.org/2001/XMLSchema-instance"
             xsi:schemaLocation="http://xmlns.jcp.org/xml/ns/javaee
                http://xmlns.jcp.org/xml/ns/javaee/web-app_3_1.xsd">
    <context-param>
     <param-name>javax.faces.PROJECT_STAGE</param-name>
     <param-value>Development</param-value>
    </context-param>
    <servlet>
     <servlet-name>Faces Servlet</servlet-name>
     <servlet-class>javax.faces.webapp.FacesServlet</servlet-class>
     <load-on-startup>1</load-on-startup>
    </servlet>
    <servlet-mapping>
     <servlet-name>Faces Servlet</servlet-name>
     <url-pattern>*.xhtml</url-pattern>
    </servlet-mapping>
    <session-config>
     <session-timeout>
        30
     </session-timeout>
    </session-config>
 </web-app>
```

The key pieces of the web.xml file to notice are the servlet and servlet-mapping elements.

The <servlet> element declares that the class javax.faces.webapp.FacesServlet is a servlet, with name FacesServlet, and must be loaded first before any other servlets in the web application. The <servlet-mapping> element asks the web container to route any HTTP requests to a resource within the web application whose resource name ends with .xhtml to the FacesServlet that was just declared.

The FacesServlet class is a class from the JavaServer Faces API and is the entry point to the JSF runtime that interprets the JavaServlet Faces in the web application. Try it out: if you comment out the servlet mapping in the web application, the .xhtml file is simply served back with none of the JSF expressions evaluated. You get something like what is shown in Figure 4-6.

This servlet and servlet mapping syntax may be used to tell the Java EE web container about any Java servlets you may create in the web application. However, they are usually not necessary because you can use the @WebServlet annotation in the servlet class declaration itself, as we did in all the examples in Chapter 2.

JavaServer Faces: Model-View-Controller

But how does this simple and fundamental example of a JSF application relate to the Model-View-Controller patterns that we noted as the basic architecture of all JSF applications?

The model is the HelloBean; it contains the data. It knows nothing about what other code is accessing and modifying its data, and it knows nothing about how the data is presented to the user.

FIGURE 4-6. *Why the Face?*

The view is the `index.xhtml` file, which reads from the data model and decides how to present it.

So is the `index.xhtml` the controller as well, since it seems to help send the request to modify the data model when the user edits the text field? In fact, the `index.xhtml` is not the controller in this model, since the request from the browser, ultimately, an HTTP POST request containing the update, is handled by the JavaServer Faces FacesServlet part of the container and declared for use in the web application via the `web.xml` and a servlet-mapping. It is responsible for interpreting the request to change the data from the web page in the browser, ensuring that the correct instance of the `HelloBean` is used to handle the request and make the modification.

This yields the JavaServer Faces version of the Model-View-Controller pattern, as shown in Figure 4-7.

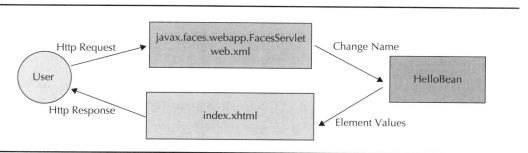

FIGURE 4-7. *JavaServer Faces Model-View-Controller*

This simple application is a template for all JavaServer Faces applications. We will elaborate on some key aspects of this application in order to explore all the possibilities of JavaServer Faces. We'll start by looking in more detail at the different tag collections available for use in JavaServer Faces, extending our knowledge from the humble `<h:textField>` tag.

JavaServer Faces Tags

The JavaServer Faces servlet performs a similar action on JavaServer Faces pages as the JSP runtime does to interpret an HTTP request against a JSP: it takes the JavaServer Faces page and compiles it down into a Java servlet that ultimately is the Java component that services the HTTP request. All the JSF tags are converted into Java object representations of the entities that they represent: text fields, buttons, and so on. Brought to life within the context of a Java servlet request/response interaction, the JSF servlet provides the runtime environment in which these components can interact with JavaBeans, have their input and output validated, fire events, and follow the prescriptions of how they should behave from the instructions in the JavaServer Faces source file. Finally, the JavaServer Faces runtime calls on this tree of components to render itself to the markup that represents this final, executed state of the component tree. This markup is written back to the client, and the user sees the results of the dynamically executed JavaServer Faces page. An easy way to think of a JavaServer Faces page is as a set of instructions for how to produce a final page of static markup from a collection of tags and various JavaBeans interpreted in the context of an HTTP request/response interaction. You can, of course, use regular HTML tags in your XHTML page, interspersed with any JSF tags you choose to use. Remember that any standard HTML tags you use will have no JSF awareness: they will not be able to interact with the JSF environment, and most importantly, with the data of your application. In terms of the component tree that the JSF runtime constructs in order to render the final markup, these elements simply "pass through" the JavaServer Faces runtime, like ghosts passing through a room but never touching anything.

All the collections of tags in JavaServer Faces are declared at the top of the XHTML file as a namespace declaration in the `<html>` tag, usually of the form

```
<html xmlns:prefix="namespace uri">
```

where `namespace uri` is the URI assigned by JSF to the tag collection, and `prefix` is the prefix you will use in all the tags you use in the page from that tag collection.

The collection of JavaServer Faces tags falls into a number of categories: those for UI components, those for control flow and string manipulation within a page, those to create UI components from other tags, "pass-through" tags and attributes that allow nonstandard markup to be used in a JSF page, and finally the core set of JSF tags that bind everything together. Let's start with the most visible of the tags: the UI components.

UI Component Tags

The UI tags in JSF are, by convention, prefixed by `h`, and so the namespace declaration for the UI tags will look like this:

```
<html xmlns:h="http://xmlns.jcp.org/jsf/html">
```

The core JSF component tags should be somewhat familiar to you already if you have written HTML before: their naming often reflects the HTML tag that they cause to render. We will see an example of some of these tags in action shortly, but for now, here is a listing of some of the most commonly used user interface components in JavaServer Faces.

Component	Tag	Example

Button	`<h:commandButton>`	`<h:commandButton`
		`    value="Submit"`
		`    action="#{bookingBean.submit}"`
		`/>`

Hyperlink	`<h:commandLink>`	`<h:commandLink`
		`    value="Learn more..."`
		`    action="learn.xhtml"`
		`/>`

Table	`<h:dataTable>`
	`<h:column>`
		`<h:dataTable`
		`    value="#{widgetBean.items}"`
		`    var="item">`
		` <h:column>`
		`    #{item.name}`
		` </h:column>`
		`  <h:column>`
		`    #{item.age}`
		`  </h:column>`
		`</h:dataTable>`

Form	`<h:form>`	`<h:form>`
		`  <h:commandButton`
		`    value="Submit"`
		`    action="#{bookingBean.submit}"`
		`  />`
		`</h:form>`

Image	`<h:graphicImage>`	`<h:graphicImage`
		`    value="#{widget.imageUri}"`
		`/>`

Text input	`<h:inputText>`
	`<h:inputArea>`
		`<h:inputText`
		`  value ="#{widget.name}"`
		`/>`

Component messages	`<h:messages>`	`<h:messages`
		`    errorStyle="color:red"`
		`/>`

Check box	`<h:selectBooleanCheckbox>`	`<h:selectBooleanCheckbox`
		`    value="#{widgetBean.working}"`
		`/>`

List, single selection	`<h:selectOneMenu>`	`<h:selectOneMenu`
		`    value="#{widget.color}">`
		`  <f:selectItem`
		`    itemValue="red"`
		`    itemLabel="Red"`
		`  />`
		`  <f:selectItem`
		`    itemValue="blue"`
		`    itemLabel="Blue"`
		`  />`
		`  <f:selectItem`
		`    itemValue="green"`
		`    itemLabel="Green"`
		`  />`
		`</h:selectOneMenu>`

Let's see some of these widgets in their native environment. To do that, we will turn to our PartyPlanner sample, which makes use of many of these widgets for the purposes of displaying and configuring a childrens' party.

The PartyPlanner

Here is the main page, as shown in Figure 4-8.

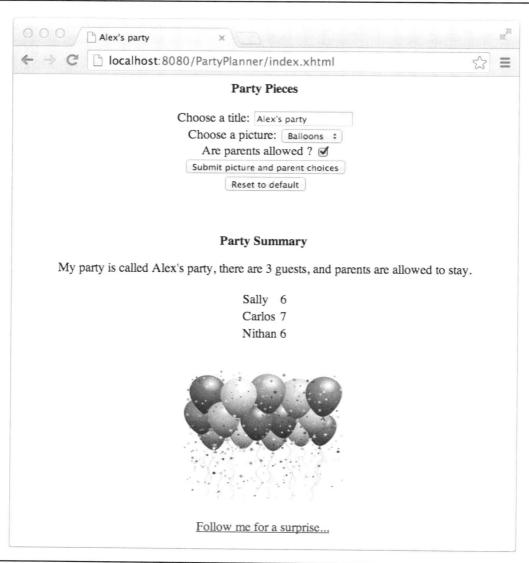

FIGURE 4-8. *PartyPlanner main page*

On this page, you can edit the title of the party, which is also the title of the web page, as seen here in the title of the tab in the browser. You can choose a picture to use for the invitation and select whether the parents of the kids are allowed to stay or not. These two pieces of information may be submitted using the `Submit` button, or the party information can be reset with the `Reset` button. You are shown a summary of the party, including a table display of the guests who have been invited. Finally, if you follow the hyperlink at the bottom of the page, you will get to the page shown in Figure 4-9. Clicking the link in this page returns you to the original page.

The data for this page is stored in a relatively straightforward JavaBean, the `PartyBean`, with the properties of the party name, a `boolean` for the parental presence, a list of invitees, and the name of an image file to use. Before we look at the JavaServer Pages that use this data, we'll look at the code for the data.

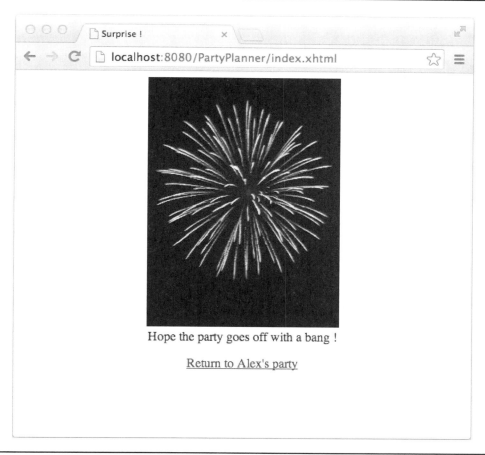

FIGURE 4-9. *Surprise, you're invited!*

Listing: *The PartyBean class*

```java
import javax.enterprise.context.*;
import javax.inject.Named;
import java.util.*;
import java.io.Serializable;

@Named("partyBean")
@SessionScoped
public class PartyBean implements Serializable {
  private String name;
  private boolean parentsAllowed;
  private List<Guest>items;
  private String imageUri;

  public PartyBean() {
   this.reset();
  }

  public String getImageUri() {
   return this.imageUri;
  }

  public void setImageUri(String imageUri) {
   this.imageUri = imageUri;
  }

  public String getName() {
   return name;
  }

  public void setName(String name) {
   this.name = name;
  }

  public boolean getParentsAllowed() {
   return parentsAllowed;
  }

  public void setParentsAllowed(boolean on) {
   this.parentsAllowed = on;
  }

  public List<Guest> getItems() {
   return this.items;
  }

  public void reset() {
   this.name = "(party title)";
   this.parentsAllowed = false;
   this.items = new ArrayList<>();
   items.add(new Guest("Sally", 6));
```

```
        items.add(new Guest("Carlos", 7));
        items.add(new Guest("Nithan", 6));
        this.imageUri = "party1.jpg";
      }


    public String getSummary() {
      StringBuilder sb = new StringBuilder();
      sb.append("My party is called " + this.name);
      sb.append(", ");
      sb.append(" there are " + items.size() + " guests");
      sb.append(", ");
      sb.append("and parents are " + (parentsAllowed ? "": "not") +
                                          " allowed to stay.");
      return sb.toString();

    }

  }
```

and the accompanying guest information

```
public class Guest {
    private String name;
    private int age;

    public Guest(String name, int age) {
      this.name = name;
      this.age = age;
    }

    public void setAge(int age) {
      this.age = age;
    }

    public int getAge() {
      return this.age;
    }

    public void setName(String name) {
      this.name = name;
    }

    public String getName() {
      return this.name;
    }

    public String toString() {
      return "Item: " + name;
    }

}
```

These two classes reflect the structure of the data shown in the application. The main things to notice are the annotations used at the top of the `PartyBean` class. The `@SessionScoped` annotation declares that this JavaBean is a managed bean, with a Java EE scope of "session." This means that this JavaBean class is instantiated exactly once for each active `HttpSession` that corresponds to an active client of the web application. In particular, this means that two different `HttpSessions` have two different instances of the `PartyBean` that HTTP interactions within each session use. This ensures that no one else other than you can change the invitation to your party, probably something that the guest of honor at your party will be pleased about. The `@Named` attribute declares that this managed bean is accessible from JavaServer Pages using the name provided, which is `partyBean`.

Now we can turn to the JavaServer Pages that use this managed bean and use UI widgets to represent and edit its values.

First and foremost is the main party page, `index.xhtml`.

Listing: *The `index.xhtml` page*

```
<?xml version='1.0' encoding='UTF-8' ?>
<!DOCTYPE html PUBLIC "-//W3C//DTD XHTML 1.0 Transitional//EN"
        "http://www.w3.org/TR/xhtml1/DTD/xhtml1-transitional.dtd">
<html xmlns="http://www.w3.org/1999/xhtml"
        xmlns:f="http://xmlns.jcp.org/jsf/core"
        xmlns:h="http://xmlns.jcp.org/jsf/html">
  <h:head>
    <title>#{partyBean.name}</title>
  </h:head>
  <h:body>
    <div align="center">
      <h:form>
      <label style="font-weight:bold"> Party Pieces </label> <br/><br/>
      <label>Choose a title: </label>
      <h:inputText value ="#{partyBean.name}" ></h:inputText><br/>
      <label>Choose a picture: </label>
      <h:selectOneMenu value="#{partyBean.imageUri}">
        <f:selectItem itemValue="party1.jpg" itemLabel="Hats" />
        <f:selectItem itemValue="party2.jpg" itemLabel="Balloons" />
      </h:selectOneMenu><br/>
      <label>Are parents allowed ? </label>
      <h:selectBooleanCheckbox value="#{partyBean.parentsAllowed}" >
      </h:selectBooleanCheckbox><br/>

        <h:commandButton value="Submit picture and parent choices"
                                        action="index" /><br/>
        <h:commandButton value="Reset to default"
                             action="#{partyBean.reset}" /><br/><br/>
      </h:form><br/><br/>
      <label style="font-weight:bold"> Party Summary </label> <br/><br/>
      <h:outputText value="#{partyBean.summary}"/><br/><br/>
      <h:dataTable value="#{partyBean.items}" var="item">
        <h:column > #{item.name}</h:column>
```

```
        <h:column>#{item.age}</h:column>
     </h:dataTable><br/><br/>
     <h:graphicImage value="#{partyBean.imageUri}" width="200" height="171" />
     <p>
     <h:form>
        <h:commandLink value="Follow me for a surprise..."
                                action="surprise.xhtml" />
     </h:form>
     </p>
   </div>
  </h:body>
 </html>
```

Notice that this page uses the standard widget library of JavaServer Faces, and also the core JavaServer Faces tags in the namespace `xmlns:f="http://xmlns.jcp.org/jsf/core"`. The title of the page is taken from the `name` property of the `partyBean`. The text field is a JSF component `h:inputText`. You will notice when you use this application that by pressing the ENTER key, the bean property to which the text field is bound, in this case, the name for the party, is updated automatically. The choice of picture for the invitation is captured in the JSF component for selecting one item from a list, the tag `<h:selectOneMenu>`, and the choice of whether to let the parents stay or liberate them to some less intensive activity is held in the check box tag for JSF: `<h:selectBooleanCheckbox>`. These widgets are bound to the `partyBean`'s `imageUri` and `parentsAllowed` properties, respectively. Two action buttons follow, using the `<h:commandButton>` tags, each specifying a different action. The first action is the JSF shorthand that causes the browser to load a given page, in this case, reloading the same page, thereby causing the JSF page to post the new attributes to the `partyBean` instance and reload itself to reflect the new state. The second action uses JSF Expression Language to call a method on a bean, in this case, the `PartyBean`'s `reset()` method. Notice the use of regular HTML tags interspersed with the JavaServer Faces tags: these simply pass through the JavaServer Faces runtime and are displayed to the output page. Next let's look at the JavaServer Faces table component in action, `<h:dataTable>`, taking a value that is a collection property and automatically iterating over the collection to generate its subelements, in this case, the two `<h:column>` subelements that form the rows of the table, thereby the attributes, name, and age of each guest.

The `imageUri` property of the `PartyBean` is used this time to display the image for the invitation, using the `<h:graphicImage>` JavaServer Faces tag. Finally, to get the surprise, a hyperlink finishes off the page, using the dynamically retrieved `imageUri` property of the bean. When you follow the link, a similar `<h:commandLink>` on the `surprise.xhtml` page generates the return link, using the name of the party to create the text of the link dynamically. You can see the code for that page in the next sample.

Listing: *The surprise.xhtml page*

```
<?xml version='1.0' encoding='UTF-8' ?>
 <!DOCTYPE html PUBLIC "-//W3C//DTD XHTML 1.0 Transitional//EN"
         "http://www.w3.org/TR/xhtml1/DTD/xhtml1-transitional.dtd">
 <html xmlns="http://www.w3.org/1999/xhtml"
      xmlns:h="http://xmlns.jcp.org/jsf/html">
  <h:head>
```

```
    <title>Surprise !</title>
  </h:head>
  <h:body>
    <div align='center'>
      <img src="surprise.jpg"/><br/>
      Hope the party goes off with a bang !
      <p>
      <h:form>
        <h:commandLink value="Return to #{partyBean.name}" action="index" />
      </h:form>
    </p>
  </div>
  </h:body>
</html>
```

Notice that the `partyBean` has retained its name value when we navigate to this page. In fact, the `partyBean` instance you accessed in the first page retains its values until such time that you edit them, or that the `HttpSession` in which your browser is participating as it accesses this application times out or is invalidated in some other way. This is because the Java EE scope of the `partyBean` is session. It also means that if someone else accesses this web application, they are working with a different instance of the `partyBean`. You can emulate this locally by accessing the same web application, but from a different browser. Note if you access the same application from a new window or tab from the same browser, you are still acting within the same `HttpSession`, so you see the same party information and the same `partyBean` instance.

Dust down that second browser you barely use, and observe that your party options are safe with JavaServer Faces managed beans!

Java EE Managed Beans

In the examples so far, you have seen two different scopes for JavaBeans that they contain: request and session. The JavaServer Faces main model for data is to use managed beans, but Java EE managed beans are used across the platform. So it is worth spending some time at this point describing all the six possible scopes available to you as a JavaServer Faces application developer, because you will likely find your knowledge of these scopes useful in other parts of the platform as well.

The Java EE managed bean scopes are an extremely simple way to be able to ask the Java EE platform to manage the lifecycle of a JavaBean that you want to use in an application. More importantly, they allow you to say when and how many instances of a JavaBean are created, or in other words, its cardinality. The managed bean scopes allow you to imbue a JavaBean with the same lifecycle and cardinality as some familiar objects in the runtime of the Java EE platform: the Java EE container, `HttpSessions`, and HTTP request and response pairs, as well as some common application-level constructs, as we shall see.

In order to declare the scope of a managed bean, the pattern is as we have seen: you annotate the JavaBean class with one of the six scope annotations found in the Java EE platform found in the `javax.enterprise.context` package. In order to make the managed bean available for use by name within a JavaServer Faces page, you must use the `@Named` annotation setting the value to the name you wish to use. You may see in older JavaServer Faces applications the `@ManagedBean` annotation: this has now been replaced in favor of the scope annotations.

@RequestScoped

The simplest scope is request scope. A managed bean in request scope is instantiated once for every new HTTP request/response interaction, created as the HTTP request arrives, and destroyed as the HTTP response leaves. Such JavaBeans are good for holding and processing information while a JSF page is being rendered, such as a bean that holds state across the generation of a single page under a single request. An example of this might be a JavaBean that backs a JavaServer Faces page that gathers contact information from a user and writes the information to a database once the user presses the Submit button.

@SessionScoped

A managed bean in session scope has the same lifecycle as the `HttpSession`. This means that if a session scoped bean is used in a JavaServer Faces page, the bean is instantiated once for each new `HttpSession` that is created for that web application and destroyed when the `HttpSession` to which the Java EE web container is associated either times out or is invalidated. This means that if you use a session scoped bean in a JavaServer Faces page, each user of your application has a unique instance of the bean backing the JavaServer Faces page that they see that lives across multiple interactions with the web application. This applies, for example, whether they reload the page, navigate somewhere else, or return at some later time. This kind of scope is useful when you want to associate the application state with a particular user that survives as long as the user is still active in the application.

@ApplicationScoped

A managed bean that is in application scope has the simplest lifecycle of all. The Java EE container instantiates the bean once prior to any users accessing the application and destroys it prior to shutting down the application. This means that a managed bean in application scope is a kind of global object that is shared by all users for the lifetime of the web application. This kind of scope is useful when you have application data that is global to the application and is shared across all users, for example, a chat transcript, a log of all the active users of an application over time, or a history of bids on an auction item.

@ConversationScoped

The conversation scope is a scope that is contained within the session scope, but the developer may control when it ends, which may be before the session ends. So a managed bean that is in conversation scope is instantiated once for every new `HttpSession`. It is active across several HTTP interactions with the web application in which it is used from a JavaServer Faces page or pages, and it is destroyed only either when the developer explicitly ends the conversation scope, or when the HTTP session with which it is associated times out or is invalidated. This makes conversation scope a useful lifecycle for a JavaBean to have if you want it to operate with a predefined set of interactions with a web application, perhaps the sequence of chat interactions on a social networking website, or a particular sequence of browsing for purchases on an online store. To end a conversation scope from a managed bean, we need access to the `javax .enterprise.context.Conversation` instance that allows us to manage the conversation scope. To do this, we use a technique called dependency injection, a topic to which we will return many times in this book, to inject the conversation instance as an instance variable into our JavaBean.

Listing: *A ConversationalBean class*

```
import javax.enterprise.context.RequestScoped;
import javax.enterprise.context.Conversation;
import javax.inject.Named;
import javax.inject.Inject;



@Named(value = "myHelloBean")
@RequestScoped
public class ConversationalBean {
  @Inject
  Conversation conversation;

  public void finishInteractions() {
   conversation.end();
  }
  ...

}
```

In this code snippet, by using the `@Inject` annotation, the Java EE container ensures that the conversation instance variable is filled out with the correct value when the `ConversationalBean` is instantiated. Then when the time comes to end the conversation, its `end()` method may be called, as is the case in the `finishInteractions()` method in the code example. The next time a JavaServer Faces page that uses this managed bean tries to call it, instead of using the original instance in use before the `end()` method was called, a new one is instantiated.

@FlowScoped

The flow scope is another managed bean scope that is contained with the session scope, like the conversation scope. The goal of the scope is for a new one to be active during a preset sequence of interactions with the web application from a given user. In this sense, it is similar to conversation scope. But instead of this scope being explicitly managed by API calls from the developer, as is the case with conversation scope, the boundaries of the flow scope are managed by a mechanism in JavaServer Faces called faces flows, which is particularly useful when creating web wizards.

@ViewScoped

The view scope is a managed bean scope that extends the request scope by starting while a particular JavaServer Faces page is being executed, and remains active while the client continues to interact with that same page. The scope becomes inactive once the client navigates to a different page. This is useful when coding pages that you expect to post back to themselves.

@Dependent

Finally, the dependent scope is a scope that says "my scope depends on where I am used." In other words, if you mark a managed bean `@Dependent`, its lifecycle and cardinality are governed by the component that uses it. This makes it a useful scope for JavaBeans that are used from components in more than one scope. For example, if you have a component that makes a currency conversion, you may wish to use this from a JavaBean that is request scope, converting currencies on a single web page, or you may wish to use it from a session-scoped managed bean that represents a shopping cart for international shoppers.

For most of the time in a JavaServer Faces application, using request, session, or application scope will be sufficient, as those scopes give the application the opportunity to wedge application state only in the time period of the request-response interaction while a page is being generated, or associate state on a per-user basis with the user session, or globally for all users, respectively. Applications that make use of wizards, or particular sets of predefined interactions, may use the finer-grained child scopes of the session scope: the conversation or flow scope.

f: Core Tags

The JavaServer Faces core tag library contains the basic tags that most JavaServer Faces pages will use. The core tags are contained in the namespace

```
xmlns:f="http://xmlns.jcp.org/jsf/core"
```

Most of the tags fall into the three important categories of tags that validate data, in other words, check that the values of data used in a tag fall within certain conditions, tags that manage events generated in the JavaServer Faces page, and tags that deal with converting data at the page level into a suitable form for consumption by the JavaBeans that back the page.

Data Validation

In a web page, it is important to make sure that data passed to you through the page by a user is in the form you expect (for example, that when you expect an email address, you don't get a telephone number) and if it isn't, to be able to inform the user of the mistake as quickly as possible. JavaServer Faces provides various levels of validation that you can use for this purpose. Often, it is enough to use the built-in tags for validation, which is the simplest approach and covers the most frequent types of validation. The validator is applied to a tag that takes input by making it a subelement of the tag whose value needs to be checked, as we shall shortly see. Let's take a look at the basic tags first.

Tag	Function
`<f:validateLength>`	Checks the minimum and/or maximum length of an input string
`<f:validateDoubleRange>`	Checks the minimum and/or maximum value of a input double
`<f:validateLongRange>`	Checks the minimum and/or maximum value of a input long
`<f:validateRequired>`	Requires some nonempty value to be input

When validation fails, JavaServer Faces generates a default error message that is displayed on the page. This message is often not very user-friendly, more an aid during development time, so it is a good idea to customize the message using the `validatorMessage` attribute of the tag that defined the input. Here is an example of simple text validation that checks whether the user is providing a username of the right length:

Listing: *Example String length validation*

```
<h:form>
  <h:inputText id="username_component"
          validatorMessage="Username must be between 4 and 10 characters">
    <f:validateLength minimum="4" maximum="10"/>
  </h:inputText>
</h:form>
```

Input values may also be validated with the Bean Validation API or with regular expressions.

Tag	Function
`<f:validateBean>`	Checks a value against an implementation of the Beans Binding API `javax.faces.validator.BeanValidator`.
`<f:validateRegex>`	Checks a value against a regular expression. Either in the form of a regex expression string: `<f:validateRegex pattern="/[0-9a-zA-Z]"/>` or as an implementation of the `javax.faces.validator.RegexValidator` class: `<f:validateRegex binding="myRegexValidator">`

You can also implement your own validator.

Listing: *Example custom validator*

```
@FacesValidator("myValidator")
public class MyValidator implements Validator {
  public void validate(FacesContext context,
                       UIComponent component,
                       Object value) throws ValidatorException {
      // check value
      // throw ValidatorException if it does not pass the check
  }
}
```

which gives you a full view into the input component to which the validator is attached, the context of the call, and the value object that has been input. To fail the validation, you simply throw a `ValidatorException` from the validate method. This kind of custom validator is wired into the input component using the

```
<f:validator validatorId="myValidator">
```

tag.

The mechanism for validations in JSF always requires a round trip to the server, where the validator code runs while the page is being regenerated. Keep this in mind when you choose to use them. There are cases where this is unavoidable, in particular, when using a custom validator that needs to check other application data elsewhere in order to determine the validity of a value. This may happen, for example, if a user enters a credit card number that must be checked for validity with an external service. For validations that require only a format check, such as the format of a telephone number, doing a round trip to the server for a JSF validation may be unnecessary: sometimes, it can be better to use JavaScript to check this kind of value locally without ever needing to send the information to the server to be checked.

Event Handling

So far in the examples we have looked at in this chapter, we have sidestepped the issue of when the data showing on the JavaServer Faces page is sent to the Java EE web container and the page refreshed with the newly generated page based on the updated information. Notice in the PartyPlanner application that there were actually two ways in which the information on the page was submitted to the Java EE web container, written to the underlying JavaBean, and the page regenerated. First, the information was submitted by pressing the ENTER key after changing the name of the party in the text field. Second, clicking the Submit button explicitly submitted the new page data and updated the PartyBean. You will notice that altering the picture choice and hitting reload in the browser to reload the page causes the picture choice to revert to the one held in the JavaBean, and a similar effect is seen if you reload the page without submitting it when you alter the choice of whether to invite parents. Even in this small example, you can see that there is explicit work you have to do to keep the data on the page in sync with the model data in the JavaBeans that back the page. We sidestepped the issue by having an explicit button, and by relying on the fact that browsers generally interpret pressing the ENTER key in a text field as a request to submit the text data to the server, as recommended by the HTML5 specification.

At times you will want the page to have a closer synchronization with the model data: even altering a selection in a list or clicking a check box button should immediately update the model data. In these common situations, JavaServer Faces provides an event handling mechanism so you can intercept events generated when the widget state on the page changes and causes an update to the corresponding model data. We examine the tags that are used in the mechanism in this section.

The overall idea is that the event handling tags can be used to register either an instance or a class that implements a certain JavaServer Faces defined event listener interface class. When the tag is used as a subelement of the appropriate user interface component, the event listener they specify is added to that user interface component. When the user interface component's state changes, the page data is submitted to the Java EE web container, the corresponding event listener is called, and the page regenerated and transmitted back to the browser.

The event handling tags in JavaServer Faces are shown in the following table.

Tag	Function

`<f:actionListener>`	For use with command buttons and links, this tag registers the given implementation of `javax.faces.event.ActionListener` which is then notified when the component's state changes.
	
	`<f:actionListener type = "`*actionlistener impl classname*`">`
	
	`<f:actionListener binding = "`*expression evaluating to actionlistener instance*`">`

Tag	Function

`<f:valueChangeListener>`	For use with all input components and lists, this tag registers the given implementation of `javax.faces.event.ValueChangeListener`, which is then notified when the component's state changes.
	
	`<f:valueChangeListener type = "valuechangelistener impl classname">`
	
	`<f:actionListener binding = "expression evaluating to valuechangelistener instance">`

`<f:setPropertyActionListener>`	For use with command buttons and links, this tag lets you directly set the value of a property on a managed bean.
	
	`<f:setPropertyActionListener`
	`  target="#{myBean.babyName}"`
	`  value="#{nameList.currentName}"`
	`/>`

We will see event listeners in action in our larger example toward the end of this chapter.

Data Converters

Data conversion is the process by which data that resides in the JavaServer Faces page, perhaps values entered into a form, is converted to and from data that resides in the data layer and the JavaBeans that back the page. There are various reasons why such conversions are necessary: primarily, the JavaBeans data layer seeks to make its data formats the easiest to process for a number of different JavaServer Faces pages, for example, `BigDecimal` for currency, while each page seeks to make the format of the data in its page layer most suited to the needs of the user of the page, a formatted `String` suitable to the locale in which the page is viewed.

JavaServer Faces allows for a number of different kinds of conversions that can cater to several different data types and conversion needs. The starting point for these conversions is the conversion tags in the JavaServer Faces core library. So again, we are looking at tags in the namespace

`xmlns:f="http://xmlns.jcp.org/jsf/core"`

Because data held in a web page is always held as a `String`, JavaServer Faces automatically converts such strings to and from strings, Java primitive data types, and `BigDecimal`.

Prebuilt tags handle the two most common data conversions, with a number of configuration options tuned to the needs of the page by the attributes on each tag.

Tag	Function
`<f:convertNumber>`	Converts a `Double` or `Long` object to and from a variety of formats, including standard currency formats, and number formats, specifying ranges for the number of integer and fractional part digits, as well as grouping patterns.
`<f:convertDateTime>`	Converts a `Date` object to and from a variety of human-readable date formats suitable for a variety of locales and time zones, and in a variety of date formats.

These two tags are the workhorses of the conversion mechanism. Like validators, used as subelements of a UI component, they register an appropriate conversion object, supplied by the JavaServer Faces runtime, which converts the data to the required specification. The `<f:convertNumber>` tag adds a converter of type `javax.faces.convert.NumberConverter` to the UI component, and the `<f:convertDateTime>` tag adds a converter of type `javax.faces.convert.DateTimeConverter` to the UI component. By browsing the `javax.faces.convert` package, you will see the other standard JavaServer Faces API classes for making the primitive Java data type to `String` conversions that are in operation by default in the JavaServer Faces runtime, such as `BigDecimalConverter`, `BooleanConverter`, and `FloatConverter`. You will also notice the `javax.faces.converter.Converter` interface. This defines the general contract for providing your own data converter by nesting the `<f:converter>` tag within a component. To do this, you implement the `Converter` interface, which requires you to implement two methods:

```
public String getAsString(FacesContext context,
                          UIComponent component,
                          Object value)

public Object getAsObject(FacesContext context,
                          UIComponent component,
                          String value)
```

for converting your data object to a string to display in the page, and for retrieving the instance of your data object corresponding to the string displayed in the page, respectively. You name your converter class using the `@FacesConverter("`*`converter-name`*`")` annotation that you have already seen in action. Then you can have a UI component pick up this converter by nesting

```
<f:converter converterId="converter-name")>
```

in the UI component tag.

JSTL Core Tags

We have encountered the Standard Tag Library already. The control flow tags are also available in JavaServer Faces. Here is a summary of these tags and their function.

Tag	Purpose
`<c:catch>`	Catches any throwable thrown within this tag, using the name of the `var` attribute to hold the throwable.
`<c:choose>`	Defines a set of mutually exclusive choices, used in conjunction with the `<c:when>` and `<c:otherwise>` tags, like a Java switch statement.
`<c:if>`	Simple conditional tag, based on the condition supplied in the test attribute evaluating to true.
`<c:forEach>`	Tag for iterating over collections.
`<c:otherwise>`	Tag for the default case in a `<c:choose>` tag.
`<c:set>`	Tag to set a page variable by name.
`<c:when>`	Simple conditional tag, for use in `<c:choose>` tags, for example.

Extensibility and Modularity

JavaServer Faces includes many ways to extend its base functionality and to modularize pieces of JavaServer Faces code to promote reuse within an application and across applications. It is beyond the scope of this foundational chapter to explore all these mechanisms fully, but let's take a whirlwind tour of the opportunities for extensibility and modularity.

Developers can create custom UI components in two main ways. First, to render a new user interface component on the page, they can provide a new subclass of `UIComponent` and associate it with a new tag and a new set of control attributes. In this way, many developers have created libraries of new HTML components and custom text components, for example, image components that include mapping functionality. Second, snippets of JavaServer Faces markup may be packaged into an XHTML file as a *composite component* and associated with a tag using a tag library descriptor. In this way, commonly occurring groupings of tags in JavaServer Faces pages, such as OK cancel button panels and image display panels, can be bundled into a single tag, thereby making it easier to reuse such commonly recurring elements in an application.

JavaServer Faces offers a couple of techniques to help web applications that have predefined user interaction pathways. A wizard that collects registration data or a sequence of web forms that help you make and pay for an online purchase are good examples of such interaction pathways.

As a general aid for navigation, JavaServer Faces defines Faces Flows. This consists of a managed bean scope, as described earlier, together with the ability to define a set of flows between JavaServer Faces pages and the ability to easily share context, such as a shopping basket or custom registration, between the pages and inject logic into the transitions.

Photo Application

We will conclude the chapter with a deeper exploration of a more sophisticated web application. It is one that we have already seen, and it puts to the test the original claim made at the very outset of this chapter: that a JavaServer Faces page is a better JSP. Let's return to the photo application, JavaServer Faces style.

The JavaServer Faces version of this application has some added functionality compared to the previous versions. Let's take a look at the home page, as shown in Figure 4-10.

The photos in the album are laid out, with each photograph having three buttons for viewing, editing, and deleting it from the album. Figure 4-11 shows the view and edit screens.

New photos are added from the album page like a wizard, leading to the sequence shown in Figure 4-12.

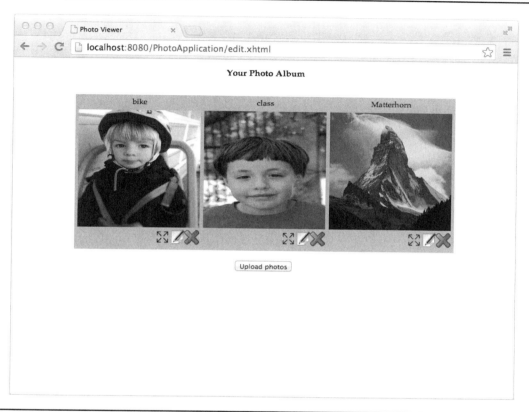

FIGURE 4-10. *The face of a photo album*

FIGURE 4-11. *Viewing and editing a photo*

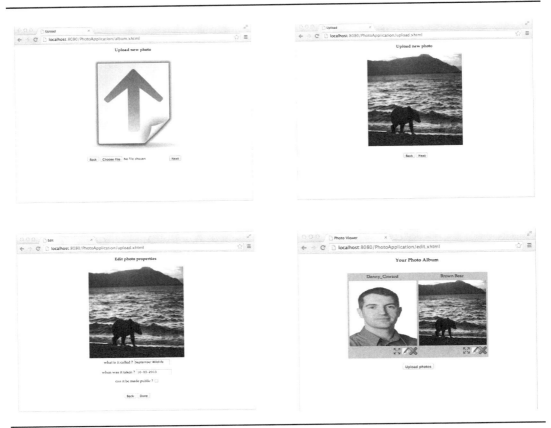

FIGURE 4-12. *Uploading a photo*

The photo application is made up of four XHTML files, two managed beans, a Plain Old Java Object class, and a servlet. The servlet is called `DisplayPhotoServlet`, and is essentially the same servlet that we saw in Chapter 2: it displays the binary image data of a photo on demand. The other application files are shown in Figure 4-13.

The diagram shows the correspondence between the XHTML files and the different screens of the application. Let's start our examination of the code by looking at the `PhotoAlbum` bean.

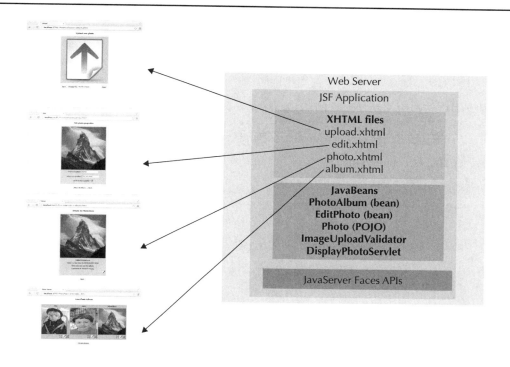

FIGURE 4-13. *Contents of the photo application*

Listing: *The PhotoAlbum class*

```
import java.util.*;
import java.io.*;
import javax.inject.*;
import javax.enterprise.context.*;

@Named(value = "photoAlbum")
@SessionScoped
public class PhotoAlbum implements Serializable {
  private List<Photo> photos = new ArrayList<>();
  private Photo currentPhoto = null;

  public PhotoAlbum() {
  }

  public void setCurrentPhoto(Photo p) {
```

```java
    this.currentPhoto = p;
  }

  public Photo getCurrentPhoto() {
    return this.currentPhoto;
  }

  public void addPhoto(Photo p) {
    if (this.containsId(p.getId())) {
      this.removePhoto(this.getPhotoById(p.getId()));
    }
    this.photos.add(p);
  }

  private Photo getPhotoById(long id) {
    for (Photo photo : this.photos) {
      if (photo.getId() == id) {
        return photo;
      }
    }
    return null;
  }

  public boolean containsId(long id) {
    return this.getPhotoById(id) != null;
  }

  public List<Photo> getPhotos() {
    return this.photos;
  }

  public void removePhoto(Photo photo) {
    this.photos.remove(photo);
  }

  public Photo getPhoto(long id) {
    for (Photo photo : this.photos) {
      if (photo.getId() == id) {
        return photo;
      }
    }
    return null;
  }

  public List getPhotoNames() {
    List<String> names = new ArrayList<>();
    for (Photo photo: this.photos) {
      names.add(photo.getName());
    }
    return names;
  }
```

```
public List getPhotoFilenames() {
  List<String> filenames = new ArrayList<>();
  for (Photo photo: this.photos) {
    filenames.add(photo.getFilename());
  }
  return filenames;
}

public int getIndexOf(String photoName) {
  for (Photo photo : this.photos) {
    if (photo.getFilename().equals(photoName)) {
      return photos.indexOf(photo);
    }
  }
  return -1;
}


public byte[] getPhotoData(int i) {
  Photo photo = this.photos.get(i);
  return photo.getData();
}

public byte[] getPhotoDataByName(String name) {
  for (Photo photo : this.photos) {
    if (photo.getFilename().equals(name)) {
      return photo.getData();
    }
  }
  return null;
}

public String getPhotoName(int i) {
  Photo photo = this.photos.get(i);
  return photo.getFilename();
}

public int getPhotoCount() {
  return photos.size();
}

}
```

We can see right away that this is a session-scoped managed bean, so the PhotoAlbum will be instantiated once for every new client of the application, and that instance will live as long as the HttpSession in use by the client during numerous interactions with the web application is active. The PhotoAlbum, as in previous incarnations of the application, holds all the Photo instances that make up the current album. So by making the PhotoAlbum session scoped, we ensure that the album lives for as long as the user interacts with the application. Of course, to take the application to the next stage, we would want to persist the photo information in a database. Notice that the `PhotoAlbum` is `Serializable`. This is a requirement of it being session scoped, ensuring that all the session-scoped managed beans in the Java EE web container can be reconstituted if an `HttpSession` moves from one web server node to another in a clustered environment. The `PhotoAlbum` is heavily used by its `@Named` name from the `album.xhtml` page. Since this is the most complicated of the pages, we will look at it in its entirety.

Listing: *The album.xhtml file*

```
<?xml version='1.0' encoding='UTF-8' ?>
 <!DOCTYPE html PUBLIC "-//W3C//DTD XHTML 1.0 Transitional//EN"
         "http://www.w3.org/TR/xhtml1/DTD/xhtml1-transitional.dtd">
 <html xmlns="http://www.w3.org/1999/xhtml"
       xmlns:h="http://xmlns.jcp.org/jsf/html"
       xmlns:c="http://xmlns.jcp.org/jsp/jstl/core">
 <h:head>
   <title>Photo Viewer</title>
 </h:head>
 <h:body style="font-family:Palatino;font-size:small">
   <div align='center'>
 <h3>Your Photo Album</h3>
 <br></br>
 <table bgcolor="99CC99" cellspacing="4">
  <tbody>
  <tr>
   <c:forEach items="#{photoAlbum.photos}" var="photo">
    <td>
    <div align='center'>
      #{photo.name}
    </div>
    </td>
    </c:forEach>
   </tr>
   <tr>
    <c:forEach items="#{photoAlbum.photos}" var="photo">
     <td>
     <h:form>
       <h:graphicImage
       height="200"
       width="200"
       value="#{photo.viewUri}"/>
       </h:form>
       <h:form>
       <div align='right'>
        <h:commandButton
       title="view"
       image="view.png"
       actionListener="#{photoAlbum.setCurrentPhoto(photo)}"
```

```
        action="photo"/>
         <h:commandButton
        title="edit"
        image="edit.png"
        actionListener="#{editPhotoBean.setPhoto(photo)}"
        action="edit"/>
         <h:commandButton
        title="delete"
        image="delete.png"
        action="#{photoAlbum.removePhoto(photo)}"/>
         </div>
        </h:form>
        </td>
      </c:forEach>

       </tr>
      </tbody>
    </table>
    <br></br>
    <h:form>
     <h:commandButton
       id="upload_button"
       value="Upload photos"
       action="upload"/>
    </h:form>
    </div>
   </h:body>
  </html>
```

This is a JavaServer Faces page that uses the core JavaServer Faces tags, the standard tag library, and the JavaServer Faces UI component tags, as you can see from the c and f and h namespace imports at the top of the file. It uses the PhotoAlbum bean, in conjunction with the <c:forEach> tag, to iterate over the photos in the album, writing out the photo names, and using the JavaServer Faces image component to display image data from the viewUri property of each photo instance. The command buttons that control the view, edit, and delete behaviors attached to each photo make use of both the actionListener attribute to take some action, as defined in an expression language expression when they are clicked, and also the action attribute to define a navigation target after the actionListener has been called. For example, when the view button is pressed, you can see from the definition of the command button tag

```
<h:commandButton
       title="view"
       image="view.png"
       actionListener="#{photoAlbum.setCurrentPhoto(photo)}"
       action="photo"/>
```

that the PhotoAlbum's current photo property is set to the photo above the button on the page, and then the photo.xhtml page is loaded once that action has been taken.

The process of uploading and adding properties to an uploaded photo in the upload wizard sequence is backed by the EditPhoto bean.

Listing: *The EditBean class*

```
import java.io.ByteArrayOutputStream;
import java.io.InputStream;
import javax.inject.Named;
import javax.inject.Inject;
import javax.servlet.http.Part;
import java.io.*;
import java.util.Date;


@Named(value = "editPhotoBean")
@javax.enterprise.context.SessionScoped
public class EditPhoto implements Serializable {
  @Inject
  PhotoAlbum photoAlbum;
  private long id = -1;
  private boolean isPublic = false;
  private String filename;
  private String photoName;
  private Date dateTaken = new Date();
  private byte[] photoData = null;

  public EditPhoto() {}

  public boolean isNew() {
   return this.id == -1;
  }

  public boolean isPublic() {
   return isPublic;
  }

  public void setPublic(boolean isPublic) {
   this.isPublic = isPublic;
  }

  public Date getDateTaken() {
   return dateTaken;
  }

  public void setDateTaken(Date dateTaken) {
   this.dateTaken = dateTaken;
  }

  public String getPhotoName() {
   return this.photoName;
  }

  public void setPhotoName(String photoName) {
   this.photoName = photoName;
```

```java
  }

  public String getFilename() {
   return this.filename;
  }

  public void reset() {
   this.id = -1;
   this.dateTaken = new Date();
   this.filename = null;
   this.photoData = null;
   this.photoName = null;
  }

  public void commit() {
   this.photoAlbum.addPhoto(this.getPhoto());
   this.reset();
  }

  private void collectData(Part uploadedPart) {
   if (uploadedPart.getSize() == 0) {return;} // dannyc
   try {
     ByteArrayOutputStream baos;
     try (InputStream is = uploadedPart.getInputStream()) {
        baos = new ByteArrayOutputStream();
        int i = 0;
        while ( (i=is.read()) != -1) {
          baos.write(i);
        }
        photoData = baos.toByteArray();
     }
     baos.close();
     } catch (Exception e) {
        photoData = null;
        throw new RuntimeException(e.getMessage());
     }
   this.filename = uploadedPart.getSubmittedFileName();
   this.photoName = this.filename.substring(0, this.filename.indexOf("."));
  }

  public byte[] getPhotoData() {
   return this.photoData;
  }

  public void setUploadedPart(Part p) {
   this.collectData(p);
  }

  public Part getUploadedPart() {
   return null;
  }
```

```
public String getPreviewUrl() {
 if (this.hasPhoto()) {
   return "DisplayPhotoServlet";
 } else {
   return "nopreview.png";
 }
}

public void setPhoto(Photo p) {
 this.id = p.getId();
 this.isPublic = p.isPublic();
 this.filename = p.getFilename();
 this.photoName = p.getName();
 this.dateTaken = p.getDateTaken();
 this.photoData = p.getData();
}

public boolean hasPhoto() {
 return (this.photoData != null);
}

public Photo getPhoto() {
  if (this.hasPhoto()) {
    Photo p = new Photo(this.id, this.getPhotoData(),
      this.getFilename(), this.photoName, this.dateTaken, this.isPublic);
    return p;
  } else {
    return null;
  }
 }
}
```

This, too, is a session-scoped bean: we need this bean to be unique to each user of our application (you do not want to upload a photo to someone else's album, after all), and it needs to live at least as long as the sequence of uploading the file and filling out the name and other properties. This bean's function is to be able to gather that data, one piece at a time. By use of dependency injection and the @Inject annotation, each instance of this EditPhoto bean has its photoAlbum instance variable assigned to the instance of the photo album that is in the same session scope (i.e., same HttpSession) as itself, thereby allowing this EditPhoto bean to add the photo it produces when all its data has been filled out to the correct photo album in scope.

Both the upload.xhtml and edit.xhtml pages use this EditPhoto bean. We won't look at both, but let us look at the upload.xhtml page.

Listing: *The upload.xhtml page*

```
<?xml version='1.0' encoding='UTF-8' ?>
<!DOCTYPE html PUBLIC "-//W3C//DTD XHTML 1.0 Transitional//EN"
         "http://www.w3.org/TR/xhtml1/DTD/xhtml1-transitional.dtd">
<html xmlns="http://www.w3.org/1999/xhtml"
      xmlns:h="http://xmlns.jcp.org/jsf/html"
      xmlns:f="http://xmlns.jcp.org/jsf/core"
      xmlns:c="http://xmlns.jcp.org/jsp/jstl/core">
<h:head>
  <title>Upload</title>
</h:head>
  <h:body style="font-family:Palatino;font-size:small">
 <div align='center'>
 <h3>Upload new photo</h3>
  <table bgcolor="FFFF99" cellspacing="4"><tbody><tr><td align='center'>
  <h:graphicImage
   height="330"
   width="330"
   value="#{editPhotoBean.previewUrl}"/>

  </td></tr></tbody></table>
  <br></br>
  <c:if test="#{!editPhotoBean.hasPhoto()}">
   <h:form id="form" enctype="multipart/form-data" prependId="false">
    <h:commandButton
    id="cancel"
    value="Back"
    actionListener="#{editPhotoBean.reset()}"
    action="album"/>
    <h:inputFile
     id="file"
     value="#{editPhotoBean.uploadedPart}">
     <f:validator validatorId="imageUploadValidator" />
    </h:inputFile>
   <h:commandButton
   id="button"
   value="Next"
   action="upload"/>

  </h:form>
 </c:if>
<c:if test="#{editPhotoBean.hasPhoto()}">
 <h:form id="navig">
 <h:commandButton
  id="cancel"
  value="Back"
  action="#{editPhotoBean.reset()}"/>
 <h:commandButton
  id="continue"
  value="Next"
```

```
     action="edit"/>
    </h:form>
  </c:if>
  <h:messages id="messages" style="color:red" />
   </div>
</h:body>
</html>
```

Notice in this page that the `EditPhoto` bean is used by the name in its `@Named` annotation and, in particular, its `uploadedPart` property is set from the `<h:inputFile>` tag. This means that the uploaded file is set on the `setUploadedPart()` method on the `EditPhoto` bean when it is uploaded. The `<h:inputFile>` tag has a nested validator: the `imageUploadValidator`. By looking at the code for `ImageUploadValidator`:

```java
import javax.faces.application.FacesMessage;
import javax.faces.component.UIComponent;
import javax.faces.context.FacesContext;
import javax.faces.validator.FacesValidator;
import javax.faces.validator.Validator;
import javax.faces.validator.ValidatorException;
import javax.servlet.http.Part;

@FacesValidator("imageUploadValidator")
public class ImageUploadValidator implements Validator {

  @Override
  public void validate(FacesContext context,
                       UIComponent component,
                       Object value) throws ValidatorException {
    Part file = (Part) value;
    if (!file.getContentType().equals("application/octet-stream")
        && !file.getContentType().equals("image/jpeg")) {
      throw new ValidatorException(new FacesMessage("The file you tried
                       to upload is not an image file. Please try again."));
    }
  }
}
```

we can see that only files of the correct MIME type will be uploaded. Try it yourself by attempting to upload a text file: you will see an error message on the page in red, thanks to the `<h:messages>` tag, and the `EditPhoto` bean will not be called.

While this application takes a simple approach to presentation in terms of color, visual styles, and layout, it should be possible to see that by using JavaServer Faces UI components, expression language, managed beans, and a variety of components such as a data validator, and a date/time converter in the `edit.xhtml` page, it is possible, even in a straightforward example, to separate the concerns of presentation from application data and logic quite cleanly. The lifecycle of the managed beans is taken care of by the Java EE web container, freeing us up to focus on the logic of photos and albums. We were able to dispose of the `UploadServlet` seen in previous versions of the application with the single `<h:inputFile>` tag.

Summary

In this chapter, we learned about the basic architecture of a JavaServer Faces application. We learned about the concepts of managed beans and how they can be used to hold a variety of different kinds of application data with differing lifecycles and cardinalities. We learned the most frequently used UI components and the mechanisms of event handling, data validation, and conversion. We saw three examples of increasing sophistication to illustrate what we learned.

We could go much further with the photo application, applying stylesheets to factor out pure presentation choices and using Faces Flows and navigation files to factor out the photo information–gathering flow in the application. We could factor out some of the common user interface elements into reusable Facelets, like the photo view table and the view, edit, delete button triples. However, even applying the mechanisms of managed beans, UI components, and expression language has brought us through the foundations of JavaServer Faces technology.

CHAPTER
5

Web Sites for
Non-browsers: JAX-RS

A JAX-RS component is a web component for non-browser clients.

In the last two chapters, we focused on web components that cater to the production of dynamic content described using a markup language. Specifically, JavaServer Faces is predominantly focused on the production of dynamic HTML pages. We have spent a good portion of our time so far looking at the features of the Java EE web container that make it easy to write a dynamic web site for browser clients.

Building a web site for browser clients entails the production not just of web components that generate dynamic markup content, but also of the design and creation of a data model and associated application logic that supports the web site. What happens if you want to expose the functionality of that application to non-browser clients? What if you want to expose some other aspect of that application data model, through some new set of logic, to non-browser clients? Suppose you have built an online store that allows customers to browse for items to purchase, fill a shopping basket, and make purchases from their desktop or smartphone. Now suppose you wish to build a rich client application that has a more interactive user experience than you can achieve when the customer is limited to using a browser, such as for a dedicated smartphone app. Suppose you wish to automate updating the inventory of items for purchase to another web application that the warehouse staff uses.

This need led to the development of web services technologies around 10 to 15 years ago. Initially growing out of the collection of existing CORBA/RPC technologies, interaction models used various XML formats and the synchronous RPC execution model, with the forerunner being SOAP/HTTP. This model paved the way for what was to come, and is well supported in the Java EE platform, using the JAX-RPC APIs in the `javax.xml.rpc.*` packages, a kind of Java RMI programming model that works with non-Java SOAP peers. But the complexity of this model was soon to be replaced with a new style of web services called Representational State Transfer web services (REST or RESTful for short). This web service technology is considerably simpler and easier to use than its predecessors. The major Internet companies of our time, Google, Amazon, Twitter, Facebook, and Yahoo!, have adopted this style for the APIs they use to expose their functionalities over the Internet. For these two reasons, this style has become the overwhelmingly predominant technology for web services.

What Are RESTful Web Services?

RESTful web services use a model wherein applications and data are exposed over HTTP as *resources*. Each resource a web service exposes has a URI that clients may use to interact with it. A web service resource may allow itself to be read by its client, updated by its clients, and deleted by its clients, and may also allow the creation of new resources. Not all web service resources allow all such operations.

In Figure 5-1, there is a web service client, which may be a rich client application on a smartphone or another web application running on a different application server. It interacts with the web service on the right, which is a lending library service. This service consists of two kinds of web service resources. One, the Library resource, of which there is one, allows browsing of the catalog and updates to the catalog information using the Read and Update operations. The second kind of resource is the Book resource, of which the Library contains many. Books may be added to the Library by using the Create operation on the Library, which creates a new Book resource to represent the new title. Individual books in the collection may be examined using the Read operation on the Book resource, while books may be removed from the Library by means of the Delete operation on the appropriate Book resource.

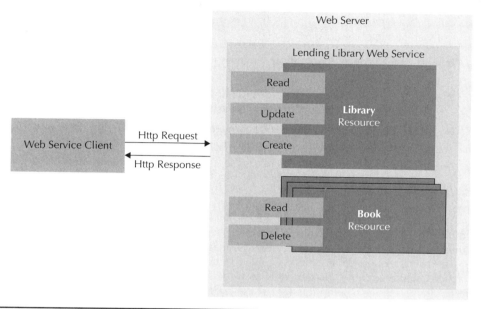

FIGURE 5-1. *A Library web service*

How are these kinds of create, read, update, and delete operations (also known collectively as CRUD operations) performed using RESTful web services? Part of the appeal of RESTful web services lies in the fact that it relies closely on well-understood and well-tested mechanisms from traditional web programming.

RESTful web services can be characterized using the following four properties.

Uses a URI Space to Address Web Service Resources

Just like a web application maps its static web pages, JSPs, and JavaServer Faces to URIs within a web application, web service resources are assigned one or more URIs on the web service, providing a means for the clients of the web service to address them in order to call their operations. Though there are no hard and fast rules about how the URI space is structured, it is common practice for the URI space to be hierarchically arranged in such a way that it reflects the hierarchy of the logical entities represented by the web resources. For example, you would reasonably expect that if the library resource in the diagram in Figure 5-1 were mapped to

```
/library
```

then the books would be mapped to URIs that shared `/library` at the root; perhaps your three favorite books in the library would correspond to Book web resources mapped to the following three relative URIs:

```
/library/books/23
/library/books/87
/library/books/1156
```

Uses HTTP Methods for Operations

RESTful web services use HTTP methods to perform operations on resources. The model for RESTful web services is to use

- HTTP GET for read operations on a resource to obtain all the information it can give about its identity.

- HTTP PUT for update operations to allow the client to pass information to the resource so that the resource can be modified as a result of the operation.

- HTTP POST to create new web services resources to allow the client to pass information to a web service resource that it uses to create a new web resource.

- HTTP DELETE for delete operations to allow the client to send an HTTP DELETE request to a web service resource, with the result that the resource is removed from the web service.

We should note at this point that this model is basically an expression of good (and common) practice. It is, of course, possible to abuse the definitions of these HTTP methods, passing data in a query string on a GET request in order to update a web service resource instead of using a PUT, or even using request parameters on a DELETE to create a new web service resource. Such practices, while possible, are generally frowned upon because they lead to web services APIs that are not very intuitive, swimming against the overwhelming stream of convention and good practice that has grown up around the use of HTTP methods in RESTful web services.

In our Library service, therefore, you would expect a

```
HTTP GET /library
```

to perform the Read operation, that is, to give you a listing of all the books in the library. You might well expect

```
HTTP PUT /library/books/87
```

together with accompanying information to update the library's records about book 87, just as you might well expect

```
HTTP DELETE /library/books/87
```

to remove book 87 from the library altogether.

RESTful Web Service Resources Are Stateless

The RESTful model is designed for highly scalable and high-performance web servers. Software components that represent web service resources are much more cleanly supported on clusters of servers with load balancing and failover if each request they service is entirely independent from the next. In other words, the RESTful model is geared toward web service resources not holding state across multiple requests. It is as though web service resources have less memory than a goldfish does: by the time the next request arrives from a new client, they have forgotten that anyone else has ever called them in the past.

Use Familiar Formats for Structured Data

RESTful web services use the MIME type to both identify the request information they will and can process and the information they will produce in response to a request. On the request side, the client uses the HTTP `Accept` header to indicate the format of the data it is sending to the web service resource. On the response side, the web service resource uses the `Content-Type` header to indicate the MIME type of the response it is giving.

RESTful web services can consume and produce any MIME type they wish; however, most web services consume and produce structured data as XML or as JavaScript Object Notation (JSON), or both.

For example, you could reasonably expect

```
HTTP GET /library/book/87, mime-type="application/xml"
```

to return something like

```
<book>
  <title>Passage to India</title>
  <author>E M Forster</author>
</book>
```

We can show these four properties of RESTful web services in a simple diagram, as seen in Figure 5-2.

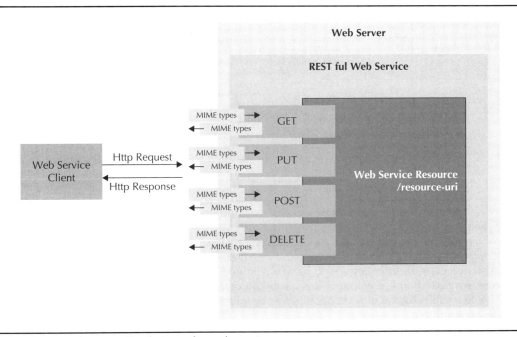

FIGURE 5-2. *A generalized view of a web service*

The Java API for RESTful Web Services

Now that we have a good understanding of the fundamental principles of RESTful web services, let us look at how they are supported in Java EE with the Java API for RESTful Web Services, or JAX-RS for short.

The starting point when representing web service resources is to take a JavaBean class and annotate it with the @javax.ws.rs.Path annotation:

```
import javax.ws.rs.Path;

@Path("hello")
public class HelloResource {
}
```

This instructs the Java EE web container to create a web service resource that is addressed at

```
http://<hostname>:<port>/<web-app-context-root>/hello
```

This is a good start, but the web service resource doesn't do anything yet. In order for it to have an operation, let's say a read operation, we need to create a Java method on the class that will be the operation and annotate it with the @GET HTTP method annotation from the javax .ws.rs package. This package is where all the other HTTP method annotations live as well.

Listing: *The HelloWorld resource*

```
import javax.ws.rs.GET;
import javax.ws.rs.Path;

@Path("hello")
public class HelloResource {

    @GET
    public String sayHello() {
       return "Hello you !";

    }

}
```

Now we have the code for a web service resource that will give the string Hello you ! when sent an HTTP GET request.

In JAX-RS terminology, the HelloResource class is a *root resource class*. You could always create web service resources as root resource classes if you wanted to, but once you have a root resource class representing a web service resource, you can use the root resource class to create web service resources whose URI is a sub-URI of the root resource class. For example, you can create a sub-resource of HelloResource by adding a new method giveGreeting() to the HelloResource class.

Listing: *The HelloWorld resource with greeting sub-resource*

```
import javax.ws.rs.GET;
import javax.ws.rs.will Path;

@Path("hello")
public class HelloResource {

    @GET
    public String sayHello() {
        return "Hello you !";
    }

    @Path("greeting")
    public GreetingResource giveGreeting() {
        return new GreetingResource();
    }

}
```

By annotating the method with the @Path annotation and setting its value to greeting, you are indicating that you want the GreetingResource class it returns to be a subresource of the HelloResource, available at the URI /hello/greeting. Now all the GreetingResource class needs to do is have a method annotated with one of the HTTP method annotations:

```
import javax.ws.rs.GET;
```

Listing: *The Greeting resource*

```
public class GreetingResource {

    @GET
    public String getGreeting() {
        return "Hail fellow well met !";
    }

}
```

Thus, there are two ways to create web service resources:

■ Create a root resource class with the @Path annotation containing the resource URI and have it declare its own operations by using one or more Java methods with HTTP method annotations.

■ From a root resource class, you declare a Java method returning a second Java class, where the Java method is annotated with @Path containing a URI relative to the URI of the root class. The second Java class implements the operations of the subresource with Java methods annotated by HTTP method annotations.

Here is a summary of the annotations to use for creating JAX-RS resources.

Annotation	Attribute	Used
@Path	Value attribute; denotes relative path where resource is deployed	At the class level to create a root resource; at the method level to create a subresource
@GET	None	To say that a Java method will handle HTTP GET requests for the web resource
@HEAD	None	To say that a Java method will handle HTTP HEAD requests for the web resource
@PUT	None	To say that a Java method will handle HTTP PUT requests for the web resource
@POST	None	To say that a Java method will handle HTTP POST requests for the web resource
@DELETE	None	To say that a Java method will handle HTTP DELETE requests for the web resource
@OPTIONS	None	To say that a Java method will handle HTTP OPTIONS requests for the web resource

Before we look at more of the JAX-RS APIs, let's look at a variation of this HelloWorld style of JAX-RS application and a couple of different ways to access it.

HelloResource Example: Server Side

In this example, we have a `HelloResource` web service resource deployed to the URI `/hello` relative to the web application that contains it. You can access the `HelloResource` resource from a browser, as we can see in Figure 5-3.

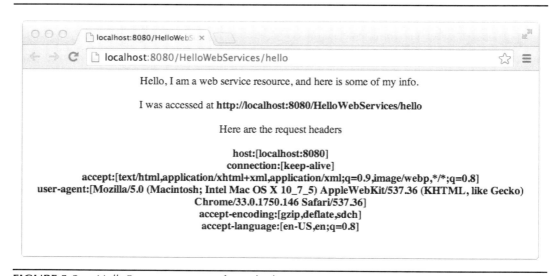

FIGURE 5-3. *HelloResource as seen from the browser*

You can see that this resource outputs some information about its configuration and how it has been accessed. Let's take a look at the code.

Listing: *The HelloResource resource*

```
import javax.ws.rs.GET;
import javax.ws.rs.PUT;
import javax.ws.rs.Path;
import javax.ws.rs.Produces;
import javax.ws.rs.core.Context;
import javax.ws.rs.core.UriInfo;
import javax.ws.rs.core.HttpHeaders;

@Path("hello")
public class HelloResource {

    @GET
    @Produces("text/html")
    public String sayHello(@Context UriInfo uri,
                        @Context HttpHeaders headers) {
        return "<html>" +
            "    <head>" +
            "      <title></title>" +
            "      <meta http-equiv='Content-Type' content='text/html'>" +
            "    </head>" +
            "    <body>" +
            "      <div align='center'>Hello, I am a web service resource," +
            "        and here is some of my info. <br></br> I am
                                                deployed at <b>"
                                        + uri.getAbsolutePath() +
                                                "</b></div><br>" +
            "         <div align='center'>Here are the request
                                            headers<br></br> "      +
            "        <b>" + this.writeHeaders(headers) + "</b></div>" +

            "    </body>\n" +
            "</html>";

    }


    private String writeHeaders(HttpHeaders headers) {

        StringBuilder buf = new StringBuilder();
        for (String header: headers.getRequestHeaders().keySet()) {
            buf.append(header);
            buf.append(":");
            buf.append(headers.getRequestHeader(header));
            buf.append("<br>");
        }
        return buf.toString();
    }
}
```

```
@PUT
@Produces("text/plain")
public String sayHelloPlain(String requestEntity) {
    return "Hello " + requestEntity + ", from JAX-RS land !";

}

}
```

Notice the use of the @Path annotation (with /hello as its URI relative to the context root of its web application) at the class level: HelloResource is therefore a root resource class. Next look at the sayHello() method. It uses the @GET annotation to declare that it will handle GET requests. This, of course, is the kind of request that the browser makes when you access this resource using the URL to the web resource. It uses a second JAX-RS annotation, @Produces, which indicates the MIME type of the content that this method will produce, in this case, HTML content. The parameter list of this method is also interesting; it asks for two objects to be passed in: an instance of UriInfo and an instance of HttpHeaders. These two JAX-RS API classes represent information about the URI used to access the web resource and the headers the client sent when requesting the resource, respectively. By virtue of the JAX-RS @Context annotation, the JAX-RS implementation knows that it (rather than anyone else who might call the method) is responsible for making sure these objects are correctly passed into this method at runtime when the method is called. We will return to the topics of accessing context and of MIME type declarations shortly. For now, we can see that the method implementation uses this information to produce the HTML content that it declares it will.

This is a rather reductive example: web service resources are not really intended for browser access. Indeed, we have better ways of generating HTML content from the Java EE platform. So what about the other web service method in this resource, sayHelloPlain()?

Before we take a look, we will pause to examine how JAX-RS resources are deployed on the Java EE server.

Deploying JAX-RS Resources

In order to deploy all the web service resource classes, and any other classes that it needs, you need to implement the javax.ws.rs.core.Application interface. The function of this interface is to let you declare in your application which of the classes it holds are resource classes and which are JAX-RS support classes, such as entity providers or exception mappers. The main contract of the class is the following method:

```
public Set<Class<?>> getClasses()
```

This method asks the straightforward question: Which JAX-RS classes would you like to deploy from this web application? When you deploy a web application containing an implementation of this application class, the JAX-RS runtime looks in the WAR file for such implementations, instantiates them, and gets the list of JAX-RS classes that it needs to deploy.

HelloResource Example and the Rich Client

Returning now to the second web service method of the HelloResource class in our example, the method sayHelloPlain(), we can see that by virtue of the @PUT annotation that decorates it, it responds to HTTP PUT requests. Therefore, it is the kind of web service resource method that

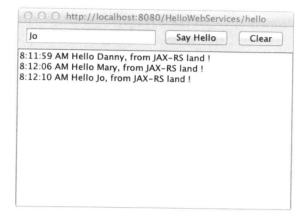

FIGURE 5-4.   *HelloResource as seen from a Java client*

accepts incoming data. We can see from its `@Produces` annotation that it produces plain text. It also has a `String` method parameter that it uses to formulate its response. Now, the HelloClient application is a second web service application, this time a Java client application, that uses a Swing window and JAX-RS to make the call to access this second method on the `HelloResource` resource on the web server, as shown in Figure 5-4.

We won't spend any time looking at Swing code; instead, let's look at the `HelloClient` Java class that the window uses to invoke the `HelloResource` web service resource running on the server.

Listing: *The HelloClient class*

```
import javax.ws.rs.client.*;

public class HelloClient {
    WebTarget wt;

    public HelloClient() {
        Client client = ClientBuilder.newClient();
        this.wt = client.target("http://localhost:8080/HelloWebServices/hello");
    }

    public String getUriAsString() {
        return this.wt.getUri().toString();
    }

    public String sayHello(String message) {
        Invocation webServiceCall = wt.request()
                .accept("text/plain")
```

```
            .build("PUT", Entity.text(message));
    String s = webServiceCall.invoke(String.class);
    return s;
}

}
```

When you click the Say Hello button in the UI, it calls the `sayHello()` method, passing in the value of the text field at the top of the window. The window appends the return value of this method to the text area in the middle of the window.

The `javax.ws.rs.client.WebTarget` class is the client-side representation of the remote resource that the client wishes to call. An instance of this is obtained from the instance of the `javax.ws.rs.client.Client` class that is bootstrapped, as shown in the code, from the `ClientBuilder` class. Once the `WebTarget` instance has been created, using the URL to the web resource in question, it can be used to create an instance of the class `javax.ws.rs` `.client.Invocation,` which represents all the data about the call that will be made. Finally, the call is actually made when the `invoke()` method of the invocation instance is called, passing in the class of the expected data type that the invocation will return, in this case, the `String` class.

Because the request that the `sayHello()` method on the client generates has been created with the `text/plain` MIME type, when the server receives the request to that URI, it looks for a method on the web service resource that can process data of that MIME type. So the incoming message is routed to the method on the server-side resource on `HelloResource` of `sayHelloPlain()`

```
@PUT
@Produces("text/plain")
public String sayHelloPlain(String requestEntity) {
    return "Hello " + requestEntity + ", from JAX-RS land !";

}
```

which was the mystery method of the `HelloResource` class earlier.

Since many web services are enacted server to server, this is no casual introduction to the JAX-RS client API. Indeed, you may well expect to use it from other Java EE components in addition to rich clients such as this Swing window. The example also introduces you rather informally to the two foundational mechanisms in JAX-RS: that of web resource content consumption and web resource production.

Content Production

All the examples that we have seen so far have web resource methods that return strings. Some were strings containing HTML, and some were strings containing regular text, but what they all had in common was that they came from Java methods whose return value was `java.lang` `.String`.

JAX-RS provides the means to model the content produced by web service resource methods with other Java classes suitable to the needs of the application and the means to describe the content to the calling client of the web resource.

The content produced by a web service resource method is called a response entity. Java methods that implement web service web resource methods create response entities in one of two ways. They may return an instance of the javax.ws.rs.core.Response class, which they can build with the Response.ResponseBuilder class, in which case the response entity is the entity property of the Response instance. Second, they may return a Java object that represents the response entity itself. The second case is a shortcut for web service methods that have no need to set other aspects of the response, for example, setting HTTP headers in the response.

You may be wondering what kinds of Java objects may be used to represent response entities: you have already seen that java.lang.String is one of them. JAX-RS supports encoding of several other Java types into response entities.

Java Type	Content Types
byte[]	Any
java.lang.String	Any
java.io.InputStream	Any
java.io.Reader	Any
java.io.File	Any
javax,activation.DataSource	Any
java.xml.transform.Source	Text/xml, application/xml application/*+xml
javax.xml.bind.JAXBElement and application-supplied JAXB classes	Text/xml, application/xml application/*+xml
javax.ws.rs.core.MultivaluedMap<String,String>	Application/x-www-form-urlencoded
javax.ws.rs.core.StreamingOutput	Any
java.lang.Boolean and boolean	Text/plain
java.lang.Character and char	Text/plain
java.lang.Number and primitive equivalents	Text/plain

Extending Response Entity Production

If this list is not convenient enough to model a response entity in an application, an application might deal in custom application-specific classes. In this case, JAX-RS has an extensibility scheme wherein any arbitrary Java type may be used in a response entity, provided there is a corresponding Java class that knows how to convert the Java type into the response type. Such conversion classes are known as response entity providers, and the contract you have to follow in creating entity providers is defined in the API class javax.ws.rs.MessageBodyWriter<T>.

In other words, if you want your web service method to return a Java object of type Foo, either directly or set as the entity of the Response instance it returns, then you provide an implementation of the interface MessageBodyWriter<Foo>, which requires you to implement the following method:

```
void writeTo(Foo entity,
        Class<?> type,
        Type genericType,
        Annotation[] annotations,
        MediaType mediaType,
```

```
MultivaluedMap<String,Object> httpHeaders,
OutputStream entityStream)
 throws IOException,

            WebApplicationException
```

The `Foo` entity parameter contains the response entity your web service method has returned, and it must be written to the `entityStream parameter`. We will see an example of such an entity provider at the end of the chapter.

@Produces

As we saw at the beginning of the chapter that when a client requests a response from a RESTful web service resource, it can use the `Accept` header to inform the resource of the MIME type of the response it wishes to receive. For the JAX-RS web service methods to be able to declare what kind of content they produce, the JAX-RS API includes the `@Produces` annotation for use on web service methods. The `@Produces` annotation's sole and mandatory attribute is the `value()` attribute, which contains the array of MIME types of the response entity of the method. This allows the same web resource method to be implemented by several Java methods, each producing a response entity of a different MIME type, as declared by the `@Produces` annotation that annotates each such Java method.

Content Consumption

Somewhat symmetrically, consumption of the body of a RESTful web service request follows many of the same mechanisms. A Java method that wishes to process the body of a web service request, known as a request entity, must have a parameter unadorned by annotations that is of a Java type suitable for holding the request entity. As we have seen, `java.lang.String` is one of the approved types for textual request entities. Just as with response entities, JAX-RS supports most of the same Java types that may be used for the request entity parameter of the Java web service method, with some limitations on the MIME types of the requests that can be used.

Java Type	Content Types
`byte[]`	Any
`java.lang.String`	Any
`java.io.InputStream`	Any
`java.io.Reader`	Any
`java.io.File`	Any
`javax,activation.DataSource`	Any
`java.xml.transform.Source`	Text/xml, application/xml application/*+xml
`javax.xml.bind.JAXBElement` and application-supplied JAXB classes	Text/xml, application/xml application/*+xml

Java Type	Content Types
`javax.ws.rs.core.` `MultivaluedMap<String,String>`	Application/x-www-form-urlencoded
`java.lang.Boolean` and `boolean`	Text/plain
`java.lang.Character` and `char`	Text/plain
`java.lang.Number` and primitive equivalents	Text/plain

Similarly, if an application wishes to consume its incoming request entities in the form of some Java type that is not on this list of supported standard types, an analogous mechanism exists for decoding incoming request entities into the given Java type. The application-provided objects that implement such decoding tasks are called request entity providers. The API contract for request entity providers is given by the `MessageBodyReader<T>` interface.

In other words, if you wish incoming web service request entities to arrive into your Java web service method as an instance of the `Foo` class, you need to create a Java class that implements `MessageBodyReader<Foo>`. This primarily requires you to implement the method

```
Foo readFrom(Class<Foo> type,
        Type genericType,
        Annotation[] annotations,
        MediaType mediaType,
        MultivaluedMap<String,String> httpHeaders,
        InputStream entityStream)
          throws IOException,

                WebApplicationException
```

which means you must read the incoming data from the `entityStream` parameter and instantiate a `Foo` instance. This instance will be passed to the Java web service method for which the request entity is destined. We will see an example of a `MessageBodyReader` later in the chapter.

@Consumes

When a resource method consumes data, the Java method that implements it expects data in a particular format. It may be that a resource wishes to implement a resource method using more than one Java method: one Java method implementation for every MIME type that it supports. The @Consumes annotation allows a Java method to declare the MIME types that it can support for incoming request entities.

Accessing Web Service Context

So far, we have seen that from a Java web service method, you have access to the request entity. We were able in the `HelloResource` example to access some more information about the context surrounding the `HelloResource` web service, namely the URL used by the client to access the web service resource, and the HTTP headers of the web service request.

Any JAX-RS resource may ask for this kind of contextual information to be passed to it by the web container by using the @Context annotation. A web service resource may obtain information about the HTTP request underlying the web service request, security information about the resource, the request and response entity providers, and other configuration information and options available to the resource. Here is a list of the JAX-RS API types that may be used in conjunction with the @Context annotation.

API Class	Purpose
javax.ws.rs.core.UriInfo	Access to the URI used to access the resource; the URI mapping of the resource.
javax.ws.rs.core.HttpHeaders	Access to the HTTP headers of the request.
javax.ws.rs.core.Request	Ability to perform content negotiation based on a client request.
javax.ws.rs.core.Application	Access to all the web service classes and properties in the same application.
javax.ws.rs.core.SecurityContext	Access to security information about the web resource, such as the user principal.
javax.ws.rs.ext.Providers	Access to all the entity providers in the application.
javax.ws.rs.container.ResourceContext	Ability to inject resources into a web service application.
javax.ws.rs.core.Configuration	Access to all the component instances in the application.

@Context may be used to annotate a parameter on a method, a constructor, or an instance variable on a resource class.

Exception Mapping

Much of the time, a web service method will function correctly and complete its work without any exceptions being raised. But this will not always be the case. Perhaps a web service method is passed content that it cannot make sense of, or perhaps some error internal to the application occurs in the middle of its execution. A Java method marked as a web service method may raise two kinds of exceptions when something unexpected happens. The method can raise a checked exception, in which case it will need to declare the exception in the throws clause of the method declaration. Or it can raise an unchecked/runtime exception. How does JAX-RS deal with these exceptions, and how does it communicate the error condition to the client?

Without any work on the developer's part, JAX-RS will transform Java exceptions thrown by web service methods into a suitable HTTP response. This may vary from implementation to implementation, but usually this will be a generic HTTP 500 - Internal Server Error. No matter what the exception, this is all the information the client will receive.

Therefore, it is often useful to be able to customize the responses your web service resource methods send back to the client in ways that depend on what kind of Java exception is raised when invoking the method and what other diagnostic information the exception is carrying. You may want to provide more descriptive information in the response about what the problem was.

In order to customize how application exceptions are mapped to HTTP responses, the `javax.ws.rs.ext.ExceptionMapper<E>` interface allows you define for a particular exception type `E` what kind of HTTP response you wish JAX-RS to make at runtime. There is only one method on this interface:

```
public Response toResponse(E exception)
```

When a class that implements this interface for a particular exception type (and, of course, one class may implement `ExceptionMappers` with many different exception types) is used in an application, and when the application throws an exception of the type specified in the generic type of the `ExceptionMapper`, then the JAX-RS runtime asks the `ExceptionMapper` to create the response that will be sent back to the client. If no `ExceptionMapper` for that type is found, then the container will send back the generic response, usually HTTP 500.

`ExceptionMappers` are useful ways to make your web service resource methods express more detail about what might go wrong when they are invoked.

Number of Instances of Resource Classes

So far, we have not talked much about how JAX-RS resources are deployed. In order to deploy all the web service resource classes, any message entity providers, or exception mapper classes, you will need to implement the `javax.ws.rs.core.Application`. The function of this interface is to let you declare in your application which of the classes it holds are resource classes or JAX-RS support classes such as entity providers or exception mappers. The main contract of the class is the method

```
public Set<Class<?>> getClasses()
```

This method asks the straightforward question: Which JAX-RS classes would you like to deploy from this web application? When you deploy a web application containing an implementation of this application class, the JAX-RS runtime looks in the WAR file for such implementations, instantiates them, and gets the list of JAX-RS classes that it needs to deploy.

This leads to the question of how many instances of each kind of JAX-RS classes are instantiated. Web service resource classes, unless they use some other scope annotation, are instantiated once for each client request. This belies the origins of RESTful web services as stateless and scalable. For developers creating resource classes, it means that any ordinary instance variables they hold in a resource class last only the lifetime of a single client request to the web service resource. It also means that JAX-RS resource class instances are called only by one thread at a time, and so do not need to deal with concurrent requests.

Provider classes, such as message body readers and writers and exception mappers, have a different lifecycle and cardinality. The JAX-RS implementation will maintain a single instance of each provider class in a web application and will share the instance among all the resource classes that use them for calls from any client. This means that multiple threads may access provider classes concurrently, so care must be taken when keeping states in such provider classes.

In the terminology of the managed beans we saw in Chapter 4, JAX-RS resource classes are request scoped and provider classes are application scoped.

It is possible to change the default scope and cardinality of resource classes, although for many web service developers, the default scopes are often the ones that their application needs. In order to change the scope of resource classes, you can declare those resource classes using the classes level `@javax.enterprise.context.RequestScoped` and `@javax.enterprise.context.ApplicationScoped` annotations, respectively. We will look at examples of managing the scope of a JAX-RS resource in this way when we look in detail at dependency injection later in the book.

Path Mapping

JAX-RS resources are mapped into the URI space using the `@Path` annotation. This annotation has one mandatory value: a path to which the resource is published for client access in the URI space of the web application in which it resides. This value may be either a relative URI or a URI template.

Relative URIs

In this case, the web service resource is published to the URI space of the web application, and a client request matches it if and only if the URI matches exactly. For example, a web service endpoint `BramleyApple` using the annotation

```
@Path("trees/apple/bramley")
public class BramleyApple {...}
```

deployed in a web application with context `root /horticulture` would only be available to clients at the URL

```
http://<hostname.port>/horticulture/trees/apple/bramley
```

URI Templates

URI templates are a fancy way of saying that one or more segments of the URI can be substituted with variables `{variable-name}`. A path variable used in the `@Path` annotation may be one of these; for example

```
@Path("/books/{book-id}")
public Book {}
```

would make the Book resource available to any of the following URIs, assuming the Book resource is deployed in a web application with a context root of `/library`:

```
http://<hostname.port>/library/books/24
http://<hostname.port>/library/books/98
http://<hostname.port>/library/books/9654
```

where the value of the path segment variable `book-id` would be 24, 98, and 9654, respectively.

In other words, any client URI that is a valid expansion of the URI template would be a match to the endpoint. If there is any contention, a match to an exact URI will always win over a match to a URI template.

This example of URI templates leads us to examine a more sophisticated application that uses and pulls together a number of the features of the JAX-RS API that we have talked about: the Library service.

The Library Service

The Library service is a client-server application. The server side is an online library that manages a collection of books that it contains. The client side is a GUI application that accesses the library and browses books in the library, adds new books to the library, and removes old books. Let's take a quick look through the main functions, as we will want to understand how the application works before we start looking at the code.

Figure 5-5 shows the main window. On the lower left, you can see a listing of the book titles in the library. When you click on a title, the panel on the right-hand side of the screen updates to give you full information about the selected book. Clicking Delete deletes the currently selected book from the library.

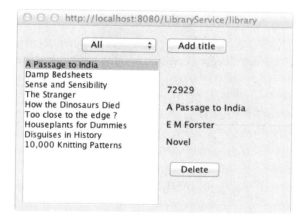

FIGURE 5-5. *The main window to the Library service*

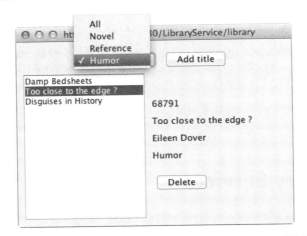

FIGURE 5-6. *Picking a genre to browse*

At the top of the window is a UI widget that allows you to filter the list of books you see by genre, as shown in Figure 5-6.

If you click the Add title button, you are asked to fill out the information about the new book you wish to add to the library, as seen in Figure 5-7.

If you forget to fill out the full information about the book properly, as in Figure 5-8, and try to add the book, the book will not be added. The Library service will tell you why, as seen in Figure 5-9.

Hopefully, you have already started to think about what kind of structure the web service resources in this application look like and the structure of the information consumed

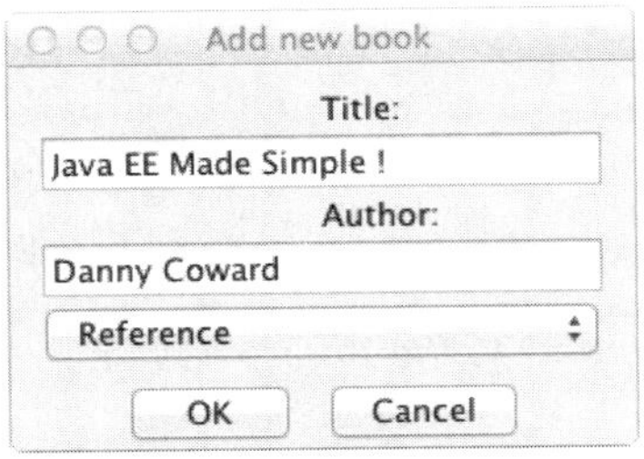

FIGURE 5-7. *Adding a new book*

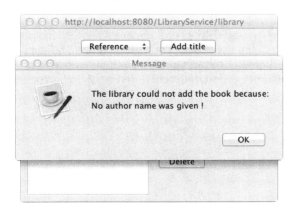

FIGURE 5-8. *Who's the author?*

and produced by its web service methods. First, let's map out the different classes in the application.

On the client side, the workhorse is the `LibraryClient` class, as shown in Figure 5-10. We will not discuss the Swing classes used to implement the user interface. The `LibraryClient` is responsible for formulating all the requests that the user interface needs to gather the information it needs to display and for unmarshaling the incoming responses to those requests from the Library service on the server. On the server side, the Library service is modeled as a single

FIGURE 5-9. *Your book is not welcome here.*

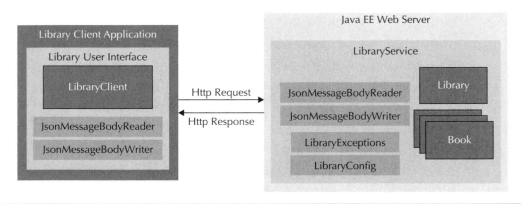

FIGURE 5-10. *Library service, class view*

instance of the `Library` class that references a list of `Book` objects that it contains. This arrangement gives us the structure of a single library containing a collection of books. As we shall see, `Library` is a root resource class, which defines itself by subresources, and, in addition, the `Book` class is a resource class. Web service calls from client to server carry payloads of entities that are JSON documents and of MIME type `application/json`. Both client and server use JSON entity providers for reading and writing JSON objects to request and response entities. The server-side application uses the addition providers `LibraryExceptions` for mapping application exceptions and the `LibraryConfig` class, which is the deployment class, for implementing `javax.ws.rs.core.Application`.

Before we look at the code, let's look at a breakdown of all the web service calls in the application in Figure 5-11, as it will prove useful to have these interactions in mind when we look at the code.

This diagram shows the five web service calls that the client makes to the server, detailing the payloads of each request and response. There are three `GET` requests, which get the list of genres that the library has, get the list of books of a given genre, and get a full description of a particular book, respectively. There is a `DELETE` request, which removes a book from the library, and there is a `POST` request containing a description of a new book to be added to the library.

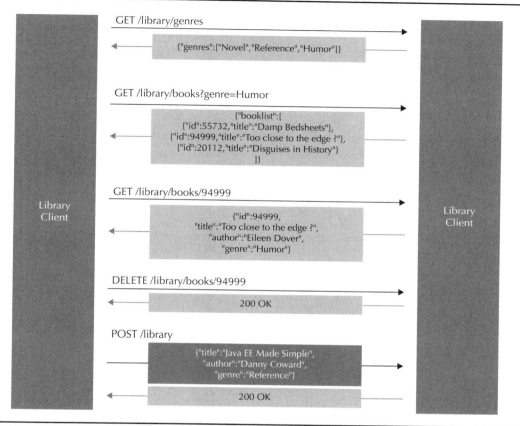

FIGURE 5-11. *Library service, interaction view*

Let's look first at the server side, starting with the Library class.

Listing: *The Library class*

```java
import javax.ws.rs.Path;
import javax.ws.rs.GET;
import javax.ws.rs.POST;
import javax.ws.rs.Produces;
import javax.ws.rs.Consumes;
import java.util.List;
import java.util.ArrayList;
import java.util.Random;
import javax.json.Json;
import javax.json.JsonObject;
```

```java
import javax.json.JsonArrayBuilder;
import javax.enterprise.context.ApplicationScoped;
import javax.ws.rs.core.MediaType;
import javax.ws.rs.core.Context;
import javax.ws.rs.core.UriInfo;
import javax.annotation.PostConstruct;

@Path("library")
@ApplicationScoped
public class Library {
    private String NOVEL = "Novel";
    private String REFERENCE = "Reference";
    private String HUMOR = "Humor";
    private List<Book> books = new ArrayList<>();

    @GET
    @Path("/books")
    @Produces(MediaType.APPLICATION_JSON)
    public JsonObject getBooks(@Context UriInfo uriInfo) {
        String genre = uriInfo.getQueryParameters().getFirst("genre");
        JsonArrayBuilder ab = Json.createArrayBuilder();
        for (Book next : this.books) {
            if (next.getGenre().equals(genre) || genre.equals("All")) {
                ab.add(next.getSummaryDescription());
            }
        }
        JsonObject model = Json.createObjectBuilder()
                .add("booklist", ab.build())
                .build();
        return model;
    }

    @Path("books/{id}")
    public Book getBook(@Context UriInfo uriInfo) {
        String idString =  uriInfo.getPathParameters().get("id").get(0);
        return this.getBook(new Integer(idString));
    }

    void removeBook(Book book) {
        this.books.remove(book);
    }

    private Book getBook(int id) {
        for (Book book : this.books) {
            if (book.getId() == id) {
                return book;
            }
        }
        return null;
    }

    @GET
    @Path("/genres")
    @Produces(MediaType.APPLICATION_JSON)
    public JsonObject getGenres() {
        JsonArrayBuilder ab = Json.createArrayBuilder()
```

```
                    .add(NOVEL)
                    .add(REFERENCE)
                    .add(HUMOR);
        JsonObject genreso = Json.createObjectBuilder()
            .add("genres", ab)
            .build();
        return genreso;
    }


    @POST
    @Consumes(MediaType.APPLICATION_JSON)
    public void addBook(JsonObject booko) throws InvalidBookException {
        String genre = booko.getString("genre");
        String title = booko.getString("title");
        String author = booko.getString("author");
        if ("".equals(author)) {
            throw new InvalidBookException("No author name was given !");
        }
        int id = (int) this.generateId();
        Book b = new Book(
                this,
                id,
                title,
                author,
                genre
                );
        this.books.add(b);
    }


    private int generateId() {
        long l = System.currentTimeMillis() * (new Random()).nextInt();
        String asString = "" + l;
        String as5String = asString.substring((asString.length()-5), (asString.
length())));
        return (new Integer(as5String)).intValue();
    }


    @PostConstruct
    private void initLibrary() {
        Book b = new Book(this, this.generateId(),
                "A Passage to India", "E M Forster", NOVEL);
        this.books.add(b);
        b = new Book(this, this.generateId(),
                "Damp Bedsheets", "I P Nightly", HUMOR);
        this.books.add(b);
        b = new Book(this, this.generateId(),
                "Sense and Sensibility", "Jane Austen", NOVEL);
        this.books.add(b);
        b = new Book(this, this.generateId(),
                "The Stranger", "Albert Camus", NOVEL);
        this.books.add(b);
        b = new Book(this, this.generateId(),
                "How the Dinosaurs Died", "P T Dactyl", REFERENCE);
        this.books.add(b);
        b = new Book(this, this.generateId(),
                "Too close to the edge ?", "Eileen Dover", HUMOR);
```

```
        this.books.add(b);
        b = new Book(this, this.generateId(),
                "Houseplants for Dummies", "G Fingers", REFERENCE);
        this.books.add(b);
        b = new Book(this, this.generateId(),
                "Disguises in History", "Ivor Beard", HUMOR);
        this.books.add(b);
        b = new Book(this, this.generateId(),
                "10,000 Knitting Patterns", "M N E Sweaters", REFERENCE);
        this.books.add(b);
    }

}
```

First, notice by virtue of the class level `@Path("library")` annotation that this is a root resource class, mapped to `/library` in the URI space of the containing web application. Second, it uses the `@ApplicationScoped` annotation to declare itself as a managed bean of application scope. This means that for each web application, there will be one and only one instance of the `Library` class that services requests from all clients. This is what this application needs: if we did not have this annotation, each time that the client makes a web service call to it, a new instance of the class would be created. In this implementation, the books are added to the library in the `initLibrary()` method at the bottom of the class. We are not using a database to store this information, and we are essentially storing the book information in the single instance of the `Library` class. When we have progressed further in our exploration of the Java EE platform, we will discover several better ways to store such information, but for now, a singleton is what we want. Notice also that the Library bean uses the `@PostConstruct` annotation to request that the Java EE web container call the `initLibrary()` method immediately after the new instance is created. This convenience hints at more of the lifecycle management of managed beans that we will be covering throughout the book.

Now to the web service method calls on the `Library` class: `getGenres()` annotated by `@GET`, `getBooks()` annotated by `@GET`, and `addBook()` annotated by `@POST`. Notice that all these methods process incoming and outgoing entities as JSON objects using the `javax.json` JSON-Processing API in the Java EE platform. For example, the return value of `getGenres()` is `JsonObject`, which contains a list of all the genres in the library in the form of a `JsonArray`. For example, the method parameter of `addBook()` is also `JsonObject`, which is expected to be a `JsonObject` containing the key-value pairs for author, title, and genres when adding a new book to the library. The marshaling and unmarshaling of JSON documents to the JSON objects that these Java methods deal in is handled by the two entity provider classes in the Library service application: `JsonMessageBodyReader` and `JsonMessageBodyWriter`. Since one is almost the mirror image of the other, let us limit our examination of these entity providers by looking at the `JsonMessageBodyReader` class.

Listing: *The JsonMessageBodyReader entity provider*

```
import javax.ws.rs.WebApplicationException;
import javax.ws.rs.ext.Provider;
import javax.ws.rs.ext.MessageBodyReader;
import javax.ws.rs.core.MediaType;
import javax.ws.rs.core.MultivaluedMap;
```

```java
import javax.ws.rs.Consumes;
import javax.json.Json;
import javax.json.JsonObject;
import java.lang.reflect.Type;
import java.lang.annotation.Annotation;

@Provider
@Consumes(MediaType.APPLICATION_JSON)
public class JsonMessageBodyReader implements MessageBodyReader<JsonObject> {

    @Override
    public boolean isReadable(java.lang.Class<?> type,
                Type genericType,
                Annotation[] annotations,
                MediaType mediaType) {
        return true;

    }

    @Override
    public JsonObject readFrom(java.lang.Class<JsonObject> type,
        Type genericType,
        Annotation[] annotations,
        MediaType mediaType,
        MultivaluedMap<java.lang.String,java.lang.String> httpHeaders,
        java.io.InputStream entityStream)
        throws java.io.IOException,

                WebApplicationException {

        JsonObject o =  Json.createReader(entityStream).readObject();
        return o;

    }
}
```

We can see that the workhorse method of the class is the readFrom() method, which uses the JSON Processing API to read the request entity from the InputStream into the expected JsonObject. The JsonMessageBodyWriter has analogous code for the reverse process of writing the JsonObject to an OutputStream, representing the response entity in its writeTo() method.

```java
public void writeTo(JsonObject t,
            Class<?> type,
            Type genericType,
            Annotation[] annotations,
            MediaType mediaType,
            MultivaluedMap<String,Object> httpHeaders,
            OutputStream entityStream)
             throws IOException,

                    WebApplicationException {
```

```
    String s = t.toString();
    byte[] bytes = s.getBytes();
    for (int i = 0; i < bytes.length; i++) {
        entityStream.write(bytes[i]);
    }
  }
}
```

Returning to the `Library` class again for a moment, notice that it has two ways to accept incoming data from the client. When the client requests the lists of books from a certain genre, the genre is passed in as a query string on the GET call to `/library/books`; for example, GET `/library/books?genre=Humor`. This call is implemented by the

```
public JsonObject getBooks(@Context UriInfo uriInfo)
```

method, which, by use of the `@Context` annotation, requires the information about the URI used to invoke it be passed in as a method parameter. You can see from the implementation that the genre request parameter is obtained from the `UriInfo` class, which is used to filter the list of books to be returned. This is quite a common pattern. Logically, the `/library/books` resource represents a list of the books in the library. It is common practice in web service APIs to use a query string to filter or order the result of a web service call. In this case, the Library service is just using the query string to filter the results, but you could equally imagine a second request parameter called `orderBy`, which would take a particular approach to order the results to a criterion.

The second way that the `Library` class accepts incoming data is in the `addBook()` method. Data is explicitly passed to this method as a request entity, represented in the Java method by the `JsonObject` method parameter. This Java method is implementing a POST request that, if successful, will lead to the creation of a new web resource for the new book. Passing this kind of information as a query string is possible but considered bad practice, as the data is not qualifying a query for information; it will be used directly to create a new resource. In general, it is good practice to use query strings to qualify querying calls and use request entities to pass into web resource creational calls.

The final piece of the puzzle is to follow the subresources representing the books. Each book is represented by a subresource at `/library/books/{id}`, where `id` is the book ID of the `Book`. The Java method

```
public Book getBook(@Context UriInfo uriInfo)
```

of the `Library` class implements this subresource, but instead of being qualified by an HTTP method annotation, it returns a `Book` instance. The `Book` class contains the web resource methods for this subresource. Before we examine this further, notice again that the use of the `@Context` annotation to require the `UriInfo` for this subresource is passed in when it is invoked. This subresource is being mapped to a `/books/{id}` URI template rather than to a URI, and the request URIs that will match this path will contain the ID of the book being requested. Therefore, the `getBook()` method needs to find out the value of the ID parameter from the matching request URI from the client to know which book to respond with information about.

The `Book` class is relatively straightforward, being a JavaBean with readable properties of ID, title, author, and genre.

Listing: *The Book resource*

```java
import javax.json.Json;
import javax.json.JsonObject;
import javax.ws.rs.DELETE;
import javax.ws.rs.GET;
import javax.ws.rs.Produces;
import javax.ws.rs.core.MediaType;

public class Book {
    private Library library;
    private int id;
    private String title;
    private String author;
    private String genre;

    public Book(Library library, int id,
                String title, String author, String genre) {
       this.library = library;
       this.id = id;
       this.title = title;
       this.author = author;
       this.genre = genre;
    }

    @DELETE
    public void removeFromLibrary() {
       this.library.removeBook(this);
    }

    @GET
    @Produces(MediaType.APPLICATION_JSON)
    public JsonObject getFullDescription() {
       JsonObject descriptiono = Json.createObjectBuilder()
           .add("id", this.getId())
           .add("title", this.getTitle())
           .add("author", this.getAuthor())
           .add("genre", this.getGenre())
           .build();
       return descriptiono;
    }

    public JsonObject getSummaryDescription() {
       JsonObject descriptiono = Json.createObjectBuilder()
           .add("id", this.getId())
           .add("title", this.getTitle())
           .build();
       return descriptiono;
    }
```

```
public int getId() {
   return this.id;
}

public String getTitle() {
   return this.title;
}

public String getAuthor() {
   return this.author;
}

public String getGenre() {
   return this.genre;
}

@Override
public String toString() {
   return "a book by " + this.author;
}
```

}

Notice its two web service methods, `GET` and `DELETE`, for querying a book's information and removing it from the library, implemented by `getFullDescription()` and `removeFromLibrary()`, respectively.

Notice throughout the `Library` and `Book` class the use of the `@Produces` and `@Consumes` annotations to qualify the formats of the incoming and outgoing entities to be JSON data.

Finally, in the server application, there is an `ExceptionMapper` implementation called `LibraryExceptions` that takes the `InvalidBookException` and maps it to an HTTP 404 Response, with a response body that contains the error message in the Java exception. This is used in the `Library.addBook()` method if the client sends a request entity whose author attribute is mistakenly empty. In this case, the `addBook()` method throws an `InvalidBookException`, which the JAX-RS implementation passes to the `LibraryExceptions` class, which in turn creates the HTTP 404 response just described. If you look carefully at the server and client code, you should be able to track the error message that pops up in the warning dialog when you try to add an authorless book to the library from the server code, where the exception is generated to the client code that displays the message.

Now that we understand the server side, the client side will be relatively straightforward.

Listing: *The LibraryClient class*

```
import javax.ws.rs.client.Client;
import javax.ws.rs.client.ClientBuilder;
import javax.ws.rs.client.WebTarget;
import javax.ws.rs.client.Invocation;
import javax.ws.rs.client.Entity;
import javax.json.JsonObject;
import javax.json.JsonArray;
import java.util.List;
```

```java
import java.util.ArrayList;
import javax.ws.rs.core.MediaType;
import javax.ws.rs.core.Response;


public class LibraryClient {
    Client wsClient;
    private static String WEBSERVICE_ROOT =
                    "http://localhost:8080/LibraryService";
    private static String LIBRARY_URI = WEBSERVICE_ROOT + "/library";
    private static String BOOKS_URI = LIBRARY_URI + "/books";
    private static String GENRES_URI = LIBRARY_URI + "/genres";



    public LibraryClient() {
        this.wsClient = ClientBuilder.newBuilder()
                .register(JsonMessageBodyReader.class)
                .register(JsonMessageBodyWriter.class)
                .build();
    }

    public String getUriAsString() {
        return LIBRARY_URI;
    }

    public List<JsonObject> getBooks(String genre) {
        WebTarget wt = this.wsClient.target(BOOKS_URI + "?genre=" + genre);
        Invocation webServiceCall = wt.request()
                .accept(MediaType.APPLICATION_JSON)
                .build("GET");
        JsonObject genreso = webServiceCall.invoke(JsonObject.class);
        List<JsonObject> bookSummaries = new ArrayList<>();

        JsonArray ar = genreso.getJsonArray("booklist");
        for (int i = 0; i < ar.size(); i++) {
            JsonObject jsono = ar.getJsonObject(i);
            bookSummaries.add(jsono);
        }
        return bookSummaries;
    }

    public JsonObject getBookById(int id) {
        WebTarget genresTarget = this.wsClient.target(BOOKS_URI + "/"+ id);
        Invocation webServiceCall = genresTarget.request()
                .accept(MediaType.APPLICATION_JSON)
                .build("GET");
        JsonObject jsono = webServiceCall.invoke(JsonObject.class);
        return jsono;
    }


    public void deleteBook(int id) {
        WebTarget genresTarget = this.wsClient.target(BOOKS_URI + "/"+ id);
        Invocation webServiceCall = genresTarget.request()
                .build("DELETE");
```

```
            webServiceCall.invoke();
    }

    public List<String> getGenres() {
        WebTarget genresTarget = wsClient.target(GENRES_URI);
        Invocation webServiceCall = genresTarget.request()
                .accept(MediaType.APPLICATION_JSON)
                .build("GET");
        JsonObject genreso = webServiceCall.invoke(JsonObject.class);
        JsonArray ar = genreso.getJsonArray("genres");
        List<String> genres = new ArrayList<>();
        for (int i = 0; i < ar.size(); i++) {
            String next = ar.getString(i);
            genres.add(next);
        }
        return genres;
    }

    public AddBookStatus addBook(JsonObject bookaddo) {
        WebTarget genresTarget = this.wsClient.target(LIBRARY_URI);
        Invocation webServiceCall = genresTarget.request()
                .header("Content-Type", MediaType.APPLICATION_JSON)
                .build("POST", Entity.json(bookaddo));
        Response response = webServiceCall.invoke();
        if (response.getStatus() == Response.Status.BAD_REQUEST.getStatusCode()) {
            return new AddBookStatus(false, response.readEntity(String.class));
        } else {
            return new AddBookStatus(true, "");
        }

    }

}

class AddBookStatus {
    boolean added = false;
    String errorMessage = "";

    AddBookStatus(boolean added, String errorMessage) {
        this.added = added;
        this.errorMessage = errorMessage;
    }
}
```

The `LibraryClient` class contains most of the JAX-RS-related code in the client application and uses a single instance of the `javax.ws.rs.client.Client` object to do its work. Notice that when this client is created, the `JsonMessageBodyReader` and `JsonMessageBodyWriter` classes are registered on it. You can see that by virtue of these entity provider classes, the `LibraryClient` deals only in message entities that are JSON objects.

The client methods all follow the same pattern: They create from the JAX-RS client object a web service `Invocation` object, using the `WebTarget` object that contains the full URL to the server resource, adding in any qualifying information about the call, such as the content type, always `application/json` in this application, and any request payload, as you can see, for example, in the `addBook()` method:

```
WebTarget genresTarget = this.wsClient.target(LIBRARY_URI);
    Invocation webServiceCall = genresTarget.request()
            .header("Content-Type", MediaType.APPLICATION_JSON)
            .build("POST", Entity.json(bookaddo));
    Response response = webServiceCall.invoke();
```

Finally, the method calls `invoke()` on the Invocation instance to obtain the response from the resource.

When there is information in the payload of the response, as there is, for example, in the method `getBooks()` that fetches the list of books in a certain genre, the response is "read" using a variant of the `invoke()` call, such as:

```
JsonObject genreso = webServiceCall.invoke(JsonObject.class);
```

This fetches the response entity in the form of a `JsonObject`, which in this case, is the JSON object containing the list of books.

Summary

The JAX-RS APIs have many features that you can continue to explore once you have fully understood the key concepts of this chapter, in particular, the model for JAX-RS filters. These filters allow you to add components to the JAX-RS application that can block or transform incoming or outgoing data to and from web service resources. These are useful for adding compression and authorization checks to a web service application.

However, this chapter is a full grounding in the essentials of JAX-RS programming, having explored all the ways Java classes can become web service resources and how their Java methods can become web service resource methods, qualified by the content types they consume and produce. The chapter looked at how such resources are mapped into the URI space of a web application and how provider classes can be created to extend the core supported request and response entity Java types to any custom Java object. We discussed the scope model for JAX-RS resources and looked at how to customize exception handling in a JAX-RS application in order to give informative error responses to clients of a RESTful API.

Finally, we looked at the Library service that pulled together all these concepts and mechanisms into a single client server RESTful application, using JSON as a content model and the JSON API to process it, showing how JAX-RS can be used to build an online library for the non-browser client.

CHAPTER
6

Adding Sparkle:
Java WebSockets

Java WebSockets are unlike other Java EE web components because can they push data out to web clients without clients having to ask for it.

Java WebSockets are a departure from the HTTP-based interaction model, providing a way for Java EE applications to update browser and non-browser clients asynchronously. The interaction model for web sites has long been the HTTP request/response interaction model, which is rich and allows for many sophisticated browser-based applications. Each interaction, however, always starts from the browser with some action on the part of the user: loading a page, refreshing a page, clicking a button, following a link, and so on.

For many kinds of web applications, having the user always in the driver's seat is not desirable. From financial applications with live market data, to auction applications where people around the world bid on items, to the lowly chat and presence applications, web developers have long sought means by which the server side of the web application can push data out to the client. A mix of ad hoc mechanisms arose out of this need that were either based around keeping long-lived HTTP connections or some form of client polling; none proved a complete solution to the problem. There was a need for a new approach, which led to the development of the WebSocket protocol.

Introduction to the WebSocket Protocol

The WebSocket protocol is a TCP-based protocol that provides a full duplex communication channel over a single connection. In simple terms, this means that it uses the same underlying network protocol as does HTTP and that over a single WebSocket connection both parties can send messages to the other at the same time. The WebSocket protocol defines a simple connection lifecycle, as we shall see, and defines a data-framing mechanism that supports binary and text-based messages. Unlike HTTP, the connections are long lived. This means that since the connection need not continually be re-established for each message transmission, as the antisymmetric HTTP protocol does, each data message in the WebSocket protocol does not need to carry all the metainformation about the connection as does HTTP. In other words, once the connection is established, the message transmission is much lighter weight than in the HTTP protocol.

Yet, this is not the primary reason WebSocket is better suited to the task of servers pushing information than are polling frameworks layered on top of the HTTP protocol. Having a dedicated TCP connection to its clients makes WebSockets an inherently more efficient way for a server to update clients because data is sent only when it is needed.

To see why, imagine an online auction where 10 people are bidding on an item over a period of 12 hours. Suppose that each bidder makes an average of two successful bids on the item. So the item price changes 20 times over the period of the auction. Suppose now that the clients have to poll to see the latest bidding information. Because you cannot know when the bidders will make a bid or how up to date the amount of the current bid is, the web application supporting the auction needs to make sure that each client is refreshed at least every minute and probably more! This means that each of the clients needs to poll 60 times an hour, giving a total of $60 \times 10 \times 12 = 7{,}200$ updates to make. In other words, 7,200 update messages get generated.

If, however, the server can push the data out to the client only when the data has actually changed, such as the case when using WebSockets, only 20 messages need to be sent to each client, giving $20 \times 10 = 200$ messages in total.

You can probably see how the relative numbers get even more divergent as, over the lifetime of an application, either the number of clients increases or the amount of time when server data could change but doesn't increases. The server push model offered by WebSockets is inherently more efficient than any polling mechanism could ever be.

The WebSocket Lifecycle

In the WebSocket protocol, a client and a server are mostly the same as each other. The only antisymmetry in the protocol is in the initial phase of the connection being established, where it matters who initiated the connection. It is somewhat like a phone call. To make the phone call happen, someone has to dial the number and someone has to answer. But once the phone call has been connected, it doesn't matter who initiated it.

For WebSockets in the Java EE platform, a WebSocket client is almost always a browser or a rich client running on a laptop, smartphone, or desktop computer, and the WebSocket server is a Java EE web application running on a Java EE application server.

Let's look now at a typical lifecycle of a WebSocket connection. First, the client initiates a connection request. This occurs when the client sends a specially formulated HTTP request to the web server. You do not need to understand every detail of the handshake request. What identifies this as a WebSocket opening handshake request over any common or garden-variety HTTP request is the use of the `Connection : Upgrade` and `Upgrade : websocket` headers, and the most important information is the request URI, /myChat in Figure 6-1.

The web server decides whether it supports WebSockets at all (which all Java EE web containers do) and, if so, whether there is an endpoint at the request URI of the handshake request that meets the requirements of the request. If all is well, the WebSocket-enabled web server responds with an equally specially formulated HTTP response called a WebSocket opening handshake response, as shown in Figure 6-2.

```
                    Handshake Request

Http Request
GET /mychat HTTP/1.1
Host: server.example.com
Upgrade: websocket
Connection: Upgrade
Sec-WebSocket-Key: x3JJHMbDL1EzLkh9GBhXDw==
Sec-WebSocket-Protocol: megachat, chat
Sec-WebSocket-Extensions : compress, mux
Sec-WebSocket-Version: 13
Origin: http://example.com
```

FIGURE 6-1. *WebSocket handshake request*

```
                        Handshake Response

Http Response
HTTP/1.1 101 Switching Protocols
Upgrade: websocket
Connection: Upgrade
Sec-WebSocket-Accept: HSmrc0sMlYUkAGmm5OPpG2HaGWk=
Sec-WebSocket-Protocol: chat
Sec-WebSocket-Extensions: compress, mux
```

FIGURE 6-2. *WebSocket handshake response*

This response confirms that the server will accept the incoming TCP connection request from the client and may impose restrictions on how the connection may be used. Once the client has processed the response and is happy to accept any such restrictions, the TCP connection is created, as shown in Figure 6-3, and each end of the connection may proceed to send messages to the other.

Once the connection is established, a number of things can occur:

■ *Either end of the connection may send a message to the other.* This may occur at any time that the connection is open. Messages in the WebSocket protocol have two flavors: text and binary.

■ *An error may be generated on the connection.* In this case, assuming the error did not cause the connection to break, both ends of the connection are informed. Such non terminal errors may occur, for example, if one party in the conversation sends a badly formed message.

■ *The connection is voluntarily closed.* This means that either end of the connection decides that the conversation is over and so closes the connection. Before the connection is closed, the other end of the connection is informed of this.

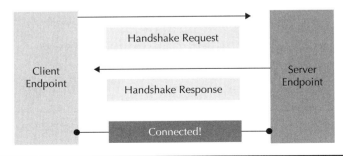

FIGURE 6-3. *Establishing a WebSocket connection*

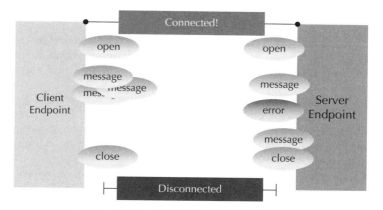

FIGURE 6-4.   *WebSocket lifecycle*

In Figure 6-4, we see an example flow of the events that can occur in the lifecycle of any WebSocket connection.

Overview of the Java WebSocket API

The Java WebSocket API provides a set of Java API classes and Java annotations that make it relatively straightforward to create WebSocket endpoints that reside in the Java EE web container. The general idea is to take a Java class that you want to implement the logic of the server endpoint and annotate it at the class level with the special Java WebSocket API annotation `@ServerEndpoint`. Next, you annotate its method with one of the lifecycle annotations, such as `@OnMessage`, which imbues the method in question with the special power of being called every time a WebSocket client sends a message to the endpoint. You then package it in the `WEB-INF/classes` directory of the WAR file. Let's see an example of just that.

 Listing: *The EchoServer sample*

```
import javax.websocket.OnMessage;
import javax.websocket.server.ServerEndpoint;

@ServerEndpoint("/echo")
public class EchoServer {

        @OnMessage
        public String echo(String incomingMessage) {
            return "I got this (" + incomingMessage + ")"
                    + " so I am sending it back !";
        }
}
```

This WebSocket endpoint is mapped to `/echo` in the URI space of the web application. Each time a WebSocket client sends it a message, it responds back immediately with a message derived from the one it received.

The Java WebSocket API contains the means to intercept all the WebSocket lifecycle events and provides the means to send messages in both synchronous and asynchronous modes. It allows you to translate WebSocket messages to and from arbitrary Java classes using decoder and encoder classes.

The Java WebSocket API also provides the means to create WebSocket client endpoints. The only time that the WebSocket protocol is asymmetric concerns who initiates the connection. The client support in the Java WebSocket API allows a client to connect to the server, and so is suitable for Java clients to connect to WebSocket endpoints running in the Java EE web container, or in fact, any WebSocket server endpoint.

Before we look at a real example of a Java WebSocket, let's take a tour of the annotations and main classes in the Java WebSocket API. Don't worry about spending too long before we get to working code: the Java WebSocket API is one of the smaller APIs of the Java EE platform.

WebSocket Annotations

The Java WebSocket annotations have two main purposes. First, they allow you to declare that you want an ordinary Java class to become a WebSocket endpoint, and second, they allow you to annotate methods on that class so that they intercept the lifecycle events of the WebSocket endpoint. First, we will take a look at the class-level annotations.

@ServerEndpoint

This is the workhorse annotation of the API, and if you create many WebSocket endpoints, you will be seeing a lot of it. The primary (and only) mandatory attribute of this class-level annotation is the value attribute, which specifies the URI path to which you want this endpoint to be registered in the URI space of the web application.

Attribute	Function	Mandatory
value	Defines URI path under which the endpoint is registered	Yes

@ClientEndpoint

The `@ClientEndpoint` annotation is used at the class level on a Java class that you wish to turn into a client endpoint that initiates connections to server endpoints. This is often used in rich client applications that connect to the Java EE web container. It has no mandatory attributes.

@ServerEndpoint and @ClientEndpoint Optional Attributes

These class-level annotations have several other attributes in common that define other configuration options that apply to the WebSocket endpoint they decorate.

@ServerEndpoint and @ClientEndpoint Attributes	Function	Mandatory
configurator	The class name of a special class the developer may provide to dynamically configure the endpoint	No

@ServerEndpoint and @ClientEndpoint Attributes	Function	Mandatory
`decoders`	List of classes used to convert incoming WebSocket messages into Java classes that represent them	No
`encoders`	List of classes used to convert Java classes into outgoing WebSocket messages	No
`subprotocols`	List of string names denoting any special subprotocols, such as "chat," that the endpoint supports	No

Now let us turn to the lifecycle annotations.

@OnOpen

This method-level annotation declares that the Java EE web container must call the method it annotates on a WebSocket endpoint whenever a new party connects to it. The method may have either no arguments or an optional Session parameter, where the class `javax.websocket.Session` is an API object that represents the WebSocket connection that has just opened, and/or an optional Endpoint config parameter, where `javax.websocket.EndpointConfig` is an API object representing the configuration information for this endpoint, and an optional WebSocket path parameter, which we will soon discuss.

@OnMessage

This method-level annotation declares that the Java EE web container must call the method it decorates whenever a new message arrives on the connection. The method must have a certain type of parameter list, but luckily, there are a number of options. The parameter list must include a variable that can hold the incoming message, can include the `Session`, and can include path parameters. A range of options exists for what kind of variables can hold the incoming message, with the most commonly used options being `String` for text messages and `ByteBuffer` for binary messages.

The method may have a specified return type or be of void return type. If there is a return type, the Java EE web container interprets the return as a message to send back immediately to the client.

@OnError

This method-level annotation declares that the Java EE web container must call the method it decorates whenever an error occurs on the connection. The method must have a `Throwable` parameter in its parameter list, and may have an optional `Session` parameter and path parameters.

@OnClose

For the final event in any WebSocket lifecycle, this method-level annotation declares that the Java EE web container must call the method it decorates whenever a WebSocket connection to this endpoint is about to close. The method is allowed to have a `Session` parameter and path parameters in its parameter list if it wants them to be passed in, as well as a `javax.websocket.CloseReason` parameter, which contains some explanation as to why the connection is closing.

The Java WebSocket API Classes

The most important API classes that the developer of Java WebSockets will encounter are the `Session`, `Remote`, and `WebSocketContainer` interfaces.

Session

The Session object is a high-level representation of an active WebSocket connection to an endpoint. It is available to any of the WebSocket lifecycle methods. It contains information about how the connection was established, for example, the request URI that the other party in the connection used to establish it, and the amount of time, if left idle, that the connection will time out after. It contains the means to close the connection programmatically. It holds a map that applications may use to hold application data that they wish to associate with the connection, perhaps a transcript of the entire message that an endpoint received from a given peer. Although different from the `HttpSession` object, it is analogous in that it represents a sequence of interactions from a particular peer of the endpoint that has access to the `Session` object instance. Additionally, it holds access to the `RemoteEndpoint` interface for the endpoint.

RemoteEndpoint

The `RemoteEndpoint` interface is available from the `Session` object and represents the endpoint at the other end of the connection. In practical terms, it is the object you call when you want to send a message to the other end of the connection. There are two subtypes of `RemoteEndpoint`. One, `RemoteEndpoint.Basic`, holds all the methods for sending WebSocket messages synchronously. The other, `RemoteEndpoint.Async`, holds all the methods for sending WebSocket messages asynchronously. Many applications only send WebSocket messages synchronously because many applications have only small messages to send, so the difference between synchronous and asynchronous sending is small. Many applications send only simple text and binary messages, so knowing that the `RemoteEndpoint.Basic` interface has the following two methods:

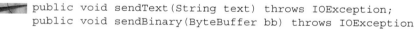

```
public void sendText(String text) throws IOException;
public void sendBinary(ByteBuffer bb) throws IOException
```

will get you a long way.

WebSocketContainer

As the `ServletContext` is to Java servlets, so is the `WebSocketContainer` to Java WebSockets. It represents the Java EE web container to the WebSocket endpoints it contains. It holds a number of configuration properties of the WebSocket functionality, such as message buffer sizes and asynchronous send timeouts.

WebSocket Clock

We have completed our tour of the Java WebSocket API, and having done so, we know more than enough to look at our first WebSocket application. The Clock application is a simple web application. When you run the application, you see the `index.html` web page, as shown in Figure 6-5.

FIGURE 6-5. *WebSocket Clock off*

When you click the Start button, the clock starts, with the current time as shown in Figure 6-6. The time updates every second.

When you click the Stop button, the clock stops until you restart it, as seen in Figure 6-7.

The application is made up of a single web page, `index.html`, and a single Java WebSocket endpoint, called `ClockServer`. When Start is pressed, the `index.html` uses JavaScript code to

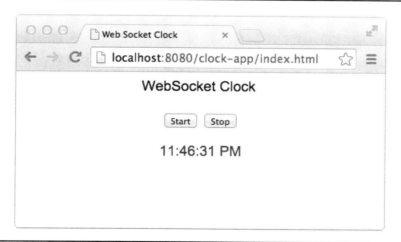

FIGURE 6-6. *WebSocket Clock on*

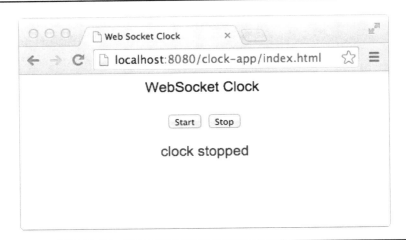

FIGURE 6-7. *WebSocket Clock stopped*

establish a WebSocket connection with the `ClockServer` endpoint. The `ClockServer` endpoint sends time update messages every second back to the browser client. The JavaScript code handles the incoming message and renders it on the page. Clicking Stop causes the JavaScript code in the `index.html` page to send a stop message to the `ClockServer`, which consequently stops sending the time updates. This architecture is shown in Figure 6-8.

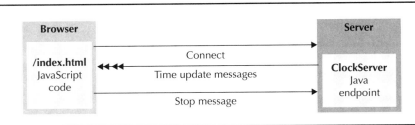

FIGURE 6-8. *Clock architecture*

Let's take a look at the code, first for the client.

Listing: *The Clock client page*

```html
<!DOCTYPE html>
<html>
 <head>
  <meta http-equiv="Content-Type" content="text/html; charset=UTF-8">
   <title>Web Socket Clock</title>
   <script language="javascript" type="text/javascript">
    var websocket;
    var last_time;

    function init() {
     output = document.getElementById("output");
    }

    function start_clock() {
     var wsUri = "ws://localhost:8080/clock-app/clock";
     websocket = new WebSocket(wsUri);
     websocket.onmessage = function (evt) {
      last_time = evt.data;
      writeToScreen("<span style='color: blue;'>" + last_time + "</span>");
     };
     websocket.onerror = function (evt) {
      writeToScreen('<span style="color: red;">ERROR:</span> ' + evt.data);
      websocket.close();
     };
    }

    function stop_clock() {
     websocket.send("stop");
    }

    function writeToScreen(message) {
     var pre = document.createElement("p");
     pre.style.wordWrap = "break-word";
     pre.innerHTML = message;
     oldChild = output.firstChild;
     if ( oldChild == null) {
      output.appendChild(pre);
     } else {
      output.removeChild(oldChild);
      output.appendChild(pre);
     }
    }
   window.addEventListener("load", init, false);

  </script>
 </head>
```

```
<body>
 <div style="text-align: center;font-family: Arial; font-size: large">
  WebSocket Clock
  <br></br>
  <form action="">
   <input
    onclick="start_clock()"
    title="Press to start the clock on the server"
    value="Start"
    type="button">
   <input
    onclick="stop_clock()"
    title="Press to stop the clock on the server"
    value="Stop"
    type="button">
  </form>
  <div id="output"></div>
 </div>
</body>
</html>
```

The HTML for this page is relatively straightforward. Notice that the JavaScript API for WebSockets uses the full URI to the WebSocket endpoint:

```
ws://localhost:8080/clock-app/clock
```

where clock-app is the context path of the web application. The start_clock() method does all the work of making the WebSocket connection and adding the event handlers, JavaScript style, particularly for handling messages that it receives from the server. The stop_clock() method simply sends the stop String to the server.

Now let's turn to the ClockServer endpoint.

Listing: *The ClockServer endpoint*

```
import javax.websocket.OnOpen;
import javax.websocket.OnClose;
import javax.websocket.OnMessage;
import javax.websocket.OnError;
import javax.websocket.Session;
import javax.websocket.server.ServerEndpoint;
import java.util.Date;
import java.text.SimpleDateFormat;
import java.io.IOException;

@ServerEndpoint("/clock")
public class ClockServer {
        Thread updateThread;
        boolean running = false;

        @OnOpen
```

```
public void startClock(Session session) {
    final Session mySession = session;
    this.running = true;
    final SimpleDateFormat sdf = new SimpleDateFormat("h:mm:ss a");
    this.updateThread = new Thread() {
        public void run() {
            while (running) {
                String dateString = sdf.format(new Date());
                try {
                    mySession.getBasicRemote().sendText(dateString);
                    sleep(1000);
                } catch (IOException | InterruptedException ie) {
                    running = false;
                }
            }
        }
    };
    this.updateThread.start();
}


@OnMessage
public String handleMessage(String incomingMessage) {
    if ("stop".equals(incomingMessage)) {
        this.stopClock();
        return "clock stopped";
    } else {
        return "unknown message: " + incomingMessage;
    }
}

@OnError
public void clockError(Throwable t) {
    this.stopClock();
}

@OnClose
public void stopClock() {
    this.running = false;
    this.updateThread = null;
}
}
```

You will notice that the ClockServer uses the @ServerEndpoint annotation to declare itself as a WebSocket endpoint, mapped to the URI /clock, relative to the context root of the web application that it is contained in. Notice that the startClock() method, called when a new client connects thanks to its @OnOpen annotation, does most of the work. It creates a thread that uses the Session object to obtain a reference to the RemoteEndpoint instance representing the client and sends it the current time, formatted into a string. If the endpoint receives a message, it is passed into the handleMessage() method, which you can identify because this method is annotated with `@OnMessage`. The `String` parameter of this method informs you that the endpoint is electing to receive its text messages in the simplest form of a Java string. This method returns a string, which is turned into a WebSocket message by the Java EE container and sent back to the client immediately.

How Many WebSocket Instances?

One question that arises even in this simple example is: How many instances will occur for a WebSocket endpoint class such as the `ClockServer`? The answer is that there will be one instance of the WebSocket endpoint class for each client that connects to it. Each client gets a unique endpoint instance. Further, the Java EE web container guarantees that no two WebSockets are sent to the same endpoint instance at once. So, in contrast to the Java servlet model, you can program your WebSocket endpoints knowing that there will only ever be one thread calling it at a time.

Java WebSocket Encoders and Decoders

The base WebSocket protocol gives us two native formats to work with: text and binary. This works well for very simple applications that exchange only simple information between client and server. For example, in our Clock application, the only data that is exchanged during the WebSocket messaging interaction is the formatted time string broadcast from the server endpoint and the `stop` string sent by the client to end the updates. But as soon as an application has anything more complicated to send or receive over a WebSocket connection, it will find itself seeking a structure into which to put the information. As Java developers, we are used to dealing with application data in the form of objects: either from classes from the standard Java APIs, or from Java classes that we create ourselves. This means that if you stick with the lowest-level messaging facilities of the Java WebSocket API and want to program using objects that are not strings or byte arrays for your messages, you need to write code that converts your objects into either strings or byte arrays and vice versa.

Fortunately, the Java WebSocket API gives us some support in this task of encoding objects to WebSocket messages and decoding WebSocket messages into objects.

First, the Java WebSocket API attempts to convert incoming messages into any Java primitive type (or its class equivalent) that you request. This means you can declare a message handling method of this form

```
@OnMessage
public void handleCounter(int newValue) {...}
```

or

```
@OnMessage
public void handleBoolean(Boolean b) {...}
```

and the Java WebSocket implementation attempts to convert any incoming message into the Java primitive parameter type you declare.

Equivalently, when sending messages, the `RemoteEndpoint.Basic` methods for sending include a general-purpose

```
public void sendObject(Object message) throws IOException, EncodeException
```

method, into which you can pass any Java primitive or its class equivalent, and the Java WebSocket implementation converts the value into the string equivalent for you.

This only gets you so far. Often, you want higher-level, highly structured objects to represent the messages in your application. In order to handle custom objects in your message handling methods, you must provide, along with the endpoint, a WebSocket `Decoder` implementation, which the runtime uses to convert the incoming message into an instance of the custom object type. To handle custom objects in your send methods, you must provide a WebSocket `Encoder` implementation that the runtime will use to convert instances of the custom object into a native WebSocket message. We can summarize this kind of scheme in Figure 6-9.

Figure 6-9 shows endpoints exchanging strings with the client at the top, and other endpoints using an encoder and a decoder for converting `Foo` objects into WebSocket text messages and vice versa.

There is a family of `javax.websocket.Decoder` and `javax.websocket.Encoder` interfaces in the Java WebSocket API to choose from, depending on what kind of conversion you wish to make. For example, to implement a `Decoder` that converts text messages into instances of a custom developer class called `Foo`, you would implement the interface `Decoder.Text<T>` using `Foo` as the generic type, which would require you to implement the method

```
public Foo decode(String s) throws DecodeException
```

This is the workhorse method of the decoder and would be called each time a new text message came in to produce an instance of the `Foo` class. The runtime would then be able to pass this class into the message handling method of your endpoint.

There are sibling `Decoder` classes for decoding binary WebSocket messages and WebSocket messages that arrive in the form of a blocking I/O stream that you may also use.

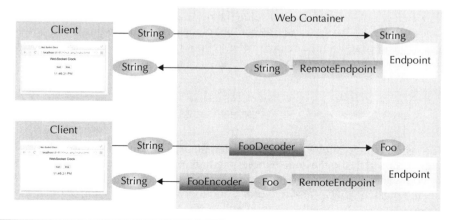

FIGURE 6-9. *Encoders and decoders*

To implement an `Encoder` that converts instances of a custom developer class `Foo` into a WebSocket text message, you would implement the `Encoder.Text<T>` interface using `Foo` as the generic type. This would require you to implement the method

```
public String encode(Foo foo) throws EncodeException
```

which does the work of converting `Foo` instances into strings, which is needed by the Java WebSocket runtime if you call the `RemoteEndpoint`'s `sendObject()` method (see earlier), passing in an instance of the class `Foo`. Like `Decoders`, there are `Encoder` siblings for converting custom objects into binary messages and for writing custom objects to blocking I/O streams in order to send the message.

This simple scheme is easy to wire into an endpoint if you wish to use it: as we saw in the definitions for `@ClientEndpoint` and `@ServerEndpoint`. You can simply list the Decoder and Encoder implementations you wish the endpoint to use in the `decoders()` and `encoders()` attributes, respectively.

If you configure your own encoders or decoders for the Java primitive types, they will override the runtime's default encoders for those types, as you would expect.

Message Processing Modes

So far, we have only discussed sending and receiving WebSocket messages one entire message at a time. Although many applications retain this simple model for message processing because they define only small messages in their application protocol, some applications will deal with large WebSocket messages, perhaps transmitting photographs or large documents. The Java WebSocket API provides a number of processing modes suited to handling larger messages gracefully and efficiently.

Receiving Large Messages

The WebSocket API has two additional modes for receiving messages that are suited to situations when you know the message will be large. The first mode exposes the endpoint to a blocking I/O API that the endpoint can use to consume the message, either `java.io.Reader` for text messages or `java.io.InputStream` for binary messages. To use this mode, instead of using either a `String` or `ByteBuffer` parameter in your message handling method, you would use a `Reader` or `InputStream`. For example:

```
@OnMessage
public void handleMessageAsStream(InputStream messageStream, Session session) {
    // read from the messageStream until you have consumed the whole binary message
}
```

The second mode allows for a kind of elementary chinking API, where the WebSocket message is passed to the message handler method in small pieces together with a `boolean` flag telling you whether there are more pieces yet to come in order to complete the message. Of course, the message pieces arrive in order, and there is no interleaving of other messages. To use this mode, the message handler method adds a `boolean` parameter; for example:

```
@OnMessage
public void handleMessageInChunks(String chunk, boolean isLast) {
    // reconstitute the message from the chunks as they arrive
}
```

In this mode, the size of the chunks is dependent on a number of factors relating to the peer that sends the message and the configuration of the Java WebSocket runtime. All you know is that you will receive the whole message in a number of pieces.

Modes for Sending Messages

As you may expect, given the symmetry of the WebSocket protocol, there are equivalent modes for sending messages in the Java WebSocket API suited to large message sizes. In addition to sending a message all in one piece, as we have seen so far in this chapter, you can send messages to a blocking I/O stream, either `java.io.Writer` or `java.io.OutputStream` depending on whether the message is text or binary. These are, of course, additional methods on the `RemoteEndpoint.Basic` interface that you obtain from the `Session` object:

```
public Writer getSendWriter() throws IOException
```

and

```
public OutputStream getSendStream() throws IOException
```

The second mode is the chunking mode, but in reverse, for sending rather than receiving. Again, an endpoint can send messages in this mode by calling either of the following methods of `RemoteEndpoint.Basic`:

```
public void sendText(String partialTextMessage,
                     boolean isLast) throws IOException
public void sentBinary(ByteBuffer partialBinaryMessage,
                       boolean isLast) throws IOException
```

depending on the type of message you wish to send.

Asynchronous Sending of Messages

Receipt of WebSocket messages is always asynchronous. An endpoint typically has no idea when messages are going to arrive; they just appear whenever the peer chooses. Now, all the methods of the `RemoteEndpoint.Basic` interface for sending messages (most all of which we have seen) are synchronous sends. In simple terms, what this means is that the `send()` method calls always block until the message has been transmitted. This is fine for small messages, but if the message is large, a WebSocket may well have better things to do than wait for it to send, such as messaging someone else, repainting a user interface, or focusing more resources on processing incoming messages. For such endpoints, the `RemoteEndpoint.Async`, obtainable from the `Session` object, as is the `RemoteEndpoint.Basic`, contains `send()` methods that take a whole message as a parameter (in various forms), but that return immediately, and before the message passed in is actually sent. For example, when sending a large text message, you may wish to use the

```
public void sendText(String textMessage, SendHandler handler)
```

method. The method returns immediately, and the `SendHandler` that you pass in to this method receives a callback when the message is actually transmitted. In this way, you know the message was sent, but you don't have to wait around until it does so. Or you may want to check in periodically on the progress of an asynchronous message send. For example, you may choose the method

```
public Future<Void> sendText(String textMessage)
```

in which case the method returns immediately and before the message is transmitted. You can query the `Future` object you obtain in return for the status of the message sent, and even cancel transmission if you change your mind.

There are binary message equivalents for these methods, as you might expect.

Before we leave the topic of sending messages in the Java WebSocket API, it's worth pointing out that the WebSocket protocol has no built-in notion of delivery guarantee. In other words, when you send a message, you don't know for sure whether it was received by the client. If you receive an error in your error handler methods, that's usually a sure sign that the message was not delivered properly. But if there is no error, the message still may not have been properly delivered. It is possible to build interactions yourself in Java WebSockets, wherein for important messages you have the peer send you an acknowledgement of receipt. But, unlike other messaging protocols, such as JMS, there is no inherent guarantee of delivery.

Path Mapping

In the Clock example, there was one endpoint and it was mapped to a single relative URI in the URI space of the web application. The client that connected to this endpoint did so by choosing a URL that was exactly that of the URI to the web application, plus the URI of the endpoint. This is an example of exact path mapping in the Java WebSocket API. In general, an endpoint is accessible at

```
<ws or wss>://<hostname>:<port>/
            <web-app-context-path>/<websocket-path>?<query-string>
```

where `<websocket-path>` is the `value` attribute of the `@ServerEndpoint` annotation and `query-string` is an optional query string.

When the `<websocket-path>` is a URI, as it is in the `ClockServer` endpoint, the only request URI that will connect to the endpoint is the one that matches it exactly.

The JavaWebSocket API also allows server endpoints to be mapped to level 1 URI templates. URI templates are a fancy way of saying that one or more segments of the URI can be substituted with variables. For example,

```
/airlines/{service-class}
```

is a URI template with a single variable called `service-class`.

The Java WebSocket API allows incoming request URIs to match an endpoint using a URI template path mapping if and only if the request URI is a valid expansion of the URI template. For example,

```
/airlines/coach
/airlines/first
/airlines/business
```

are all valid expansions of the URI template

```
/airlines/{service-class}
```

with variable `service-class` equal to `coach`, `first`, and `business`, respectively.

URI templates can be very useful in a WebSocket application, since the template variable values are available within the endpoint that matches the request URI. In any of the lifecycle methods of a server endpoint, you can add as many String parameters annotated with the `@PathParam` annotation to obtain the value of the variable path segments in the match. Continuing this example, suppose we had the following server endpoint:

Listing: *A Booking notifier endpoint*

```
@ServerEndpoint("/airlines/{service-class}")
public class MyBookingNotifier {

@OnOpen
public void initializeUpdates(Session session,
                    @PathParam("service-class") String sClass) {
    if ("first".equals(sClass)) {
            // open champagne
    } else if ("business".equals(sClass)) {
            // heated nuts
    } else {
            // don't bang your head on our aircraft
    }
}
...
}
```

which would yield different levels of service, depending on which request URI a client connects with.

Accessing Path Information at Runtime

An endpoint has full access to all of its path information at runtime. First, it can always obtain the path under which the WebSocket implementation has published it. Using the

`ServerEndpointConfig.getPath()`

call for the endpoint holds this information, which you can easily access wherever you can get hold of the `ServerEndpointConfig` instance, such as we see in this example.

Listing: *An endpoint accessing its own path mapping*

```
@ServerEndpoint("/travel/hotels/{stars}")
public class HotelBookingService {

        public void handleConnection(Session s, EndpointConfig config) {
            String myPath = ((ServerEndpointConfig) config).getPath();
            // myPath is "/travel/hotels/{stars}"
        ...
        }
}
```

This works equally well for exact URI-mapped endpoints.

The second piece of information you may wish to access at runtime from within an endpoint is the URI with which the client to your endpoint connected. This information is available in a variety of forms, as we shall see later, but the workhorse method that contains all the information is the

```
Session.getRequestURI()
```

method. This gives you the URI path relative to the web server root of the WebSocket implementation. Notice that this includes the context root of the web application that the WebSocket is part of. So, in our hotel booking example, if it is deployed in a web application with context root `/customer/services` and a client has connected to the `HotelBookingService` endpoint with the URI

```
ws://fun.org/customer/services/travel/hotels/3
```

then the request URI the endpoint receives by calling `getRequestURI()` is

```
/customer/services/travel/hotels/3
```

Two more methods on the `Session` object parse out further information from this request URI when the request URI includes a query string. So let's take a look at query strings.

Query Strings and Request Parameters

As we saw earlier, following the URI path to a WebSocket endpoint is the optional query string

```
<ws or wss>://<hostname>:<port>/
            <web-app-context-path>/<websocket-path>?<query-string>
```

Query strings in URIs originally became popular in Common Gateway Interface (CGI) applications. The path portion of a URI locates the CGI program (often `/cgi-bin`), and the query string appended after the URI path supplies a list of parameters to the CGI program to qualify the request. The query string is also commonly used when posting data using an HTML form. For example, in a web application, in the HTML code

```
<form name="input" action="form-processor" method="get">
    Your Username: <input type="text" name="user">
                    <input type="submit" value="Submit">
</form>
```

clicking the Submit button produces an HTTP request to the URI

```
/form-processor?user=Jared
```

relative to the page holding the HTML code and where the input field contains the text `Jared`. Depending on the nature of the web resource located at the URI path `/form-processor`, the query string `user=Jared` can be used to determine what kind of response should be made. For example, if the resource at form processor is a Java servlet, the Java servlet can retrieve the query string from the `HttpServletRequest` using the `getQueryString()` API call.

In a similar spirit, query strings can be used in the URIs used to connect to WebSocket endpoints created using the Java WebSocket API. The Java WebSocket API does not use a query string sent as part of the request URI of an opening handshake request to determine the endpoint to which it might match. In other words, whether or not a request URI contains a query string or not makes no difference to whether it matches a server endpoint's published path. Additionally, query strings are ignored in paths used to publish endpoints.

Just as CGI programs did and other kinds of web components do, WebSocket endpoints can use the query string to further configure a connection that a client is making. Because the WebSocket implementation essentially ignores the value of the query string on an incoming request, any logic that uses the value of the query string is purely inside the WebSocket component. The main methods that you can use to retrieve the value of the query string are all on the `Session` object

```
public String getQueryString()
```

which returns the whole query string (everything after the ? character) and

```
public Map<String,List<String>> getRequestParameterMap()
```

which gives you a data structure with all the request parameters parsed from the query string. You'll notice that the values of the map are lists of strings; this is because a query string may have two parameters of the same name but different values. For example, you might connect to our `HotelBookingService` endpoint using the URI

```
ws://fun.org/customer/
        services/travel/hotels/4?showpics=thumbnails&description=short
```

In this case, the query string is `showpics=thumbnails&description=short`, and to obtain the request parameters from the endpoint, you might do something like this:

Listing: *Accessing request parameters*

```
@ServerEndpoint("/travel/hotels/{stars}")
public class HotelBookingService2 {

        public void handleConnection(Session session, EndpointConfig config) {
            String pictureType = session.getRequestParameterMap()
                                            .get("showpics").get(0);
            String textMode = session.getRequestParameterMap()
                                            .get("description").get(0);
            ...
        }
        ...
}
```

where the values of `pictureType` and `textMode` would be `thumbnails` and `short`, respectively.

NOTE
You can also get the query string from the request URI. In the Java WebSocket API, the `Session.getRequestURI()` call always includes both the URI path and the query string.

Deployment of Server Endpoints

Deployment of Java WebSocket endpoints on the Java EE web container follows the rule that easy things are easy. When you package a Java class that has been annotated with `@ServerEndpoint` into a WAR file, the Java WebSocket implementation scans the WAR file and finds all such classes and deploys them. This means there is nothing special you have to do in order to get your server endpoints deployed except package them in the WAR file. However, you may wish to more tightly control which of a collection of server endpoints gets deployed in a WAR file. In this case, you may provide an implementation of the Java WebSocket API interface `javax.websocket .ServerApplicationConfig`, which allows you to filter which of the endpoints get deployed.

The Chat Application

A good way to test a push technology is to build an application that has frequent, asynchronous updates to make to a number of interested clients. Such is the case with a Chat application. Let's take a look in some detail at how to apply what we have learned about the Java WebSocket API to build a simple chat application.

Figure 6-10 shows the main window of the Chat application, which prompts for a username when you sign in.

Several people can be chatting all at once, typing their messages in the text field at the bottom and clicking the Send button. You can see the active chatters on the right side and the shared transcript recording everyone's messages in the middle and left. In Figure 6-11, there is an uncomfortable triad of people chatting.

In Figure 6-12, we can see that one of the chatters left rather suddenly, and the other has left slightly more gracefully, leaving just one chatter in the room.

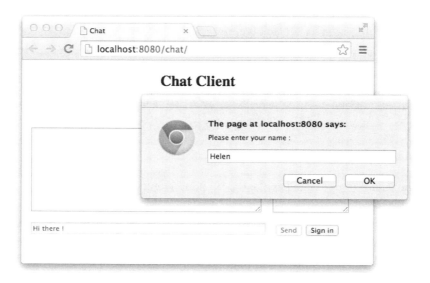

FIGURE 6-10. *Logging in to chat*

FIGURE 6-11. *Chat in full flow*

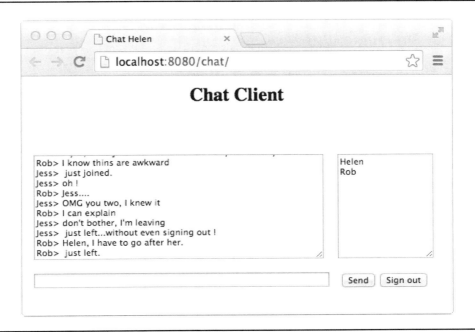

FIGURE 6-12. *Leaving chat*

Before we look at the code in detail, let's get the big picture of how this application is built. The web page uses the JavaScript WebSocket client to send and receive all the chat messages. There is a single `ChatServer` Java WebSocket endpoint on the web server, which is handling all chat messages from multiple clients, keeping track of those clients that are actively chatting, maintaining the transcript, and broadcasting updates to all connected clients whenever someone enters or leaves the chat room and whenever any one of them sends a message to the group. The application uses custom objects with WebSocket `Encoders` and `Decoders` to model all the chat messages.

Let's look at the `ChatServer` endpoint.

Listing: *The `ChatServer` endpoint*

```java
import java.io.IOException;
import java.util.*;
import javax.websocket.*;
import javax.websocket.server.*;
import jwsp.chapter4.data.*;

@ServerEndpoint(value = "/chat-server",
        subprotocols={"chat"},
        decoders = {ChatDecoder.class},
        encoders = {ChatEncoder.class})
public class ChatServer {
    private static String USERNAME_KEY = "username";
    private static String USERNAMES_KEY = "usernames";
    private Session session;
    private Transcript transcript;
    private EndpointConfig endpointConfig;

    @OnOpen
    public void startChatChannel(EndpointConfig endpointConfig, Session session) {
        this.endpointConfig = endpointConfig;
        this.transcript = Transcript.getTranscript(endpointConfig);
        this.session = session;
    }

    @OnMessage
    public void handleChatMessage(ChatMessage message) {
        switch (message.getType()){
            case NewUserMessage.USERNAME_MESSAGE:
                this.processNewUser((NewUserMessage) message);
                break;
            case ChatMessage.CHAT_DATA_MESSAGE:
                this.processChatUpdate((ChatUpdateMessage) message);
                break;
            case ChatMessage.SIGNOFF_REQUEST:
                this.processSignoffRequest((UserSignoffMessage) message);
        }
    }

    @OnError
    public void myError(Throwable t) {
        System.out.println("Error: " + t.getMessage());
```

```java
    }

    @OnClose
    public void endChatChannel() {
        if (this.getCurrentUsername() != null) {
            this.addMessage(" just left...without even signing out !");
            this.removeUser();
        }
    }

    void processNewUser(NewUserMessage message) {
        String newUsername = this.validateUsername(message.getUsername());
        NewUserMessage uMessage = new NewUserMessage(newUsername);
        try {
            session.getBasicRemote().sendObject(uMessage);
        } catch (IOException | EncodeException ioe) {
            System.out.println("Error signing " + message.getUsername() +
                                        " into chat : " + ioe.getMessage());
        }
        this.registerUser(newUsername);
        this.broadcastUserListUpdate();
        this.addMessage(" just joined.");
    }

    void processChatUpdate(ChatUpdateMessage message) {
        this.addMessage(message.getMessage());
    }

    void processSignoffRequest(UserSignoffMessage drm) {
        this.addMessage(" just left.");
        this.removeUser();
    }

    private String getCurrentUsername() {
        return (String) session.getUserProperties().get(USERNAME_KEY);
    }

    private void registerUser(String username) {
        session.getUserProperties().put(USERNAME_KEY, username);
        this.updateUserList();
    }

    private void updateUserList() {
        List<String> usernames = new ArrayList<>();
        for (Session s : session.getOpenSessions()) {
            String uname = (String) s.getUserProperties().get(USERNAME_KEY);
            usernames.add(uname);
        }
        this.endpointConfig.getUserProperties().put(USERNAMES_KEY, usernames);
    }

    private List<String> getUserList() {
        List<String> userList =
        (List<String>) this.endpointConfig.getUserProperties().get(USERNAMES_KEY);
        return (userList == null) ? new ArrayList<String>() : userList;
    }
```

```java
    private String validateUsername(String newUsername) {
        if (this.getUserList().contains(newUsername)) {
            return this.validateUsername(newUsername + "1");
        }
        return newUsername;
    }

    private void broadcastUserListUpdate() {
        UserListUpdateMessage ulum =
                new UserListUpdateMessage(this.getUserList());
        for (Session nextSession : session.getOpenSessions()) {
            try {
                nextSession.getBasicRemote().sendObject(ulum);
            } catch (IOException | EncodeException ex) {
                System.out.println("Error updating a client : " + ex.getMessage());
            }
        }
    }

    private void removeUser() {
        try {
            this.updateUserList();
            this.broadcastUserListUpdate();
            this.session.getUserProperties().remove(USERNAME_KEY);
            this.session.close(new CloseReason(CloseReason.CloseCodes.NORMAL_CLOSURE,
"User logged off"));
        } catch (IOException e) {
            System.out.println("Error removing user");
        }
    }

    private void broadcastTranscriptUpdate() {
        for (Session nextSession : session.getOpenSessions()) {
            ChatUpdateMessage cdm = new
                ChatUpdateMessage(this.transcript.getLastUsername(),
                            this.transcript.getLastMessage());
            try {
                nextSession.getBasicRemote().sendObject(cdm);
            } catch (IOException | EncodeException ex) {
                System.out.println("Error updating a client : " + ex.getMessage());
            }
        }
    }

    private void addMessage(String message) {
        this.transcript.addEntry(this.getCurrentUsername(), message);
        this.broadcastTranscriptUpdate();
    }

}
```

There is a lot to notice in this code. First, notice that this is a server endpoint that is mapped to the relative URI /chat-server. The endpoint uses an encoder and a decoder class, ChatEncoder and ChatDecoder, respectively.

The best way to look at Java WebSocket endpoints for the first time is to look at the lifecycle methods: These, as you know, are the methods annotated by @OnOpen, @OnMessage, @OnError, and @OnClose. We can see by looking at the ChatServer class in this way that the first thing the ChatServer WebSocket does when a new client connects is to set up instance variables that reference the chat transcript, the session, and the EndpointConfig. Remember that there is a new instance of the endpoint for each client that connects. So each chatter in the chat room will have a unique chat server instance associated with it. There is always a single EndpointConfig per logical WebSocket endpoint, so the endpointConfig instance variable on each instance of the ChatServer points to the single shared instance of the EndpointConfig class. This instance is a singleton, and it holds a user map that can hold an arbitrary application state. Thus, it is a good place to hold global state in an application. There is always a unique session object per client connection, so each ChatServer instance points to its own Session instance representing the client to which the instance is associated by following the code to the Transcript class.

Listing: *The Transcript class*

```
import java.util.ArrayList;
import java.util.List;
import javax.websocket.*;

public class Transcript {
    private List<String> messages = new ArrayList<>();
    private List<String> usernames = new ArrayList<>();
    private int maxLines;
    private static String TRANSCRIPT_ATTRIBUTE_NAME = "CHAT_TRANSCRIPT_AN";

    public static Transcript getTranscript(EndpointConfig ec) {
        if (!ec.getUserProperties().containsKey(TRANSCRIPT_ATTRIBUTE_NAME)) {
            ec.getUserProperties()
                        .put(TRANSCRIPT_ATTRIBUTE_NAME, new Transcript(20));
        }
        return (Transcript) ec.getUserProperties().get(TRANSCRIPT_ATTRIBUTE_NAME);
    }

    Transcript(int maxLines) {
        this.maxLines = maxLines;
    }

    public String getLastUsername() {
        return usernames.get(usernames.size() -1);
    }

    public String getLastMessage() {
        return messages.get(messages.size() -1);
    }

    public void addEntry(String username, String message) {
        if (usernames.size() > maxLines) {
            usernames.remove(0);
            messages.remove(0);
        }
```

```
            usernames.add(username);
            messages.add(message);
        }
    }
```

We can see that there is a single transcript instance per `EndpointConfig`. In other words, there is a single `Transcript` instance and it is shared across all `ChatServer` instances. This is good because we need the transcript to show the group chat messages to all clients.

The most important method on the `ChatServer` is the message handling method, annotated with `@OnMessage`. You can see from its signature that it deals with `ChatMessage` objects rather than text or binary WebSocket messages, thanks to the `ChatDecoder` that it uses. The `ChatDecoder` it uses has already decoded the message into one of the subclasses of `ChatMessage`. In the interest of brevity, rather than listing all the `ChatMessage` subclasses, here is a summary of the different `ChatMessage` subclasses and the function of each.

ChatMessage subclass	Purpose
`ChatUpdateMessage`	Message holding a username and a chat message that user sent
`NewUserMessage`	Message holding the name of a new user signing on
`UserListUpdateMessage`	Message holding a list of the names of the current active chatters
`UserSignoffMessage`	Message holding the name of a user who has signed off

Now we can easily see that the `ChatServer`'s message handling method, `handleChatMessage()`, which is called by the client every time a new chat-related action occurs, is designed to handle situations when a new user signs in, when a user posts a new chat message to the board, and when a user signs out.

Let's follow the code path when a `ChatServer` is notified that the user has posted a new chat message. This leads us from the `handleChatMessage()` method to the `processChatUpdate()` method, which calls `addMessage()`, which adds the new chat message to the shared transcript. Then it calls `broadcastTranscriptUpdate()`.

Listing: *Broadcasting a new chat message*

```java
private void broadcastTranscriptUpdate() {
    for (Session nextSession : session.getOpenSessions()) {
        ChatUpdateMessage cdm = new ChatUpdateMessage(
                            this.transcript.getLastUsername(),
                            this.transcript.getLastMessage());

        try {
            nextSession.getBasicRemote().sendObject(cdm);
        } catch (IOException | EncodeException ex) {
            System.out.println("Error updating a client : " +
                                            ex.getMessage());
        }
    }
}
```

This method uses the very useful API call `Session.getOpenSessions()`, allowing one endpoint instance to gain a handle on all the open connections to the logical endpoint. In this case, the method uses that list of all the open connections to broadcast the new chat message out to all the clients so that they can update their user interfaces with the latest chat message. Notice that the message that is sent is in the form of a `ChatMessage`, here, the `ChatUpdateMessage`. The `ChatEncoder` takes care of marshaling the `ChatUpdateMessage` instance into a text message that is actually the one sent back to the client with the news of the new chat message contained within.

Since we did not look at the `ChatDecoder` when we were looking at incoming messages, let's pause to look at the `ChatEncoder` class.

Listing: *The ChatEncoder class*

```
import java.util.Iterator;
import javax.websocket.EncodeException;
import javax.websocket.Encoder;
import javax.websocket.EndpointConfig;

public class ChatEncoder implements Encoder.Text<ChatMessage>  {
    public static final String SEPARATOR = ":";

    @Override
    public void init(EndpointConfig config) {}
    @Override
    public void destroy() {}

    @Override
    public String encode(ChatMessage cm) throws EncodeException {
        if (cm instanceof StructuredMessage) {
            String dataString = "";
            for (Iterator itr = ((StructuredMessage) cm)
                              .getList().iterator(); itr.hasNext(); ) {
                dataString = dataString + SEPARATOR + itr.next();
            }
            return cm.getType() + dataString;
        } else if (cm instanceof BasicMessage) {
            return cm.getType() + ((BasicMessage) cm).getData();
        } else {
            throw new EncodeException(cm, "Cannot encode messages of type: " +
                                          cm.getClass());
        }
    }
}
```

You can see that the `ChatEncoder` class is required to implement the `Encoder` lifecycle methods `init()` and `destroy()`. Although this encoder does nothing with these callbacks from the container, other encoders may choose to initialize and destroy expensive resources in these lifecycle methods. The `encode()` method is the meat of the class and takes the message instance and turns it into a string, ready for transmission back to the client.

Returning now to the `ChatServer` class, we see from the `handleChatMessage()` method that this endpoint has a graceful way of dealing with clients that sign off in the proper way: by sending a `UserSignoffMessage` prior to closing the connection. It also has a graceful way of dealing with clients who simply close the connection unilaterally, perhaps by closing the browser or navigating away from the page. The `@OnClose` annotated `endChatChannel()` method broadcasts a message to all connected clients informing them when someone leaves the chatroom without saying goodbye. Looking back at the screenshots, we can now see the difference between the manner in which Jess and Rob left the room.

Summary

In this chapter, we have learned how to create a Java WebSocket endpoint. We have explored the basic concepts of the WebSocket protocol and what kinds of situations demand their true server push nature. We have looked at the lifecycle of a Java WebSocket endpoint, examined the main classes of the Java WebSocket API, and looked at encoding and decoding techniques, including the variety of messaging modes supported in the Java WebSocket API. We looked at how server endpoints are mapped to the URI space of a web application and how client requests are matched to endpoints therein. We concluded with a look at a Chat application that exercises many of the features of the Java WebSocket API.

CHAPTER
7

Securing Web
Applications

Medieval castles usually had high walls and gates that were guarded by soldiers who checked who was allowed entry. So the notions of authentication, authorization, and protection of what is valuable are not new to the Internet age after all! If your Java EE web application has any interesting data in it, then it probably needs securing.

There are many aspects of securing a web application: You may wish simply to ensure that you know who is interacting with resources in an application, or you may wish to use the identity of the user of your application to customize the interactions. You may wish to allow only certain kinds of users to access an application, or you may wish to provide different levels of access to an application to different kinds of users. You may wish to ensure that some or all of the interactions with the application are encrypted to foil eavesdroppers. You may want to combine any or all these kinds of approaches in your application.

In this chapter, we will look at the security mechanisms available in the Java EE web container for securing web applications. As we explore the mechanisms, we see how they apply to all the web components we have studied so far: Java servlets, JSPs, JavaServer Faces, JAX-RS resources, and WebSocket endpoints. The primary security mechanism is the declarative security model. This describes in metadata the protection model that you want the web container to apply to your web application. The metadata is mostly held within the deployment descriptor of the web application, but can also be held within certain security annotations in source code. The second security mechanism is the roll-your-own model: the Java EE web APIs collectively hold a number of APIs that web components can use in order to build their own security model.

Before we get into the declarative and programmatic security mechanisms in the Java EE web container, let's review the core security concepts we will be using.

Security Concepts

Let's start by looking at our basic deployment scenario, someone using a web browser or a rich client application with access to a web component that is hosted on a web server. The starting point for all interactions with web components on the Java EE web container is an HTTP request; this is true whether the web component is a servlet, JAX-RS resource, or WebSocket. Even in the case of WebSocket, the client may not establish a WebSocket session until the opening HTTP handshake interaction has completed.

In Figure 7-1, the user is initiating an HTTP request from a browser or rich client for a web component that is protected by a security model on the server. Before the request can be fulfiled, the server's security model must consider the following three questions:

- *Who is asking for the resource?* If the user has not previously logged into the web server, and if the HTTP request is not carrying some indication of that state, the request is anonymous. It may be that the security model allows anonymous access to the web component, or it may be that the web server must know the identity of the user requesting the resource in order to answer the next question.

- *May this person have it?* If the web server does not allow anonymous access to the web component, then it has the information necessary to determine whether this particular user is allowed access to the resource or not. Once the server has made this determination, the server needs to consider the next question.

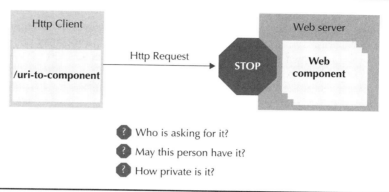

FIGURE 7-1. *The three security questions*

- *How private is its data?* The server may have decided that the data the web component yields in response to the request must be delivered back to the client in such a way that guarantees that the information has not been altered en route. Or the server may wish to ensure with some level of certainty that anyone intercepting the data it sends from the web component to the client cannot read it.

The processes of determining the answers to these questions are more commonly known as

- **Authentication**   Establishing the identity of a user making a request
- **Authorization**   Granting or denying access to a web component by a user
- **Establishing data privacy**   Determination the privacy level of the communication channel used to transmit data between the web component and the client

Java EE Web Container Security

The Java EE web container supports a declarative security model, wherein the container acts as the gatekeeper to all the web components that elect to be protected by it, intercepting all HTTP requests to the application and deciding whether they are allowed to continue and, if so, over what channel the interaction may proceed. A web application that chooses to use the Java EE web container's declarative security model does so by adding security declarations to its deployment descriptor, in combination with certain annotations in certain cases. This kind of static configuration generally allows the security model for an application to be configured and defined separately from the application logic itself. The second security model that a web application may choose to use is the programmatic one. In this model, the application itself is responsible for determining whether an HTTP request issued by a user to one or more of its web components is allowed to execute the application logic of the web component. In this case, the application developer is essentially responsible for programming the web application security in the application itself. In this chapter, our focus is mainly on the declarative security model. However, there are a number of runtime APIs concerned with different aspects of security in a web application that are useful to developers, whether they choose to use a built-in declarative model or a programmatic one. We will cover these APIs as well.

Of course, every good security model has many more features in addition to the core three we have just described, including auditing, nonrepudiation, and interoperability. Every implementation of the Java EE platform will have some level of support for these features, but the level of support is likely to differ from implementation to implementation. We will focus on the three core features of authentication, authorization, and establishing data privacy, since they are supported in a standard way by the Java EE web container and because they cover the security needs of a majority of Java EE web applications.

The Declarative Security Model

The declarative security model is declared in the web.xml deployment descriptor of the web application. We will see many examples of relevant syntax, but let's start with the models that allow you to ensure that only known, or authenticated, users are allowed access to the web components in a Java EE web application.

Authentication

We will look at three standard types of authentication for Java EE web applications in this section, starting with the simplest.

Basic Authentication   This is the simplest HTTP-based authentication scheme. Basic authentication is initiated when the client sends its credentials in the form of a username and password pair encoded in an HTTP header. The client may either send this preemptively or in reaction to a challenge from the server, if the client sends an unauthenticated request. Because the credentials in the HTTP Basic scheme are encoded only with Base 64 encoding, they are vulnerable to being intercepted and decoded. This is a good scheme to use in a web application where you need a sign-in and need to know which user is accessing the application, but you do not necessarily have a strong concern about the privacy of the data in the application. In other words, basic authentication is useful in applications where you wish to tailor the content to the users because you already know something about them, but you do not necessarily need a strong security scheme to protect the data that you are sending or receiving. Other web applications that wish to protect the credentials and the application data may choose to use basic authentication, but only when the communication occurs over an encrypted or private connection.

Browsers typically use a basic modal username password dialog to retrieve the user credentials, so the user experience from a browser is simple, but it is also not easy to customize.

Form-Based Authentication   Form-based authentication is a mechanism that allows the user credentials to be gathered by a highly customizable HTML form in a login page created by the developer. The mechanism defines the pair of HTTP request parameters that signify the username and password that are encoded in a `<form>` element in the web page. Like basic authentication, the credentials are vulnerable to interception, so this suits the same class of applications. The main difference between form authentication and basic authentication is that the look and placement of the login form is customizable, and thus suits applications that are more conscious of the user experience. Again, applications that are doing more than a casual personalization based on the user identity and that are concerned about maintaining the integrity of credentials supplied by the user will choose to use only form-based authentication over an encrypted or private connection.

Client Certificate Authentication   Client certificate authentication is a process by which the server and, optionally, the client authenticate one another using a digital certificate, which acts as a kind of encrypted passport that verifies the agent's identity. The process is more secure than either basic or form-based authentication because the credentials are always transferred using HTTP over SSL and because the client is able to verify the server identity.

Configuring Authentication Mechanisms   Once you have decided which scheme you wish to use, configuring it is relatively easy: you specify it in the `web.xml` deployment descriptor of the WAR file in which your web components are packaged. The key element to include in the deployment descriptor is the `<login-config>` element. It has the following subelements.

Element Name	Value	Meaning
auth-method	BASIC, FORM, or CLIENT-CERT	Defines the authentication scheme
realm-name	Name of the user realm used for basic authentication	Defines which server realm is used to verify the basic authentication credentials
form-login-config	Subelements login-page and error-page	For form login only, defines the relative location within the web application of the page containing the login form and the page to which the user is redirected if the login fails

Authentication Examples   Here are some excerpts of `web.xml` files that specify each of the three types of authentication that you can use for web applications.

For basic authentication, including this snippet of XML under the top-level web-app element of the `web.xml` configures an application to receive an HTTP basic authentication challenge when attempting to access a protected web component. The server verifies the credentials that the client sends in response with matching user credentials in the server's `file` authentication realm.

Listing: *Basic authentication*

```
<login-config>
        <auth-method>BASIC</auth-method>
        <realm-name>file</realm-name>
</login-config>
```

To specify your application, use form authentication if you include the following XML under the top-level `web-app` element of the `web.xml`

Listing: *Form login authentication*

```
<login-config>
        <auth-method>FORM</auth-method>
```

```
<form-login-config>
    <form-login-page>/login.html</form-login-page>
    <form-error-page>/error.html</form-error-page>
</form-login-config>
</login-config>
```

then the server redirects any unauthenticated requests to protected resources within the web application to the `login.html` page located at the root of the web application's URI namespace. The `login.html` page needs to include a form of the shape shown next.

Listing: *A login <form>*

```
<form method=POST action="j_security_check">
        User ID
    <input type="text" size="10" name="j_username"> <br>
        Password
    <input type="password" size="10" name="j_password">
    <input type="submit" name="login" value="Login">
 </form>
```

And so the form submission posts request parameters named j_username and j_password containing the values of the username and password that the user enters to a specially reserved name, j_security_check, on the server that processes the authentication request. If the authentication succeeds, the user is redirected to the protected resource he requested in the first place. If the authentication fails, the user is redirected to the error.html page that was specified in the form-login-config element and that is located at the root of the web application's URI space.

Finally, here is the login-config snippet you need to include in your web application if you would like the server to initiate a client-certificate challenge when an unauthenticated user of the web application attempts to access a protected resource.

Listing: *Client certificate authentication*

```
<login-config>
        <auth-method>CLIENT-CERT</auth-method>
</login-config>
```

Being able to specify an authentication scheme for the web component isn't any use unless you know how to protect those server-side endpoints in the first place. Thus, we turn to the language of *authentication* in Java EE web applications.

Authorization

Authorization is the process by which the Java EE web container decides whether a particular user is permitted access to a particular endpoint. The Java EE platform uses a level of indirection in defining users by using the idea of a *user role*, or simply a *role*. A role is a kind of abstraction of a user that allows authorization rules to be set up in the application without actually having to put real usernames in the application configuration.

When an authenticated HTTP request for a web component arrives at the web container, the web container must decide three things in order to determine whether it will grant access to the web component the request is for.

First, the web container must determine to which role or roles the authenticated user belongs. How users are associated with roles is not a standard part of the Java EE platform, and therefore will vary from Java EE implementation to Java EE implementation. In the GlassFish 4.0 application server, you can make the association between the user and the roles to which he belongs in a GlassFish-specific deployment descriptor called the `glassfish.xml` file that you co-package with the WAR file containing your endpoints. Other application servers, however, use different schemes.

Next, the web container looks at the web application's deployment descriptor (the `web.xml` file co-packaged in the WAR file). The definition of which roles are allowed access to which URI in the URI space of a web application is expressed in a number of XML elements called security constraints, which have been written by the developer. We will look at some specific examples of this later. Once the web container has examined the deployment descriptor, it knows which roles are allowed access to the URI that the original HTTP request is for.

Finally, since the web container knows the association between the requested URI and the web component, whether it be a static file, Java servlet, JSP, JavaServer Faces page, JAX-RS resource, or Java WebSocket, it can now determine whether the user has access to the web component. Figure 7-2 shows this process of authorization.

With these three pieces of information, the server can then decide for a given user and HTTP request URI whether the user is allowed access to the web component.

Now the mapping of URIs to web components is handled by the individual component technologies, so we already know one part of the three. The question of the role to which the user

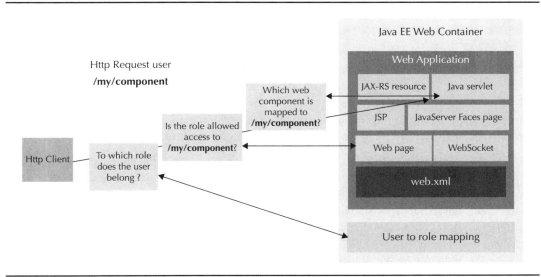

FIGURE 7-2. *The process of authorization*

issuing the HTTP request belongs, as we already mentioned, is defined in the Java EE implementation. To consider the question "Are users in this role allowed access to this URI?," we need to look at the `<security-constraint>` element of the web.xml, as this is where that question will be answered for a web application.

Security Constraints   The security constraint element contains two pieces of information:

- **A web resource collection in the web resource collection subelement**   This is composed of a list of URL patterns, which define a portion of the URI space within the web application to which the containing security constraint applies. The second component is a list of HTTP methods that defines the HTTP operations on the URIs covered in the URL patterns to which you wish this security constraint to apply.
- **An authorization constraint in the auth-constraint subelement**   This is composed of a list of the names of roles to which the security constraint will apply.

The `security-constraint` element also may contain a third subelement, `user-data-constraint`, which defines how data is transported between client and server for the web component operations defined in the containing security constraint. We will examine this shortly.

Let's look in some detail at the semantics of `web-resource-collection` and of `auth-constraint`. The next table contains a description of each of the subelements.

web-resource-collection Sub Element	Multiplicity	Value
web-resource-collection-name	Single	Optional text name of this collection of URIs for display in tools
description	Single	An optional text description of this collection of URIs for display in tools
url-pattern	Multiple	A path designation indicating a URL or group of URLs
http-method	Multiple	The HTTP method (GET, POST...) used to access the web component

The `url-pattern` element contains a string that indicates a URI or signifies some matching set of URIs. There are three ways you can define a `uri-pattern` value:

- **exact path**   This is a path relative to the context root of the web application, for example, `/airlines/booking.xhtml`. This path matches one and only one web component in the web application.
- **wildcard**   This is a path that defines a group of URLs relative to the context root of the web application. For example `/airlines/*` indicates all URIs starting with `airlines`, including, for example, `/airlines/booking.xhtml`.
- **filename ending**   This is a URL pattern that looks for a particular endpoint pattern in a URI. For example, if you decided to protect all the JavaServer Faces pages ending in `.xhtml` in your application, you could use the filename extension URL pattern `*.xhtml` in the URL pattern element.

The `auth-constraint` element is much simpler: it simply contains a list of the names of user roles that are allowed access under the limits of these security constraints.

`auth-constraint` Sub Elements	Multiplicity	Value
`role-name`	multiple	The name of a role to which the security constraint applies

The values of the user roles in the `role-name` element may be drawn from the list of security roles that has been previously defined for this `web.xml`. This list is held in a list of `<security-role>` subelements of the root `web-app` element of the `web.xml`, with the name of the role the text value of the `role-name` subelement.

Note that there is a special role name, "`*`," which denotes any user. Using `*` in a security constraint allows any user to access the resources matched under the URL pattern, provided they have authenticated. This is different from allowing open access to resources: in this latter case, access is granted to anyone, authenticated or not.

This gives us the answer to our question: To which roles is a given HTTP request URI (including the HTTP method) allowed access in my web application?

Before we look at an example of the security constraint in action, we will finish off the exploration by looking at the final question in the security model: how to ensure data privacy.

User Data Constraints   The user data constraint of a security constraint defines the level of privacy the web application needs in order for users to access it. This is defined in the subelement `user-data-constraint` of the `security-constraint`. It takes a text value, either NONE, INTEGRAL, or CONFIDENTIAL. A value of NONE allows the Java EE server to interpret this as allowing access over HTTP, which is the default mode if non-user-data-constraint is included. The risk to application data is that a third party can intercept the HTTP interactions and read potentially sensitive data (such as HTTP basic authentication information and credentials, which are held in the headers of HTTP requests and responses). A value of INTEGRAL or CONFIDENTIAL is, in practice, interpreted by Java EE web containers as meaning the web components need an encrypted connection.

We can summarize the structure of the security constraint syntax in Figure 7-3, where `web-app` is the root element of the `web.xml` deployment descriptor.

Example   Let's take a look at an example using security constraints. In this example, we have a web application that is an online book store. It allows any Internet user to browse its online catalog of books, which is displayed in a JavaServer Faces page called `store-front.xhtml`. It allows customers to create accounts with another JavaServer Faces page called `create-account.xhtml`. Once a user has created a customer account, he or she is then allowed to purchase books from the store, either through a browser by viewing the `/purchase /purchase.xhtml` page, or on a custom smartphone app by accessing a JAX-RS endpoint mapper to `/purchase/PurchaseResource`. Another type of user is the user who is working in the warehouse where the books for sale are kept and new ones delivered. Through a browser interface, they are able to upload new book information, using the `BookUpload` servlet that is mapped to `/inventory/BookUploader`. As a real-time check on what inventory exists across all the warehouses, a web page called `/inventory/inventory.xhtml` is always up to date

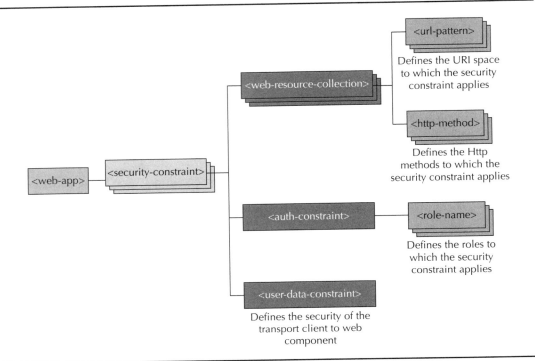

FIGURE 7-3. *Security constraints in the deployment descriptor*

with regard to what books are in stock. This page uses a Java WebSocket mapped to the URI `/inventory/TrackingMonitor` to remain up to date without needing the warehouse manager to keep refreshing the page. Let's see that web application and the URI space it occupies in Figure 7-4.

Like any Internet user, the site would be able to browse the catalog of books, would like only registered customers to be able to purchase books, and only the team across the warehouses would be able to access inventory information and update the catalog as new books arrive. Last, it would like its own team of administrators to have access to all the functions of the web site.

Let's look at how we express those constraints in the `web.xml` deployment descriptor. First, we will create three different roles for each of the different types of users that have access to parts of the web application: `customer`, `backoffice`, and `administrator`. So to the `web.xml`, we add the following security role elements that are described in the listing:

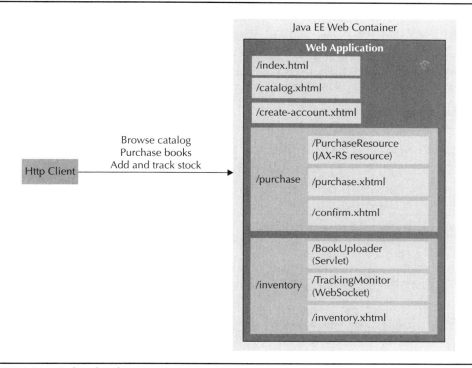

FIGURE 7-4. *Online book store*

Listing: *Security roles*

```
<web-app>
...
    <security-role>
        <role-name>backoffice</role-name>
    </security-role>
    <security-role>
        <role-name>client</role-name>
    </security-role>
    <security-role>
        <role-name>administrator</role-name>
    </security-role>
...
<web-app>
```

Now, let's look through the URI space of the application. In order to restrict access to the purchasing web components (JAX-RS resource, JavaServer Faces pages), all we need to do is make sure that any user trying to access

/purchase/PurchaseResource
/purchase/purchase.xhtml
/purchase/confirm.xhtml

must belong to either the customer or administrator role. In order to restrict access to the inventory-related web components (TrackingMonitor WebSocket, and inventory.xhtml page), we need to make sure that any user trying to access

/inventory/TrackingMonitor
/inventory/inventory.xhtml

has to belong to either the backoffice or administrator role. These restrictions can be enforced by adding the following two security constraints to the web.xml:

Listing: *Security constraints*

```
<web-app>
...
    <security-constraint>
        <display-name>Customer Constraint</display-name>
        <web-resource-collection>
            <web-resource-name>inventory</web-resource-name>
            <url-pattern>/inventory/*</url-pattern>
        </web-resource-collection>
        <auth-constraint>
            <role-name>backoffice</role-name>
            <role-name>administrator</role-name>
        </auth-constraint>
    </security-constraint>
    <security-constraint>
        <display-name>Client Constraint</display-name>
        <web-resource-collection>
            <web-resource-name>purchase</web-resource-name>
            <url-pattern>/purchase/*</url-pattern>
        </web-resource-collection>
        <auth-constraint>
            <role-name>client</role-name>
            <role-name>administrator</role-name>
        </auth-constraint>
    </security-constraint>
...
<web-app>
```

Notice that the index.html, catalog.xhtml, and create-account.xhtml pages are not matched by any of the URL patterns in the security constraints in the example. Therefore, they are available to any user, whether they are authenticated or not.

Finally, we have not specified in this example how the users are to be authenticated. Once the scheme has been decided on, the authentication scheme can be requested in the `web.xml` by adding the suitable `login-config` element, as we covered earlier.

A Note on WebSockets

A final note on WebSockets: as you read in Chapter 6, Java WebSockets use an underlying protocol that is not the same as HTTP. Java WebSockets are mapped by the Java WebSocket API to URIs within a web application, and are in fact covered by the security constraints in a web application. How can this be possible? You will recall that a WebSocket connection can be established only by the client initiating a specially formatted HTTP request called a WebSocket opening handshake. It is this HTTP response interaction that is gated by the security model of the web application that contains it: if the opening handshake returns an HTTP 403 Forbidden response, the WebSocket connection is not established. This means that the authorization model of the Java EE web container applies to Java WebSockets just as it does to the other HTTP components in the platform. How does a Java WebSocket authenticate the opening handshake request so that the Java EE web container can check the caller identity and determine whether to authorize the interaction? Unfortunately, the WebSocket protocol does not include any standard mechanism for authentication. Fortunately, WebSocket connections in web applications are typically initiated by JavaScript code within a web page. So when a WebSocket attempts the opening handshake with the Java EE web container, the Java EE web container knows the authorization state of the opening handshake HTTP request because it knows the authorization state of the web page in which the JavaScript code is executing. In this way, provided the web page in which the WebSocket connection is trying to be established is authenticated, so is the opening handshake, and the converse is also true. The upshot of this is that everything in the Java EE web container security model carries through for Java WebSockets, except that in order to know that a WebSocket client in a web page is authenticated with the Java EE web container, you must ensure that the web page that contains it is authenticated.

Security Constraints in Java Servlets

One type of web component does not need the `web.xml` deployment descriptor to define the security constraints under which it wishes to operate: Java servlets.

The original goal of the deployment descriptor in the WAR file was to be able to simultaneously standardize information about the web application needed by the web container in order to deploy it, while at the same time making sure that such deployment information was separate from the source code. Thus, the information could, in theory, be created (or at least tweaked) after all the application code was written, possibly by someone other than the developer of the application and someone more familiar with the setup of the web server. But editing the `web.xml` can be somewhat onerous, in part because you are maintaining a global view of all the web components in the web application. This is why the Java servlet API includes several security annotations that allow developers to annotate a Java servlet with the information needed to define the security model under which it operates. The annotations control the same security model we have already examined, so they should be easy to pick up.

In order to apply a security constraint to a Java servlet, the starting point is to add an annotation of type `@ServletSecurity` from the package `javax.servlet.annotation` to the servlet class. The `@ServletSecurity` annotation is the same as a security constraint, with a single URL pattern matching the path of the Java servlet in question. The `@ServletSecurity` allows two attributes that are themselves annotations from the same package. First, `@HttpConstraint` annotation allows you to define the list of roles allowed to access all of the servlet's HTTP methods by listing the role names in its `rolesAllowed` attribute, or to grant access to all authenticated users using `ServletSecurity.EmptyRoleSemantic` in the value attribute. The attribute `transportGuarantee` allows you to specify in this annotation the level of data privacy this servlet needs. Second, the `@HttpMethodConstraint` annotation has the value attribute, which is the name of one of the standard HTTP methods, GET, POST, and so forth, together with the same attributes as the `@HttpConstraint` element. In this way, the `@HttpMethodConstraint` annotations allow you to define per-HTTP method constraints, while the `@HttpConstraint` annotation enables you to define security constraints that apply to all of the HTTP methods of the Java servlet. We summarize the structure of the servlet security annotations in Figure 7-5.

We'll conclude this section with a simple example of the `@ServletSecurity` annotation in action. In this example, we have a Java servlet that can display a web page containing information about all the uploaded photos, and can also upload a photo to add to the catalog.

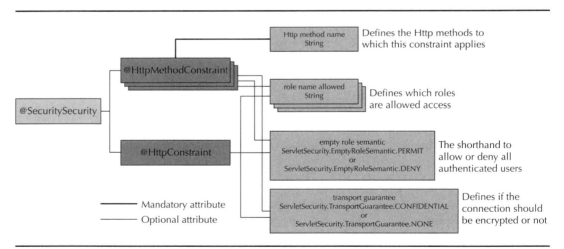

FIGURE 7-5. `@ServletSecurity annotation`

Listing: *A secure servlet using security annotations*

```java
import java.io.IOException;
import javax.servlet.ServletException;
import javax.servlet.annotation.MultipartConfig;
import javax.servlet.annotation.WebServlet;
import javax.servlet.http.*;
import javax.servlet.annotation.ServletSecurity;
import javax.servlet.annotation.HttpMethodConstraint;

@WebServlet(name = "UploadPhoto", urlPatterns = {"/photo/upload"})
@MultipartConfig()
@ServletSecurity(httpMethodConstraints={
    @HttpMethodConstraint(
            value="GET",
            emptyRoleSemantic=ServletSecurity.EmptyRoleSemantic.PERMIT),
    @HttpMethodConstraint(
            value="POST",
            rolesAllowed={"administrator", "photographer"},
            transportGuarantee=ServletSecurity.TransportGuarantee.CONFIDENTIAL)
    })
public class UploadPhoto extends HttpServlet {

    @Override
    protected void doGet(HttpServletRequest request,
                    HttpServletResponse response)
                        throws ServletException, IOException {
        // create the photo catalog page
    }

    @Override
    protected void doPost(HttpServletRequest request,
                    HttpServletResponse response)
                        throws ServletException, IOException {
        // upload a photo
    }
}
```

This servlet uses the `@ServletSecurity` with two `@HttpMethodConstraints` to define access restrictions on the two HTTP methods, GET and POST, implemented by the servlet. You can see from the first of the `@HttpMethodConstraints` that all authenticated users are allowed access to the HTTP GET method implemented by the servlet. From the second `@HttpMethodConstraint`, you can see that only users that are in the administrator role or in the photographer role are allowed to upload photos to the servlet, and only over an encrypted connection.

Programmatic Security

When a web application has declared a security model that causes its users to be authenticated, web components can do several interesting things with this information. Within a particular request to web components, it is often useful to know programmatically who is calling, how they authenticated, and in which of the application-defined roles they belong. Perhaps you wish to use their identity to pull up and display private information particular to that user. Perhaps you wish to provide different output from your web component depending on which roles they belong to. Anyone who has peered forward to the meal and entertainment service available to first-class passengers on a plane can probably relate to that idea. Second, it is useful to be able to manage the authentication model explicitly, perhaps being able to programmatically initiate an authentication interaction, even if the user has not requested a protected resource, or to explicitly log a user out of an application.

So we will take a look at the APIs available at runtime to web component developers to perform these functions.

Understanding the Caller

Java represents a user identity using the `javax.security.Principal` class. The `Principal` of the client calling a web component is available to all web components, as shown in the following table.

Who's Calling?	Object	Method
Java Servlet	`javax.servlet.http.HttpServletRequest`	`Principal getUserPrincipal()`
JSP	The `request` implicit object	`Principal getUserPrincipal()`
JavaServer Faces	The `request` implicit object	`Principal getUserPrincipal()`
JAX-RS	The `javax.ws.rs.core.SecurityContext` object, injected with the @Context annotation	`Principal getUserPrincipal()`
Java WebSocket	The `javax.websocket.Session` object	`Principal getUserPrincipal()`

This is useful information to have at runtime, allowing a range of possibilities for personalizing the output of a web component based on knowing information about the user and his or her previous interactions.

As we have seen, however, web applications often partition their users into roles. This allows applications a simplified view of their users, being able to divide a large number of users into a small set of known roles that can be used to control access, as we have already seen. Exposing the knowledge concerning the current user's role allows applications to offer different functionality to different user groups or roles. The source of the defined list of roles for a web application, as we have seen, is defined in the list of `<security-role>` elements in the `web.xml` deployment descriptor. The function

```
boolean isUserInRole(String rolename)
```

occurs in a number of places in the Java EE web APIs, and is the means by which you can tell whether a caller is in a given role. The following table shows you the locations for each of the web component types.

The Caller Is in Which Role?	Object	Method
Java Servlet	`javax.servlet.http.HttpServletRequest`	`boolean isUserInRole(String role)`
JSP	The `request` implicit object	`boolean isUserInRole(String role)`
JavaServer Faces	The `request` implicit object	`boolean isUserInRole(String role)`
JAX-RS	The `javax.ws.rs.core.SecurityContext` object injected with the @Context annotation	`boolean isUserInRole(String role)`
Java WebSocket	The `javax.websocket.server.HandshakeRequest` object	`boolean isUserInRole(String role)`

The role name you pass into this method is checked by the Java EE web container against role names that appear in the `web.xml`. If you wish to decouple the hard-coded role names from code calling `isUserInRole()` from the role names that appear in the `web.xml`, you can take advantage of the `<security-role-ref>` syntax in the `web.xml` to map role references in code to role names in the `web.xml` deployment descriptor.

If the current request is not authenticated (i.e., there is no user identity associated with the request), then the method returns false.

It is often useful to know whether or not the current connection of the current underlying HTTP request, or the WebSocket connection that is invoking the web component, is encrypted. The

```
boolean isSecure()
```

method is available to make this determination, and the following table summarizes the locations of the API call on the various Java EE web APIs.

The Caller Is in Which Role?	Object	Method
Java Servlet	`javax.servlet.http.HttpServletRequest`	`boolean isSecure()`
JSP	The `request` implicit object	`boolean isSecure()`
JavaServer Faces	The `request` implicit object	`boolean isSecure()`
JAX-RS	The `javax.ws.rs.core.SecurityContext` object injected with the @Context annotation	`boolean isSecure()`
Java WebSocket	The `javax.websocket.Session` object	`boolean isSecure()`

Finally, you can determine the authentication scheme used, for the HTTP components by means of the `String getAuthenticationScheme()` calls. As you might imagine, it is available on the `HttpServletRequest`, JSP and JSP request implicit objects, and the JAX-RS `SecurityContext`.

HttpSessions, login(), and logout()

Many Java EE web containers use the `HttpSession` mechanism not only to track a sequence of interactions from the same browser, but also to track authenticated state. Unfortunately, as a Java EE developer, you cannot rely on all containers taking this approach. For example, some web containers may expire the authenticated state of a user while allowing the `HttpSession` to continue unexpired. Equally, explicitly invalidating an `HttpSession` using the `HttpSession.invalidate()` call may not log out the user, even if on many Java EE implementations it does.

The Java Servlet API does allow you to control `HttpSession` state and authenticated state separately, however, and most importantly, provides a means to reliably log a user out of an application no matter what the underlying mechanism a web container is using to track the authenticated state.

The `HttpServletRequest` provides three useful methods to explicitly control authenticated state. First and foremost, however, if a user has authenticated, calling

```
public void logout() throws ServletException
```

causes that user to be logged out: that is, all authenticated state associated with that user is removed. If the same client calls the web application again and the web component requested is protected, a new authenticated challenge will be issued.

Second, some applications that have decided on using a username/password scheme of authentication may wish to further customize the login process, more than is allowed by the form login mechanism. Such applications can manage their own authentication process, from the gathering of the credentials from the user to the call to a web component, and call the `HttpServletRequest` API

```
void login(String username,
           String password)


           throws ServletException
```

passing in the username and password that it gathered from the client. The method returns without exception if the authentication succeeds; otherwise, the exception is raised.

To complete the trio of controls on the authentication mechanism in the Java EE web container, the method

```
public boolean authenticate(HttpServletResponse response)
                             throws IOException, ServletException
```

can be called from application code to explicitly cause the Java EE web container to attempt to authenticate the caller, based on the mechanism defined in the web application deployment descriptor. This method returns true if and only if the authentication succeeds. This can be a useful method to know about if you wish to make decisions on your web component based on the caller's identity, but you do not necessarily want to have to use security constraints to protect the web component just to do so.

In order to pull together some of the ideas and mechanisms we have explored in this example, it's high time we looked at an example.

Photo Application Example

We will apply the Java EE web container's declarative security model to an application we already know: the photo application we studied in Chapter 4.

You will recall that the photo application allows its users to view the contents of a photo album, the photos themselves, and the metadata about the photo, for example, the date that the photo was taken. The application also allows its users to upload new photos to the photo album, adding the associated descriptive information, and to delete photos from the photo album.

This version of the application is updated to require all users to authenticate with the Java EE web container before the user is able to use the application. The application defines two kinds of users. One, the viewer user, is allowed to log in and browse the photo album, but not to make any changes to it. The second kind of user, the photographer user, is allowed to view the photo album and upload new photos, as well as edit or delete existing photos in the album. The URI space of the application has changed a little, so let's take a look at it in Figure 7-6.

You can see that the JavaServer Faces pages concerned with viewing the photo album are in the /main directory in the URI space of the web application, and all the JavaServer Faces pages concerned with altering the photo album or its photos are in the /main/edit directory in the URI space of the web application. This makes it easier to express the security constraints on the application, as we shall see.

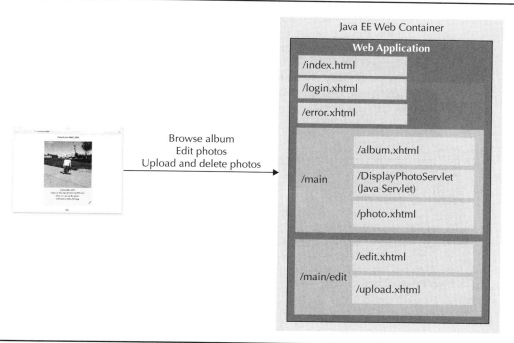

FIGURE 7-6. *The secured photo application*

When you run the application, you will see a number of new things. In order to run the application, you will need to set up at least two user accounts on your application server and note the username and passwords. Second, you will need to associate one of the users to each of the security roles that have been defined in the Photo application. Creating users in the Java EE server and associating them with application-defined roles are tasks that are done differently depending on the Java EE server you are using.

You can find the declarations of the roles for the photo application in the web deployment descriptor.

Listing: *Photographer and viewer roles*

```
<web-app>
...
    <security-role>
        <role-name>viewer</role-name>
    </security-role>
    <security-role>
        <role-name>photographer</role-name>
    </security-role>
</web-app>
```

You can see the role names are viewer and photographer. In the GlassFish 4.0 server, you can associate the users you have created with these roles by adding a `glassfish-web.xml` file containing the mappings to the web application.

Once you run the application, as shown in Figure 7-7, having provisioned these user accounts and associated them with the viewer and photographer roles, you will see that the first page of the application has changed.

Pressing the image of a key attempts to access the `main/album.xhtml` page. Now, you will notice that the deployment descriptor of this application contains a directive to use the form login mechanism, as we can see from this excerpt from the `web.xml` file.

Listing: *Form login for photos*

```
<web-app>
...
    <login-config>
        <auth-method>FORM</auth-method>
        <form-login-config>
            <form-login-page>/login.xhtml</form-login-page>
            <form-error-page>/error.xhtml</form-error-page>
        </form-login-config>
    </login-config>
...
</web-app>
```

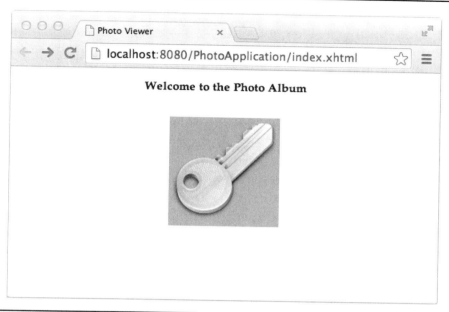

FIGURE 7-7. *Welcome to security*

We shall see that the `main/album.xhtml` page is protected by the security constraints in the deployment descriptor, and so when you attempt to access it, the form login mechanism redirects you to log in in the `login.xhtml` page specified in the deployment descriptor, as shown earlier. This is shown in Figure 7-8.

Filling out one of the user accounts you had created and associated with one of the security roles grants you access to the photo album page. If the user account you use to authenticate is the viewer account, you should see something like what is shown in Figure 7-9.

On the other hand, if you authenticated using a user account that is associated with the photographer role, you should see something like Figure 7-10.

Notice that the `main/album.xhtml` page knows the name of the user account in its Welcome title. Notice also that for either user, you can log out of the web application. Notice that for both account types, you can view the photos and click the view icon to get a more detailed view. Only the users that have the role of photographer see the Upload photos button and see the icons for editing or deleting the photos. In fact, if a user in the viewer role tried to access some of the editing functionality despite it not being available in the UI, by typing the `/main/edit/photo.xhtml` URI to edit a photo, they are forbidden from accessing the resource and receive an HTTP 403 response.

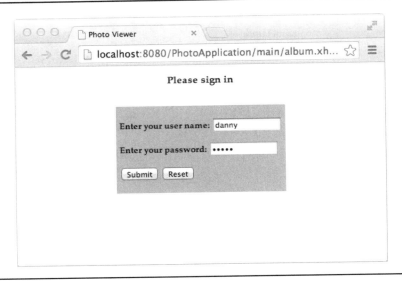

FIGURE 7-8. *Logging in*

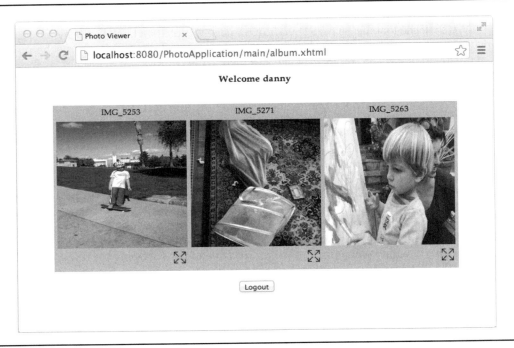

FIGURE 7-9. *Photo album as a viewer*

FIGURE 7-10. *Photo album as a photographer*

Two things are occurring here: first, the declarative security model is enforcing the different access rights to the resources in the web application to users in the viewer role versus users in the photographer role. And second, the JavaServer Faces pages are using the programmatic access to the underlying security model in order to display only those options to the user that are allowed.

Let's look at the two security constraints that protect the web components in the application and divide the access rights between the two roles.

Listing: *Security constraints for the photo application*

```
<web-app>
...
    <security-constraint>
        <display-name>ViewAndEdit</display-name>
        <web-resource-collection>
            <web-resource-name>ViewableAndEditable</web-resource-name>
            <url-pattern>/main/*</url-pattern>
        </web-resource-collection>
        <auth-constraint>
            <role-name>photographer</role-name>
        </auth-constraint>
```

```
    </security-constraint>
    <security-constraint>
        <display-name>ViewOnly</display-name>
        <web-resource-collection>
            <web-resource-name>Viewables</web-resource-name>
            <url-pattern>/main/album.xhtml</url-pattern>
            <url-pattern>/main/photo.xhtml</url-pattern>
            <url-pattern>/main/DisplayPhotoServlet</url-pattern>
        </web-resource-collection>
        <auth-constraint>
            <description/>
            <role-name>viewer</role-name>
            <role-name>photographer</role-name>
        </auth-constraint>
    </security-constraint>
...
</web-app>
```

We see that the first security constraint, `ViewAndEdit`, grants access to photographers to all the web components in the application: the ones that display and also those that edit the photo album. It does so using a `url-pattern` in the wildcard matching style.

The second security constraint, `ViewOnly`, grants access to viewers to only the web components in the application that display photos and the album. It does so using an explicit list of url-patterns that use the exact URI style.

The programmatic APIs for security are used in the photo application to display the current username on the album page, to decide whether to display the various edit functions to the user based on knowing the role to which he or she belongs, and to perform the logout. The code that uses these APIs is collected together into a request-scoped managed bean that various JavaServer Faces pages in the photo application can use. Let's take a look at the code for this, the SecurityBean:

Listing: *The SecurityBean*

```
import javax.enterprise.context.RequestScoped;
import javax.faces.FacesException;
import javax.inject.Named;
import javax.faces.context.FacesContext;
import javax.servlet.http.HttpServletRequest;
import javax.servlet.ServletException;

@Named(value = "securityBean")
@RequestScoped
public class SecurityBean {
    private static String VIEWER_ROLE = "viewer";
    private static String PHOTOGRAPHER_ROLE = "photographer";

    private HttpServletRequest getHttpServletRequest() {
        return (HttpServletRequest) FacesContext.getCurrentInstance()
                                    .getExternalContext().getRequest();
```

```
    }

    public String getUsername() {
        HttpServletRequest request = this.getHttpServletRequest();
        if (request.getUserPrincipal() != null) {
            return request.getUserPrincipal().getName();
        } else {
            return "";
        }
    }

    public boolean isUserAbleToEdit() {
        HttpServletRequest request = this.getHttpServletRequest();
        return request.isUserInRole(PHOTOGRAPHER_ROLE);
    }

    public boolean isLoggedIn() {
        return (this.getHttpServletRequest().getUserPrincipal() != null);
    }

    public void logout() {
        try {
            this.getHttpServletRequest().logout();
            this.getHttpServletRequest().getSession().invalidate();
        } catch (ServletException se) {
            throw new FacesException("Failure on logout", se);
        }
    }
}
```

The managed bean is in request scope, and is named `securityBean` so it can be accessed with that name from any of the JavaServer Faces pages in the application. The central object it uses to support its messages is the `HttpServletRequest` object from the underlying Java servlet API. It obtains this from its `FacesContext` object, as you can see from the `getHttpServletRequest()` method, and uses it to perform `logout()` on demand, and to present the key bean properties that allow a client of the bean to determine whether the current user is authenticated, what the current user's username is, and whether the current user is allowed to edit the photo album by checking the user's membership in the roles defined for the application. These properties are defined in the methods `isLoggedIn()`, `getUsername()`, and `isUserAbleToEdit()`, respectively.

We won't look at all the places in the application where the security bean is used, but let's look just at the `main/album.xhtml` to see where it is used.

Listing: *The album JavaServer Faces page*

```
<?xml version='1.0' encoding='UTF-8' ?>
<!DOCTYPE html PUBLIC "-//W3C//DTD XHTML 1.0 Transitional//EN" "http://www.w3.org/TR/
xhtml1/DTD/xhtml1-transitional.dtd">
<html xmlns="http://www.w3.org/1999/xhtml"
      xmlns:h="http://xmlns.jcp.org/jsf/html"
```

```
    xmlns:c="http://xmlns.jcp.org/jsp/jstl/core">
<h:head>
    <title>Photo Viewer</title>
</h:head>
<h:body style="font-family:Palatino;font-size:small">
    <div align='center'>
        <h3>Welcome #{securityBean.username}</h3>
    <br></br>
    <table bgcolor="99CC99" cellspacing="4">
        <tbody>
            <tr>
                <c:forEach items="#{photoAlbum.photos}" var="photo">
                    <td>
                    <div align='center'>
                            #{photo.name}
                    </div>
                    </td>
                </c:forEach>
            </tr>
            <tr>
                <c:forEach items="#{photoAlbum.photos}" var="photo">
                    <td>
                        <h:form>
                            <h:graphicImage
                                height="200"
                                width="200"
                                value="#{photo.viewUri}"/>
                        </h:form>

                        <h:form>
                            <div align='right'>

                            <h:commandButton
                             title="view"
                             image="../view.png"
                             actionListener="#{photoAlbum.setCurrentPhoto(photo)}"
                             action="photo"/>
                            <c:if test="#{securityBean.userAbleToEdit}">
                                <h:commandButton
                                 title="edit"
                                 image="../edit.png"
                                 actionListener="#{editPhotoBean.setPhoto(photo)}"
                                 action="edit/edit"/>
                                <h:commandButton
                                    title="delete"
                                    image="../delete.png"
                                    action="#{photoAlbum.removePhoto(photo)}"/>
                            </c:if>
                            </div>
                        </h:form>

                    </td>
                </c:forEach>

            </tr>
          </tbody>
```

```
            </table>
            <br></br>
            <c:if test="#{securityBean.userAbleToEdit}">
                <h:form>
                    <h:commandButton
                        id="upload_button"
                        value="Upload photos"
                        onclick="window.open('edit/upload.xhtml')"/>
                </h:form>
            </c:if>
            <c:if test="#{securityBean.loggedIn}">
                <h:form>
                    <h:commandButton
                        id="logout_button"
                        value="Logout"
                        actionListener="#{securityBean.logout()}"
                        onclick="window.open('../index.xhtml')"/>
                </h:form>
            </c:if>
        </div>
    </h:body>
</html>
```

You should be able to locate quite easily in the code the point where the security bean is used to display the username, where it is used to hide or display the `edit` and `delete` icons under each photo in the album, where it is used to show or hide the `Upload` button, and where it is used for the logout function. You will find the security bean used for similar purposes, that is to say, hiding functionality that the declarative security model forbids, throughout the rest of the photo application.

Summary

In this chapter, we looked at the general principles of security models for web applications, the concepts of authenticating users, allowing access to resources only to certain authenticated users, and determining communication channels that are more or less easy to intercept and decode.

We looked at the mechanisms in the Java EE web container for configuring the declarative security model, covering the techniques for defining the login mechanism for a web application, using security constraints to shut off access to web components based on their position in the URI space of the web application to unwanted users, and ensuring an encrypted communication channel for access to web components. We looked at the programmatic APIs for security available to the different types of web components, and in a final example, we applied all we learned to a familiar application, showing how the security mechanisms can protect resources in an application, allow for different levels of access to that application to different types of users, and how to use the programmatic APIs to make the user experience adapt to the constraints of the security model.

CHAPTER
8

The Self-Contained Web Site: Java EE Web Application

Now that we have looked at all the web component technologies in the Java EE web container, it's time to take a step back and look at the mechanisms in the web container that apply not to individual web components, but to the web application as a whole.

In this chapter, we will examine how the URI space of a web application is composed. This will lead us to look in some detail at the WAR file format, and in particular, the web.xml deployment descriptor. We have already encountered some aspects of this important piece of metadata, in particular, the security directives it contains. We will now look more deeply at two kinds of web components: servlet context listeners and web filters. The former category is never called by a client, and the latter category never produces its own content. We will conclude our examination by looking at how asynchronous processing is modeled in the web component APIs, using examples throughout.

The WAR File

The WAR file is a special kind of ZIP archive that contains all the static and dynamic content, class files, text files, images, libraries, and other resources that make up a web application, together with the deployment information that the web container needs to know in order to know how to configure the application at runtime. This deployment information is held in part in Java annotations in code and/or the WAR file's web.xml deployment descriptor.

Let's take a look at the structure of a WAR file.

There are three main areas:

■ **Web resources, rooted at** /   The web resources section is the home to all of the static content in the web application, together with any of the web components that are held in a text file containing a markup language, such as JSPs and JavaServer Faces pages. Unless explicitly protected by a security constraint, any web resource put into this area will be exposed into the URI space of the web application, and so will be visible to clients when deployed to the Java EE web container.

■ **Java classes and code libraries, rooted at WEB-INF/classes and WEB-INF/lib**   This section contains all the Java class files that constitute top-level web components, or that are used by web components in the application. Therefore, this is the location for all Java servlet class files, JAX-RS resources, WebSocket endpoints, and any other classes used by any of the web components such as managed beans and tag libraries. The classes may be placed directly under the WEB-INF/classes entry in the WAR file. Or, if the classes have been packaged into a JAR file as a self-contained library, they may be placed under the WEB-INF/lib entry. Anything placed under the WEB-INF entry will not be directly exposed to HTTP clients of the web application when deployed to the Java EE web container.

■ **The web deployment descriptor at WEB-INF/web.xml**   This XML document contains deployment information describing how the Java EE web container is to deploy the web application contained in the WAR file. This configuration file is not available to be viewed by HTTP clients when the web application is deployed to the Java EE web container.

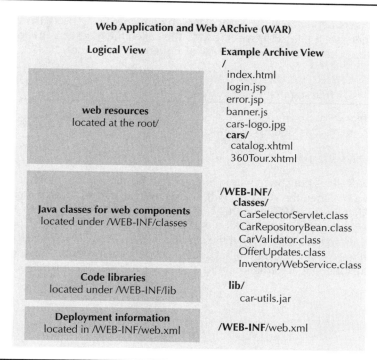

FIGURE 8-1. *Example of WAR file showing structure*

In Figure 8-1, the example application is a car dealership web site. The application contains a number of web components: JavaServer Faces components for browsing the catalog of available models, and the ability to take a 3D tour of a particular vehicle. It uses JSPs to implement a form login for repeat viewers of the web site. It uses various Java web components, for example, a servlet and a JAX-RS resource to update the inventory, and a Java WebSocket to keep the user's web page up to date with regard to current offers. It has a class library specially for displaying car information as HTML. Finally, it uses the web deployment descriptor to map the Java servlet to a URI in the URI space of the application and configure the form login, among other things.

What other things can it configure? We begin by looking at a global property of the web application that is not always straightforward to derive from the WAR file.

The URI Space of a Web Application

The URI space of a web application is the collection of URIs relative to the root URL of the web container under which the web container publishes all the web components and static resources in the application. When a web application is deployed to a Java EE web container, it must be accompanied by a relative URI that the web container uses to place the root of all web resources in the web application. This relative URI is called the context root of the web application. If the web application is deployed directly to the web container, then how the context root for that web application is set depends on the particular web container being used. For example, the GlassFish web container uses a GlassFish-specific XML file called the `glassfish-web.xml`, which resides under the `WEB-INF/` entry in the WAR file to hold the context root.

Listing: *GlassFish descriptor*

```
<glassfish-web-app>
  <context-root>car-app</context-root>
...
</glassfish-web-app>
```

If the WAR file is contained within a larger Java EE application (perhaps because it uses Enterprise Beans), then the WAR file will be deployed as part of a larger archive called an Enterprise ARchive, or EAR file. In this case, the EAR file has its own deployment descriptor that contains the context root of the WAR file. We will see more of the Java EE deployment descriptor and EAR file format later. For now, if the car web site is packaged in a WAR file called `car-site.war`, then the Java EE application that contains it defines the context root for the WAR file by including the following information in its `application.xml` deployment descriptor:

```
<application>
  ....
  <module>
    <web>
      <web-uri>car-site.war</web-uri>
      <context-root>/car-app</context-root>
    </web>
  </module>
 ...
</application>
```

However the context root is established, the root of the web application when deployed to the Java EE web container is

```
http://<hostname:port>/<context-path>/
```

which means that any web component with a relative path of `/web-component` will be available at

```
http://<hostname:port>/<context-path>/web-component
```

This means that once we have fully understood all the ways that web components can be mapped in a web application, we will fully understand the complete URI space of a web application.

So let us take a look at all the different web components and how they are mapped into the URI space of a web application.

Static Content

The relative URI of a static content file (HTML file, XML file, text file, sound file, image file) within the web application is simply its entry name in the WAR file.

So, for example, if the index page of a web application is named `index.html`, and it is located in the WAR file at the entry `/index.html`, then, it is available to clients at the URL

```
http://<hostname:port>/<context-path>/index.html
```

Similarly, if a file named `classroom.jpg` is located at the WAR file entry `/kids/classroom.jpg`, then it is available to clients at the URL

```
http://<hostname:port>/<context-path>/kids/classroom.jpg
```

JavaServer Faces

In terms of path mapping, JavaServer Faces pages are treated like static content, so their URI paths within the deployed web application are the same as their WAR file entry names. In the car web site example earlier, the JavaServer Faces page at the WAR file entry `/cars/catalog.xhtml` is available to clients at the URL

```
http://<hostname:port>/<context-path>/cars/catalog.xhtml
```

Java Servlets

As we saw in Chapter 2, the path mapping for a Java servlet can be achieved by using the `@WebServlet` annotation. The `urlPatterns` attribute of this annotation takes an array of Strings, each of which can be a kind of path called a servlet URL pattern. We encountered the definition of a URL pattern in Chapter 7, where we learned that URL patterns are used to define the paths covered by a security constraint.

Definition of URL Patterns

There are three kinds of URL patterns to map a Java servlet. They are

- **An exact path**   For example, `cars/InventoryUploadServlet`. Only request URIs that are the same as this path, including case, will match this path.
- **Path with wildcard**   For example, `cars/*`, which will match any request URI that begins with `/cars`; for example, `cars/InventoryUploadServlet`, or `cars/InventoryDownload`.
- **Filename ending**   This is a URLpattern that is matched by any request URI whose last segment includes the same filename ending pattern. For example, a filename endpoint URLpattern of `*.web` will match the request URI `index.web`, `/cars/inventory.web` and `/cars/make/models.web`.

In this way, a single Java servlet may use the `@WebServlet` annotation to map to one or a collection of different possible URIs within the web application.

There is a second way in which a Java servlet may declare its position in the URI space of a web application: by using the servlet mapping mechanism in the web deployment descriptor.

Using this mechanism occurs in two steps. First, you have to declare the Java servlet in the web application using a `<servlet>` element. This element has the sub elements `<servlet-name>` and `<servlet-element>`, which require you to give the servlet a logical name that will be used elsewhere in the deployment descriptor, and the fully qualified classname of the servlet. For example, if the servlet has classname

```
com.acme.cars.CarSelectorServlet
```

then it can be given the logical name `CarSelector`, and so would be declared in the web deployment descriptor as shown in the following listing.

Listing: *Web deployment descriptor with servlet declaration*

```
<web-app>
    <servlet>
        <servlet-name>CarSelector</servlet-name>
        <servlet-class>com.acme.cars.CarSelectorServlet</servlet-class>
    </servlet>
...
</web-app>
```

Now that the servlet has a logical name, it can be used in an element called the `<servlet-mapping>` element to associate the servlet with one or more URL patterns, using the `<url-pattern>` element, which takes one of the three forms of the URL pattern described earlier. For example, to map the `CarSelectorServlet` to the URL pattern `/cars/CarSelectorServlet`, you would need fragment in the deployment descriptor that this listing shows.

Listing: *Web deployment descriptor with servlet mapping*

```
<web-app>
    <servlet>
        <servlet-name>CarSelector</servlet-name>
        <servlet-class>com.acme.cars.CarSelectorServlet</servlet-class>
    </servlet>
      <servlet-mapping>
        <servlet-name>CarSelector</servlet-name>
        <url-pattern>/cars/CarSelectorServlet</url-pattern>
      </servlet-mapping>

...
</web-app>
```

Finally, if you define both a servlet mapping in the web deployment descriptor and a URL pattern in the `@WebServlet` annotation for a Java servlet, then mapping in the web deployment descriptor replaces the mapping defined in the annotation. This can often be a useful implementation technique to create a reasonable default URL pattern in the annotation, which can be overridden later by servlet mappings in the deployment descriptor as the servlet is assembled into the web application.

JavaServer Pages

JavaServer Pages are simple to map into the URI space of the web application: like Java Server Faces pages, the relative URI of a JavaServer Page is the same as the archive entry name in the WAR file.

Like servlets, however, you can provide additional mappings to the JavaServer Page by declaring the JSP in the deployment descriptor, using the `<servlet>` element. The `<servlet>` element has an alternative sub element, `<jsp-file>`, which can be used in place of the `<servlet-class>` element. Once the JSP has been declared using the servlet element, you can add a `<servlet-mapping>` element to add any number of `<url-pattern>` elements that will expose the JSP to more URIs in the URI space of the web application. For example, suppose that you want to expose the `login.jsp` page in the car web site example not simply as `/login.jsp`, which is the default, but as `login.html` as well. Then you would need to add the following servlet and servlet mapping elements to the deployment descriptor.

 Listing: *Web deployment descriptor with JSP mapping*

```
<web-app>
    <servlet>
        <servlet-name>LoginPage</servlet-name>
        <jsp-file>login.jsp</jsp-file>
    </servlet>
      <servlet-mapping>
        <servlet-name>LoginPage</servlet-name>
        <url-pattern>/login.html</url-pattern>
      </servlet-mapping>

...
</web-app>
```

JAX-RS Resources and Java WebSockets

JAX-RS resources and Java WebSocket endpoints are mapped to their positions in the URI space of the web application using the `@Path` annotation from the `javax.ws.rs` package and by using the `@ServerEndpoint` annotation from the `javax.websocket.server` package, respectively. As we saw in Chapters 5 and 6, both kinds of components can be mapped using these annotations with either a relative URI or a URI template. Neither web component technology defines any syntax in the web deployment descriptor for mappings to the URI space of the web application.

Summary: Web Components and Their URI Paths

We'll end this section by summarizing the ways in which web applications define the URI space that they expose to their clients.

Category	Path Type	URI Path Defined
Static content	Exact path	Same as WAR archive entry
JavaServer Faces	Exact path	Same as WAR archive entry

Category	Path Type	URI Path Defined
JavaServer Pages	Exact path and URL pattern	Same as WAR archive entry; additional paths defined using `<servlet-mappings>`
Java servlets	URL pattern	Either using `@WebServlet` annotation in servlet class OR using `<servlet-mappings>`
JAX-RS resources	Exact path or URI template	Using `@Path` annotation in the resource class or method
Java WebSocket endpoint	Exact path or URI template	Using `@ServerEndpoint` annotation in the endpoint class

Global Web Components: Web Filters and Web Listeners

We turn our attention next to two kinds of web components that we have not yet covered: web filters and web listeners. Each kind of component is global in a different way. Web filters are a way to adapt incoming HTTP requests and adapt outgoing HTTP responses to any HTTP web component in a web application. Thus, their global quality is that they can apply equally to a Java servlet or to a JavaServer Faces page. Web listeners are global in the sense that they are instantiated once for the lifetime of the web application. Both are useful additions to web applications and offer a degree of modularity in dividing up the functionality of a web application and making some of the functionality available for use in other web applications.

Web Filters

Web filters are very powerful web components that intercept the HTTP interactions to any HTTP component in a web application. The web filter model may be used to implement a wide range of filtering tasks, from filters that simply monitor interactions with web components such as logging filters, to filters that selectively block or allow interactions based on some dynamic decision making, such as authentication filters, to filters that can transform any aspect of the incoming request and/or any aspect of the outgoing HTTP response, including compression filters and XML transformation filters.

The web filter model enables you to write a Java component that intercepts the underlying `HttpServletRequest` object as it arrives at the web container. The filter is responsible for passing a possibly read and modified `HttpServletRequest` and possibly a modified response object to the next web component in the interaction, which may be another web filter, or may be the destination web component of the interaction. The strategy used for modifying `HttpServletRequests` and `HttpServletResponses` is by wrapping them: in other words, a filter will create an implementation of `HttpServletRequest` or `HttpServletResponse` that delegates most of its method implementations to the instance it wraps, but modifies the behavior of other calls in order to implement the filtering behavior. We can see this kind of approach in Figure 8-2.

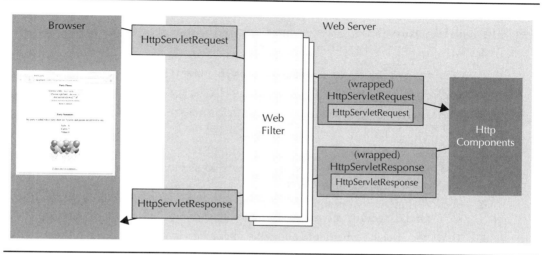

FIGURE 8-2.   *Web filters*

We can see that by the time the HTTP components in the web application call the read methods on the `HttpServletRequest`, they are calling it on an `HttpServletRequestWrapper` object that wraps the original `HttpServletRequest`, and so has the opportunity to modify and/or delegate the behavior of reading the original content of the request. Similarly, by the time the HTTP component writes data to the response, the `HttpServletResponseWrapper` object to which it writes is wrapping the `HttpServletResponse` object that the container created in order to send the content back to the caller, and so has a similar opportunity to modify and delegate the behavior of those write methods to the real response. If more than one filter applies to a particular interaction (we shall see shortly how they are configured), then the collection of filters that apply is called a filter chain. Each filter in the chain may wrap the request and response objects passed to the next filter in the chain, just as the last filter in the chain can wrap the request and response objects for the destination HTTP component.

Let us look first at some pseudocode that illustrates how a web filter works. The starting point for creating a web filter is to implement the class `javax.servlet.Filter`. This class has two lifecycle methods to implement:

`void init(FilterConfig filterConfig) throws ServletException`

which is called by the container when the web filter is being called into service, and

`void destroy()`

which is called by the web container when the web filter instance is being taken out of service.

These two methods give the web filter instances the chance to call up and clean up any potentially expensive resources they may need to work, for example, database or external connections.

The main method of the filter interface is the `doFilter()` method:

```
void doFilter(ServletRequest request,
              ServletResponse response,
              FilterChain chain)
                  throws IOException, ServletException
```

The `FilterChain` object is the web container's object reference to the next web component that this filter needs to call, either another filter if this is not the last filter in the chain, or the destination HTTP component. All web filters implement the `doFilter()` method according to the following recipe:

- First, they may examine the request that was passed in, for example, reading headers and logging the request with the time.
- Second, they may wrap the request or the response object or both in order to perform some kind of request and/or response modification as part of their filtering job.
- Third, they decide whether to allow the interaction to continue by choosing whether or not to invoke `doFilter()` on the `FilterChain` object. For example, an authentication filter may decide whether to allow the interaction to continue based on customer request headers it is looking for when invoked.
- Finally, it may directly add or change headers on the response object after it has invoked the filter chain. Just as in the servlet model, whether this change makes an effect will depend on whether the headers of the response have already been sent back to the client.

All web filters follow some subset of these steps in their `doFilter()` implementations. Here is a simple example of a filter that makes no modification or requests and responses, but simply logs HTTP interactions it receives.

Listing: *Log filter*

```
import java.io.IOException;
import javax.servlet.Filter;
import javax.servlet.FilterChain;
import javax.servlet.FilterConfig;
import javax.servlet.ServletException;
import javax.servlet.ServletRequest;
import javax.servlet.ServletResponse;
import javax.servlet.annotation.WebFilter;
import javax.servlet.http.HttpServletRequest;
import java.util.logging.*;


@WebFilter(filterName = "LogFilter", urlPatterns = {"/*"})
public class LogFilter implements Filter {
    private Logger logger;
    @Override
```

```
public void init(FilterConfig filterConfig) {
    this.logger = Logger.getLogger(LogFilter.class.getName());
}

@Override
public void doFilter(ServletRequest request,
                     ServletResponse response,
                     FilterChain chain)
                 throws IOException, ServletException {


    this.logger.log(Level.INFO, "Request for " +
            ((HttpServletRequest)request).getRequestURI());
    try {
        chain.doFilter(request, response);
    } catch (ServletException se) {
        this.logger.log(Level.SEVERE, "Error fulfilling request " +
                                                se.getMessage());
        throw new ServletException("Error invoking the " +
                "rest of the filter chain: " + se.getMessage());
    }
    this.logger.log(Level.INFO, "Request complete.");
}

@Override
public void destroy() {
    this.logger = null;
}

}
```

Web Filter Configuration

The configuration model for web filters is similar to that of Java servlets. Logically, each web filter may be assigned a list of URL patterns whose match to an incoming request governs whether the filter is invoked or not.

Just as with Java servlets, a web filter can be declared either using an annotation or in the web deployment descriptor.

The annotation for declaring web filters is @javax.servlet.annotation.WebFilter, which has attributes of name, the logical name of the web filter, and an array of url-patterns; for example,

```
@WebFilter(name="LogFilter", url-pattern="/*")
```

maps a filter to any request URI to the web application.

Alternatively, the filter may be equivalently declared in the deployment descriptor, using the `<filter>` and `<filter-mapping>` elements as follows.

Listing: *Web deployment descriptor with filter mapping*

```
<web-app>
    <filter>
        <filter-name>LogFilter</filter-name>
        <filter-class>javaeems.chapter8.filters.LogFilter</filter-class>
    </filter>
    <filter-mapping>
        <filter-name>LogFilter</filter-name>
        <url-pattern>/*</url-pattern>
    </filter-mapping>
...
</web-app>
```

If you have a web application in which you wish to configure a number of filters and the order in which the chain is called is significant, then you should always declare the filter mappings in the deployment descriptor. The Java EE web container assembles the filter chain following the order in which matching URL patterns appear in the web deployment descriptor. If you use the annotation approach, there is no guaranteed order in which the filters are called.

Let's look now at a slightly more complicated filter. This filter injects additional content into the response from static content in a web application to let the client know it has been operating and converts the static content to all uppercase letters.

This filter requires that the caller be an authenticated user, so to run it, you need to add a user to your Java EE application server and associate it with the user role that it defines in the web deployment descriptor. Each Java application server has a different mechanism for adding users and associating them with application-defined roles.

Back to the example: let's see what happens when the `UppercaseFilter` is applied to the following HTML code.

Listing: *Unfiltered HTML code*

```
<html>
  <head>
    <title></title>
  </head>
  <body>
    <title></title>
      <div align="center">
        <h3>Web filters are really Wonderful !</h3>
      </div>
  </body>
</html>
```

The result for the user `becky` is shown in Figure 8-3.

FIGURE 8-3.   *Filtered output of the HTML content*

This application requires all users be authenticated, and applies the `UppercaseFilter` to all the HTML pages in the application. Let's take a look at the code.

Listing: *The UppercaseFilter content filter*

```java
import java.io.IOException;
import java.io.PrintWriter;
import javax.servlet.http.*;
import javax.servlet.Filter;
import javax.servlet.FilterChain;
import javax.servlet.FilterConfig;
import javax.servlet.ServletException;
import javax.servlet.ServletRequest;
import javax.servlet.ServletResponse;
import javax.servlet.annotation.WebFilter;
import java.security.Principal;


@WebFilter(filterName = "Uppercase", urlPatterns = {"*.html"})
public class UppercaseFilter implements Filter {

    @Override
    public void init(FilterConfig filterConfig) {
    }

    @Override
    public void doFilter(ServletRequest request,
                         ServletResponse response,
                         FilterChain chain)
                            throws IOException, ServletException {
```

```
            Principal principal = ((HttpServletRequest) request).getUserPrincipal();
            PrintWriter writer = new PrintWriter(response.getWriter());
            writer.println("<p><b>The page is filtered for: " +
                                        principal.getName() + "</b></p>");
            try {
                UppercaseResponse uResponse =
                        new UppercaseResponse((HttpServletResponse) response);
                chain.doFilter(request, uResponse);
            } catch (Throwable t) {
                throw new ServletException("Error during filtering: " +
                                                t.getMessage());

            }
        }

        @Override
        public void destroy() {
        }

}
```

We can see immediately from the use of the `@WebFilter` annotation that it uses the filename ending style of URL pattern to map itself to all the HTML files in the web application. The `UppercaseFilter` has no state associated with its instances; therefore, it has nothing to initialize or tear down in its lifecycle methods `init()` and `destroy()`. The meat of the filter is in the `doFilter()` method.

We can see that by reading the user principal out of the request, it first writes a header line to the response, which we can see in the web page. Second, in order to convert all the content of the web page it is filtering to uppercase, it uses a custom class, `UppercaseResponse`, to wrap the real response from the web page. The request remains unmodified by this filter. Let's look at the `UppercaseResponse`, which makes the character conversion.

Listing: *Filter response wrapper*

```
import java.io.IOException;
import java.io.PrintWriter;
import java.util.Arrays;
import javax.servlet.http.HttpServletResponse;
import javax.servlet.http.HttpServletResponseWrapper;


public class UppercaseResponse extends HttpServletResponseWrapper {

    UppercaseResponse(HttpServletResponse response) {
        super(response);
    }

    @Override
    public PrintWriter getWriter() throws IOException {
        return new UppercaseWriter(super.getWriter());
    }
}
```

```
class UppercaseWriter extends PrintWriter {

    public UppercaseWriter(PrintWriter w) {
        super(w);
    }

    @Override
    public void write(char[] cbuf, int off, int len)  {
        char[] charsToConvert = Arrays.copyOfRange(cbuf, off, off+len);
        String convertedString = (new String(charsToConvert)).toUpperCase();
        super.write(convertedString.toCharArray(), 0, len);
    }

    }
}
```

The Java Servlet API includes the helper classes `HttpServletRequestWrapper` and `HttpServletResponseWrapper`. These classes are wrapper classes on `HttpServletRequest` and `HttpServletResponse`, respectively, with the default behavior of doing nothing to the objects they wrap. In other words, they implement all the methods of `HttpServletRequest/ Response` simply by calling the same method on the class that they wrap. What this means is that if you wish to provide your own request or response wrapper, all you have to do is subclass one of the wrapper classes, overriding only the methods where you wish to modify some behavior. The behavior we wish to override is in converting the characters written to the response writer of the HTML page. Therefore, the `UppercaseResponse` wrapper overrides the `getWriter()` method, inserting another wrapper around the `PrintWriter`. The only method that needs to be overridden on the `PrintWriter` is the `write(char[] cbuf, int off, int len)` method, as all other `write()` methods on this class ultimately call this one. You can see that the implementation of this wrapper method takes the incoming characters as they are being written and converts them to uppercase. You might equally see this kind of character manipulation working for word substitution or eliminating certain character combinations for a range of other filters that can modify the text content of a static (or dynamic!) web page.

Web filters are enormously powerful. With a web filter, you have ultimate control over the request and response interactions between an HTTP client and an HTTP component. While Java WebSockets are unaffected by web filters, their opening handshake interactions are not. Since a WebSocket opening handshake is the beginning of each and every WebSocket connection, in this way, even WebSockets can be affected by web filters.

Web Listeners

A variety of important events occurs in the ordinary functioning of the Java EE web container that web applications can sign up to hear about. These events concern changes in state in either the `ServletContext` or the `HttpSession` objects.

The first two types of event listeners are concerned with the global lifecycle of the `ServletContext`. The web container creates a unique instance of the `ServletContext` for each new web application that it deploys. The lifetime of this instance begins at some point before the web container allows the web application to accept its first HTTP request, and ends after the web container has allowed the web application to make its last HTTP response. The ServletContextListener interface allows a web application to intercept the events that are generated as the web container creates the ServletContext instance for a web application and as the web container releases the ServletContext instance for a web application. This makes the ServletContextListener the ultimate global timekeeper for a web application: it is called right after a new web application comes to life, and right before an old one is about to die. This is a very useful event listener when you have some heavy initialization and/or cleanup to do before you start up a web application and after you are done, for example, readying a database for use by the web components in the web application.

The ServletContextAttributesListener interface is designed to allow web applications to be notified when attributes are added to or removed from the ServletContext. They do so simply by having any application object that will be set as a ServletContext attribute implement that interface.

The other three event listeners in the web container are all concerned with the activities of HttpSessions. The HttpSessionListener allows a web application to listen in to all session creation and destruction events in the web container: by implementing this interface with a Java class, the container will instantiate one instance of the Java class and notify it whenever an HttpSession is created or destroyed. This can be a really useful interface to implement if you want to keep a handle on all the different clients of your application; as we shall see shortly, you can easily use this listener to keep an up-to-date list of all the active sessions in an application.

HttpSessions may change IDs during their lifetime. This is often done when a user authenticates in the middle of an active session. It can be useful to know about changes in the HttpSession ID in case you have code that is relying on the relationship between the current session and its ID. If you need to know when an active session changes its ID, then your application can implement the HttpSessionIdListener interface to be notified when such an event occurs.

Like the ServletContext, HttpSessions have an attribute map where applications may store application data in the form of key-value pairs. Like the ServletContext, it can be useful to know when application data is added to or removed from or changed in the attribute map of the HttpSession. A number of events can occur: it may be the case that an attribute is newly added, changed, or removed by one of the web components or listener objects in the web application. For these kinds of events, all the attribute needs to do to be notified of such changes is to implement the HttpSessionAttributesListener. The web container may have to temporarily store the state of the HttpSession so that it can replicate the state of the web application at a later time, or even on a different machine. This is often the case for distributed application servers where the web server runs on a number of VMs. In such deployments, there is a special server called a load balancer that is sharing out the work of the web server across those VMs. The load balancer may choose to move an HttpSession from one VM to another to ensure that the load of the web application is borne evenly among the VMs in the web server. In such cases, any attributes bound to the HttpSession are also stored with the HttpSession and restored as part of the HttpSession when it is revived. To be notified when application data is stored or restored in this way, the attribute need only implement HttpSessionActivationListener and it will be told. Let's look at a summary of all these listeners in Figure 8-4.

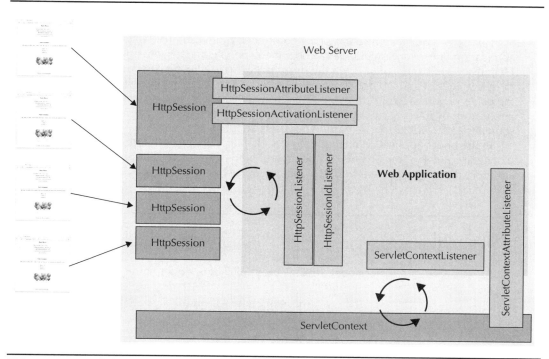

FIGURE 8-4.   *All the web listeners*

Configuring Web Listeners

As we have discussed, to configure web listeners that listen to changes to the state of attributes on either the `ServletContext` or the `HttpSession`, simply have the attribute implement the relevant web listener interface.

The three other web listeners, the `ServletContextListener`, the `HttpSessionListener`, and the `HttpSessionIdListener`, must be configured using a different mechanism. As usual with the Java EE web APIs, you have some choices. You can use the `@javax.servlet` `.annotation.WebListener` annotation at the class level to mark the listener implementation as a web listener, or you can add a

```
<listener>
    <listener-class> fully qualified classname of
                     the listener implementation </listener-class>
</listener>
```

to the web deployment descriptor. As for web filters, if the order of invocation of web listeners is important to your application, then if you use the annotation approach, there is no guaranteed order of invocation. However, with the deployment descriptor approach, the web container for each listener type invokes the listeners in the order that they are declared in the deployment descriptor.

Let's look a quick application of a web listener for an example we already know: the photo application. It is often useful to know how many people are actively using your web application. Of course, you cannot always tell the difference when a client is idle for a few minutes if they have lost interest and are doing something else, or if they are avidly reading every word on one of the pages of your web site, but you get a reasonable idea of how many people are using your application by tracking the active `HttpSessions`, as seen in Figure 8-5. It may sometimes be something you would like to inform your users about.

In the photo application example for this chapter, the photo album used is a group album: the managed bean that implements the album and holds the pictures has application scope. In addition, the main page tells you how many other active users are looking at the group album.

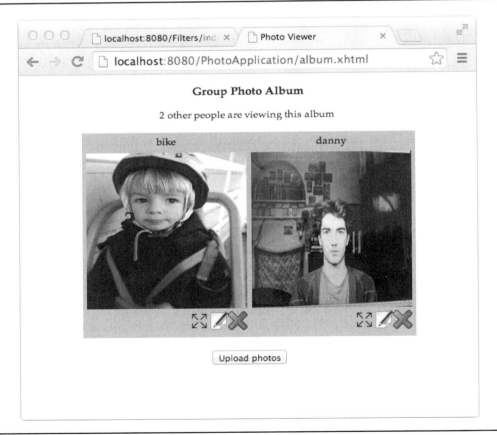

FIGURE 8-5. *Who's watching?*

This is achieved by means of the UserCounter class, which implements the HttpSessionListener interface.

Listing: *UserCounter session listener*

```
import javax.servlet.http.HttpSessionEvent;
import javax.servlet.http.HttpSessionListener;
import javax.servlet.annotation.WebListener;
import java.util.List;
import java.util.ArrayList;
import javax.servlet.http.HttpSession;
import javax.servlet.ServletContext;

@WebListener
public class UserCounter implements HttpSessionListener {
    private List<HttpSession> sessions = new ArrayList<>();
    public static String SERVLET_CONTEXT_SESSION_LIST =
                         "servlet_context_session_list";


    @Override
    public void sessionCreated(HttpSessionEvent se) {
        this.sessions.add(se.getSession());
        this.updateServletContext(se.getSession().getServletContext());
    }

    @Override
    public void sessionDestroyed(HttpSessionEvent se) {
        this.sessions.remove(se.getSession());
        this.updateServletContext(se.getSession().getServletContext());
    }

    private void updateServletContext(ServletContext sc) {
        sc.setAttribute(SERVLET_CONTEXT_SESSION_LIST, new ArrayList(sessions));

    }
}
```

The UserCounter is registered by the web container as a web listener because, as you can see, it includes a @WebListener annotation. It maintains a list of the active sessions in the photo application by adding newly activated sessions as it receives notification as they start, and removing recently destroyed sessions as they are terminated by the web container as it receives notification of that event. Whenever the UserCounter changes the list of active sessions, it updates a ServletContext attribute that holds a copy of the list. This is the list that is accessed by the PhotoAlbum class in its new property viewerCount.

Listing: *Viewer count property of the photo album*

```
public int getViewerCount() {
    ServletContext servletContext = (ServletContext) FacesContext
                .getCurrentInstance().getExternalContext().getContext();
    List sessions = (List) servletContext
                .getAttribute(UserCounter.SERVLET_CONTEXT_SESSION_LIST);
    if (sessions != null) {
        return sessions.size();
    } else {
        return 0;
    }
}
```

This is used by the JavaServer Faces page `album.xhtml` to display the active user count, as shown in the following listing.

Listing: *Album JavaServer Faces page displaying the viewer count*

```
...
<c:if test="#{photoAlbum.viewerCount == 2}">
   one other person is viewing this album
</c:if>
<c:if test="#{photoAlbum.viewerCount != 2}">
  #{photoAlbum.viewerCount - 1} other people are viewing this album
</c:if>

...
```

Asynchronous Modes in Web Applications

All the programming models and APIs for HTTP components we have looked at so far have followed the underlying synchronous nature of the underlying HTTP request and response interaction. In other words, when a client has made a request, the thread that the container uses to invoke the web component with the request, and that the web component uses to read the request, is the same as the thread the web component uses to formulate the data it uses to write to the response. There are a number of situations where this synchronous programming model is not ideal. Examples include cases where either the reading of the request or the formulation of the response is a lengthy or expensive process, such as gathering a large data set from a database, or doing some kind of post-processing on a large amount of data that will be used in the response. In such cases, such as AJAX programming, the client is deliberately setting up long-lived HTTP connections to the web server in order to receive small updates from the web component over a period of time. Since the web container generally uses a finite thread pool to fund its web components, the one-thread-per-client interaction model can lead to situations in which there are more active client interactions than threads in the thread pool, causing new client interactions to be put on hold until threads that are tied up doing slow response processing or holding persistent

HTTP connections become freed up. So, you may wish to separate the request reading and the response formulation onto two separate threads, and even use your own thread pool to allocate the threads you wish your web application to use for formulating its HTTP responses.

In this section, we look at two examples of asynchronous support in the Java EE web container. First, let us see how to create an asynchronous servlet.

Asynchronous Java Servlets

In the traditional servlet model, the processing of the incoming `HttpServletRequest` and the formulation of the `HttpServletResponse` all occur within the servlets `service()` method in one block of code that can be executed only by one thread provided by the container. The state of the objects available within the service methods, for example, the request and the readability of the headers, and the response and the availability of its output stream, can be described as the *execution context* of the servlet interaction. If you have tried to store the `HttpServletRequest` or `HttpServletResponse` that you obtained from within a servlet `service()` call and tried to use them after the service method has completed, you may well have seen some very unusual behavior: these objects are not supposed to be used outside their execution context.

The key to being able to process a servlet call asynchronously is the ability to extend the execution context of a call beyond the bounds of the servlet's `service()` invocation. The Java Servlet API provides a call called the `javax.servlet.AsyncContext`, which can be understood as a place to hold the `HttpServletRequest` and `HttpServletResponse` pair passed into a servlet's `service()` method that extends the execution context of the call to wherever the `AsyncContext` object is. Once the `HttpServletRequest` and `HttpServletResponse` are in the `AsyncContext`, the `service()` method may finish without any processing having occurred, and the `AsyncContext` passed to another thread can retrieve them for processing at leisure.

The key points of using the `AsyncContext` in this manner include the following: The servlet must be marked as using the asynchronous programming mechanism, either by using the `asyncSupported=true` attribute of the `@WebServlet` annotation or adding `<async-supported>true</async-supported>` to the `<servlet>` element in the web deployment descriptor. This allows the web container to treat this servlet differently in terms of how it allocates its threads.

The `AsyncContext` object for the interaction is obtained from the `HttpServletRequest` using the `request.startAsync()` method. This places the active request and response into the context so that it can be passed to a different thread to process the interaction.

This is accomplished by passing the thread you wish to use to do the actual request processing to the `AsyncContext` using the `AsyncContext.start(Thread)` method. Now the `service()` method can complete and the web container thread that called it can finish its work.

On the worker thread used to process the interaction, the request and response objects can be retrieved from the `AsyncContext` using

```
asyncContext.getRequest()
asyncContext.getResponse()
```

and used just as if they were within the usual confines of the `service()` call.

Once the processing is complete, the `complete()` method must be called on the `AsyncContext` to commit the response and allow the web container to garbage-collect the request and response objects.

This is the flow with which you can dissect the execution context of a servlet invocation and pass it to a different thread for processing. Let us take a look at a simple example of this in action.

Locked Servlet

The Locked Servlet example uses a servlet that uses the AsyncContext to delegate processing of its invocation to a different thread. The thread that the Locked Servlet application uses to process interactions with the servlet, however, always waits until a second web component has "unlocked" a servlet context attribute. Once the servlet context attribute has been unlocked, at some arbitrary time after the call to the locked servlet was made, the thread proceeds to process the request. Let's see what this looks like.

The lock.xhtml page is the first web page, as shown in Figure 8-6.

Clicking the thunderbolt button invokes the LockedServlet in a second window, as shown in Figure 8-7, which waits on the LockedServlet's response. The LockedServlet is locked until the padlock button is clicked in the original window, which releases the waiting asynchronous thread and completes execution of the Locked Servlet, as shown in Figure 8-8.

The code for the lock.xhtml reveals simply the two actions on the page, given in the following excerpt.

FIGURE 8-6.   *Locked servlet home page*

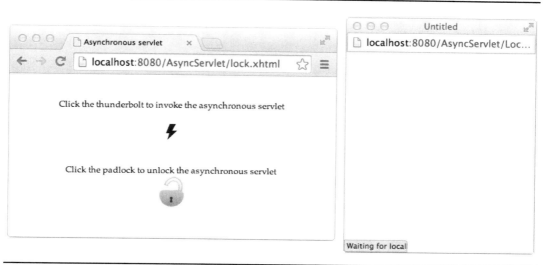

FIGURE 8-7. *Locked servlet locked*

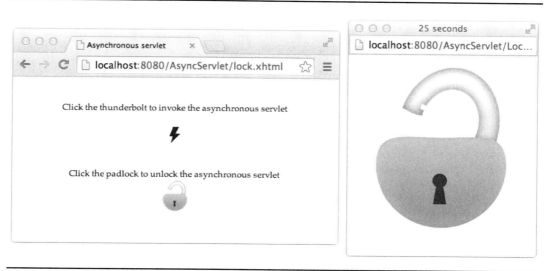

FIGURE 8-8. *Locked servlet unlocked*

Listing: *lock.xhtml JavaServer Faces page*

```
<h:form> Click the thunderbolt to invoke the asynchronous servlet <br><br>
  <h:commandbutton
    id="async_button"
    value="Call async servlet"
    image="lightening_sm.png"
    onclick="window.open('LockedServlet','_blank',
                         'height=300,width=275')"/> <br><br>
  <br><br>
  Click the padlock to unlock the asynchronous servlet <br><br>
  <h:commandbutton
    id="upload_button"
    value="Unlock async servlet"
    image="unlock_sm.png"
    action="#{application.setAttribute('lock', 'unlocked')}"/>
</h:form>
```

You can see that the first button causes the LockedServlet to be called, and the second causes the ServletContext, represented by the implicit object called application in the JSF environment, to have an attribute called lock set to the value unlocked.

Now let us look at the LockedServlet itself.

Listing: *The asychronous LockedServlet*

```
import java.io.IOException;
import java.io.PrintWriter;
import javax.servlet.ServletException;
import javax.servlet.annotation.WebServlet;
import javax.servlet.http.HttpServlet;
import javax.servlet.http.HttpServletRequest;
import javax.servlet.http.HttpServletResponse;
import javax.servlet.AsyncContext;
import javax.servlet.ServletContext;

@WebServlet(urlPatterns = {"/LockedServlet"}, asyncSupported=true)
public class LockedServlet extends HttpServlet {
    public static String LOCK = "lock";
    public static String LOCKED = "locked";
    public static String UNLOCKED = "unlocked";


    @Override
    protected void doGet(HttpServletRequest request,
                         HttpServletResponse response)
                            throws ServletException, IOException {
        final AsyncContext asyncContext = request.startAsync();
        asyncContext.start(new Runnable() {
            @Override
            public void run() {
                performProcessing(asyncContext);
```

```
            }
        });
        ServletContext context = request.getServletContext();
        context.setAttribute(LOCK, LOCKED);
    }

    protected void performProcessing(AsyncContext asyncContext) {
        HttpServletResponse response =
                    (HttpServletResponse) asyncContext.getResponse();
        response.setContentType("text/html");
        HttpServletRequest request =
                    (HttpServletRequest) asyncContext.getRequest();
        ServletContext context = request.getServletContext();
        int wait = 0;
        for (wait = 0; wait < 100; wait++) {
            if (!"locked".equals(context.getAttribute(LOCK))) {
                break;
            } else {
                try {
                    Thread.sleep(250);
                } catch (Exception r) {}
            }
        }
        int waitSecs = (int) (wait /4);
        try (PrintWriter out = response.getWriter()){
            out.println("<!DOCTYPE html>");
            out.println("<html>");
            out.println("<head>");
            out.println("<title>" + waitSecs + " seconds</title>");
            out.println("</head>");
            out.println("<body>");
            out.println("<image src='unlock_lg.png'/>");
            out.println("</body>");
            out.println("</html>");
        } catch (IOException ioe) {
            System.out.println("There was an IOException");
        }
        asyncContext.complete();
    }

}
```

The overall structure of the LockedServlet is simple. In the doGet() method, instead of performing the request/response processing, it obtains the AsyncContext from the request object and creates a worker thread, the runnable anonymous class, that is passed to the AsyncContext instance to perform the actual work of the servlet. Once this is done, it ensures the special lock attribute on the ServletContext is locked. The worker thread simply makes a call to the performProcessing() method of the LockedServlet. The action of passing the worker thread into the start() method of the AsyncContext kicks the thread off. Notice that by the time the performProcessing() method is called, the doGet() method of the servlet will have completed, without sending any response back to the client.

The `performProcessing()` method obtains the request and response objects that were passed into the `doGet()` method of the `LockedServlet`, and otherwise looks like a regular servlet method in terms of how it uses the request and response objects. It waits in a loop until the `ServletContext` attribute used as a lock is unlocked, at which point it renders the page containing the image of an unlocked padlock. It keeps a note of the time at which the worker thread first enters the `performProcessing()` method, and uses that to set the title of the page to the number of seconds it had to wait to be unlocked.

Asynchronous Web Resources

The JAX-RS uses a similar mechanism to separate out the execution context of a web service call on the server from the execution context of a single Java method used to implement the web service resource. We will explore that mechanism in this section. There is a similar, if not greater, need in web applications that expose a RESTful web service API to be able to manage processing of the web service requests in separate threads from those that produce the response entities. Web service resources may represent large data sets, or may be used to initiate operations that take a long time and/or a large amount of computing power to complete, such as installing software or transforming or analyzing large amounts of data.

On the server side, the class `javax.ws.rs.container.AsyncResponse` represents the execution context of a web service call that can be lifted out of a single synchronous Java method call and used in a different thread. Like the Java servlet API's `AsyncContext`, the JAX-RS's `AsyncResponse` allows you to delegate formulating the response to another thread.

Here are the steps to using the `AsyncResponse` in a web service resource.

First, you must get hold of the `AsyncResponse` instance associated with a particular resource call. To do this, you declare a parameter of type `AsyncResponse` in the resource method, decorating the parameter with the `@javax.ws.rs.container.Suspended` annotation.

Inside the resource method, you can then establish the thread you wish to use to do the actual response processing and have it reference the `AsyncResponse` to start the work by calling its `resume()` method, or you can cancel the request by means of the `cancel()` method. We will see an example of this in action shortly.

Since the JAX-RS API also includes a client API, we should mention that the client API also contains a mechanism for handling returning responses from web service calls asynchronously. This is equally useful for client applications of web services that call web service APIs that represent long-lived operations as the server-side mechanism is. Client applications typically will invoke a potentially lengthy web service call in response to a GUI event initiated by a user. The client application will certainly not want the GUI to freeze while the event thread waits for the web service it is calling to formulate a response. Instead, it may wish to dispatch the request and assign a different thread from the GUI event thread to poll for the result, or opt to receive a callback when the response has arrived.

In the JAX-RS client API, the web service invocation may be made asynchronous while building the `Invocation` object from the `WebTarget`; for example:

```
WebTarget resourceTarget = client.target("http://acme.com/webservice/bigdata/");
```

where instead of building a synchronous `Invocation` object on which the web service method, in this case, `get()`, is called:

```
String responseString = resourceTarget
                .request("text/plain")
                .get(String.class);
```

instead, the asynchronous mode builds an `AsyncInvoker` object by using the `async()` method on the `Invocation.Builder` on which the web service method, in this case `get()`, is called:

```
Future<String> responseFuture = resourceTarget
                        .request("text/plain")
                        .async()
                        .get(String.class);
```

In the asynchronous case, what you get back is a `java.util.concurrent.Future<V>` object, where `V` is the Java type of the response entity you are expecting. You get the `Future` object back immediately, before the response is received from the server. The `Future` object is a holder for the ultimate response that will return from the server, and you can interrogate it in order to determine the state of the call, cancel it, and obtain the actual response entity when it arrives. These tasks are accomplished by calling the following methods:

```
boolean isDone()
boolean cancel(boolean mayInterruptIfRunning)
V get()
```

where `V` is the Java type of the result you expect.

Hello Asynchrony

Let us look at a familiar example that we saw in Chapter 5: the HelloWorld web service with rich client. But now this example has been updated so that the client makes its call to the web service and awaits the response on a separate thread, and the server side creates the response it will make to the client call on a separate thread from that which handled the incoming request from the client.

The client window looks the same as before, as seen in Figure 8-9, until you press the Say Hello button, when you will notice a couple of things, as seen in Figure 8-10. First, the response

FIGURE 8-9.   *Hello Asynchronous Client main window*

FIGURE 8-10. *Hello Asynchronous Client call complete*

takes a few seconds to arrive. And second, the client application lets you know every second that it is waiting on the response to return. Those of you who are very practiced in the arts of GUI programming will also notice that the activities of making the web service request, awaiting the reply, and processing the response do not tie up the GUI event thread. The Say Hello button repaints once the request is made, the window may be resized mid-operation, and so on.

Let's take a look at the code on the server side first.

Listing: *The HelloResource asynchronous web resource*

```
import java.text.SimpleDateFormat;
import javax.ws.rs.PUT;
import javax.ws.rs.Path;
import javax.ws.rs.Produces;
import javax.ws.rs.container.AsyncResponse;
import javax.ws.rs.container.Suspended;
import java.util.*;

@Path("hello")
public class HelloResource {
    SimpleDateFormat dateFormatter = new SimpleDateFormat("h:mm:ss a");

    @PUT
    @Produces("text/plain")
    public void sayHelloPlain(@Suspended final AsyncResponse asyncResponse,
                                              final String requestEntity) {
        final Date requestTime = new Date();
        Thread workerThread = new Thread() {
            @Override
            public void run() {
                try {Thread.sleep(2000);} catch (Exception r) {}
                asyncResponse.resume(processResponse(requestTime, requestEntity));
```

```
                }
            };
            workerThread.start();
    }

    private String processResponse(Date requestTime, String requestEntity) {
        return "Replying to your message ("+ requestEntity +")
                            I got at " + dateFormatter.format(requestTime);
    }

}
```

Notice now that the web service resource method `sayHelloPlain()` no longer formulates the response. Instead, it takes the `AsyncResponse` object that it has asked the container to pass it, using the `@Suspended` annotation, and submits a new worker thread that it creates to a thread pool that the class is using. It starts the worker thread, and before waiting for any particular work on that thread to be done, the method is finished and completes. The worker thread does the work of formulating the response by invoking the `processResponse()` method, which contains the response. Notice that the worker thread emulates a slow process by pausing for two seconds before calling the `processResponse()` method. In this way, the work of responding to the web service client is delegated to a thread that is managed by, in this case, the application, but could equally be drawn from a thread pool.

Unlike the Java Servlet API, the execution context in this case need not be explicitly closed: the `AsyncResponse.resume()` method that you can see in the worker thread's `run()` method writes the response entity in a one-shot deal and also commits the underlying response object. The `AsyncResponse` may be used to set timeouts for the operation and to listen to events pertaining to the progress of the response formulation.

Turning to the client side, the GUI thread that initiates the call to this web service call that will take two seconds to complete does not wait on the response. Let's see how in the following listing.

Listing: *The Asynchronous HelloClient*

```
import javax.ws.rs.client.*;
import java.util.concurrent.Future;
import javax.ws.rs.core.Response;

public class HelloClient {
    WebTarget wt;

    public HelloClient() {
        Client client = ClientBuilder.newClient();
        this.wt =
          client.target("http://localhost:8080/HelloAsyncWebServices/hello");
    }

    public String getUriAsString() {
        return this.wt.getUri().toString();
    }

    public Future<Response> sayHelloFuture(String message) {
        Future<Response> futureResponse = wt
```

```
                    .request()
                    .accept("text/plain")
                    .async()
                    .method("PUT", Entity.text(message));
            return futureResponse;
        }
    }
```

We can see from the `HelloClient` class's `sayHelloFuture()` method that instead of using the `Invocation` class to invoke the put, by virtue of the `async()` call it makes on the `Invocation.Builder`, it obtains an `AsyncInvoker` on which to call the put. This in turn immediately returns a `Future<Response>` object, where Response is the JAX-RS API's `javax.ws.rs.core.Response` object representing the returning response from the call. In this way, this method returns before the web service call has actually completed, allowing the `ClientWindow` to check in on the Future object to establish the status of the response. In this excerpt from the `ClientWindow` code, the `sayHello()` method is the one called when the Say Hello button is pressed, and the `jta` variable is the text area it uses to display information to the user.

Listing: *Excerpt from the `ClientWindow` class*

```java
    public void sayHello() {
        final Future<Response> futureResponse =
                this.helloClient.sayHelloFuture(this.jtf.getText());
        this.jta.append(dateFormatter.format(new Date()) +
                                    " " + "sent request." + "\n");
        Thread pollingThread = new Thread() {
            @Override
            public void run() {
                pollForResponse(futureResponse);
            }

        };
        pollingThread.start();
    }

    void pollForResponse(Future<Response> futureResponse) {
        while(!futureResponse.isDone()) {
            jta.append(dateFormatter.format(new Date()) + " " +
                                            "waiting..." + "\n");
            try {Thread.sleep(1000);} catch (InterruptedException ie) {}
        }
        String s = "";
        try {
            Response r = futureResponse.get();
            s = r.readEntity(String.class);
            jta.append(dateFormatter.format(new Date()) + " " + s + "\n");
        } catch (ExecutionException | InterruptedException e) {
            jta.append(e.getMessage() + "\n");
        }
    }
```

In the sayHello() method, the ClientWindow initiates the web service call on the HelloClient instance it uses and obtains the Future<Response> object. After printing status to the window saying the request has been made, it creates a polling thread that calls the pollForResponse() method. This method remains in a loop, checking every second whether the Future<Response> has completed by calling its isDone() method and printing a message each time it checks. When the Future is done, it means that the Response has been received and can be read. The isDone() method then returns true, and the method reads the response entity and prints it out to the window.

In this way, the work of waiting for the response and informing the user is delegated to a special thread, instead of the work having to occur on the same thread as is used to paint the user interface.

Summary

In this chapter, we looked at some of the global aspects of a web application: the URI space, the deployment descriptor, and the global components that are web filters and web listeners. We also looked at how in applications where web components model potentially long and expensive operations, the execution context of a web component call can be moved into threads under the control of the application for an asynchronous programming model.

In all our explorations of the web layer, we have found some useful structures such as the ServletContext and HttpSession in which we can hold application- and user-specific information, but only for the lifetime of the application. In order to keep application data around longer than the short time of an application session, we need to dig deeper into the next layer of the Java EE platform. In the next chapter, we start moving out of the work of markup, XML, and HTTP and into the world of data, transactions, and persistence.

PART
II

The Brain of Java EE:
The Middle Tier

CHAPTER
9

The Fundamentals of
Enterprise Beans

If Enterprise Beans were airline passengers, they would all fly first class.

Enterprise Beans are application components that run on the Java EE server in the most cosseted components in any of the Java platforms. Like regular Java classes, they have constructors to instantiate them, and methods to process information and perform tasks. Unlike regular Java classes, they run in the luxurious environment of the Enterprise Bean container, which takes care of a variety of potentially complicated tasks that typically confront the developer of a server application.

Introduction to Enterprise Beans

The services that an Enterprise Bean container offers to its components include

- Managing the lifecycle and number of instances of the Enterprise Bean, from instantiation through various phases to destruction.

- Managing the concurrency of access to methods exposed by the Enterprise Bean, allowing the Enterprise Bean to determine whether the Enterprise Bean container should allow multiple threads to access its methods at the same time, or whether such threads should wait in line to access methods one at a time.

- Allowing Enterprise Beans to implement asynchronous methods, wherein the component's method can return immediately while the container thread waits on the actual process of the method to complete.

- Allowing multiple Enterprise Bean method calls to be handled atomically within a single transaction, guaranteeing the integrity of common data being handled by more than one method at a time.

- Gating calls to Enterprise Beans to allow them to declare which users are allowed access to their methods.

In Figure 9-1, we can see a summary of the services enjoyed by an Enterprise Bean.

These features of the Enterprise Bean component model mean that as a Java EE developer, you should consider using them in an application if

- *Your application needs to scale to a large number of users.* Because the Enterprise Bean's lifecycle is managed by the container, containers can instantiate a suitable number of them to meet the current demand made by the active clients at any one time. Additionally, because many Enterprise Bean containers are distributed across more than one Java VM, the work of running the application can be evenly shared across Java VMs and even across server machines. In this way, the load borne by the application due to the varying client demand can be effectively balanced by the container. Finally, the clients of Enterprise Beans do not need to know the details of how many instances there are nor where physically (i.e., on which Java VM) they are located; the methods with which a client can locate an Enterprise Bean are independent of these details. Therefore, it is generally easier to let Enterprise Bean containers perform this kind of load balancing rather than trying to write it yourself in a Java EE application.

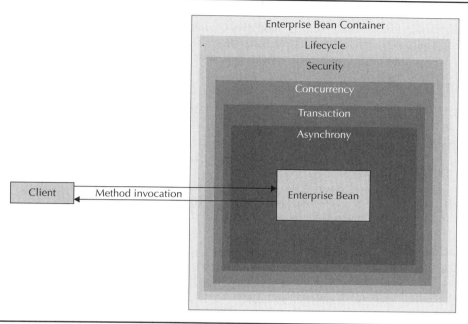

FIGURE 9-1. *Services enjoyed by Enterprise Beans*

- *Your application is managing relatively complex data that requires transactional support.* Because the Enterprise Bean container is managing concurrent threads, it is clear in the programming model where there may be contention while reading and writing data from and to a database or databases. The Java Transaction API that supports the transactional capabilities of Enterprise Beans allows you to demarcate where you need multiple Enterprise Bean operations to be considered as one atomic action. In other words, you get to decide whether a group of method calls that manipulate application data must either all complete without a hitch in order to succeed, or whether the collective action will be rolled back if a constituent method fails. Like load balancing, the controls that allow you to control concurrent access to Enterprise Beans and demarcate transactions involving application data are generally much easier to use than trying to code these kinds of safeguards by yourself.

- *Your application has a variety of different clients.* There are a number of different client types that can call an Enterprise Bean. Enterprise Beans may be called from other Enterprise Beans, from Java EE web components, from client applications using the Java EE Application Client container, and from web service clients. By implementing application logic in one or more Enterprise Beans, you do not need to change the application logic in order to add a new client type, which is always a big timesaver in application development and maintenance.

The main ways that these clients connect with Enterprise Beans are over RMI/IIOP (described next), HTTP, JMS, and local Java method invocation.

RMI/IIOP

Short for Java Remote Method Invocation over the Internet Inter-Orb Protocol, this is the primary and general-purpose means for clients to talk to Enterprise Beans in a different Java VM, for example, a Java servlet in the web container calling an Enterprise Bean in the Enterprise Bean container.

HTTP

You can declare that an Enterprise Bean be callable as a RESTful web service, meaning its methods are exposed to clients making the kind of RESTful web service calls over HTTP that we observed in Chapter 5.

JMS Protocol

One of the flavors of Enterprise Beans is called the message-driven bean. Clients of this kind of bean use one of the many wire protocols for message transmission supported under the Java Message Service to make calls.

Local Java Method Invocation

In some situations, clients of an Enterprise Bean may be colocated in the same container. It is actually possible to run certain kinds of Enterprise Beans in the web container, in which case calls to this kind of Enterprise Beans from a web component in the same web container may occur using plain old Java object-to-Java object method calls. Developers usually opt for this kind of setup if they want the performance advantages of local calls.

Figure 9-2 provides a summary of the ways different clients connect to an Enterprise Bean.

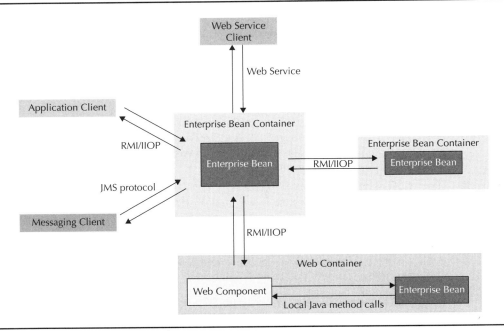

FIGURE 9-2. *Enterprise Bean clients*

Flavors of Enterprise Bean

There are two essentially different types of Enterprise Bean. They are known as session beans and message-driven beans.

Session beans are a general-purpose kind of Enterprise Bean, accessible through RMI/IIOP and web service protocols, as well as local Java method invocations. They are the most commonly used kind of Enterprise Beans. Message-driven beans are a special kind of Enterprise Bean for use with clients that make calls on them by sending messages using the Java Messaging Service (JMS). While session beans and message-driven beans share some properties, for example, the way in which they are packaged and deployed to the Java EE server, their interaction models are quite different. We will examine these categories of Enterprise Beans separately.

Before we explore the different kinds of Enterprise Beans, we start with a very simple example.

Hello Enterprise Beans

This example is a Java EE application containing a single Enterprise Bean, which is called by a Java servlet. We use this example to highlight some of the core concepts of Enterprise Beans.

When you run the application, the web browser calls the Java servlet. You will see something like Figure 9-3.

There are three Java classes in this application: the Java servlet, called `ServletClient`, and two Java classes that make up the Enterprise Bean: `HelloBean` and `HelloBeanImpl`.

FIGURE 9-3. *Hello Enterprise Beans client view*

The `HelloBean` Java class is actually an interface.

Listing: *The `HelloBean` remote interface*

```
import javax.ejb.Remote;

@Remote
public interface HelloBean {
    public String getMessageFor(String caller);
}
```

It defines a single method, and other than the `@Remote` annotation at the class level, it is just like an ordinary Java interface. What the `@Remote` annotation does is turn this interface into an Enterprise Bean remote interface, which is to say, this is an interface that is used by an Enterprise Bean to publish its methods to all its potential clients, whether they be application clients, web components, or other Enterprise Beans.

Figure 9-4 shows the architecture of the Hello Enterprise Beans application, showing its implementation classes.

Figure 9-5 shows the logical arrangement of the Enterprise Bean and its Java servlet client.

Listing: *The `HelloBean` implementation class*

```
import javax.ejb.Stateful;

@Stateful
public class HelloBeanImpl implements HelloBean {

    @Override
    public String getMessageFor(String caller) {
        return "hello to you, " + caller + " !";
    }
}
```

We can see from the code that the Enterprise Bean implementation class implements the remote interface. The only extra thing over a regular Java class that implements an interface is the use of the

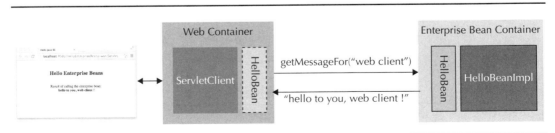

FIGURE 9-4.   *Hello Enterprise Beans architecture*

@Stateful annotation from the javax.ejb package. This marks the implementation class as a particular kind of session bean called a stateful session bean. In short, the Enterprise Bean container creates exactly one instance of this kind of bean for each client that makes calls to it.

Finally, let us see how the Enterprise Bean is called from the Java servlet client.

Listing: *The HelloBean client:* ServletClient

```
import java.io.IOException;
import java.io.PrintWriter;
import javaeems.chapter9.hello.HelloBean;
import javax.ejb.EJB;
import javax.servlet.ServletException;
import javax.servlet.annotation.WebServlet;
import javax.servlet.http.HttpServlet;
import javax.servlet.http.HttpServletRequest;
import javax.servlet.http.HttpServletResponse;


@WebServlet(name = "ServletClient", urlPatterns = {"/ServletClient"})
public class ServletClient extends HttpServlet {
    @EJB
    private HelloBean helloBean;

    @Override
    protected void doGet(HttpServletRequest request, HttpServletResponse response)
                                      throws ServletException, IOException {
        response.setContentType("text/html;charset=UTF-8");
        PrintWriter out = response.getWriter();
        try {
            out.println("<html>");
            out.println("<head>");
            out.println("<title>Hello Java EE</title>");
            out.println("</head>");
            out.println("<body>");
            out.println("<br>");
            out.println("<div align='center'>");
            out.println("<h2>Hello Enterprise Beans</h2>");
            out.println("<br>");
            String displayMessage;
            String message = helloBean.getMessageFor("web client");
            out.println("Result of calling the enterprise bean: <br><b>"
                                              + message + "</b>");
            out.println("</div>");
            out.println("</body>");
            out.println("</html>");
        } finally {
            out.close();
        }
    }
}
```

The `ServletClient` accesses the Hello Enterprise Bean by declaring an instance variable, `helloBean`, to store a reference to the bean's remote interface and by annotating the instance variable declaration with the `@EJB` annotation from the `javax.ejb` package. What this annotation does is ask the web container to inject a suitable instance of the Enterprise Bean whose remote interface is `HelloBean` at the time that the servlet is being instantiated. Then, as you see from the `doGet()` method of the servlet, the `HelloBean's getMessageFor()` method is called when the browser makes its request.

This example shows one particular type of Enterprise Bean, a stateful session bean, being accessed through its remote interface from a Java servlet that is using dependency injection by virtue of the `@EJB` annotation to locate an instance of the Enterprise Bean and then calling its method.

We now explore the four avenues that this example opens up: the different types of Enterprise Beans, how Enterprise Beans are located from the clients that use them, different modes for accessing Enterprise Beans, both local and remote, and what kinds of Java methods an Enterprise Bean can expose.

Flavors of Enterprise Beans

As you now know, there are two main kinds of Enterprise Beans: session beans and message-driven beans, and we have already hinted at different kinds of session beans. Let's look at the three types of session beans: stateless, stateful, and singleton.

Stateless Session Beans: @Stateless

A stateless session bean is so called because, from the client's perspective, it cannot hold a state between calls. In other words, this bean can be extremely forgetful! A stateless session bean is one whose implementation class is marked `@Stateless`. The reason it cannot hold a state is that two separate calls to this kind of Enterprise Bean may be handled by two different instances of the Enterprise Bean's implementation class. This is true whether the calls are from the same client or from totally different clients. Thus, if the Enterprise Bean implementation instance attempts to hold state in its instance variables based on the first method call, because subsequent calls to the Enterprise Bean may be handled by a different instance of the implementation class, the retained state from the first call is lost. This model allows Enterprise Bean containers to choose how many instances to create a running Enterprise Bean, and typically to manage a pool of them. This means that applications that use this kind of bean scale well to many clients. Thus, developers often choose to use this kind of bean for performance reasons. That is the case, of course, in applications where they do not need to hold any kind of application state in the Enterprise Beans. Such applications might include beans that model execution of stateless processes, such as deleting files, sending messages, and performing mathematical calculations. We could in fact have used a stateless session bean for our HelloBean example, as it holds no application state. For holding application state, we need to move to the next kind of session bean, stateful session beans.

Stateful Session Beans: @Stateful

Stateful session beans are the most common kind of Enterprise Bean. A stateful session bean is one whose implementation class is marked @Stateful. The Enterprise Bean container instantiates a stateful session bean once for each client that calls it. This means that if, for example, a particular web component calls a stateful session bean multiple times, it will actually be calling the same instance of the Enterprise Bean implementation class. Equally, if a different web component calls the same stateful session bean, it will call a different instance of the bean's implementation class.

This model allows such Enterprise Beans to hold state in the instance variables of its implementation class that it wishes to associate with its clients across multiple method calls from that client. This makes this kind of bean very useful for applications such as shopping carts, applications that collect user data over a sequence of interactions, or any kind of application containing personalization features, adapting the application based on previous interactions. The downside of stateful session beans is that they do not scale quite so well as stateless session beans: the Enterprise Bean container must maintain as many instances of the stateful session bean as it has active clients. Sometimes, however, applications need to hold state that is common to all clients of the application. This brings us to singleton session beans.

Singleton Session Beans: @Singleton

Singleton session beans are instantiated once in the application and last for as long as the application is deployed. They are marked using the annotation @Singleton. Singleton session beans, or singletons for short, can be accessed by multiple clients concurrently, and can hold state in their instance variables for the lifetime of the application. This makes this type of Enterprise Bean good for modeling global properties of the application, for example, a group chat transcript, a record of all the bids on an item in an online auction, or a repository of all posted news articles in an aggregation site.

Message-Driven Beans

Message-driven beans are a type of Enterprise Bean that responds to Java Message Service (JMS) messages. They are marked using the @MessageDriven annotation, and receive messages through the javax.messaging.MessageListener interface with its single method

 `void onMessage(Message inMessage)`

where javax.messaging.Message represents the incoming message. This makes its interaction model fundamentally different from session beans. For session beans, clients call Java methods on the Enterprise Bean. For message-driven beans, clients push JMS messages into a JMS queue, which delivers them to the message-driven bean asynchronously.

Session beans are generally accessed through a remote interface (though, as we shall see, there are cases where a remote interface is not required), while message-driven beans have only a bean implementation class.

Message-driven beans are stateless, that is to say, clients of message beans may not rely on the same instance being used to process a message to be the same on subsequent messages. Message-driven beans are useful in applications where clients need to be able to initiate some action or task, but do not want to wait around for the task or action to complete.

Exposing Enterprise Beans

Let us look now at how Enterprise Beans expose their functions to the clients that wish to use them.

Java Methods

Generally speaking, there are two ways in which an Enterprise Bean implementation class may expose its Java methods: remotely or locally. Message-driven beans are the exception: they expose only their callable method remotely. All types of session beans, however, can expose remote or local views to their Java methods.

When an Enterprise Bean exposes its Java methods remotely, it can be accessed from application clients, from web components, and from other Enterprise Beans in the same or other applications. At the heart of this remote access model is the ability for the Enterprise Bean to reside on a different Java VM and a different computer altogether.

When an Enterprise Bean exposes its Java methods locally, it can be accessed from web components and other Enterprise Beans within the same Java EE application, a more limited scope, but one that comes with an important advantage.

The wide exposure granted to an Enterprise Bean's remote view comes at a price: when a client calls an Enterprise Bean through its remote methods, it does so using the remote protocol RMI/IIOP. This means that every Java object passed as a method parameter or return value has to be serialized in order to be transmitted over the wire. This incurs a performance penalty when compared with ordinary local Java method invocation. For this reason, some Enterprise Beans choose to expose a local view when they are sure their clients fall within the more limited scope of the same Java EE application because clients can call them more quickly.

So how does an Enterprise Bean expose a remote view and a local view?

Exposing a Remote View

An Enterprise Bean exposes a remote view by providing one or more remote interfaces. A remote interface is a regular Java interface that contains methods that the container is to expose to clients of the Enterprise Bean and that is marked with the `@Remote` annotation from the `javax.ejb` package. An Enterprise Bean implementation class provides the implementations for the methods exposed remotely on a remote interface. The Enterprise Bean implementation class declares its remote interfaces in one of two ways:

- By implementing the remote interface(s) directly
- By using the class-level annotation `@Remote` using the value attribute to list the remote interface classes it wishes to expose.

In the Hello example, we saw that the Hello Enterprise Bean exposes a remote interface called `HelloBean`,

```
@Remote
public interface HelloBean { ... }
```

while its implementation class exposes the `HelloBean` remote interface by implementing it directly:

```
@Stateful
public class HelloBeanImpl implements HelloBean {...}
```

However, the Hello Enterprise Bean implementation class could equivalently have declared its remote interface by using the `@Remote` annotation:

```
@Stateful
@Remote(HelloBean.class)
public class HelloBeanImpl {...}
```

Exposing a Local View

When an Enterprise Bean wishes to expose its methods through a local view, it has a couple of ways of doing this. The first and more formal way is for it to define a local interface, which is a regular Java interface that declares the methods of the bean's implementation class that it wishes to expose and that is marked with the `@Local` annotation. Then the bean's implementation class declares its local interface, or interfaces if it wishes to expose more than one local view, either by implementing the local interface or interfaces, or by using the `@Local` annotation, listing the local interface classes in the value attribute. This is analogous to the way the Enterprise Bean exposes its remote view. So, for example, if our Hello Enterprise Bean wishes to expose a local view, it might do this

```
@Local
public interface LocalHelloBean { ... }
```

and declare the local view like this

```
@Stateful
@Local(LocalHelloBean.class)
public class HelloBeanImpl {...}
```

or like this

```
@Stateful
public class HelloBeanImpl implements LocalHelloBean {...}
```

The second way to expose a local view on an Enterprise Bean is to add the `@LocalBean` annotation to the bean's implementation class. This gives the Enterprise Bean what is called a no-interface view, a type of local view that does not require the definition of a local interface. For example, here's how you would declare a no-interface view on our Hello Enterprise Bean:

```
@Stateful
@LocalBean
public class HelloBeanImpl {...}
```

This says that all the methods of the `HelloBeanImpl` class will be available to local clients. In fact, if the bean implementation class does not implement any other interfaces, you can omit the `@LocalBean` entirely.

```
@Stateful
public class HelloBeanImpl {...}
```

and this becomes the definition of an Enterprise Bean that exposes all the methods on `HelloBeanImpl` to local clients.

In general, it is better to be explicit about the views that your Enterprise Beans export, particularly if exposing both a local and a remote view. Calling methods on an Enterprise Bean locally and remotely have a subtly different semantic, and it is best to be clear about that by defining remote and local views.

Pass by Value and Pass by Reference

When a client calls methods on an Enterprise Bean, if it calls it as a local bean, the method invocation is a local one. This means that when objects are passed into the method call, they are passed by reference. In other words, if the bean's method implementation calls methods on the object passed in, it is calling methods on exactly the same object that the client passed to it. Changes that the bean makes to the object are observed by the client when the method completes. However, if the client is remote, the objects it passes to the bean's methods are first serialized, sent on the wire, deserialized, and then passed in. This means the objects that the bean methods process are copies of the ones sent by the client. So changes the bean makes to the object are not observed by the client. In other words, objects used in method invocations made by local clients are passed by reference, and objects used in method invocations made by remote clients are passed by value.

Web Services View

In addition to remote and local views of its Java methods, stateless session beans and singleton session beans may expose a web service view by turning one or more of the methods on its implementation as web service resources. To do so, the bean class must be marked with the `@WebService` annotation, and the methods to expose with the `@WebMethod` annotation. Here is a short example.

Listing: *Enterprise Bean with web service view*

```
import javax.jws.WebMethod;
import javax.jws.WebService;

@WebService
@Stateless
public class HelloServiceBean {

    public void HelloServiceBean() {}

    @WebMethod
    public String getMessageFor(String caller) {
        return "hello to you, " + caller + " !";
    }
}
```

We summarize the different types of views on Enterprise Beans in Figure 9-5.

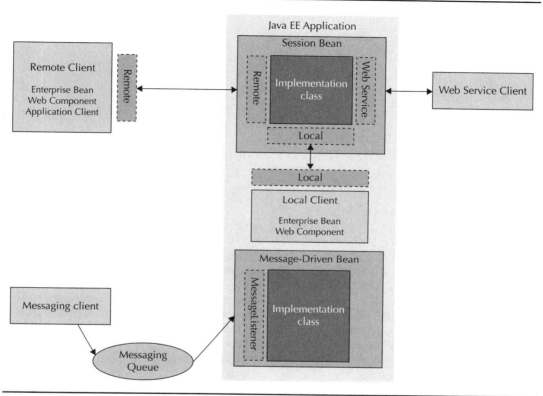

FIGURE 9-5. *The various views onto Enterprise Beans*

Finding Enterprise Beans

Now that we have seen how an Enterprise Bean can make its functions available for clients to use, we will look at how clients that wish to use these functions can locate the Enterprise Bean.

Finding Message-Driven Beans

Message-driven beans listen to the messages that are received by a JMS messaging queue; message-driven beans are not called by direct Java method invocation. The @MessageDriven bean annotation that you use to declare a Java class as a message-driven bean calls for you to include a JNDI name of a JMS messaging queue to connect to this bean. Supposing the messaging queue is available at the JNDI name `jms/myQueue`, then the following message-driven bean receives a callback each time a client of the JMS queue sends in a message.

 Listing: *Mapping a message-driven bean*

```
import javax.ejb.MessageDriven;
import javax.jms.Message;
```

```
@MessageDriven(mappedName = "jms/myQueue")
public class MyMessageDrivenBean {
    ...
    public void onMessage(Message incoming) {
      // process message
    }
...
}
```

Finding Session Beans

There are two ways to find a reference to a session bean. The first is by looking up the Enterprise Bean in the Java Naming and Directory Interface (JNDI) service that is part of the Java EE platform. The second method is to use dependency injection.

Enterprise Bean Lookup in JNDI

The JNDI service in the Java EE platform is a handy repository of interesting platform objects, which can also be used to store application objects. We will return to the topic of JNDI in a later chapter. For now, it is enough to understand that objects may be stored in JNDI under a unique name, which can be used later to look up and locate them.

Any Enterprise Bean you deploy in Java EE is given a name in the JNDI namespace where it can be looked up later by any other Java class running in the same Java EE environment. This lookup may occur in the same EJB module. It may occur in a different module in the same Java EE application, for example, if the client looking up the Enterprise Bean is in a web application or application client module within the same Java EE application. Additionally, the lookup may occur from a client located in an entirely different Java EE application.

All of the Enterprise Bean annotations have a name attribute that allows you to name the bean explicitly. For example, to name the `HelloBean` in the preceding example, we would use

```
@Stateful(name="hello-bean")
public class HelloBeanImpl implements HelloBean {
...
}
```

The most general form of the JNDI name of an Enterprise Bean is

```
java:global/app-name/module-name/ejb-name
```

where `app-name` is the name of the application containing the Enterprise Bean, `module-name` is the name of the module containing the Enterprise Bean, and `ejb-name` is the name of the Enterprise Bean. If an Enterprise Bean does not declare a name explicitly in its Enterprise Bean annotation, then the `ejb-name` in the JNDI lookup may be formed using the short classname of the bean implementation class and short remote interface classname.

```
ejb-name = <bean-implementation-class>!<remote-interface>
```

Therefore, to locate the `HelloBean` Enterprise Bean in the JNDI namespace from any other application, you could use either of the JNDI names

```
java:global/<hello-app-name>/<hello-ejb-module-name>/hello-bean
```

or

```
java:global/<hello-app-name>/<hello-ejb-module-name>/HelloBeanImpl!HelloBean
```

The lookup itself occurs programmatically using the JNDI APIs. For example, to look up the HelloBean, you could use

```
import javax.naming.InitialContext;
```

. . .

```
HelloBean hello = (HelloBean) InitialContext.doLookup("java:global/
                  <hello-app-name>/<hello-ejb-module-name>/hello-bean");
```

If the client of the Enterprise Bean resides in the same application, it can be accessed with the shortened JNDI name of

```
java:app/module-name/ejb-name
```

and if the client of the Enterprise Bean resides in the same module, it can be accessed with the shortened JNDI name of

```
java:module/ejb-name
```

We illustrate this naming scheme in Figure 9-6.

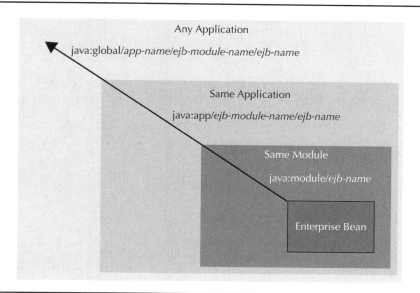

FIGURE 9-6. *Enterprise Beans in the JNDI namespace*

Enterprise Bean Injection

It is important to understand the global naming scheme for Enterprise Beans. However, the simplest way to locate an Enterprise Bean and use it from client code is to inject it using the @EJB annotation. As with many mechanisms in Enterprise Beans technology, there are several ways this can be done!

The first approach is simply to inject the Enterprise Bean by its remote classname. Looking back to our example:

Listing: *The HelloBean implementation class and remote interface*

```
@Remote
public interface HelloBean {
    public String getMessageFor(String caller);
}


@Stateful(name="hello-bean")
public class HelloBeanImpl implements HelloBean {

    @Override
    public String getMessageFor(String caller) {
        return "hello to you, " + caller + " !";
    }
}
```

We could inject a reference to this Enterprise Bean into an instance variable by using the remote classname:

```
import javax.ejb.EJB;
import javaeems.chapter9.hello.HelloBean;
...
@EJB
HelloBean hello;
```

or we could inject a reference to this Enterprise Bean into an instance variable by using the formal name of the Enterprise Bean:

```
import javaeems.chapter9.hello.HelloBean;
...
@EJB(name="hello-bean")
HelloBean hello;
```

or we could do an explicit JNDI lookup:

```
import javaeems.chapter9.hello.HelloBean;
...
@EJB(lookup=" java:global/<hello-app-name>/
                <hello-ejb-module-name>/hello-bean")
HelloBean hello;
```

Dependency injection of this type limits you to using the Enterprise Bean as an instance variable, and also can be used only when the Java class is a Java EE managed bean. We will return to the topic of Java EE managed beans in Chapter 13, but for now, we will just note that Enterprise Beans, Java servlets, JSF managed beans, application clients, JAX-RS resource classes, and Java WebSocket endpoints are all Java EE managed beans, and thus can use this mechanism. For an ordinary Java class, you need to use the JNDI API lookup described in the previous section.

EJB Lifecycle

One thing to notice about Enterprise Beans is that you never instantiate them yourself; the Enterprise Bean container manages the lifecycle and cardinality of Enterprise Beans. In this section, we look at the different lifecycles of the different kinds of Enterprise Bean.

Singleton and stateless session beans together with message-driven beans have the same lifecycle. There are two states: Out of Service and Active. When such beans are being brought into service, they start in the Out of Service state. At this point, all the Enterprise Bean container has is the class definitions of the Enterprise Beans. When the container needs to bring a bean into service, it invokes the constructor, injects any dependencies such as other Enterprise Bean references made using the `@EJB` annotation, prepares other container-level resources in support of the bean instance, and then brings the instance into the Active state. In this state, the bean instance can accept and service incoming calls from clients. When the container has no more need for the bean instance, it brings the instance out of service, cleans up any supporting resources, and releases the bean instance for garbage collection. This happens, for example, if the container is itself shutting down.

Stateless session beans and message-driven bean instances are required to exist only for the duration of a client call, and Enterprise Bean containers may bring them into service only as a client makes a call to them. Equally, Enterprise Bean containers may destroy such bean instances as soon as the client call is serviced. On the other hand, singleton session beans are created only once prior to any client calls being serviced, and then destroyed only once all the client calls have been completed, for example, when the container shuts down.

You may intercept all these state changes on your Enterprise Beans, from Out of Service to Active, and from Active to Out of Service. To do so, you implement a Java method that you wish to be called when the state change occurs and mark it with one of the Enterprise Bean state change annotations. In order for the container to call your Enterprise Bean when it is moving from the Out of Service to the Active state, you use the `@PostConstruct` annotation. Note that at this point, the bean instance has been constructed and any dependency injection has already occurred. For the container to call your Enterprise Bean when it is moved from the Active state to the Out of Service state, you use the `@PreDestroy` annotation.

Stateful session beans have a lifecycle that includes these same states, Out of Service and Active, and you can use `@PostConstruct` and `@PreDestroy` annotations to ask the container to call you when it transitions your Enterprise Beans between these states. Additionally, stateful session beans contains a third state: the Passive state. The Passive state is one in which the Enterprise Bean instance is taken out of service temporarily. The container will not pass any client calls to the Enterprise Bean while it is in this state. When a call comes in for a bean in the Passive state, the container brings it back into the Active state in order to respond to the call. The container may bring the same Stateful session bean instance in and out of the Passive state many times. The reason for this extra state in the case of Stateful session beans is as follows: for this kind of bean, the container must create a new instance for each and every client that uses it. This means that for such stateful session beans with large numbers of clients, the container needs to support correspondingly large numbers of instances. The Passive state allows the container to put beans that are not currently being called onto the back burner, thereby saving valuable computing resources. You may participate in this kind of optimization by intercepting the state transitions between Active and Passive, using the `@PrePassivate` and `@PostActivate` events to annotate methods so the container calls them during the transitions.

One final note on singleton beans: the Enterprise Bean container has a choice as to when to instantiate the single instance it uses of a singleton bean: it can do it at any time between the deployment of the application containing the singleton bean and the moment immediately prior to a client call needing a response. You can use the class-level `@Startup` annotation on a singleton bean to direct the container to instantiate the bean upon application deployment, rather than allow the container to leave it to the last minute. This, in combination with a method annotated with `@PostConstruct`, is a useful way to have the container run code for you right after the application is deployed and before any calls, whether they be to this singleton bean or to any others in the application that have been serviced.

We summarize the lifecycles of Enterprise Beans and the annotations that allow them to be called back at the key stages in Figure 9-7.

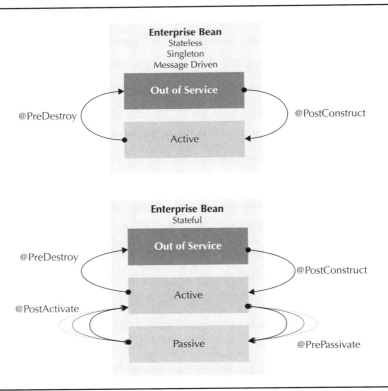

FIGURE 9-7. *Lifecycles of Enterprise Beans*

Packaging Enterprise Beans

Packaging of Enterprise Beans is similar to, though simpler than, the packaging of web components into WAR files. The packaging format for Enterprise Beans is the Enterprise Beans JAR file. This is a regular JAR file that contains all the Enterprise Bean classes and their supporting classes located at the root, together with the JAR's manifest file, and an optional Enterprise Bean deployment descriptor, located in a file called `ejb-jar.xml`, under the `META-INF` entry in the JAR file.

Like the web deployment descriptor, the Enterprise Bean deployment descriptor is often not needed: much of the information the container needs to know about the Enterprise Beans in the JAR file is contained within the annotations embedded within the code for the beans. In fact, as we shall see shortly, relatively complicated Enterprise Bean applications might have no need for the Enterprise Bean deployment descriptor. We return to this descriptor in the next chapter.

We illustrate the Enterprise Bean JAR format in Figure 9-8.

Enterprise Bean applications may also be packaged inside a WAR file. This can be convenient when the Enterprise Beans it contains are used by a web application only as it allows all the application logic to be located in the same file.

As you might expect, the Enterprise Bean JAR may simply be added to the `WEB-INF/lib` entry in the WAR file, or the Enterprise Bean classes added to the `WEB-INF/classes` directory, and the `ejb-jar.xml` deployment descriptor, if used, added to the `WEB-INF` directory.

We have learned much about Enterprise Beans, and now it is time to put what we have learned into practice.

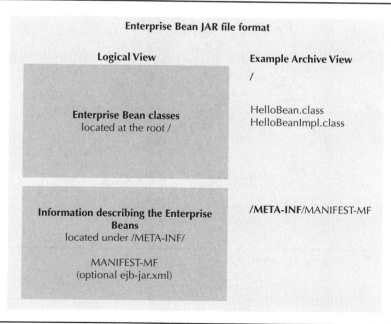

FIGURE 9-8. *The Enterprise Bean JAR file format*

Banking Example

The Banking Example application comes in two pieces. The customer-facing piece is a Java EE application, containing a web application and Enterprise Beans that power an online banking website. You can use the website to check your balance (as shown in Figure 9-9), make a payment by entering the amount (shown in Figure 9-10), confirm the payment (shown in Figure 9-11), submit the payment (shown in Figure 9-12), and see the new account balance after the payment has been made (shown in Figure 9-13).

There is a second application, the Banking Backoffice application. As clients make payments through the website, this application displays confirmation of each payment as it comes in, as you can see in Figure 9-14. Let's take a look at the applications in Figure 9-15.

We can see that the Bank Account application is made up of a web application containing three JavaServer Faces pages. These are using a JSF managed bean called the AccountBean, which is in turn making calls to the Checking bean and the BillPay bean. We won't spend any time looking at the JavaServer Faces code, but we will look at the AccountBean code as this is where the first Enterprise Bean calls are made.

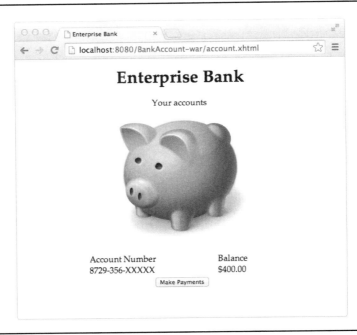

FIGURE 9-9. *Banking Application home page*

FIGURE 9-10. *Making a payment*

FIGURE 9-11. *Confirm payment*

FIGURE 9-12. Payment confirmed

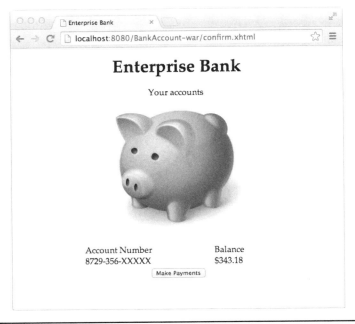

FIGURE 9-13. Banking Application, new account balance

Backoffice at Sun May 04 22:26:08 PDT 2014

```
8729-356-XXXXX:energy paid 15.0 [1399267424933]
8729-356-XXXXX:cable paid 76.87 [1399267496566]
8729-356-XXXXX:water paid 35.91 [1399267512550]
```

FIGURE 9-14. *Banking Backoffice status window*

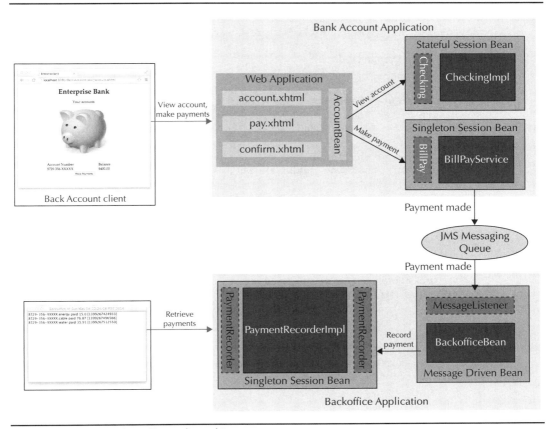

FIGURE 9-15. *Banking Example architecture*

Listing: *The AccountBean JavaServer Faces managed bean*

```java
import javax.faces.bean.ManagedBean;
import javax.faces.bean.SessionScoped;
import javax.faces.FacesException;
import javax.ejb.EJB;
import javaeems.chapter9.bank.Checking;
import javaeems.chapter9.bank.BillPay;
import javaeems.chapter9.bank.PaymentException;
import java.util.*;

@ManagedBean
@SessionScoped
public class AccountBean {
    @EJB
    private Checking checking;
    @EJB
    private BillPay billPay;

    private String currentPayee;
    private double amount = 15;
    private boolean paymentOK = false;
    private String paymentConfirmation = null;

    public AccountBean() {
    }

    public String getCheckingAccountNumber() {
        return this.checking.getAccountNumber();
    }

    public double getCheckingBalance() {
        return this.checking.getBalance();
    }

    public List<String> getPayees() {
        return this.billPay.getPayees();
    }

    public String getCurrentPayee() {
        if (this.currentPayee == null) {
            this.currentPayee = this.billPay.getPayees().get(0);
        }
        return this.currentPayee;
    }

    public void setCurrentPayee(String payee) {
        this.currentPayee = payee;
    }
```

```
public double getAmount() {
    return this.amount;
}

public void setAmount(double amount) {
    this.amount = amount;
}

public void reset() {
    this.paymentOK = false;
    this.paymentConfirmation = null;
}

public String getPaymentConfirmation() {
    return this.paymentConfirmation;
}

public boolean getPaymentOK() {
    return this.paymentOK;
}

public void makePayment() {
    try {
        this.checking.doDeduct(this.amount);
        String confirmation = this.billPay.doPay(
                    this.checking.getAccountNumber(),
                    currentPayee,
                    this.amount);
        this.paymentOK = true;
        this.paymentConfirmation = confirmation;
        this.amount = 15;
        this.currentPayee = null;
    } catch (PaymentException pe) {
        throw new FacesException(pe.getMessage());
    }
}
```

}

Note first that the AccountBean locates the Checking and BillPay beans by asking the Java EE container to inject them into its instance variables by means of the @EJB annotation. The lookup is occurring by virtue of the remote interfaces that are specified as the type of instance variables to be filled out by injection. Notice also that the AccountBean is session scoped, meaning that each client of the JavaServer Faces pages using this AccountBean sees its own instance of the AccountBean. The AccountBean uses the Checking Enterprise Bean to obtain the account number and current balance of the account for this client, and to deduct money from the account as a bill is being paid. It uses the BillPay Enterprise Bean to list out all the potential bill payees and to make the call to make a payment in a specific amount to a specific payee.

So now let us turn our attention to the Enterprise Beans, first the Checking bean.

Listing: *The Checking bean implementation class*

```java
import javax.ejb.Stateful;
import javax.annotation.PostConstruct;


@Stateful
public class CheckingImpl implements Checking {
    private double balance;
    private String accountNumber;

    @PostConstruct
    private void init() {
        this.balance = 400;
        this.accountNumber = "8729-356-XXXXX";
    }

    @Override
    public double getBalance() {
        return this.balance;
    }

    @Override
    public String getAccountNumber() {
        return this.accountNumber;
    }

    @Override
    public void doDeduct(double amount) throws PaymentException {
        if (amount > this.balance) {
            throw new PaymentException("Not enough cash in the account
                                        to deduct " + amount);
        } else {
            balance = balance - amount;
        }
    }

}
```

Notice that the `Checking` bean is a stateful session bean. This means that the Enterprise Bean container creates a new instance for each client of the bean. In this application, since the only client of this bean is the `AccountBean` in the web application, and since there is one `AccountBean` instance per web client, it means that each web client has one and only one `Checking` bean associated with it. This is what we want, because this bean represents a user's own bank account. Notice also that the `Checking` bean implements the calls of its remote interface `Checking` as used by the `AccountBean` for returning the current balance, account number, and deducting money from the account. The `Checking` bean also takes advantage of the `@PostConstruct` annotation to initialize its account information. In a more complete application, this method would likely connect to a database to retrieve this information, using the identity of the caller to find the correct account information.

Listing: *The BillPay bean implementation class*

```java
import javax.ejb.Singleton;
import java.util.*;
import javax.annotation.Resource;
import javax.jms.Connection;
import javax.jms.ConnectionFactory;
import javax.jms.JMSException;
import javax.jms.MessageProducer;
import javax.jms.Session;
import javax.jms.TextMessage;

@Singleton
public class BillPayService implements BillPay {
    @Resource(mappedName = "jms/myConnectionFactory")
    private ConnectionFactory connectionFactory;
    @Resource(mappedName = "jms/myQueue")
    private javax.jms.Queue queue;

    @Override
    public List<String> getPayees() {
        List<String> l = new ArrayList<>();
        l.add("energy");
        l.add("water");
        l.add("mortgage");
        l.add("cable");
        return l;
    }

    @Override
    public String doPay(String accountNumber, String payee, double amount)
                                            throws PaymentException {
        // process the payment in the credit system
        String confirmation = new Long(System.currentTimeMillis()).toString();
        this.updateBackofficeRecords(accountNumber, payee,
                            amount, confirmation, new Date());
        return confirmation;
    }


    private void updateBackofficeRecords(String accountNumber, String payee,
double amount, String confirmation, Date d) {
        try (Connection connection = connectionFactory.createConnection()){
            Session session = connection.createSession(false,
                                        Session.AUTO_ACKNOWLEDGE);
            MessageProducer messageProducer = session.createProducer(queue);
            TextMessage message = session.createTextMessage();
            message.setText(accountNumber + ":" + payee + " paid " + amount +
                                        " ["+confirmation+"]");
```

```
                messageProducer.send(message);

        } catch (JMSException e) {
            System.out.println("Exception occurred: " + e.toString());
        }


    }
}
```

The `BillPay` bean is a singleton session bean, meaning that there is only one instance of this bean per application. Therefore, the instance of this bean in the application processes all payments from all accounts.

Aside from returning the current list of payees, this bean sends a JMS message notification to the JMS queue located at `jms/myQueue` using a connection obtained from the JMS `ConnectionFactory` located at the JNDI address `jms/myConnectionFactory`. In order for these operations to succeed, the Java EE server must be configured with these objects registered in the JNDI namespace at those addresses. The way to set up this JMS environment depends on which Java EE server you are using. Please refer to the introduction for more information on how to set up the JMS environment in the GlassFish server. The message that the BillPay bean sends to the JMS queue contains a confirmation of the payment made, from which account, to which payee, and the amount.

Where does this message go?

In order to answer this question, we must now look at the Backoffice application. This application contains two Enterprise Beans, as we saw in Figure 9-15. One is a message-driven bean; let's take a look.

Listing: *The Backoffice bean implementation class*

```java
import javax.ejb.MessageDriven;
import javax.jms.Message;
import javax.jms.TextMessage;
import javax.jms.JMSException;
import javax.ejb.EJB;

@MessageDriven(mappedName = "jms/myQueue")
public class BackofficeBean {
    @EJB(lookup="java:module/payment-recorder")
    private PaymentRecorder recorder;

    public BackofficeBean() {
    }

    public void onMessage(Message incoming) {
        try {
            if (incoming instanceof TextMessage) {
                TextMessage message = (TextMessage) incoming;
                this.recorder.recordPayment(message.getText());
            } else {
                System.out.println("Unexpected message type: " +
```

```
                                         incoming.getClass().getName());
                }
        } catch (JMSException jmse) {
            System.out.println("Exception recording incoming message: "
                                        + jmse.getMessage());
        }

    }
}
```

This message bean's mapped name is `jms/myQueue`, the same JNDI name as the JNDI name used by the `BillPay` bean to look up the queue into which it sends its messages. So this message-driven bean receives a callback into its `onMessage()` method every time anyone sends a JMS message to that queue. In other words, this bean receives all the payment confirmations from the Bank Account application.

When it gets this kind of message, we can see that it invokes the other Enterprise Bean in the application, the `PaymentRecorder` bean, passing it the payment confirmation. It locates this bean by using the lookup variant of the `@EJB` annotation and using the module-wide name `java:module/payment-recorder`.

Now we look at the code for the `PaymentRecorder` bean.

Listing: *The `PaymentRecorder` bean implementation class*

```
import javax.ejb.Singleton;
import java.util.List;
import java.util.ArrayList;


@Singleton(name="payment-recorder")
public class PaymentRecorderImpl implements PaymentRecorder {
    List<String> payments = new ArrayList<>();

    @Override
    public void recordPayment(String payment) {
        this.payments.add(payment);
    }

    @Override
    public List<String> getPayments() {
        return this.payments;
    }
}
```

We can see that it is a singleton session bean, which is appropriate as it records confirmations for all accounts managed by this Bank application, and that it declares a formal Enterprise Bean name, payment-recorder, tallying with the JNDI name used by the `BackofficeBean` to locate it. In addition to exposing the method that receives the confirmation, it exposes a method that lists all the confirmations it has received. This brings us to the last part of the Backoffice application, and the last part of the overall example: the Java EE application client that calls the `PaymentRecorder` bean.

Listing: *The application client for the `PaymentRecorder` bean*

```
import javax.swing.*;
import javaeems.chapter9.backoffice.PaymentRecorder;
import java.util.*;
import javax.naming.InitialContext;
import javax.naming.NamingException;

public class Main extends JFrame {
    JTextArea jta = new JTextArea();
    PaymentRecorder recorder;


    public Main() {
        try {
            recorder = (PaymentRecorder) InitialContext
                    .doLookup("java:app/BankBackoffice-ejb/payment-recorder");
        } catch (NamingException ne) {
            System.out.println("Could not connect to payment
                        recorder bean, exiting. " + ne.getMessage());
            return;
        }
        JScrollPane jsp = new JScrollPane(jta);
        this.getContentPane().add(jsp);
        Thread t = new Thread() {
            @Override
            public void run() {
                while (true) {
                    List<String> l = recorder.getPayments();
                    updateUI(l);
                    setTitle("Backoffice at " + new Date());
                    try {sleep(5000);} catch (InterruptedException r) {}

                }
            }

        };
        t.start();
    }

    public static void main(String[] args) {
        Main m = new Main();
        m.setBounds(20,20, 450, 300);
        m.setVisible(true);
        m.setDefaultCloseOperation(JFrame.EXIT_ON_CLOSE);
    }
```

```
void updateUI(List<String> l) {
    this.jta.setText("");
    for (String next : l) {
        jta.append(next + "\n");
    }
}
```

}

This simple swing application uses the JNDI API method for locating the `PaymentRecorder` bean in the JNDI namespace, looking it up from the `InitialContext` class. Once it has done so, it polls the Enterprise Bean and displays all its confirmations.

In this application, we have exercised many of the features we have explored so far in Enterprise Bean technology. One question that may have come up in your mind as you looked at this application is: what happens if something goes wrong during the bill payment process? Is it possible for money to be deducted from a bank account successfully, but for the bill payment not to complete?

The answer is, yes. This example needs some more work to ensure the integrity of the bill payment process in the face of error. In the next chapter, we will see how to correct this kind of situation by using one of the many features of Enterprise Beans we have not yet explored: their transactional capabilities.

Summary

In this chapter we introduced Enterprise Beans, the middleware component model of the Java EE platform. We explored some of the common services supplied to Enterprise Bean components by the Java EE server, such as lifecycle management, security, and transactions. We looked at the different types of Enterprise Beans and how to declare them and package them in an application. We examined the different ways Enterprise Beans can be located and called from clients within the same application and also from different applications. We looked at the lifecycle and cardinality of Enterprise Beans and how to intercept state transitions during the lifetime of a bean. We finished the chapter with an exploration of a multi–Enterprise Bean banking application that used a variety of Enterprise Bean types and lookup methods by application clients, web components, and other Enterprise Beans.

CHAPTER
10

Advanced Thinking
with Enterprise Beans

The goal of the Enterprise Bean container is to allow Enterprise Beans to do what they are best at: thinking.

Everyone knows that in order to think best, it's best to have peace and quiet. You need to be relieved temporarily of the details of everyday life that interrupt the thought process. So it is with Enterprise Beans: the Enterprise Bean container manages several aspects of programming a server-side component that clears a path for the bean to focus on its intended application logic. Let's look again at Figure 10-1, which we first saw in Chapter 9.

We have already covered in some detail the lifecycle of the various kinds of Enterprise Beans, and we will thoroughly explore security with Enterprise Beans in Chapter 15. In this chapter, we look at the topics of asynchronous programming, transactions, and concurrency in Enterprise Beans, while also covering topics such as timers and interceptors.

Multi-threading and Enterprise Beans

Session and message-driven bean instances are single threaded: that is to say that for each instance of any Enterprise Bean of this type, the Enterprise Bean container ensures that only one thread is calling the Enterprise Bean at any one time. There is one case where the developer can override this behavior, as we shall see next later, but without special work on the developer's part,

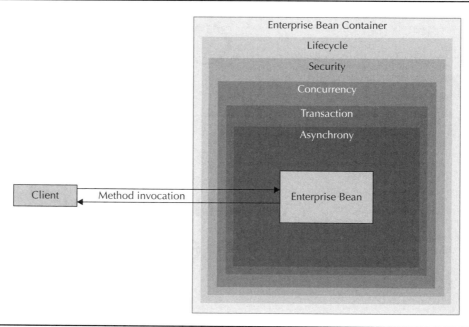

FIGURE 10-1. *The services of the Enterprise Bean container*

this single-threaded behavior is the case. From the client's perspective, however, the Enterprise Bean appears to be multi-threaded. Multiple clients of an Enterprise Bean may call it simultaneously; the same client of an Enterprise Bean may spawn multiple threads to call it and start them all at the same time. What is happening in this case is that the Enterprise Bean container is the first to receive the client requests. It is in charge of how to pass the request to the correct bean instance, and if multiple requests are destined for the same bean instance, it will deliver them one at a time, as shown in Figure 10-2.

There's a big benefit of this approach and also a drawback. The benefit of this approach is for the developer. Enterprise Beans do not need to be coded defensively against simultaneous access by more than one thread; no race conditions to worry about, for example. The drawback is that there is a performance price to be paid. If an Enterprise Bean receives 10,000 simultaneous requests (for example, it is handling online votes in a TV talent show contest), then either the container has to form a queue of all the requests, or it has to instantiate enough separate instances of the Enterprise Bean so that there is one instance to handle each request, or some combination of the two approaches. Either approach, or hybrid of the two, has a computation cost. The type of the Enterprise Bean matters in how the container chooses its approach: for example, for stateless session beans, it is free to instantiate as many instances as it judges suitable to handle the requests, but for singleton session beans, since the rule is that there can only be one instance of the singleton bean in the application, the container has no choice but to form a queue of requests and deliver them one at a time to the single instance. Anyone who has been on a multilane freeway that suddenly narrows to a single lane can appreciate the performance penalty.

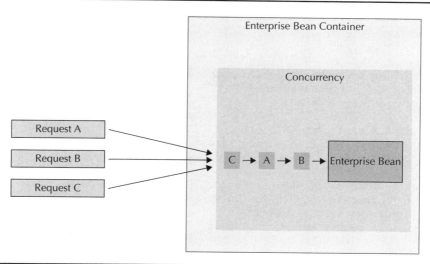

FIGURE 10-2. *Delivering requests one at a time*

Multi-threading and Singleton Beans

In the case of the singleton session bean, however, the developer, with some extra work, can override this threading restriction. This is achieved by opening up the bean to concurrent threads, either on a per-method basis or to all of the methods on the bean at once.

The class-level annotation `@javax.ejb.ConcurrencyManagement` controls the overall concurrency scheme for a singleton bean. Its value attribute is either `ConcurrencyManagementType.CONTAINER` or `ConcurrencyManagementType.BEAN`.

The annotation `@ConcurrencyManagement(ConcurrencyManagementType.CONTAINER)` indicates that the Enterprise Bean container manages concurrent client requests for the bean, passing them one at a time to it. This is the same as the default behavior if the annotation is not included. The annotation `@ConcurrencyManagement(ConcurrencyManagementType.BEAN)` indicates that the container is to pass concurrent requests to the bean instance, and it is up to the bean itself to synchronize its own data.

When a singleton bean uses container-managed concurrency, it may declare how concurrent access is managed on a method-level basis. The method-level `@javax.ejb.Lock` governs this behavior. A method of a singleton using container-managed concurrency annotated with `@Lock(LockType.READ)` may be called while other threads are calling the bean, while a method of a singleton bean using container-managed concurrency that is marked with `@Lock(LockType.WRITE)` can be called by a thread only when there are no other active threads calling the bean. Finally, the `@Lock` annotation can be used at the class level to provide the desired level of concurrency methods to all methods that are not already marked with the `@Lock` annotation.

Let's look at an example.

Listing: *A non-concurrent singleton bean*

```
import javax.ejb.Singleton;

@Singleton
public class VotingBeanSingleThreaded {
    private String contestant;
    private long voterId;

    public String getLastVote() {
        return "Voter: " + voterId + " vote for " + contestant;
    }

    public void doVote(long voterId, String contestant) {
        // process vote in voting system
        this.voterId = voterId;
        this.contestant = contestant;
    }
}
```

In this example, the singleton bean is responsible for both accepting and processing votes coming in from viewers for contestants in a TV talent show. The bean can also report who the last voter was and which contestant he or she voted for.

In a talent show with hundreds of thousands of votes, you would expect there to be many concurrent requests to vote. Assuming there are as many viewers accessing the show's website as the votes flood in, you might also expect as many, if not more, requests for the last vote report. Now, as written, the VotingBeanSingleThreaded bean can respond only to one request at a time, whether it is to vote or to get a vote report. We would not want two people to vote at the same time, since the recording data in the bean might be corrupted. But it would be okay, and in fact desirable, if the bean could serve multiple requests for the vote report at the same time. In terms of the method calls, we would prefer that all requests wait while a thread is in the doVote() method, but that if no one was calling doVote(), requests to getLastVote() could be served concurrently. In the next listing, you will see that we have used the @ConcurrencyManagement and @Lock annotations to do just that.

Listing: *A partially concurrent singleton bean*

```
import javax.ejb.Singleton;
import javax.ejb.ConcurrencyManagement;
import javax.ejb.ConcurrencyManagementType;
import javax.ejb.Lock;
import javax.ejb.LockType;

@Singleton
@ConcurrencyManagement(ConcurrencyManagementType.CONTAINER)
public class VotingBeanConcurrentReadAccess {
    private String contestant;
    private long voterId;

    @Lock(LockType.READ)
    public String getLastVote() {
        return "Voter: " + voterId + " vote for " + contestant;
    }

    @Lock(LockType.WRITE)
    public void doVote(long voterId, String contestant) {
        // process vote in voting system
        this.voterId = voterId;
        this.contestant = contestant;
    }
}
```

Threading Restrictions

Aside from this type of more specialized case, the typical case of the Enterprise Bean not having to concern itself with concurrent access to its methods comes with another larger benefit, though one that can be less tangible during development. By handing over responsibility for thread management to the Enterprise Bean container, the container is free to apply all sorts of hard-earned lessons in order to balance the load on an Enterprise Bean application (in other words, the number and frequency of client requests) with the computing resources it has at hand. This means that Enterprise Bean containers are taking on some of the burden of optimizing application performance. But this benefit also comes with a tradeoff: if the Enterprise Bean container is to manage the threads used to invoke its Enterprise Beans, it has to manage *all* the threads in the application. This means that Enterprise Beans are restricted from creating, stopping, and suspending threads, and from altering thread priorities of container threads. Some applications find this restriction too onerous and the type of optimizations that Enterprise Bean containers perform not specific enough to their needs. We will return to the topic of concurrent processing in the Java EE platform in Chapter 16.

Asynchronous Enterprise Beans

Enterprise Beans model a wide variety of programming tasks. Some of those tasks are long lived, such as analysis of large amounts of data, or may take periods of time that are difficult to determine at the time of calling, such as operations that depend on some external service whose response time is unpredictable. When the initiators of such tasks kick them off, it can often be useful if they are not required to wait on the response coming: they might have better things to do with their resources while they await the result, or they may wish to cancel the task if the task ends up taking longer than they thought it would at the start. For such cases, Enterprise Beans support an asynchronous invocation model. Let's take a closer look at how it works.

Suppose we have an Enterprise Bean that analyzes examination results for a school district. Such analyses are potentially slow since the datasets will be large.

Listing: *A synchronous SlowBean*

```
@Stateful
public class SlowBean {
    public String getAverageExamScore(String criteria) {
        String score;
        // unpredictably long operation calculating the score
        return score;
    }

}
```

A client of the `SlowBean` makes a regular invocation, such as

```
String score = slowBean.getAverageExamScore("11<age<13&F&county");
```

But rather than wait while the calculation is performed, the client would rather be getting on with something else. We can therefore rewrite the `SlowBean` a little, adding the `@javax.ejb.Asynchronous` annotation to the method, changing its return type to `java.util.concurrent.Future`, and using the `javax.ejb.AsyncResult` class to model the return value of the calculation.

Listing: *An asynchronous SlowBean*

```
@Stateful
public class SlowBeanAsync {

    @Asynchronous
    public Future<String> getAverageExamScore(String criteria) {
        String score;
        // unpredictably long operation calculating the score
```

```
        return new AsyncResult<String>(score);
    }
}
```

When this method is called, it immediately returns the `Future` object while the calculation starts as shown here:

```
Future<String> futureScore =
            slowBeanAsync.getAverageExamScore("11<age<13&F&county");
```

The client can test the `Future` object to see whether the method is complete:

```
boolean calculationComplete = futureScore.isDone();
```

The client can cancel the operation if it is taking too long:

```
if (impatient) {
    futureScore.cancel(true);
}
```

or await the result:

```
String score = futureScore.get();
```

The `@Asynchronous` annotation can be applied to synchronous Enterprise Bean methods with a `void` return value, but the new return value is also `void`, so the client has no way to track the completion of the method.

If an exception is raised during the execution of the asynchronous method with a return value, then the result of the `get()` call on the Future object that the client receives upon invoking the asynchronous method is a `java.util.ExecutionException` whose cause, obtainable by calling `getCause()`, is the exception generated in the method.

Let's walk through a less generic example.

The Async Example

When you run the Async example, you are using a Java EE application client, wrapped in a Java Swing window, to connect to an asynchronous method on an Enterprise Bean running on the server that is making a calculation. The calculation is to calculate the largest prime number less than a given upper bound. When you start the application, you see a window as shown in Figure 10-3.

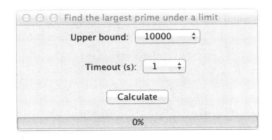

FIGURE 10-3. *Async example on startup*

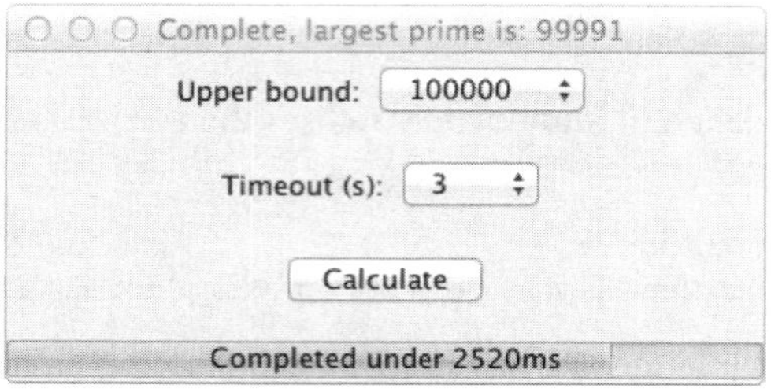

FIGURE 10-4. *Async example, calculating a large prime*

If you choose a smaller upper bound and a generous timeout, when you press the Calculate button you should see something like Figure 10-4.

However, if you increase the upper bound and do not give a large enough timeout, you will see something like Figure 10-5.

In this case, instead of getting a result from the asynchronous method call, the client window has timed out and stopped waiting for the result to arrive.

In the Async example there is a stateless session bean called `PrimeCalculator` that is able to calculate the largest prime number under a given maximum bound. Let's take a look at the code.

Listing: *Calculating primes*

```
import javax.ejb.AsyncResult;
import javax.ejb.SessionContext;
import javax.ejb.Stateless;
import javax.ejb.Asynchronous;
import javax.annotation.Resource;
import java.util.concurrent.Future;

@Stateless
public class PrimeCalculator implements PrimeCalculatorRemote {
    @Resource
    SessionContext context;
```

FIGURE 10-5. *Async example, timed out, calculation canceled*

```
@Asynchronous
public Future<Long> calculateMaxPrimeBelow(long upperLimit) {
    Long current = null;

    for (long candidate = 2; candidate < upperLimit+1; candidate++) {
        if (isPrime(candidate)) {
            current = candidate;
        }
        if (context.wasCancelCalled()) {
            System.out.println("Cancel was called....");
            break;
        };
    }
    return new AsyncResult<>(current);
}

private boolean isPrime(long l) {
    for (long i = 2; i <= (long) l/2; i++) {
        if ((l % i) == 0) {
            return false;
        }
    }
    return true;
}

}
```

Don't worry that the algorithm it uses to determine whether a number is prime is not at all: the point of this example is to be slow!

The main method of interest here is the method `calculateMaxPrimeBelow()`. It takes the upper bound as a method parameter and returns a `Future<Long>` that will hold the largest prime number less than the upper bound provided, if all goes well. When the calculation completes, the method returns an instance of the `AsyncResult` class, containing the prime number. Notice that this result is returned only after the calculation has completed. Notice also the injection of an object of type `SessionContext` using the `@Resource` annotation. The `SessionContext` is an object representing various information that the Enterprise Bean container keeps current while this session bean is active. When the `calculateMaxPrimeBelow()` method calls the `context.wasCancelCalled()` method, it is querying whether the client of the call has cancelled the asynchronous method invocation.

We will not look at all of the client code, but the client initiates the calculation by the call

```
Future<Long> calculationFuture = calculatorBean.calculateMaxPrimeBelow((long) max);
```

and creates a thread that loops on the test

```
while (!calculationFuture.isDone()) {..}
```

to test whether the calculation is complete. If the time exceeds the timeout, the client code calls

```
calculationFuture.cancel(true);
```

which can be picked up in the `PrimeCalculator` bean in its call to `context.wasCancelCalled()`.

If the timeout is not exceeded, then the prime number is returned from the `get()` on the `Future` object:

```
Long prime = calculationFuture.get();
```

In this way, the client window does not have to hang while the calculation is made.

Enterprise Bean Contexts

In the middle of the last example, we discovered that session beans have access to some useful information that the Enterprise Bean container keeps while the session bean is active. This is a good point to look more closely at the `SessionContext` and at the contextual information available to other kinds of beans.

Session beans have access to an instance of the `javax.ejb.SessionContext` that the container associates with it, while message-driven beans have access to an instance of the `javax.ejb.MessageDrivenContext` that the container associates with it. Both contexts inherit from `javax.ejb.EJBContext`. This interface contains a variety of useful methods concerning security, to look up objects in the JNDI namespace, for example. Here is a selection of the more commonly used ones:

EJBContext Method	Purpose
`Principal getCallerPrincipal()` and `boolean isCallerInRole(String rolename)`	Obtain the identity of the caller associated with the calling thread, and test whether the caller belongs to the given role.
`Object lookup(String jndiName)`	Look up an object (for example, another Enterprise Bean) in the JNDI namespace.
`TimerService getTimerService()`	Obtain a reference to the timer service associated with the context for registering scheduled callbacks.
`UserTransaction getUserTransaction()`	If the calling thread is associated with a bean-created transaction, return it.

We will soon be covering the timer service and the topic of transactions. The `MessageDrivenContext` in fact adds no new methods to what is provided in this common super interface, but the `SessionContext` adds several methods, two of which we highlight here.

SessionContext Method	Purpose
`Class getInvokedBusinessInterface()`	Obtain the remote or no-interface type through which the caller accessed the bean.
`boolean wasCancelCalled()`	Determine for asynchronous calls whether the client cancelled the operation before it completed.

The relevant context object is injected into an instance variable of the bean, for example, as we saw in the Async example.

Listing: *Accessing the* `SessionContext`

```
import javax.annotation.Resource;

public class PrimeCalculator implements PrimeCalculatorRemote {
    @Resource
    SessionContext context;
...
}
```

and equally for a message-driven bean:

Listing: *Accessing the* `MessageDrivenContext`

```
import javax.annotation.Resource;

@MessageDriven(mappedName = "jms/myQueue")
public class NotifyBean {
    @Resource
    MessageDrivenContext context;
...
}
```

The Timer Service

So far, all the examples and scenarios we have discussed concerning Enterprise Beans have been based on the idea that there is always a calling client outside the Java EE application that causes activity (such as a method call) to an Enterprise Bean. Whether it has been a user action conveyed through an application client, through a web component calling, or in reaction to a JMS message, the Enterprise Beans have had work to do only in reaction to some external event. Enterprise Beans can also have another client: the Enterprise Bean Timer Service can invoke them automatically according to some preset schedule.

The Timer Service has a variety of uses in applications that need some kind of periodic heartbeat activity or task. Such tasks include periodic backup of data, regular notifications or reporting of the current state in an application, and background cleanup of old application data at preset intervals. All such tasks can be scheduled by the Enterprise Bean container according to a timetable set by the application.

The basic mechanism of the Timer Service comprises the following pieces:

- A *Timer object* created according to the schedule the application needs
- The *timeout event* of the Timer object expiring as it follows the stipulations of its schedule
- The timeout method of the Enterprise Bean that the container calls when the timer generates a timeout event

We can illustrate this general mechanism in Figure 10-6.

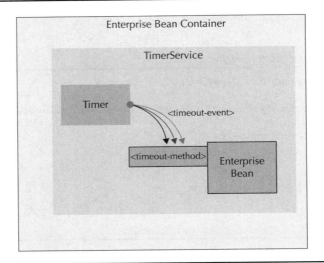

FIGURE 10-6. *The Timer Service*

The Timer Service can be used in conjunction with any type of session or message-driven bean. Timer objects may be created with a variety of schedules, from simple one-time expiry timers, to timers that expire at regular intervals, or according to calendar-specified times. There are two ways in which timers may be associated with a timeout method: programmatically and using an annotation.

In the programmatic approach, a `Timer` object is created using one of the methods on the `javax.ejb.TimerService` obtained from the EJBContext associated with the bean. For example, this snippet of code

```
TimerService timerService = ejbContext.getTimerService();
Timer myTimer = timerService.createSingleActionTimer(60 * 1000,
                              new TimerConfig("just a minute", false));
```

creates and starts a `Timer` object that will create one timeout event after one minute.

When the `Timer` object creates a timeout event, the Timer Service looks for a method on the bean that is annotated with `@javax.ejb.Timeout`. Such timeout methods must have a void return value and either no arguments or a single method parameter of type `javax.ejb.Timer`.

```
@Timeout
    private void closeAuction(Timer t) {
        // close the auction to bids, the time has come.
    }
```

Using the annotation approach, the creation of the `Timer` object and the assignment of the timeout method are both achieved by annotating a suitable timeout callback method (subject to the same restrictions as described in the programmatic approach) with the `@Schedule` annotation. Under this approach, the Timer object used by the container is created and started as soon as the Enterprise Bean is deployed. The `@Schedule` annotation contains a number of attributes, which we will look at shortly, that allow you to define the timetable under which you wish the associated `Timer` object to create expiry events. For example, the snippet

```
@Schedule(dayOfWeek = "*")
public void backupCustomerData() {
      // make the daily backup of the customer's data
}
```

causes this method to be called every day at the turn of midnight. Finally, timeout callback methods may be assigned more than one Timer object by annotating it with the composite `@Schedules` annotation, which may contain one or more `@Schedule` annotations, each of which creates a `Timer` object.

The Language of Schedules

The `@Schedule` annotation's many time attributes allow for a wide range of values to be given for a schedule. In the next table, we summarize all the allowable values that may be used in the annotation.

@Schedule Attribute	Allowable Values
second	0,1,...,59 *, meaning every second
minute	0,1,...,59 *, meaning every minute
Hour	0,1,...,23 *, meaning every hour
dayOfMonth	1,2,...,31 -1, -2, ..., -31 (counted back) "Last" (last day of month) {"1st", "2nd", "3rd", "4th", "5th", "Last"} {"Sun", "Mon", "Tue", "Wed", "Thu", "Fri", "Sat"} *, meaning every day
Month	[1,12] {"Jan", "Feb", "Mar", "Apr", "May", "Jun", "Jul", "Aug", "Sep", "Oct", "Nov", Dec"} *, meaning every month
dayOfWeek	0,1,...,7, where 0 and 7 are Sunday. {"Sun", "Mon", "Tue", "Wed", "Thu", "Fri", "Sat"} *, meaning every day
Year	NNNN *, meaning every year
timezone	Zone Name(TZ), defaults to time zone of server
Info	String used to identify the schedule
persistent	True (default) or false, depending on whether you want the timer to survive Java EE server crashes and restarts

The values for the time-relative attributes, such as hour and month, may be used as single values. For example

```
@Schedule(hour="2")
```

means "every day at 2 a.m.," and

```
@Schedule(dayOfWeek="5", hour="17")
```

means "every Friday at 5 p.m."
Alternatively, they may be used in a list, separated by comments, such as

```
@Schedule(dayOfWeek="Mon,Wed,Fri", hour="9")
```

meaning "every Monday, Wednesday, and Friday at 9 a.m."
They may also be used in a range of values, with the minimum and maximum values separated by -, for example

```
@Schedule(dayOfMonth="1-7")
```

which means "every day for the first seven days of the month."
Finally, the values for the time-relative attributes may be used in increment expressions, using / to denote a range and an interval. For example

```
@Schedule(minute="*/5")
```

which means "every five minutes," or

```
@Schedule(dayOfMonth="10/2")
```

which means "every other day from the 10th of the month to the end of the month."
Under the programmatic approach, the `Timer` object can be created using the `TimerService` call

```
Timer createCalendarTimer(ScheduleExpression schedule)
```

where the `ScheduleExpression` object can be created from the same attributes used in the `@Schedule` annotation.
For example,

```
new ScheduleExpression()
        .dayOfWeek("Mon,Wed,Fri")
        .hour(9);
```

And if you are reading this at the time denoted by the following expression

```
ScheduleExpression happyHour = new ScheduleExpression()
        .dayOfWeek("Fri")
        .hour(18)
        .minute("*");
```

then perhaps it is time to put down this book and go and do something else.

Timers at Runtime

Enterprise Beans running under a time can programmatically control the `Timer` object. The timeout callback method, as we have already seen, can elect to receive the `javax.ejb.Timer` object as a method parameter. Even if an Enterprise Bean has set up multiple timers, the Timer instance that has just created a timeout event is the one that is passed into the method.

From this `Timer` object you can cancel the timer and find out full information about its schedule. `Timer` objects are by default persistent and so are persisted in the event of a Java EE server restart or failure. This means that such timers continue to operate if and when the Java EE server and its applications are restored. You can make the Timer objects you create not persistent, either programmatically in the `TimerConfig` object passed to the `TimerService`'s Timer creation methods, or through the use of the `@Schedule` annotation, setting the persistent attribute to `false`.

Finally, you can access all the timers for the current bean, or all the timers for the current bean's containing module from the `TimerService`, by calling `getTimers()` or `getAllTimers(,)` respectively.

Transactions and Enterprise Beans

Enterprise Beans are the thinking layer in the Java EE platform. This means that they are often handling, processing, and synthesizing application data whose resting place is in the data layer of the Java EE platform, managed either through the JDBC or Java Persistence APIs. It is therefore very important that while Enterprise Beans are interacting with application data held in one or more databases, the integrity of the data is maintained across operations. Simple data operations, such as incrementing a counter or adding an employee record to a database can easily be modeled as single Enterprise Bean methods. If the method fails, the data write fails and vice versa. But in real-world applications, many operations, such as adding a new employee to a company's HR system, involve interactions with more than one database table. And returning to the bank account example we studied in Chapter 8, making a payment is a classic example of a two-step operation: withdrawing money to make the payment, and making the payment. When everything goes well, it doesn't matter whether these operations have multiple steps. But when something does go wrong in the middle of a multistep operation, extra work needs to happen to make sure that the system is left in a consistent state. In the bank account example, if something goes wrong with the payment step, we really should return the money that we withdrew from the bank account.

Java transactions are an answer to this problem. In a multistep operation, often coded in an application as several method calls that result in read-and-write operations to one or more data sources, a Java transaction turns the operations into a single unit of action that either succeeds or fails. If the transaction succeeds, all the data sources involved move to the new state. If the transaction fails due to any of the constituent steps failing, the data sources involved are all rolled back to their state as it was at the beginning of the operation. In the bank account example, either the payment goes through and the money is withdrawn from the account, or no payment is made and no money is removed from the account.

With that background, an easier way to think of a transaction is a way to treat multiple Java methods that update data sources as a single atomic operation that either succeeds or fails.

To help visualize, let's look at the bank account example in Figure 10-7.

In Figure 10-7, the operations of making the payment and debiting the checking account are wrapped in a transaction. Before anything happens, the transaction, the atomic payment operation, begins. Then the payment is made and the account debited. If anything goes wrong in these

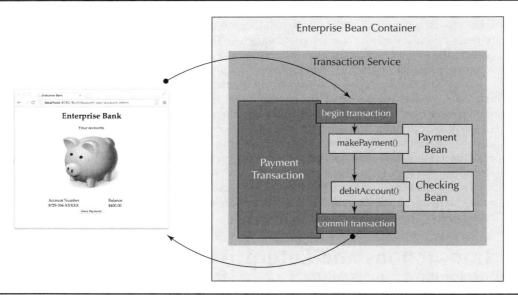

FIGURE 10-7. *A transactional bank account*

operations that are part of the payment transaction, the transaction is rolled back, and everything returns to the beginning state. If both the operations complete successfully, then and only then can the payment transaction complete.

Since you have already written some Enterprise Beans and called their methods, you have already used Java transactions: by default, every Enterprise Bean method invocation occurs within a Java transaction. This is not very useful in the kind of scenario earlier, because every Enterprise Bean method invocation occurs within its own Java transaction. Transactions are only really useful when you can group Enterprise Bean method invocations together into the same transaction so that they can act as one atomic and indivisible operation.

There are two ways to use Java transactions in Enterprise JavaBeans: the first is to use them programmatically, defining the transaction boundaries by hand using API calls to the Java Transaction API. The second method is to annotate the Enterprise Bean methods to govern their transactional properties.

Programmatic Transactions

When Enterprise Beans want to control their own transactions explicitly, they declare the class-level annotation `@javax.ejb.TransactionManagement` with value `TransactionManagementType.BEAN`. Then they must use the `javax.transaction.UserTransaction` object to perform transactions. This object can be injected into an Enterprise Bean using resource injection, the `@Resource` annotation, just as we saw, for example, when injecting the `SessionContext` into a session bean earlier. Or it can be accessed from the Enterprise Bean's `EJBContext`. `UserTransaction` has three methods that control the transaction behavior in scope in which it is used.

▰▰▰ `UserTransaction.begin()`

causes a new transaction to be created. Any Enterprise Bean method call that follows this will now be a part of this transaction.

▰▰▰ `UserTransaction.rollback()`

causes the current transaction to roll back to its original state, causing any data source updates that have been made by any of the bean method calls in this transaction (and so are pending being committed permanently) to be removed. Enterprise Beans call `rollback()` when one of the Java methods they call as part of the transaction goes wrong: all it takes is one missing link in the chain for it all to break, and the `rollback()` ensures that no permanent damage is done.

▰▰▰ `UserTransaction.commit()`

causes any data source updates that have been made by any of the bean method calls in this transaction to be committed permanently to the data sources.

The following code excerpt shows how you might apply the `UserTransaction` to the bank account example to ensure that the payment operation is processed as a single transaction.

▰▰▰ **Listing:** *Paying a bill within a transaction*

```
import javax.transaction.UserTransaction;
import javax.annotation.Resource;
import javax.ejb.TransactionManagement;
import javax.ejb.TransactionManagementType;

@Stateful
@TransactionManagement(value=TransactionManagementType.BEAN)
public class PaymentBean implements Payment {
@Resource
private UserTransaction userTransaction;
...
    public String makePayment(double amount,
                        String accountNumber,
                        String payee)
                            throws ApplicationException {
        try {
            userTransaction.begin();
            this.checkingBean.doDeduct(amount, accountNumber);
            String confirmation =
                this.billPay.doPay(amount, accountNumber, payee);
            userTransaction.commit();
            return confirmation;
        } catch (PaymentException pe) {
            userTransaction.rollback();
            throw new ApplicationException(pe.getMessage());
        }
    }
...
}
```

Transaction by Annotation

When an Enterprise Bean wants the Enterprise Bean container to manage its transactions instead of having to handle them explicitly with the `UserTransaction` object, it omits any class-level `@TransactionManagement` annotation altogether, since by default the container manages Enterprise Bean transactions. Equivalently, it may include the `@TransactionManagement` annotation, but this time with value `TransactionManagementType.CONTAINER`.

`@TransactionManagement(value=TransactionManagementType.CONTAINER)`

Without further intervention, such an Enterprise Bean is assigned a new transaction for every call that the container makes to its methods. As we noted, transactions are really useful only when they allow you to group a number of method invocations together, so let us look at how you can annotate the Enterprise Bean methods to define how they participate in Java transactions.

Suppose a bean client C calls a method on Enterprise Bean B. C could be a web component, an application client, or another Enterprise Bean. Either the call C makes is already in a transaction or it isn't. Now when C calls B, B has some choices it can make. If C's call is already in a transaction, does B want to be part of it? Does B always want to have a new transaction to operate in? Does B never want to be in a transaction at all? B can make such choices, and more, by annotating its method in question with the annotation `@javax.ejb.TransactionAttribute`. `@TransactionAttribute` has one mandatory value attribute, which takes one of the values of the `TransactionAttributeType` enum: `MANDATORY`, `NEVER`, `NOT_SUPPORTED`, `REQUIRED`, `REQUIRES_NEW`, and `SUPPORTS`. Let's look at what each attribute means in the next table.

Method on B Uses the `TransactionAttributeType`:	If the Call from C Is Already Part of a Transaction:	If the Call from C Is Not Part of a Transaction:
MANDATORY	The call to B is part of C's transaction.	Invocation to B's method throws an `EJBException`.
NEVER	Invocation to B's method throws an `EJBException`.	Invocation to B's method proceeds with no transaction.
NOT_SUPPORTED	C's transaction is suspended while the call to B proceeds with no transaction.	Invocation to B's method proceeds with no transaction.
REQUIRED	The call to B is part of C's transaction.	The container creates a new transaction for the call to B to be part of.
REQUIRES_NEW	C's transaction is suspended while the container creates a new transaction for the call to B to be part of.	The container creates a new transaction for the call to B to be part of.
SUPPORTS	The call to B is part of C's transaction.	Invocation to B's method proceeds with no transaction.

In order to see the power of transactions and Enterprise Beans together, we need to connect with some data sources to see the effects of transaction commits and rollbacks. So for now, we will defer a detailed example. But we will return to transactions in the next two chapters.

Interceptors

Enterprise Bean interceptors are Java components that wrap around invocations to Enterprise Beans. Interceptors are useful because they allow you to write separate Java classes that you can attach to one or more Enterprise Beans that intercept all method invocations on the bean. This kind of component has a variety of uses: from logging and auditing, to security checks, to allowing application development frameworks to modify the behaviors of Enterprise Beans by modifying the objects they consume and produce. We can get a general picture of how interceptors work in Figure 10-8.

You can flag that a Java class will be an interceptor by marking it with the class annotation `@javax.interceptor.Interceptor`.

And in order to intercept regular Enterprise Bean invocations, you write a method that you will use to implement the intercepting logic and annotate it with `@javax.interceptor.AroundInvoke`. The method must have an `Object` return value, throw `java.lang.Exception`, and take a class called `javax.interceptor.InvocationContext` as its single method

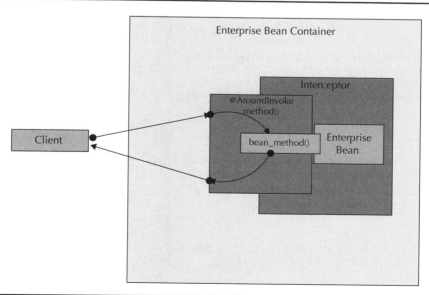

FIGURE 10-8. *An interceptor attached to an Enterprise Bean*

parameter. In other words, all the @AroundInvoke interceptors you might write look something like this:

Listing: *Template for an interceptor*

```
import javax.interceptor.AroundInvoke;
import javax.interceptor.InvocationContext;
import javax.interceptor.Interceptor;

@Interceptor
public class MyInterceptor {
     @AroundInvoke
     public Object myInterceptMethodName(InvocationContext ic)
                                               throws Exception {
          ...
     }
}
```

The InvocationContext is the key to implementing the @AroundInvoke method. From the InvocationContext, you can determine the java.lang.reflect.Method object of the Enterprise Bean method being intercepted. Using the getMethod() call, you can obtain the values of the method parameters with getParameters(), and even modify them with the setParameters() call. Most importantly, the proceed() method causes the Enterprise Bean (or next interceptor in the chain) to be called, either throwing an exception or returning, with a value or null if the Enterprise Bean method has void return. So the typical flow of an @AroundInvoke method implementation is something like this:

Listing: *Template for an @AroundInvoke method*

```
@AroundInvoke
public Object myInterceptMethodName(InvocationContext ic)
                                          throws Exception {
     // look at InvocationContext to obtain information
     // about the Enterprise bean being called, and information
     // about the method
     // modify parameters if necessary
     try {
          Object result = ic.proceed();  // call the bean
     } catch (Exception e) {
          // rethrow, wrap, or consume exception e
     }
     // clean up, record interception complete
     return result;
}
```

In order to attach an interceptor to an Enterprise Bean or to any of its methods, all you need to do is list the interceptor class in the class or method-level annotation @Interceptors, whose value attribute takes a list of classnames of interceptors. The Enterprise Bean container calls the interceptors attached to an Enterprise Bean in the order they appear in the @Interceptors annotation. If the `@Interceptors` annotation is applied at the class level, it applies to all methods of the Enterprise Bean.

The AuditInterceptor Example

Let's look at a short example. Consider the `AuditInterceptor`, which logs every method call to an Enterprise Bean.

Listing: *The `AuditInterceptor`*

```
import javax.interceptor.AroundInvoke;
import javax.interceptor.InvocationContext;
import javax.interceptor.Interceptor;
import java.util.*;

@Interceptor
public class AuditInterceptor {
    @AroundInvoke
    public Object intercept(InvocationContext context) throws Exception {
        Object result = null;
        String ebClassname = context.getTarget().getClass().getSimpleName();
        String methodName = context.getTarget().getClass().getSimpleName();
        String parameterString =
                    Arrays.asList(context.getParameters()).toString();
        System.out.println("AuditInterceptor: The call to " +
                                ebClassname +
                                "." + methodName +
                                parameterString + "...");
        try {
            result = context.proceed();
        } catch (Exception e) {
            System.out.println("AuditInterceptor: ....which raised " + e);
            throw e;
        }
        System.out.println("AuditInterceptor: ....has returned " + result);
        return result;
    }

}
```

Now let us attach this to the critical methods of a pair of Enterprise Beans we have already met in Chapter 8: the `BillPay` and `Checking` beans from the bank account example. We will attach the `AuditInterceptor` to the payment and debit methods on those beans, respectively.

Listing: *Attaching the `AuditInterceptor` (1)*

```
@Stateful
public class CheckingImpl implements Checking {
...
```

```
@Interceptors(AuditInterceptor.class)
public void doDeduct(double amount) throws PaymentException {
    ...
    }
...
}
```

and

Listing: *Attaching the `AuditInterceptor` (2)*

```
@Stateful
public class BillPayService implements BillPay {
@Interceptors(AuditInterceptor.class)
    public String doPay(String accountNumber,
                        String payee,
                        double amount) throws PaymentException {
...
}
```

Then when we make a payment through the web interface, the `AuditInterceptor` produces output, as you can see in the next excerpt.

Listing *Output from the `AuditInterceptor`*

```
Info:    AuditInterceptor: The call to CheckingImpl.CheckingImpl[15.0]...
Info:    AuditInterceptor: ....has returned null
Info:    AuditInterceptor: The call to BillPayService.BillPayService[8729-356-
XXXXX, energy, 15.0]...
Info:    AuditInterceptor: ....has returned 1399960391941
```

Interceptors can be used to catch invocations to the timeout methods that we introduced in the previous section, using the `@AroundTimeout` annotation applied to any method of the same shape as required by the `@AroundInvoke` annotation. An interceptor may have at most one `@AroundInvoke` and one `@AroundTimeout` method. Otherwise, if there is more than one of either, the container does not know which one you want it to call!

The Enterprise Bean container creates one instance of the interceptor for each instance of an Enterprise Bean that declares it. This makes the lifecycle of interceptor instances easy: they live and die with the Enterprise Bean instance they are attached to. They are truly the WebFilters of the Enterprise Bean container.

Summary

In this chapter, we have explored some of the various services that Enterprise Beans can enjoy. We looked at what the threading model is for Enterprise Beans and at how they can depend on single-threaded access, while, in the case of singleton session beans, for performance reasons, some of the methods may be allowed to have access by concurrent threads. We looked at how Enterprise Bean methods can work asynchronously, what that looks like, and what can be controlled about the asynchronous process both from the perspective of the bean and its client. We looked at how the Enterprise Bean container can automatically invoke a bean according to a wide variety of different application-provided schedules with the Timer Service. We looked at the EJBContext of an Enterprise Bean and how it can be used to access caller information and the JNDI naming directory and timers on a bean. We explored the world of transactions from the perspective of an Enterprise Bean developer and concluded by looking at the very useful and general-purpose Interceptor model.

However, we are running short on new examples of Enterprise Beans, because as much as we have seen how good they are at thinking, we haven't really given them anything interesting to think *about*. For that, we need to delve deeper into the platform and the data layer, which are the subjects of the next two chapters.

PART
III

The Collective Memory:
The Information Tier

CHAPTER
11

Classic Memories: JDBC

Relational databases form the majority of databases today, and JDBC is the traditional way to access data in a relational database.

A relational database is a storage system for information that is based on storing the information in tables. The term *relational* comes from the idea that when you define the columns in a table, for each row of data in the table you are defining a relationship between the pieces of information in the row. For example, if you define a table to have columns for name, age, and height for each row, you are defining a relationship between the name of a person, her age, and her height. In relational databases, tables themselves are created to have relationships between them: in a relational database containing information about employees, you might define a table to contain all personal information about an employee: their hire date, home address, and so on. You might define a second table to contain information about their job: their title, salary, and grade level. You need to have a way to uniquely identify each row in the personal information table in a relational database, usually in the form of a unique identifier called a primary key. With these, you can link the information from the personal information table with the table containing the job-related information by using an identifier in the job table, called a foreign key, to match the primary key. Using this basic scheme of tabular information and a way to link tables together, relational databases store most of the information used in computer systems today.

In order to interact with a relational database, to write information to and read information from its tables, relational databases use query languages. There are several such languages, but the most popular for many years is Structured Query Language (SQL). The JDBC APIs use SQL to create, delete, and update tables in the relational databases that it uses.

JDBC is not the only API through which to access the database in the Java EE platform; in the next chapter we will examine the Java Persistence API. The JDBC API provides a simple approach, where data is modeled through SQL statements and a generic object called a `ResultSet`, which represents the results of a query for data. In contrast, the Java Persistence API offers a higher-level view of relational data in terms of application objects. In the next two chapters, we will explore both approaches in some detail.

In this chapter, we look at the JDBC APIs, focusing on the key abstractions needed to interact with a relational database. We review the SQL language, introducing or refamiliarizing you with this relatively straightforward query language. We also present some examples to illustrate the concepts we discuss.

Introduction to JDBC

The Java Database Connectivity APIs (JDBC) enable you to connect to a relational database for the following principal tasks:

- To connect to a database configured in the Java EE server
- To define, set up, and create tables in which to hold data
- To add, remove, and edit data held within tables in the database

You can use the JDBC APIs from either the web container or the EJB container, as you can see in the Figure 11-1.

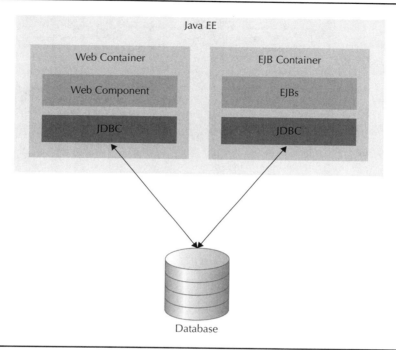

FIGURE 11-1. *Accessing JDBC APIs from Java EE components*

Because of the relative simplicity of the JDBC APIs, there are many Java EE applications that use JDBC in combination with one or more kinds of web components and do not use Enterprise Beans at all. This two-tier approach has many advantages of simplicity, particularly for smaller applications, not requiring knowledge of the Enterprise Bean container at all. In this chapter, our examples all have this simple two-tier architecture. However, the kind of access to relational data you see in this chapter from web components through the JDBC APIs also works equally well from Enterprise Beans.

In Figure 11-2, we see the typical JDBC objects in play in a typical JDBC application.

The JDBC client application, either a web component or Enterprise Bean, obtains an instance of a `javax.sql.DataSource`. The `DataSource` object is the entry point for access to a relational database, acting as a factory for `java.sql.Connection` objects. Java EE components may either look up preconfigured `DataSource` objects in the JNDI namespace, or they can be injected into the Java EE component, as we shall see. A `Connection` object represents a single session with a database, encompassing a series of interactions to update the database or retrieve data from it. Applications pass SQL statements to the `Connection` object in order to create `java.sql.Statement` objects representing the operation they wish to perform. There are various different kinds of `Statement` objects, as we shall see, depending on how the SQL statement will be processed. The application causes the SQL statement held by a `Statement` object to be run against the database by calling one of the `execute()` methods on the `Statement` object. The result of the execution of the `Statement` is either a status in the case of operations

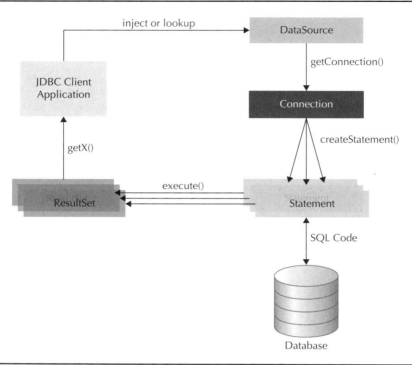

FIGURE 11-2. *Anatomy of a JDBC application*

like table creation or updating a row in a table that does not return table data, or an instance of the `ResultSet` object in the case of operations that retrieve data. The `java.sql.ResultSet` object is a representation of general tabular information based on the concepts of traversing through each row of data with a cursor and reading each piece of data from the row based on a `get()` call using the name of the column. You might immediately see from this description that much of the work in an application that uses JDBC to hold its data is in formulating the correct SQL statements and in reading data from `ResultSet` objects and converting them into application-level Java objects.

Hello JDBC Example

With this general description of the JDBC API, let us look at a simple example: Hello JDBC.

In this example, from the initial page we see in Figure 11-3 we create a table as can be seen in Figure 11-4, add a message to it as we see in Figure 11-5, retrieve the message as seen in Figure 11-6, and then delete the table, shown in Figure 11-7.

FIGURE 11-3. *The HelloJDBC home page*

FIGURE 11-4. *Creating a table in HelloJDBC*

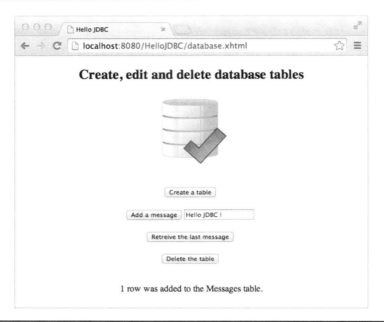

FIGURE 11-5. *Adding a message to the database*

FIGURE 11-6. *Fetching a message from the database*

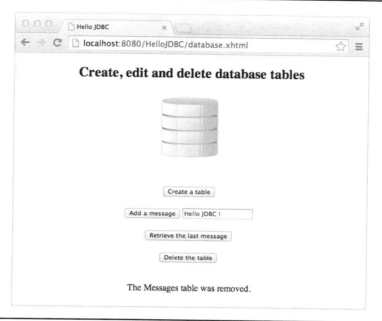

FIGURE 11-7. *Deleting the table*

The Hello JDBC application is a JavaServer Faces page called `database.xhtml`, calling into a request-scoped managed bean with classname `HelloJDBCBean`. This managed bean could equally be a Java servlet or Enterprise Bean in terms of its use of the JDBC APIs.

Before we turn to the source code in this example, we cover the topic of how it is configured. The main two steps in the configuration are first to set up a schema in the database where the table in the example will be written, and second to configure a data source that the application will use and that will contain all the configuration information necessary for the application to connect through this data source to the schema set up in the database.

How these two tasks are accomplished varies depending on which database and which Java EE application server you use. From the Netbeans tool, using the Derby Java database and GlassFish 4.0 in order to create the schema, the first step is to locate the JavaDB NetBeans and choose the Create Database option, supplying a name for the database and a username and password that can be used to connect to it. Second, to configure a data source in an application, add a New GlassFish JDBC DataSource to the application. This process prompts you to select a JNDI name under which to register the data source, guiding you through the available schema (one of which you should just have created) to which the data source will connect. NetBeans will store a `glassfish-resources.xml` file with the application that contains the configuration information about the data source. In this example, we have set up a data source registered to the JNDI name `jdbc/helloJDBCDatasource`, which connects to the schema called `hello-jdbc` with the username hello and password hello1. Here is the `glassfish-resources.xml` file for this example.

Listing: *A DataSource configuration in GlassFish the* `glassfish-resources.xml` *file*

```xml
<?xml version="1.0" encoding="UTF-8"?>
<!DOCTYPE resources PUBLIC
 "-//GlassFish.org//DTD GlassFish Application Server 3.1 Resource Definitions//EN"
 "http://glassfish.org/dtds/glassfish-resources_1_5.dtd">
<resources>
  <jdbc-resource enabled="true"
                 jndi-name="jdbc/helloJDBCDatasource"
                 object-type="user"
                 pool-name="helloConnectionPool">
    <description/>
  </jdbc-resource>
  <jdbc-connection-pool allow-non-component-callers="false"
                        associate-with-thread="false"
                        connection-creation-retry-attempts="0"
                        connection-creation-retry-interval-in-seconds="10"
                        connection-leak-reclaim="false"
                        connection-leak-timeout-in-seconds="0"
                        connection-validation-method="table"
                        datasource-classname="org.apache.derby.jdbc.ClientDataSource"
                        fail-all-connections="false"
                        idle-timeout-in-seconds="300"
                        is-connection-validation-required="false"
                        is-isolation-level-guaranteed="true"
                        lazy-connection-association="false"
                        lazy-connection-enlistment="false"
                        match-connections="false"
                        max-connection-usage-count="0"
                        max-pool-size="32" max-wait-time-in-millis="60000"
                        name="helloConnectionPool"
                        non-transactional-connections="false"
                        ping="false" pool-resize-quantity="2"
                        pooling="true"
                        res-type="javax.sql.DataSource"
                        statement-cache-size="0"
                        statement-leak-reclaim="false"
                        statement-leak-timeout-in-seconds="0"
                        statement-timeout-in-seconds="-1"
                        steady-pool-size="8"
                        validate-atmost-once-period-in-seconds="0"
                        wrap-jdbc-objects="true">
    <property name="URL" value="jdbc:derby://localhost:1527/hello-jdbc"/>
    <property name="serverName" value="localhost"/>
    <property name="PortNumber" value="1527"/>
    <property name="DatabaseName" value="hello-jdbc"/>
    <property name="User" value="hello"/>
    <property name="Password" value="hello1"/>
  </jdbc-connection-pool>
</resources>
```

We will not look at the source code for the `database.xhtml` JavaServer Faces page because it is backed by the managed bean `HelloJDBCBean`, which contains all the code relating to the JDBC APIs. We will look only at the following listing.

Listing: *The HelloJDBCBean*

```java
import java.sql.Connection;
import java.sql.ResultSet;
import java.sql.Statement;
import javax.annotation.Resource;
import javax.enterprise.context.RequestScoped;
import javax.sql.DataSource;
import java.sql.SQLException;
import javax.inject.Named;

@Named("databaseBean")
@RequestScoped
public class HelloJDBCBean {
    @Resource(lookup="jdbc/helloJDBCDatasource")
    DataSource ds;
    String statusString = "";
    String message = "Hello JDBC !";
    String iconString = NO_TABLE_ICON;
    static String NO_TABLE_ICON = "database-icon.png";
    static String EMPTY_TABLE_ICON = "database-add-icon.png";
    static String FULL_TABLE_ICON = "database-check-icon.png";
    static String ERROR_TABLE_ICON = "database-error-icon.png";

    public HelloJDBCBean() {
    }

    public String getIcon() {
        return this.iconString;
    }

    public String getStatus() {
        return this.statusString;
    }

    public void setMessage(String message) {
        this.message = message;
    }

    public String getMessage() {
        return this.message;
    }

    private void setStatus(String statusString, String icon) {
        this.statusString = statusString;
        this.iconString = icon;
    }

    public void createTable() {
        try (Connection connection = ds.getConnection()) {
                Statement smnt = connection.createStatement(
                        ResultSet.TYPE_SCROLL_INSENSITIVE,
                            ResultSet.CONCUR_READ_ONLY);
                int result = smnt.executeUpdate(
                  "CREATE TABLE Messages ( MessageID int, Message varchar(255))");
                this.setStatus(
                  "The Messages table was created. You can now add your message.",
```

```java
                EMPTY_TABLE_ICON);

        } catch (SQLException e) {
            this.setStatus("Error: " + e.getMessage(), ERROR_TABLE_ICON);
        }
    }

    public void writeValue() {
        try (Connection connection = ds.getConnection()) {
            Statement smnt = connection.createStatement(
                    ResultSet.TYPE_SCROLL_INSENSITIVE,
                        ResultSet.CONCUR_READ_ONLY);
            int result = smnt.executeUpdate(
                            "INSERT INTO Messages (MessageID,Message)
                            VALUES (1,'"+this.message+"')");
            this.setStatus(
                result + " row was added to the Messages table.",
                FULL_TABLE_ICON);
        } catch (SQLException e) {
            this.setStatus("Error: " + e.getMessage(), ERROR_TABLE_ICON);
        }
    }


    public String retrieveValue() throws SQLException {
        ResultSet rs = null;
        try (Connection connection = ds.getConnection()) {

            Statement smnt = connection.createStatement(
                    ResultSet.TYPE_SCROLL_INSENSITIVE,
                        ResultSet.CONCUR_READ_ONLY);
            rs = smnt.executeQuery("SELECT Message FROM Messages");
            rs.last();
            String s =  rs.getString("Message");
            rs.close();
            this.setStatus(
                "Retrieved the value [" + s + "] from the Messages table.",
                FULL_TABLE_ICON);
            return s;
        } catch (SQLException e) {
            rs.close();
            this.setStatus("Error: " + e.getMessage(), ERROR_TABLE_ICON);
        }
        return "";
    }

    public void dropTable() {
        try (Connection connection = ds.getConnection()) {
            Statement smnt = connection.createStatement(
                    ResultSet.TYPE_SCROLL_INSENSITIVE,
                        ResultSet.CONCUR_READ_ONLY);
            int result = smnt.executeUpdate("DROP TABLE Messages");
            this.setStatus("The Messages table was removed.", NO_TABLE_ICON);
        } catch (SQLException e) {
            this.setStatus("Error: " + e.getMessage(), ERROR_TABLE_ICON);
        }
    }
}
```

Notice that this request scope bean injects the `DataSource` as an instance variable into itself, using the JNDI name to locate it in the JNDI name `@Resource(lookup="jdbc/helloJDBCDatasource")`. The methods that are invoked when the four buttons on the main page are pressed are `createTable()`, `writeValue()`, `retrieveValue()`, and `dropTable()`. Each method follows the same pattern of obtaining a new connection from the data source. Notice that the call `getConnection()` takes no arguments: as we saw from the particular configuration of the data source in NetBeans, the `DataSource` object already contains the location of the database and the account credentials needed to connect to it; no such configuration information is needed in code that will use the connection. Each of the four methods creates a Statement object that is ready to accept the SQL statement. The options used to create the statement, `ResultSet.TYPE_SCROLL_INSENSITIVE` and `ResultSet.CONCUR_READ_ONLY`, indicate that the `ResultSet` coming from a SQL statement executed on this `Statement`, if it returns data, will return data that will not be changed while the result set is open. Then the four methods use SQL `CREATE TABLE`, `INSERT`, `SELECT`, and `DELETE TABLE` statements to create a table called `Messages`, add a row containing a custom message to the table, retrieve the last row of the `Messages` table, and delete the `Messages` table, respectively. The SQL statement is executed against the database when the relevant `execute()` method is called: either `executeQuery()` or `executeUpdate()` depending on whether the SQL statement will return data or not. In the case where the SQL statement does result in returning data, in the `retrieveValue()` method, the `ResultSet` object contains all the rows of the table, and the value of the `Message` column in the row last added to the `Messages` table is returned. The `HelloJDBCBean` maintains a status string and a link to the appropriate icon depending on the state of the proceedings.

You can see in this very simple example the building block steps of creating and adding to a table and of retrieving values and deleting the table. You can start to see some of the main themes of a JDBC application even in this simple application: managing connections, managing SQL code embedded within Java JDBC API calls, and the beginnings of how to use statements and navigate through the `ResultSets` that return data that application has requested.

Now we are ready to expand on these foundational themes and explore in more detail how to use JDBC for more sophisticated application data storage and retrieval. But first we will present a quick overview of the SQL language.

Structured Query Language

SQL is a simple language for interacting with relational databases. It has proved extremely durable, having been first created in the early 1970s. In this section, we will look at the most common commands.

SQL statements fall into two basic categories: ones that manipulate the shape of the data that can be stored in the database, and ones that manipulate the data itself. In other words, there are statements that create or alter the tables that will hold the data, and there are statements that create or alter the data held within the tables.

Statements That Alter Table Structure

The most frequently used statements are `CREATE TABLE` and `DROP TABLE`. We have already seen two of these in action in the Hello JDBC example.

The CREATE TABLE statement is used to create a new table in the database, for example:

```
CREATE TABLE Employees (
Employee_Number Integer,
First_Name Text,
Last_Name Text)
```

The syntax

```
CREATE TABLE <table-name> (
      <column-name1> <data-type(size)>,
      <column-name2> <data-type(size)>,
      ....
      <column-nameN> <data-type(size)>
)
```

creates a new table in the database with the name table name, and with N columns, named column-name1...column-nameN, each with the specified data type for holding information. Each relational database defines a slightly different set of allowed data types, which can cause problems when moving from database to database. All relational databases support data types for text; various number, date, and time formats; and binary formats such as blob. The examples in this chapter are limited to commonly supported data types, in particular, those supported by the Apache Derby database.

The statement

```
DROP TABLE <table-name>
```

deletes the table called <table-name1> in the database and all the data it holds. For example,

```
DROP TABLE Employees
```

removes the Employees table and all the employee records that it holds.

Statements That Store or Retrieve Data Into and From Tables

The SELECT statement is the workhorse statement for retrieving data from a table in a relational database. The statement is composed of the table name or names from which you want to get information and the column names of the data you want to access together.

The statement

```
SELECT <column-name1>, <column-name2>...<column-nameN>
FROM <table-name1>, ..., <table-nameM>
```

will retrieve the data held within all the named columns in the given tables. You can use table-name.column-name to disambiguate column names if more than one table uses the same column name. For example,

```
SELECT First_Name, Last_Name FROM Employees
```

will return the first and last names of all the employees in the Employees table.

The WHERE clause can be used at the end of the SELECT statement to filter the results according to some given criteria:

```
SELECT <column-name1>, <column-name2>...<column-nameN>
FROM <table-name1>, ..., <table-nameM>
WHERE <column-name> <sql-operator> <value>;
```

and where `sql-operator` can be = (equal), <> (unequal), > (greater than), < (less than), >= (greater than or equal), <= (less than or equal), BETWEEN (within an inclusive range), LIKE (matching a pattern), or IN (to specify multiple possible values for a column).

For example:

```
SELECT Last_Name FROM Employees WHERE First_Name='John'
```

would fetch all the last names of employees whose first name is John.

The INSERT statement allows you to add a record to an existing table. The syntax is

```
INSERT INTO <table-name> (<column-name1>, <column-name2>,...,<column-nameN>)
VALUES (<value1>,<value2>,...<valueN>)
```

where `table-name` is the name of the table to which you wish to add new information, the `column-names` are the names of the columns you wish to update, and the values list contains the values you wish to update in the columns you have specified.

For example:

```
INSERT INTO Employees (Employee_Number, First_Name, Last_Name)
VALUES (398, 'John', 'Robles')
```

There are more commands in the SQL language, such as the UPDATE statement for editing rows within a table or ALTER for changing the columns in a table. However, if you are not already familiar with them, CREATE TABLE, INSERT, SELECT, and DROP TABLE will take you a long way.

The JDBC APIs

Now we can take a look at the main classes of the JDBC APIs.

The DataSource Object

From the perspective of an application using the JDBC APIs, the `DataSource` object is a factory object for creating connections that the application can use to interact with the database. The `DataSource` interface hides away a number of complexities concerning locating and connecting with a relational database from the JDBC application. It encapsulates all the configuration information that the application needs to connect to the database, including the driver information and location, any driver-specific properties, and optionally, the credentials that will be used when connecting to the database through the driver. The `DataSource` also hides away the implementation of the connection pool used and the transactional support of the driver, if it is supported. This leaves the application free of such configuration options, and leaves the `DataSource` object with only two methods for creating connections, one using the credential setup in the `DataSource`, and one using an application-supplied credential.

```
Connection getConnection() throws SQLException
Connection getConnection(String username,
                         String password)
                            throws SQLException
```

DataSources are configured into applications in different ways by different development environments. The Hello JDBC example showed how NetBeans and GlassFish configure a DataSource into an application. Once configured, the DataSource can either be injected into a web component or Enterprise Bean in the application, or looked up in the JNDI namespace. Supposing the DataSource has been registered under the name my/jdbcDataSource, then the following examples show the two modes that can be used to locate it and find it in an application.

Listing: *Two ways to locate a DataSource*

```
@Stateless
public class MySessionBean {
    @Resource(lookup="jdbc/helloJDBCDatasource")
    private DataSource ds;
...
}
```

or

```
@Stateless
public class MySessionBean {
        private DataSource ds;
        public void init() {
            try {
                DataSource ds = (DataSource) InitialContext
                        .doLookup("jdbc/helloJDBCDatasource");
            } catch (NamingException ne) {
                // time for plan B
            }
        }
    ...
}
```

The Connection Object

The JDBC Connection object represents an active session with a database fronted by a DataSource object. The connection is either active or it is closed. This state can be tested with its isClosed() method, and the application can close the connection with the close() method. The Connection object contains a number of methods that allow the JDBC application to query the configuration of the database, for example, the DatabaseMetaData object returned from its getMetaData() call. Most critically for JDBC applications, the Connection object holds the means to Statement objects, which will be used to invoke SQL statements on the database. As we will soon see, there are different kinds of Statement objects, which vary in terms of how the SQL statement they embody is executed (though the results are the same whichever Statement type you choose). Let us look at the most general-purpose Statement object. Any empty Statement object is created from the Connection object using the method

```
Statement createStatement() throws SQLException
```

with variants that control the properties of the `ResultSet` object that is returned in the cases where the `Statement` is used to execute queries that return data.

Statement Objects

There are three kinds of `Statement` objects, represented by the `Statement`, `PreparedStatement`, and `CallableStatement` interfaces. `CallableStatement` inherits from `PreparedStatement`, which inherits from `Statement`.

The `Statement` interface represents an object that executes arbitrary SQL statements. The statements are executed by one of the `execute()` methods that takes an SQL statement as a parameter, for example

```
int executeUpdate(String sql) throws SQLException
```

for SQL statements that do not return table data, such as TABLE CREATE or INSERT statements, and

```
ResultSet executeQuery(String sql) throws SQLException
```

for SQL statements that do return table data, in the form of a `ResultSet` object such as SELECT statements.

You will notice that the SQL statement is known only to JDBC and the database at the time it is being executed. Using the `Statement` object to run SQL statements is perfectly adequate for many programs. It does, however, offer the JDBC API and database few opportunities for optimizing frequently used queries.

The `PreparedStatement` interface represents an SQL statement that has been precompiled into a Java class and so saves a step in the process of running the statement against the database. For frequently used SQL statements in an application, using a `PreparedStatement` instead of a `Statement` can lead to performance improvements. `PreparedStatements` are created from the `Connection` objects by passing in an SQL statement, for example, the `Connection` method

```
PreparedStatement prepareStatement(String sql) throws SQLException
```

The SQL statement passed in can be parameterized with the ? character so that the same `PreparedStatement` can be reused easily with different parameterized values. For example,

```
PreparedStatement ps = prepareStatement("SELECT Last_Name FROM
                         Employees WHERE First_Name = ?")
ps.setString(1, "Sarah");
..
ps.setString(1, "Ian");
```

shows the same `PreparedStatement` being used with two different values of the last name in the WHERE clause of its SELECT statement.

`PreparedStatements` are executed using

```
int executeUpdate();
```

and

```
ResultSet executeQuery()
```

depending on whether the SQL statement will return table data or not.

The `CallableStatement` interface represents the next and final step in optimization of SQL statement execution. Most relational databases can store queries themselves. More efficient than the precompiled `PreparedStatements`, the queries, being local to the database, are usually much more efficiently processed. They are created from the `Connection` object, using, for example, the method

```
CallableStatement prepareCall(String sql) throws SQLException
```

Similar to `PreparedStatements`, `CallableStatements` may be created with SQL statements that are parameterized. `CallableStatements` are executed by the same method calls as its super-interface `PreparedStatement executeQuery()` or `executeUpdate()`, depending on the nature of the SQL statement it represents.

Which style of `Statement` you use depends very much on the nature of your application. It is a simple and valid approach to stick with the `Statement` interface until you understand where your application may benefit from optimization. Figure 11-8 shows the three different types of statements.

ResultSets

The `ResultSet` object is a representation of table data that is returned from an SQL query such as a `SELECT` statement. JDBC applications can read data from a `ResultSet` object and can also update the data in a `ResultSet`. `ResultSets` are returned from `Statement` objects as a result of executing a query that returns table data, such as a `SELECT` statement. A `ResultSet` is not

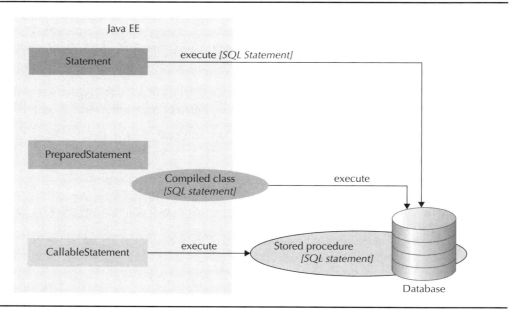

FIGURE 11-8. *Statement, PreparedStatement, and CallableStatement*

simply a data structure containing table data: it represents an active session with a table or tables in the database. `ResultSets` must be closed when the JDBC application has finished using them.

In reading data, there are two ideas: the first is that the `ResultSet` contains a notion of a cursor, or a current row. The cursor position is the index of the row in the table, and a new `ResultSet` will have its cursor set at the first row of the table. The `ResultSet` API contains various methods to read data from the cell in the table data corresponding to the value in the current row given a column name or index. For example, if the cursor position in a `ResultSet` is at the first row of our Employees table, the call `getString("First_Name")` returns the first name of the first employee in the table. The cursor position in a `ResultSet` may be moved around using the row navigation methods, for example, `next()` and `previous()`. We can illustrate this kind of navigation around the data in a `ResultSet` in Figure 11-9.

The API is quite large, so we do not include a listing of all the methods. The accessor methods for cell data are typed according to the SQL datatype requested in the column containing the cell, for example: `getString(String columnName)`, `getByte(String columnName)`, `getDate(String columnName)`, and `getInt(String columnName)`. Additionally, there are several methods for moving the cursor through the rows of the table in addition to `next()` and `previous()` as shown.

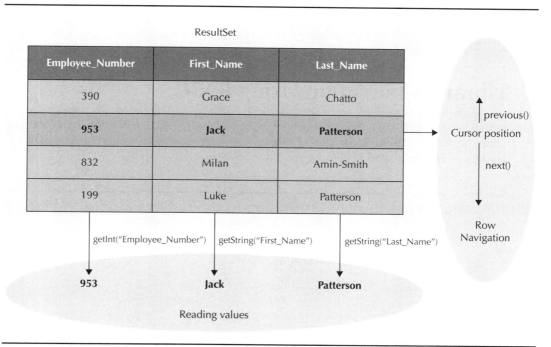

FIGURE 11-9. *Navigating a* `ResultSet`

You may have noticed that when creating `Statement` objects from the `Connection` object, there are variants on the `create()` methods that allow any or all of three options that can be set. For example,

```
Statement createStatement(int resultSetType,
                          int resultSetConcurrency,
                          int resultSetHoldability)
                                    throws SQLException
```

These options govern aspects of the `ResultSet` objects that are returned when the `Statements` are executed.

The `resultSetType` governs how the cursor can be moved through the set. The default value `ResultSet.TYPE_FORWARD_ONLY` allows only the cursor to move down the table. The `resultSetConcurrency` value governs whether the `ResultSet` can be updated or not. If you wish to change the underlying data tables in the `ResultSet` by calling its write methods, you need to use the `ResultSet.CONCUR_UPDATABLE` option as the default. `ResultSet.CONCUR_READ_ONLY` does not allow for anything but reading the `ResultSet`. The `resultSetHoldability` value governs what happens to the `ResultSet` if the statement is executed within a transaction.

For `ResultSets` that are writable, there are write methods that are analogous to the read methods for accessing data. The methods `updateString(String columnName, String value)`, `updateByte(String columnName, byte b)`, `updateDate(String columnName, Date date)`, and `updateInt(String columnName, int i)` are some of the most commonly used.

We now have enough knowledge of the JDBC APIs to revisit a familiar application and find a permanent storage place for its precious data.

Library Application Using JDBC

In Chapter 5 we created a Library application. The Library application is a JAX-RS application with a Swing client. With the JAX-RS client, you can browse books in the library, filtering by the genre of the book, and you can add or delete books to and from the Library, as you can see in Figures 11-10, 11-11 and 11-12.

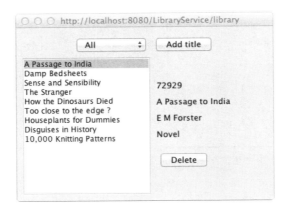

FIGURE 11-10. *Browsing books in the Library*

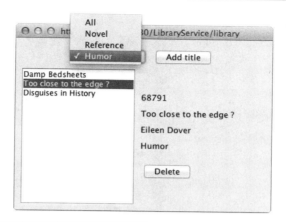

FIGURE 11-11. *Browsing books in the library by genre*

In Chapter 5, the data held in the application was held in the code of the application: the books that are displayed when you first start up the application are added to a list upon initialization of the library endpoint class.

By now, we have enough knowledge of the JDBC APIs to use them to keep the book data that the Library application uses in a database. Before we look at any code, let's look at a picture of the architecture of this application.

In Figure 11-13, we can see that the client is using REST calls to the `LibraryEndpoint` and `BookEndpoint` JAX-RS resources in order to query and modify the library service. In turn, these JAX-RS resources are using a singleton session bean called the `LibraryManager`. The `LibraryDataManager` Enterprise Bean is using the JDBC APIs to fulfill the requests to search for books by genre and add and delete books from the database. The `Book` data object represents

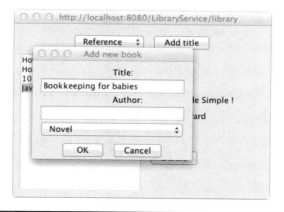

FIGURE 11-12. *Adding a book to the library*

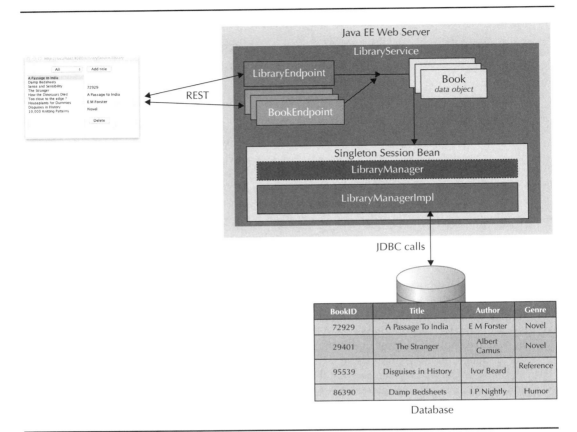

FIGURE 11-13. *Anatomy of the Library application*

each book inside the Library Service application. Since we have already covered the JAX-RS aspects of this application in Chapter 5, we will not repeat it here. We will instead just focus on the `LibraryDataManager` bean and look at how it uses JDBC. First, we will take a quick look at the `Book` data object.

Listing: *The Book data object*

```
public class Book {
    private final int id;
    private final String title;
    private final String author;
    private final String genre;

    public Book(int id, String title, String author, String genre) {
        this.id = id;
        this.title = title;
```

```
        this.author = author;
        this.genre = genre;
    }

     public int getId() {
        return this.id;
    }

    public String getTitle() {
        return this.title;
    }

    public String getAuthor() {
        return this.author;
    }

    public String getGenre() {
        return this.genre;
    }

    @Override
    public String toString() {
        return "a book by " + this.author;
    }
}
```

This is a simple immutable Java object containing the attributes of a book in the Library application. The LibraryEndpoint and BookEndpoint JAX-RS resources talk to the LibraryDataManager bean through its remote interface LibraryDataManager.

Listing: *The LibraryDataManager remote interface*

```
import java.util.List;
import javax.ejb.Remote;

@Remote
public interface LibraryDataManager {
    public static String NOVEL = "Novel";
    public static String REFERENCE = "Reference";
    public static String HUMOR = "Humor";

    public boolean removeBook(int id);
    public List<Book> getBooks(String searchGenre);
    public List<Book> getBooks();
    public boolean addBook(Book book);
    public int generateId();
}
```

Notice that this remote interface makes heavy use of the Book data object.

Now we turn to the JDBC calls and the `LibraryDataManagerImpl` class. The prerequisite for running this Enterprise Bean is that there must be a preconfigured `DataSource` registered under the name `jdbc/myLibraryDatasource`, such as we set up for the HelloJDBC example earlier.

Listing: *The `LibraryDataManagerImpl` Enterprise Bean implementation*

```java
import java.sql.Connection;
import java.sql.ResultSet;
import java.sql.SQLException;
import java.sql.Statement;
import java.sql.PreparedStatement;
import javax.annotation.Resource;
import javax.ejb.Singleton;
import javax.sql.DataSource;
import javax.ejb.Startup;
import javax.annotation.PostConstruct;
import javax.annotation.PreDestroy;
import java.util.*;

@Singleton
@Startup
public class LibraryDataManagerImpl implements LibraryDataManager {
    @Resource(lookup="jdbc/myLibraryDatasource")
    private DataSource ds;

    @PostConstruct
    public void initializeData()  {
        try {
            this.initDatabase();
        } catch (SQLException er) {
            System.out.println("Error initializing: " + er.getMessage());
        }
    }

    @PreDestroy
    private void deleteData() {
        try (Connection connection = ds.getConnection()) {
            Statement smnt = connection.createStatement(
                    ResultSet.TYPE_SCROLL_INSENSITIVE,
                        ResultSet.CONCUR_READ_ONLY);
            smnt.executeUpdate("DROP TABLE Books");
        } catch (SQLException e) {
            System.out.println(e.getMessage());
        }
    }

    @Override
    public boolean removeBook(int id) {
        try (Connection connection = ds.getConnection()) {
            Statement smnt = connection.createStatement(
                    ResultSet.TYPE_SCROLL_INSENSITIVE,
                        ResultSet.CONCUR_READ_ONLY);
            int result = smnt.executeUpdate("DELETE FROM Books WHERE BookID="+ id);
            return true;
```

```java
        } catch (SQLException e) {
            return false;
        }
    }
}

@Override
public List<Book> getBooks(String searchGenre)  {
    List<Book> books = new ArrayList<>();

    try (Connection connection = ds.getConnection()) {
        String getAllQuery = "SELECT BookID, Title, Author, Genre FROM Books";
        String getByGenreQuery = getAllQuery  + " WHERE Genre=?";

        PreparedStatement getAllStatement =
                connection.prepareStatement(getAllQuery,
                    ResultSet.TYPE_SCROLL_INSENSITIVE,
                    ResultSet.CONCUR_READ_ONLY);

        PreparedStatement getByGenreStatement =
                connection.prepareStatement(getByGenreQuery,
                     ResultSet.TYPE_SCROLL_INSENSITIVE,
                     ResultSet.CONCUR_READ_ONLY);

        PreparedStatement ps;
        if (!"All".equals(searchGenre)) {
            ps = getByGenreStatement;
            ps.setString(1, searchGenre);
        } else {
            ps = getAllStatement;
        }
        try (ResultSet rs = ps.executeQuery()) {
            while (!rs.isLast()) {
                rs.next();
                int id = rs.getInt("BookID");
                String title = rs.getString("Title");
                String author = rs.getString("Author");
                String genre = rs.getString("Genre");
                Book b = new Book(id, title, author, genre);
                books.add(b);
            }

        }
        return books;
    } catch (SQLException e) {
        System.out.println(e.getMessage());

    }
    return new ArrayList<>();

}

@Override
public List<Book> getBooks()  {
    return this.getBooks("All");
}
```

```java
    @Override
    public boolean addBook(Book book) {
        try (Connection connection = ds.getConnection()) {
            Statement smnt = connection.createStatement(
                    ResultSet.TYPE_SCROLL_INSENSITIVE,
                    ResultSet.CONCUR_READ_ONLY);
            smnt.executeUpdate("INSERT INTO Books
                (BookID, Title, Author, Genre) VALUES
                ("+book.getId()+",'"+book.getTitle()+"', '"+book.getAuthor()+"',
                '"+book.getGenre()+"')");
            return true;
        } catch (SQLException e) {
            System.out.println(e.getMessage());
            return false;
        }
    }

    private void initDatabase() throws SQLException {
        try (Connection connection = ds.getConnection()) {
            Statement smnt = connection.createStatement(
                    ResultSet.TYPE_SCROLL_INSENSITIVE,
                    ResultSet.CONCUR_READ_ONLY);
            smnt.executeUpdate("CREATE TABLE Books "
                    + "( BookID int, Title varchar(255), "
                    + "Author varchar(255), Genre varchar(255))");
            for (Book b : this.getDefaultBooks()) {
                this.addBook(b);
            }
        }
    }




    @Override
    public int generateId() {
        long l = System.currentTimeMillis() * (new Random()).nextInt();
        String asString = "" + l;
        String as5String = asString.substring((asString.length()-5),
                                              (asString.length()));
        return (new Integer(as5String)).intValue();

    }

    private List<Book> getDefaultBooks() {
        List<Book> books = new ArrayList<>();
        Book b = new Book(this.generateId(), "A Passage to India", "E M Forster",
                                            LibraryDataManager.NOVEL);
        books.add(b);
        b = new Book(this.generateId(), "Damp Bedsheets", "I P Nightly",
                                            LibraryDataManager.HUMOR);
        books.add(b);
        b = new Book(this.generateId(), "Sense and Sensibility", "Jane Austen",
                                            LibraryDataManager.NOVEL);
        books.add(b);
        b = new Book(this.generateId(), "The Stranger", "Albert Camus",
                                            LibraryDataManager.NOVEL);
```

```
        books.add(b);
        b = new Book(this.generateId(), "How the Dinosaurs Died", "P T Dactyl",
                                        LibraryDataManager.REFERENCE);
        books.add(b);
        b = new Book(this.generateId(), "Too close to the edge ?", "Eileen Dover",
                                        LibraryDataManager.HUMOR);
        books.add(b);
        b = new Book(this.generateId(), "Houseplants for Dummies", "G Fingers",
                                        LibraryDataManager.REFERENCE);
        books.add(b);
        b = new Book(this.generateId(), "Disguises in History", "Ivor Beard",
                                        LibraryDataManager.HUMOR);
        books.add(b);
        b = new Book(this.generateId(), "10,000 Knitting Patterns",
                        "M N E Sweaters", LibraryDataManager.REFERENCE);
        books.add(b);
        return books;
    }


}
```

Notice first that this singleton bean is taking advantage of its lifecycle in order to provide the convenience of setting up the database table, called Books, and populating it with default values on application startup. You can see that through the use of the

```
@PostConstruct
public void initializeData() {...}
```

method. Similarly, the application "cleans up" after itself by using the @PreDestroy annotation to mark the deleteData() that deletes the Books table when the application shuts down.

Other than these two methods, which exist to make the Library application easy to run without having to set up the tables separately, this class contains all the methods to search the Books database table and edit it. Let's take a look, for example, at the addBook() method.

You can see that the method obtains a connection to the data source, which is injected into this Enterprise Bean into the ds variable. Then the method creates a Statement object containing the SQL to add a row to the Books table. It does so using the supplied Book object, which is to be added to fill out the values in the row in the SQL statement. Next it calls the executeUpdate() method to call the database. This method either succeeds or throws an exception.

Since adding books is not likely to be such a frequently used operation, using a Statement object should be perfectly adequate. The search operation that searches for lists of books is likely to be called more frequently, so let's look at the getBooks(String searchGenre) method that implements that.

Instead of using a Statement object, this method creates PreparedStatements to accommodate the two kinds of SQL statements that will be executed: one that returns all the books if the search criteria is All, and one that returns only the books that match a given genre. In the latter case, notice how the genre is set on the SQL statement using the setString() method. Once the ResultSet is obtained, when the appropriate PreparedStatement is executed, the navigation of the ResultSet is simple: looping through the ResultSet using the next() method and the isLast() method to terminate the loop when all the data is read. By using the PreparedStatement object, the execution of the SQL statement avoids the step inside the JDBC implementation of creating and compiling a Java object to represent the query.

Summary

In this chapter, we learned about the most traditional method for accessing relational databases from Java EE. Based on SQL statements, a connection framework, and APIs for reading tabular data from the database, we worked through the fundamental concepts of this important API. We reviewed the basic SQL syntax and looked at how the JDBC API allows for precompilation of statements and access to stored procedures on the database in order to increase the efficiency of frequently used database queries. We did not show all the possibilities for modeling data in a relational database, since this is a book about Java APIs. But we worked through two examples that highlight the most common types of queries, in the second case, to use the JDBC APIs to take a RESTful web application and move its data into a relational database.

Even with the two relatively simple example JDBC applications we looked at, it is clear that much of the code in a JDBC application is devoted to modeling the data held in the tables (such as in the `Book` class defined for the Library application), or to maintaining SQL statements embedded in code, or to navigating `ResultSet` objects to extract the data in the shape the application needs. This is in addition to dealing with some of the lower-level connection issues such as having to close `Connection` objects and `ResultSets`.

Wouldn't it be nice if there was code that could map Java objects more directly to and from their equivalent form as rows of relational data in a database? In the next chapter, we will see how the Java Persistence API does just that.

CHAPTER
12

Modern Memories:
The Java Persistence API

The Java Persistence API enables applications to extend the life of regular Java objects by persisting them in a relational database.

As we saw in the JDBC APIs, much of the work of a JDBC application is concerned with formulating the correct SQL statements that will write an application's data objects into a relational database, manage them there, and reconstruct application-level data objects by interpreting the generic `ResultSet` objects that represent the result of a data query against the database.

The Java Persistence API (JPA) provides a very convenient shortcut to some of these steps. JPA helps applications in the process of storing and retrieving data from a relational database with the following key features:

- It allows application data objects to be easily converted into objects that can be persisted in a relational database. Such data objects are called persistence entities or simple entities.

- It contains APIs to manage the transition of entities between the application layer and the relational database, with a simple method protocol for simple tasks. This API is called the `EntityManager`.

- It includes both a query language called Java Persistence Query Language (JPQL) and a Criteria API for creating queries against the data.

Figure 12-1 shows a simple architecture of the Java Persistence API.

In this chapter, we explore what kind of Java classes are eligible to be persistence entities, and we look in some detail at how such Java classes can be mapped to tables in a relational database, in particular when there are numerous Java classes that model an application's data and that have

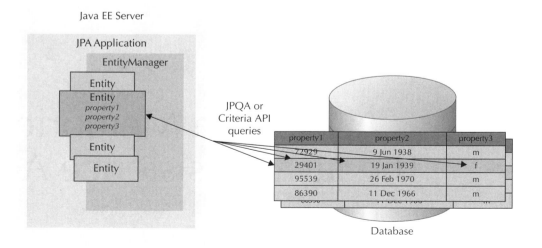

FIGURE 12-1. *Anatomy of the Java Persistence API*

relationships with one another, either by referencing one another in instance variables, or by having inheritance relationships with each other. We look at how to use Java objects as primary keys in the relational tables. We look in some detail at the `EntityManager` APIs, and we take a high-level view, with examples from the JPQL language.

The Java Persistence API is one of those APIs in the Java EE platform that has been designed to make the simple things simple. In that spirit, we use a familiar application with fairly straightforward application data as our "Hello World" application.

The Library Service, with Java Persistence

We last saw the Library service application in Chapter 11. We had extended this JAX-RS client/ server application from its incarnation in Chapter 5 to store its book data in a relational database, and we used the JDBC APIs to store and retrieve the book data.

As a reminder, here is the Library service in action, shown in Figure 12-2(a) and 12-2(b).

As we touched on at the end of Chapter 11, a portion of the JDBC data management layer of the Library service is taken up with SQL statements to create, update, and delete from the table used to store the book data, and another portion is concerned with reading book data out of the generic JDBC `ResultSet` object. As we look at the Library service application here that uses the Java Persistence API, notice how much simpler the application code is.

To start with, much of the application is the same. In fact, the application modifies the `Book` data object, which represents the application data about a single book to make it a persistence entity. Then, the application replaces the `LibraryDataManager` Enterprise Bean implementation class with a new implementation that uses the Java Persistence API. We can see the general architecture of the application in Figure 12-3.

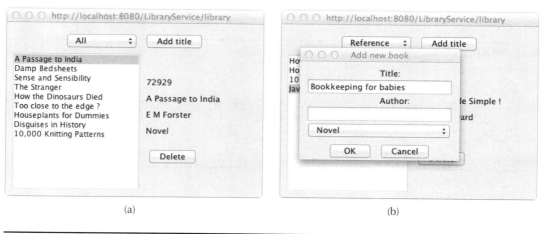

(a)   (b)

FIGURE 12-2. *(a) Library service browsing; (b) Library service adding a book*

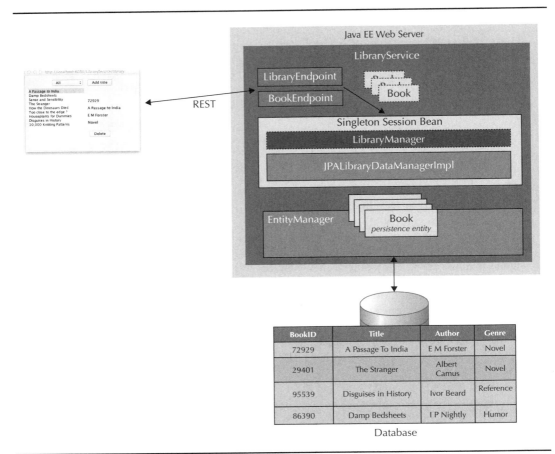

FIGURE 12-3. *Architecture of the Library service*

Therefore, we need not revisit the client code or the code for the JAX-RS endpoints: they are all unchanged. Let's look first at the new Book class.

Listing: *The Book class*

```
import javax.persistence.Entity;
import javax.persistence.NamedQueries;
import javax.persistence.NamedQuery;
import javax.persistence.Id;
import java.io.*;


@Entity
@NamedQueries({
```

```
    @NamedQuery(
        name="findAllBooks",
        query="select b from Book b"
    ),
    @NamedQuery(
        name="findBooksByGenre",
        query="select b from Book b where b.genre = :genre"
    )
    }
)
public class Book implements Serializable {
    @Id
    private int id;
    private String title;
    private String author;
    private String genre;

    public Book() {}

    public Book(int id, String title, String author, String genre) {
        this.id = id;
        this.title = title;
        this.author = author;
        this.genre = genre;
    }

    public int getId() {
        return this.id;
    }

    public String getTitle() {
        return this.title;
    }

    public String getAuthor() {
        return this.author;
    }

    public String getGenre() {
        return this.genre;
    }

    @Override
    public String toString() {
        return "a book by " + this.author;
    }
}
```

The overall data structure of the Book class is unchanged: it still has an ID and slots for the book's title, author name, and genre. But you can see from the class declaration that it uses a number of annotations to transform it into a persistence entity. It uses `@Entity` annotation to declare that this class is a persistence entity. It also defines at the class level two `NamedQueries`. Notice that a `NamedQuery` has a name (which will be used to execute it as we shall see) and a query string. The query strings are in the JPQL language. Notice, with the exception of the query parameters, for example, the `:genre`, in the `NamedQuery` named `findBooksByGenre`, the query strings look very like SQL statements. Finally, notice that the ID instance variable has been marked with the `@Id` annotation. The Java Persistence API will map this Book entity to a single table called Book. Each instance variable that the `Book` class has will be a column in the table, and each Book instance that is persisted will be a new row in the table. The `@Id` annotation says that the ID instance variable of the `Book` class will be used as the primary key for the table, and that the column name in the table for the ID will be called `ID`, the name attribute of the `@Column` annotation.

Therefore, this `Book` class contains all the information needed by the Java Persistence API to map its instances into a table in a relational database.

Now we can use this persistent data. Let's look at the `JPALibraryDataImpl` class.

Listing: *The JPALibraryDataImpl class*

```
import javax.ejb.Singleton;
import javax.ejb.Startup;
import javax.annotation.PostConstruct;
import java.util.*;
import javax.persistence.EntityManager;
import javax.persistence.PersistenceContext;
import javax.persistence.Query;

@Singleton
@Startup
public class JPALibraryDataManagerImpl implements LibraryDataManager {
    @PersistenceContext
    private EntityManager em;

    @PostConstruct
    public void initializeDefaultData()  {
        for (Book b : this.getDefaultBooks()) {
            this.addBook(b);
        }
    }

    @Override
    public void removeBook(int id) {
        Book book = this.em.find(Book.class, id);
        this.em.remove(book);
    }

    @Override
    public List<Book> getBooks(String searchGenre)  {
        List<Book> books;
        if (LibraryDataManager.ALL.equals(searchGenre)) {
```

```
            books = em.createNamedQuery("findAllBooks").getResultList();
        } else {
            Query query = em.createNamedQuery("findBooksByGenre");
            query.setParameter("genre", searchGenre);
            books = query.getResultList();
        }
        return books;
    }

    private void addBook(Book book) {
        this.em.persist(book);
    }

    @Override
    public void addBook(String title, String author, String genre) {
        Book book = new Book(this.generateId(), title, author, genre);
        this.addBook(book);
    }

    public int generateId() {
        long l = System.currentTimeMillis() * (new Random()).nextInt();
        String asString = "" + l;
        String as5String = asString.substring((asString.length()-5),
                                              (asString.length()));
        return new Integer(as5String);
    }

    private List<Book> getDefaultBooks() {
        List<Book> books = new ArrayList<>();
        Book b = new Book(this.generateId(), "A Passage to India",
                          "E M Forster", LibraryDataManager.NOVEL);
        books.add(b);
        b = new Book(this.generateId(), "Damp Bedsheets",
                          "I P Nightly", LibraryDataManager.HUMOR);
        books.add(b);
        b = new Book(this.generateId(), "Sense and Sensibility",
                          "Jane Austen", LibraryDataManager.NOVEL);
        books.add(b);
        b = new Book(this.generateId(), "The Stranger",
                          "Albert Camus", LibraryDataManager.NOVEL);
        books.add(b);
        b = new Book(this.generateId(), "How the Dinosaurs Died",
                          "P T Dactyl", LibraryDataManager.REFERENCE);
        books.add(b);
        b = new Book(this.generateId(), "Too close to the edge ?",
                          "Eileen Dover", LibraryDataManager.HUMOR);
        books.add(b);
        b = new Book(this.generateId(), "Houseplants for Dummies",
                          "G Fingers", LibraryDataManager.REFERENCE);
        books.add(b);
        b = new Book(this.generateId(), "Disguises in History",
```

```
                                      "Ivor Beard", LibraryDataManager.HUMOR);
        books.add(b);
        b = new Book(this.generateId(), "10,000 Knitting Patterns",
                     "M N E Sweaters", LibraryDataManager.REFERENCE);
        books.add(b);
        return books;
    }
}
```

This singleton bean injects an instance of the `javax.persistence.EntityManager` into itself. All the data operations on books performed by this class use this instance of the `EntityManager`. The `JPALibraryDataImpl` class uses the following API methods on the `EntityManager`:

- `find()` to locate an instance of an entity by primary key, for example,

  `Book b = this.em.find(Book.class, id)`

  which finds the instance of the Book class with the given ID

- `remove()` to remove an entity from the database, for example,

  `this.em.remove(book)`

  which removes the `Book` instance from the database

- `persist()`, which adds an entity to the database if it is not already there, or updates the database version of the entity if it was added previously, for example,

  `this.em.persist(book)`

  which puts a new `Book` instance into the Book table.

- `createNamedQuery()`

  which makes a `Query` object from the supplied named query that can be executed, for example,

  `books = em.createNamedQuery("findAllBooks").getResultList()`

  yields a `List` of Book objects, and also, when the named query contains a parameter, such as the `findBookByGenre` query, it can be set on the `Query` object, as you can see here:

  ```
  Query query = em.createNamedQuery("findBooksByGenre");
  query.setParameter("genre", searchGenre);
  books = query.getResultList();
  ```

Even in this simple example where the application data is a list of book objects, there are a few additional things to notice:

- The mapping of the `Book` object to and from its database table is wholly contained within the `Book` class by means of the persistence annotations. There is no translation code.

- The simple operations of adding and removing a `Book` to and from the database are one-line calls.

- For more complicated data queries, `NamedQueries` look very much like SQL code.

This example shows the fundamental properties of a Java Persistence application: the transformation of an application class into a persistence entity, the use of the `EntityManager` to move entities in and out of the database, and the use of queries (in this case, JPQL queries) to question the data.

We are now in a position to look at all the variations on these three central themes.

Persistence Entities

The starting point for a JPA application is to decide which application data you wish to persist. Let's look first at how to turn a regular Java class into a persistence entity.

The candidate Java class must be a non-final, top-level class with a public or protected constructor. The data held within the class that you wish to be persisted must be held in its non-public, non-transient instance variables. The candidate class must have an instance variable (or combination of instance variables as we shall see later) that can be used by the Persistence API as a primary key in the table it will use to store instances of this class. The candidate class may be turned into a persistence entity by adding the `@javax.persistence.Entity` annotation at the class level and marking the instance variable used for the primary key (assuming for now the simplest case of a single instance variable key) with the `@javax.persistence.Id` annotation. The data held within the Java class's qualifying instance variables are called the persistence attributes of the persistence entity. For example, the following `Author` has been turned into a persistence entity.

Listing: *An Author entity*

```
@Entity
public class Author {
    @Id
    private int id;
    private String firstName;
    private String lastName;

    public Author() {}

    public Author(int id, String firstName, String lastName) {
        this.id = id;
        this.firstName = firstName;
        this.lastName = lastName;
    }

}
```

The `Author` persistence entity has persistence attributes `id`, `firstName`, and `lastName`, and uses the `id` attribute as the primary key.

A persistence entity by default is mapped to a primary table whose name is the same as the name of its Java class, and the names of the qualifying instance variables are used as the names of the columns in the primary table. For example, the `Author` entity is mapped to a relational table called `Author` with columns `id`, `firstName`, and `lastName`.

These names can be changed by adding the `@Table` and `@Column` annotations. For example, look at the following the `Author` entity.

Listing: *An `Author` entity with adjusted table and column names*

```
@Entity
@Table(name="Author_Table")
public class Author {
    @Id
    @Column(name="Key")
    private int id;
    @Column(name="First_Name")
    private List<String> firstName;
     @Column(name="Last_Name")
       private String lastName;
...
}
```

This maps the `Author` entity to a table called `Author_Table` with columns named `Key`, `First_Name`, and `Last_Name`.

The type of the instance variables that may be used in a persistence entity is quite long. Here are the allowed types in a persistence entity:

- Java primitives their class equivalents, strings, and Java collections thereof
- Anything `Serializable`

  ```
  java.math.BigInteger and java.math.BigDecimal
  java.util.Date java.util.Calendar
  java.sql.Date, java.sql.Time, java.sql.Timestamp
  byte[], Byte[], char[], Character[]
  ```
- Java enums
- Other persistence entities and collections of other persistence entities
- Embeddable classes and collections thereof

In particular, you will notice that other persistence entities may be used, which expands the range of persistence entities to include graphs of Java classes with a variety of relationships between the members. Before we get to the complexity of how entities can be mapped to one another, we will cover the last type in the list of allowed types embeddable classes.

Embeddable Classes

Sometimes, it is convenient to model some of an object of type A's private data as an instance of another class B. In such cases, the data modeled in class B is wholly owned by class A and has no meaning outside the context of class A. When A is a persistence entity, this means that the data in an instance of B can be "flattened" into the same table as for A. In this situation, class B is called an embeddable class and is marked with the class-level `@javax.persistence.Embeddable` annotation. The instance variable that the persistence entity A uses to reference its instance of B is correspondingly marked with the `@javax.persistence.Embedded` annotation to complete the persistence relationship. For example, for convenience, in our Author example, we could define a new class `Name` to hold the first and last names of our authors:

Listing: *An embeddable class*

```
@Embeddable
public Name {
      private String firstName;
      private String lastName;
...
}
```

and then use `Name` in the `Author` persistence entity:

Listing: *Embedding and embeddable class*

```
@Entity
public class Author {
    @Id
    private int id;
    @Embedded
    private Name name;
...
}
```

In this case, the Author entity would be mapped to the same single table, and the embedded Name attribute would be flattened into two columns to accommodate its data.

Entity Relationships

Now suppose we have a `Book` entity, with an ID and a title, and now we want each book to have an instance of `Author` associated with it.

```
@Entity
public class Book implements Serializable {
    @Id
    private int id;
    private String title;
    private Author author;
...
}
```

In this case, since each author may have written more than one book, the `Author` instance is not suitable to be modeled as an embedded class. We would like all the books that were written by the same author to share the same `Author` instance. In this case, we want both the book and the author to be entities, and we wish to define the relationship between the two so that the correct instance graph is reconstructed when entities are retrieved from the database.

This simple example introduces us to the world of entity relationships. An entity relationship is a state that exists between two persistence entities. One side of the relationship is the owning side, and the other side is called the target. The owning entity in the relationship decides how its target is updated in the relational database, as we shall see.

Persistence entities define their relationships with each other by the owning entity referencing the target in an instance variable. If the target does not reference the owning entity in any of its instance variables, this is called a unidirectional relationship. If the target entity does reference the owning entity with an instance variable, it is called a bidirectional relationship, and the target is sometimes called the inverse entity of the relationship.

There are four different kinds of entity relationships, whether unidirectional or bidirectional: one-to-one, one-to-many, many-to-one, and many-to-many.

In a one-to-one relationship, the owning entity relates to a single instance of the target. If we were to model cats with a `Cat` entity and their collars with a `Collar` entity, since each cat has one collar, we would model the owning entity `Cat` as having a one-to-one relationship with its target `Collar` entity.

In a one-to-many relationship, the owning entity relates to one or more instances of the target entity. If we were to model the `Author` as the owning entity, since each author has written more than one book, we would model the `Author` as having a one-to-many relationship with the `Book` entity.

In a many-to-one relationship, one or more instances of the owning entity would relate to a single target entity. For example, if we were modeling cars as an owning `Car` entity, with a target `Owner`, since each `Car` has a single owner, but each owner may own several cars, the `Car` entity would have a many-to-one relationship with the `Owner` entity.

In a many-to-many relationship, one or more instances of the owning entity have a relationship to one or more instances of the target entity. For example, if we were modeling people and families, each family has one or more persons, and each person may belong to more than one family, so we could model the owning `Person` entity as having a many-to-many relationship with the target `Family` entity.

We can see the four types of entity relationships in Figure 12-4.

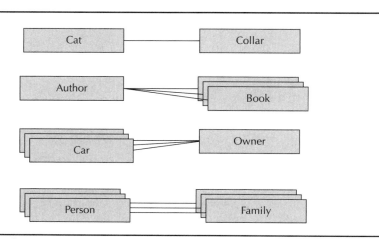

FIGURE 12-4. *The four entity relationship types*

When an owning entity wishes to declare its relationship with a target entity, it must annotate its attribute with one of the following four annotations from the `javax.persistence` package: `@OneToOne`, `@OneToMany`, `@ManyToOne`, or `@ManyToMany`, depending on the type of the relationship. For example, the Book entity has a unidirectional many-to-one relationship with the `Author` entity, so we would need to annotate the `Book` entity's author field with the `@ManyToOne` annotation.

```
public class Book implements Serializable {
    @Id
    private int id;
    private String title;
    @ManyToOne
    private Author author;
...
}
```

When the relationship is bidirectional, the inverse side must refer to its owning side by using the `mappedBy` attribute of the `@OneToOne`, `@OneToMany`, or `@ManyToMany` annotation. The `mappedBy` element designates the property or field in the entity that is the owner of the relationship. In a bidirectional relationship, if one side is "many," that side must be the owning side. Thus, there cannot be a one-to-many bidirectional relationship.

These annotations must be added to the persistence entities so that the Java Persistence API knows what to do when part of a graph of related persistence entities is modified. What happens to the books, for example, if the author is deleted?

Before we can understand how graphs of persistent objects are affected by operations on their members, we will first take a look at the different states entities can have in the Java Persistence API.

Persistent States

Persistent entities have two existences: one is in the form of a Java object, marked with the `@Entity` annotation, running in a JPA application. The other is spread as a row across one or more tables in a relational database. The persistent states in a JPA application refer to the relationship between the Java object form of a persistent entity and its representation in the relational database managed by the Java Persistence entity manager.

In the `New` state, the persistent entity (or graph of persistent entities) has been created, but has not yet been persisted by the entity manager into the database. At this point, there is no data in the database reflecting the state of the persistent entity. When the entity is persisted, it moves to the `Managed` state. In this state, it has an equivalent representation as relational data in the database. Changes to the persistent entity in the managed state are reflected in the database. If the entity is moved to the `Detached` state, it has a representation in the relational database, but that representation is only up-to-date with the Java object representation at the time it became detached. Further changes to the Java objects do not cause updates to the relational data in the database. A detached entity may be put back into the `Managed` state by performing a merge operation, which updates the relational data in the database with the new state of the Java object representation of the entity. Finally, the entity may be in the `Removed` state, in which case, its representation in the relational database has been deleted. Figure 12-5 gives a pictoral summary of the states of persistent entities. We will look shortly at how the `EntityManager` API allows JPA applications to manage these states through API calls, but now we can return to the topic of what happens to graphs of related persistent entities when member entities are modified.

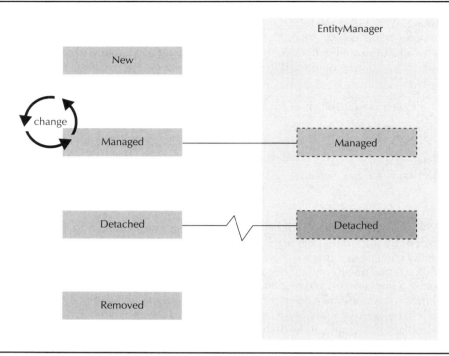

FIGURE 12-5. *The persistent states of persistent entities*

Cascading in Entity Relationships

The entity relationship annotations @OneToOne, @OneToMany, @ManyToOne, and @ManyToMany each have a cascade attribute that defines what is to happen when there is an end of the relationship, where the annotation applied is modified by the EntityManager in some way. The options for this control include what happens to the target entity when the owning entity becomes detached, is merged, or is removed or deleted, when it is refreshed, and when it is persisted. The CascadeType enumeration defines all the possible options, as the following table shows.

CascadeType	
CascadeType.PERSIST	If the EntityManager persists the owning entity, it will also persist the target entity.
CascadeType.REFRESH	If the EntityManager refreshes the owning entity, it will also refresh the target entity.
CascadeType.DETATCH	If the EntityManager detaches the owning entity, it will also detach the target entity.
CascadeType.MERGE	If the EntityManager merges the owning entity, it will also merge the target entity.

CascadeType

CascadeType.REMOVE	If the EntityManager removes the owning entity, it will also remove the target entity.
CascadeType.ALL	If the EntityManager performs any of the operations listed on the owning entity, it will perform the same operation on the target.

The Entity Manager

Now that we have explored some of the most common options for setting up persistent entities with the Java Persistence API, it's time to look at the controller of the show: the EntityManager. This interface is the gateway to all the operations that store, retrieve, synchronize, and remove the persistent data from the relational database that corresponds to persistent entities in a JPA application.

The main functions of an EntityManager are to manage the lifecycle of persistence entities and to formulate query operations to query the data. Each EntityManager has a lifecycle of its own: it is either open or closed. EntityManagers typically cache persistent entities, with a flush() operation that writes the persistent entity to the database. The main methods of an open EntityManager used in an application are as follows:

void persist(Object entity)

which persists the given entity;

void merge(Object entity)

which updates the persistent state of the given entity;

void refresh(Object entity)

which changes the state of the given entity to match that of its persistent state;

void detach(Object entity)

which detaches the given entity from its persistent state;

void remove(Object entity)

which deletes the given persistent entity's persistent state;

<T> T find(Class<T> entityClass, Object primaryKey), and variants

which find the instance of the given persistent entity class with the matching key; and

Query createQuery(String qlString), and variants

which creates a Query object from the given query string, which can be executed to obtain the query results.

We can see the main functions of the EntityManager in Figure 12-6.

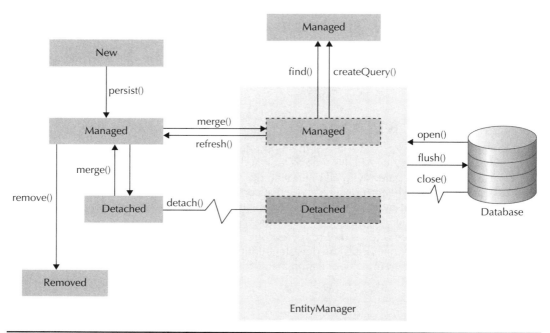

FIGURE 12-6. *EntityManager operations*

EntityManagers may be instantiated programmatically or be injected into Java EE components. When EntityManager instances are injected, the Java EE container manages their lifecycles, whereas programmatically instantiated EntityManagers must be explicitly opened and closed. This makes injecting the EntityManager instance the easier option, and, when programming with standard Java EE components, the obvious choice for using the Java Persistence API.

In order to inject an EntityManager, all you need to do is add an instance variable of type EntityManager annotated with @PersistenceContext, for example

```
@Singleton
public class Library {
    @PersistenceContext
    private EntityManager em;


..
}
```

EntityManager instances may be created programmatically using the EntityManagerFactory interface, which is obtained from an instance of the PersistenceUnit class that may be injected:

```
@PersistenceUnit
EntityManagerFactory emf;
...
EntityManager em = emf.createEntityManager();
```

Java Persistence Query Language

The Java Persistence API defines an SQL-like query language that can be used to formulate queries against persistent data managed by an `EntityManager`. It is beyond the scope of this chapter and this book to discuss every aspect of the language, so this section will limit itself to the main and most commonly used features as they apply to querying data with the Java Persistence API.

JPQL is heavily inspired by SQL, and anyone already familiar with a SQL variant will find JPQL very easy to use. The basic statements are `SELECT`, `UPDATE`, and `DELETE`. For example,

```
SELECT a.firstName FROM Author a WHERE a.lastName = "Coward" ORDER BY a.firstName
```

would return all the first names of authors in alphabetical order from the `Author` table with last name `Coward`.

```
DELETE from Author WHERE lastName = "James"
```

would delete all authors from the `Author` table where the last name is `James`.

Most pertinently to JPA applications, JPQL statements may contain named parameters. A named parameter in a JPQL statement always begins with a colon.

JPA queries are created with the EntityManager. There are two primary ways this can be done: either dynamically using the `createQuery()` API, for example

```
Query q = myEntityManager.createQuery("SELECT a.firstName,
                    a.lastName FROM Author a ORDER BY a.lastName");
```

or by using named queries. Named queries are precompiled JPQL statements that are declared using the @NamedQuery annotation. For example, the following `Author` entity holds a named query with the name `findAuthors`:

```
@Entity
    @NamedQuery(
        name="findAuthors",
        query="select a from Author a"
    )
public class Author implements Serializable {
    @Id
    private int id;
    ...
}
```

When the JPA application wishes to call the query, it creates the `Query` object using the `createNamedQuery()` method on the `EntityManager`, passing in the name of the named query. For example,

```
Query q = myEntityManager.createNamedQuery("findAuthors");
```

However the query is created, whether dynamically or as a precompiled named query, the query is executed by calling the `Query` object's

```
executeUpdate()
```

method if the query is a `CREATE` or an `UPDATE` statement.

When the query is created from a `SELECT` statement, the query is executed by calling either the `Query` object's

```
List getResultList()
```

method, which returns a `List` of result objects of the type expected when multiple are expected, or the

```
Object getSingleResult()
```

method, which returns a single result object of the type expected in the case when a single result is expected.

Most usefully, JPQL statements may be parameterized with named parameters. A named parameter is a string that starts with a colon and whose value can be set on the `Query` object created from the `EntityManager` at runtime. So, for example, if we wished to create a named query that searched for authors with the same last name, but wanted to defer which last name until the JPA application chose it at runtime, we could create the named query

```
@NamedQuery(
    name="findAuthorsByLastName",
    query="select a from Author a where a.lastName = :ln"
)
```

Then when we create the `Query` in the JPA application,

```
Query q = myEntityManager.createNamedQuery("findAuthorsByLastName");
```

we can set the ln parameter by calling

```
q.setParameter("ln", "Jones");
```

prior to executing the query. You can use named parameters in the other JPQL clauses, such as `ORDER BY` or `GROUP BY`. There are also many other ways to use and set parameters on JPA queries, but this named form is the most basic and useful to master. We will see some more examples of this style of formulating queries shortly.

Configuring JPA Applications

The `PersistenceContext` is a kind of high-level abstraction of a data source used by a JPA application. You will recall that when injecting the `EntityManager` into a Java EE application, the annotation `@PersistenceContext` is used to make the injection. This injection says that all the `EntityManager` instances will be created from the same `PersistenceContext`. In fact, an application may have more than one persistence context, in which case, using the name attribute of the `@PersistenceContext` annotation can disambiguate them. In many cases, applications have only one `PersistenceContext`, so the name attribute is frequently omitted.

The Java Persistence API defines a file format that contains the configuration information for the `PersistenceContexts` in an application, called the `persistence.xml` file. It resides in the `META-INF` directory of the containing Java EE archive. So, for example, if an Enterprise Bean application uses a persistence context, the `persistence.xml` will reside in the Enterprise Bean JAR's `META-INF` entry. Usually, the `persistence.xml` file is set up for you if you are using an IDE, so you only need concern yourself with the name if you are using more than one persistence context in an application. However, here is an example.

Listing: *An example `persistence.xml` file*

```xml
<?xml version="1.0" encoding="UTF-8"?>
<persistence version="2.1"
             xmlns="http://xmlns.jcp.org/xml/ns/persistence"
             xmlns:xsi="http://www.w3.org/2001/XMLSchema-instance"
             xsi:schemaLocation="http://xmlns.jcp.org/xml/ns/persistence
             http://xmlns.jcp.org/xml/ns/persistence/persistence_2_1.xsd">
  <persistence-unit name="myPersistenceContextName" transaction-type="JTA">
    <exclude-unlisted-classes>false</exclude-unlisted-classes>
    <properties>
      <property name="javax.persistence.schema-generation.database.action"
             value="drop-and-create"/>
    </properties>
  </persistence-unit>
</persistence>
```

This `persistence.xml` file defines a persistence context with name `myPersistenceContextName`. Notice in particular the property `javax.persistence.schema-generation.database.action`. This property has three options: `none`, `create`, and `drop-and-create`. When a JPA application is being deployed, this property governs whether the JPA runtime attempts to create tables for the persistence entities within the application and whether it deletes the tables when the application is undeployed. If the property is absent, the application takes neither action. If the property is present with the `create` value, the tables are created at deployment time, and if present with the `drop-and-create` value, the tables are created at application deployment and deleted when the application is undeployed.

With this understanding of the primary features of the Java Persistence API, we are now in a position to revisit the Library application.

The Persistent Library Service

The Persistent Library service builds on the concept of the Library service introduced earlier, but adds the notion of book authors and genres to which books can belong. Instead of a Swing client, the JavaServer Faces web front end is used. This web UI allows you to browse books by genre (shown in Figure 12-7), list all the books by a given author (shown in Figure 12-8), add a new book (shown in Figure 12-9) and add a new author (shown in Figure 12-10).

FIGURE 12-7. *Browsing the Sci-Fi catalog*

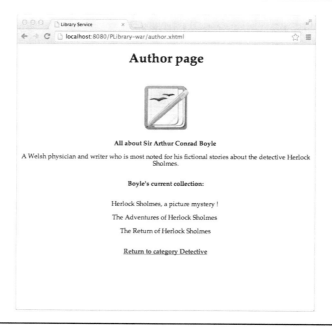

FIGURE 12-8. *All about the author*

FIGURE 12-9. *Adding a new book*

FIGURE 12-10. *Adding a new author*

The core of this application is its collection of persistence entities: Book with its subclass ChildrensBook, and Author and Genre. First let's look at the Book class.

Listing: *The Book class*

```
import javax.persistence.Entity;
import javax.persistence.NamedQueries;
import javax.persistence.NamedQuery;
import javax.persistence.Id;
import javax.persistence.GeneratedValue;
import javax.persistence.ManyToOne;
import javax.persistence.OneToMany;
import javax.persistence.CascadeType;
import java.io.*;
import java.util.List;

@Entity
@NamedQueries({
    @NamedQuery(
        name="findAllBooks",
        query="select b from Book b order by b.title"
    ),

    @NamedQuery(
        name="findAllBooksBy",
        query="select b from Book b where b.author.id = :aId order by b.title"
    )
    }
)
public class Book implements Serializable {
    @GeneratedValue
    @Id
    private int id;
    private String title;
    @ManyToOne(cascade={CascadeType.PERSIST, CascadeType.REFRESH})
    private Author author;
    @OneToMany(cascade={CascadeType.PERSIST, CascadeType.REFRESH})
    private List<Genre> genres;

    public Book() {}

    public Book(String title, Author author, List<Genre> genres) {
        this.title = title;
        this.author = author;
        this.genres = genres;
    }

    public int getId() {
        return this.id;
    }

    public String getTitle() {
        return this.title;
    }
```

```
    public Author getAuthor() {
        return this.author;
    }

    public List<Genre> getGenres() {
        return this.genres;
    }

    public boolean isInGenre(String name) {
        for (Genre g : this.genres) {
            if (g.getName().equals(name)) {
                return true;
            }
        }
        return false;
    }

    @Override
    public String toString() {
        return "a book called " + this.title + " by " + this.author + " in " + this.
genres;
    }
}
```

We can see from its class declaration that it is a persistence entity thanks to its `@Entity` annotation, and it declares two named queries, one that fetches all books in the library, and one that fetches all the books by a given author `id`, ordered by `title`. It has persistence attributes ID, its primary key, and title. It also has a many-to-one entity relationship with the `Author` entity, and a one-to-many entity relationship with the `Genre` entity. So this library allows only single-author books, but each book may belong to multiple genres. We can see from the cascade attribute of the relationship annotations that under the operations `persist()` and `refresh()` the `Book` entity will cause its associated author and genres to be persisted and refreshed. But if the `Book` entity is removed, the associated author and genres will not be removed. If we did want those target entities removed in that situation, we could have used `CascadeType.REMOVE` in the entity relationship annotations to have the `EntityManager` do it automatically.

Notice also that compared with the previous version of the `Book` class, this `Book` class does not require a unique `id` to be passed in order to create an instance from it. Instead, the `Book` entity uses the `@GeneratedValue` annotated from the Java Persistence API to request that its `id` variable be generated automatically by the Java Persistence runtime, a unique one for each instance. This means that this version of the library no longer has to worry about creating unique `id`s for the books it houses. The `@GeneratedValue` annotation has optional attributes that allow applications to control the generation strategy for the IDs.

Listing: *The Author class*

```
import java.util.*;
import java.io.*;
import javax.persistence.Entity;
import javax.persistence.NamedQueries;
import javax.persistence.NamedQuery;
import javax.persistence.Id;
```

```java
import javax.persistence.GeneratedValue;

@Entity
@NamedQueries({
    @NamedQuery(
        name="findAllAuthors",
        query="select a from Author a"
    ),
    @NamedQuery(
        name="findAuthorById",
        query="select a from Author a where a.id = :aId"
    )
}
)
public class Author implements Serializable {
    @Id
    @GeneratedValue
    private int id;
    private List<String> foreNames;
    private String lastName;
    private String description = "";

    public Author() {}

    public Author(List<String> foreNames,
                  String lastName,
                  String description) {
        this.foreNames = foreNames;
        this.lastName = lastName;
        this.description = description;
    }

    public Author(String firstName, String lastName, String description) {
        this(new ArrayList<String>(), lastName, description);
        List<String> foreNames = new ArrayList<>();
        foreNames.add(firstName);
        this.foreNames = foreNames;
    }


    public int getId() {
        return this.id;
    }

    public List<String> getForeNames() {
        return this.foreNames;
    }


    public String getLastName() {
        return this.lastName;
```

```
        }

        public String getDescription() {
            return this.description;
        }

        @Override
        public String toString() {
            return "Author:(" + this.foreNames + " " + this.lastName + ")";
        }

    }
```

In the `Author` class, we can see the `Book`'s relationship to it is unidirectional, since the `Author` class has no instance variable for Books. The `Author` class makes use of `NamedQueries`, in particular, using a named parameter for the `findAuthorById` query to allow the author `id` to be supplied dynamically. The `Genre` entity is along the same lines, with `NamedQueries`, showing that its relationship from `Book` is also unidirectional, having primary key as the name of the genre and having an attribute to hold the description of the genre.

Notice that, like the `Book` class, the `Author` class now requests its `id` be generated by the Java Persistence runtime, relieving the application of the job of generating a new one each time it creates a new `Author` instance.

Listing: *The Genre class*

```
import java.io.Serializable;
import javax.persistence.*;

@Entity
@NamedQueries({
    @NamedQuery(
        name="findAllGenres",
        query="select g from Genre g"
    ),
    @NamedQuery(
        name="findByGenreName",
        query="select g from Genre g where g.name = :gName"
    )
}
)
public class Genre implements Serializable {
    @Id
    private String name;
    private  String description;

    public String toString() {
        return "genre: " + name + " " + description;
    }
```

```
    public Genre(String name, String description) {
        this.name = name;
        this.description = description;
    }

    public String getName() {return this.name;}

    public String getDescription() {return this.description;}
    public Genre() {}
}
```

Finally, regarding the entities, the `ChildrensBook` entity is a subclass of `Book`, adding an integer age attribute to denote a guide age for the audience of the book. You will see the childrens' books are shown in the library front page with different icons depending on whether they are for adults or younger or older children.

Listing: *The ChildrensBook class*

```
import java.io.Serializable;
import java.util.List;
import javax.persistence.Entity;

@Entity
public class ChildrensBook extends Book implements Serializable {
    private int bestAge;

    public ChildrensBook() {}

    public ChildrensBook(String title, Author author,
                         List<Genre> genres, int bestAge) {
        super(title, author, genres);
        this.bestAge = bestAge;
    }

    public int getAge() {
        return bestAge;
    }

        @Override
    public String toString() {
        return "a kids book called " + super.getTitle() +
          " by " + super.getAuthor() + " in " + super.getGenres() +
                                            "age " + bestAge;

    }

}
```

In this application, we have configured the persistent unit such that the tables are created on application deployment and dropped when the application is removed. The tables are populated by a `Singleton` bean, which is marked with the `@javax.ejb.Startup` annotation to ensure that it runs when the application is deployed. We will not look at the code, except to note that it uses the ordinary Java constructors for Book, ChildrensBook, Author, and Genre to set up the data, and the EntityManager persist() call to write each Book to the database; for example

```
Book b = new Book("The Adventures of Herlock Sholmes", a, genres);
entityManager.persist(b);
```

We could equally create SQL scripts to populate the tables on startup. This is a more advanced configuration option in the persistence.xml than we need to show in this example.

Now we come to the thinking part of the application, the LibraryBeanImpl that uses the Entity Manager to query and manage the book, author, and genre data.

Listing: *The LibraryBeanImpl class*

```java
import javaeems.chapter12.library.entities.*;
import javaeems.chapter12.library.LibraryBean;
import java.util.*;
import javax.ejb.*;
import javax.persistence.EntityManager;
import javax.persistence.PersistenceContext;
import javax.persistence.Query;


@Singleton
public class LibraryBeanImpl implements LibraryBean {
    @PersistenceContext
    private EntityManager em;

    @Override
    public Genre getGenreByName(String name) {
        Query query = em.createNamedQuery("findByGenreName");
        query.setParameter("gName", name);
        return (Genre) query.getSingleResult();
    }

    @Override
    public List<Book> getBooksByGenre(String genreName) {
        Query query = em.createNamedQuery("findAllBooks");
        List<Book> books = query.getResultList();
        List<Book> genreBooks = new ArrayList<>();
        for (Book b : books) {
            if (b.isInGenre(genreName)) {
                genreBooks.add(b);
            }
        }
        return genreBooks;
    }

    @Override
    public List<Book> getBooksByAuthor(int authorID) {
        Query query = em.createNamedQuery("findAllBooksBy");
        query.setParameter("aId", authorID);
        return query.getResultList();
    }
```

```java
@Override
public List<Author> getAuthors() {
    Query query = em.createNamedQuery("findAllAuthors");
    List<Author> authors = query.getResultList();
    return authors;
}

private List<Genre> getGenres(List<String> genreNames) {
    List<Genre> genres = new ArrayList<>();
    for (String name : genreNames) {
        genres.add(this.getGenreByName(name));
    }
    return genres;
}

@Override
public void addBook(String title, int authorId,
                    List<String> genreNames, boolean isChildrens, int age) {
    Author author = this.getAuthorForId(authorId);
    if (author == null) {
        throw new RuntimeException("bad author");
    }
    List<Genre> genres = this.getGenres(genreNames);
    Book newBook;
    if (isChildrens) {
        newBook = new ChildrensBook(title, author, genres, age);
    } else {
        newBook = new Book(title, author, genres);
    }
    em.persist(newBook);

}

@Override
public List<String> getGenreNames() {
    Query query = em.createNamedQuery("findAllGenres");
    List<Genre> genres = query.getResultList();
    List<String> names = new ArrayList<>();
    for (Genre g : genres) {
        names.add(g.getName());
    }
    return names;
}

@Override
public void deleteBook(int id) {
    Book b = em.find(Book.class, id);
    em.remove(b);
}

@Override
public Author getAuthorForId(int id) {
    Query query = em.createNamedQuery("findAuthorById");
    query.setParameter("aId", id);
    return (Author) query.getSingleResult();
```

```
        }

        @Override
        public void addAuthor(List<String> foreNames, String lastName, String description) {
            Author a = new Author(foreNames, lastName, description);
            em.persist(a);
        }

    }
```

Take some time to look through all the operations. Note in particular the use of `persist()` to persist an entity, such as can be seen in the `addAuthor()` method.

And note the use of named queries throughout, in particular, the use of named parameters therein, for example, in `getAuthorForId()` and `getBooksByAuthor()`.

Note in particular, and in contrast to the JDBC examples, how the results of the `SELECT`-based queries return with all the entity type information. There is no need to cast the elements of a result list to a `Book` object. If you look carefully around the rest of the application, in particular, the managed bean that supplies the icons that signify the guide age for the books, you see that the `EntityManager` preserves the polymorphism in the `Book/ChildrensBook` hierarchy, retrieving instances of `ChildrensBook` where appropriate.

Summary

In this chapter, we have examined the primary features of the Java Persistence API. Starting with a Hello World-style application, we set out by looking at how the Java Persistence API offers a higher level and more compact approach than does JDBC to storing and retrieving application data in and from a relational database. We explored the mechanisms to turn a regular Java class into a persistence entity that can be used with the JPA APIs and how to define embeddable classes and relationships with other persistence entities. We toured the EntityManager API, understanding its main operations and how they relate to the different states persistence entities can be in. We looked at queries and the JPQL language. We concluded with an examination of an updated library with a more complete application dataset, including persistence entities within a class hierarchy and with a variety of entity relationships.

PART
IV

The Java EE Toolbox:
Java EE Environment

CHAPTER
13

The Big Picture Revisited:
Java EE Applications

The Java EE application model is the combination and culmination of the web, Enterprise Bean, and data models in the Java EE platform.

Up to this point in the book, we have focused mainly on the individual enterprise technologies that make up the Java EE platform. We have examined all the major point technologies in Java EE. Now we will consider some of the mechanisms and concepts that bring the point technologies together.

Although we have already seen some of these ideas in action, this chapter will explore the packaging and deployment mechanisms of Java EE applications, and will look at some of the services common to Java EE components. We will finish with a description of Java EE profiles.

The Java EE Application

A Java EE application is a single deployable unit of code, resources, and deployment information. It is composed of any or all of the following elements.

Web Application WARs

As discussed in Chapter 8, a web application is a collection of static content, markup pages, and images, together with dynamic web components such as Java servlets, JSPs, JavaServer Faces, JAX-RS resources, and Java WebSocket endpoints, with any resources that these web components need such as managed beans or tag libraries and their collective deployment information.

Enterprise Bean JARs

As we saw in Chapter 9, an Enterprise Bean JAR is a collection of one or more related Enterprise Beans and any resources or libraries they need, along with their collective deployment information.

Application Client JARs

An application client JAR is a Java EE application client application, containing a main class, any other classes, libraries, and resources it needs together with its deployment information. We will discuss application clients in more detail shortly.

Resource Adapter Archives

A Resource Adapter Archive (RAR) is something that implements the Java EE Connector architecture. This architecture is the standard way by which the Java EE server can be extended to connect to other enterprise information systems such as ERP systems, transaction processing systems, and non-Java systems of many kinds. A Resource Adapter Archive allows the rest of the Java EE application of which it is part to call into these systems. Creating RARs is usually done by developers with a high degree of familiarity with the system to which it connects, and is a specialty that is beyond the scope of this book.

Java EE Modules

Each of these elements: a web application WAR, Enterprise Bean JAR, application client JAR, and Resource Adapter Archive is known more generically as a Java EE module.

In addition, a Java EE application may contain deployment information that is not already contained in its constituent Java EE modules.

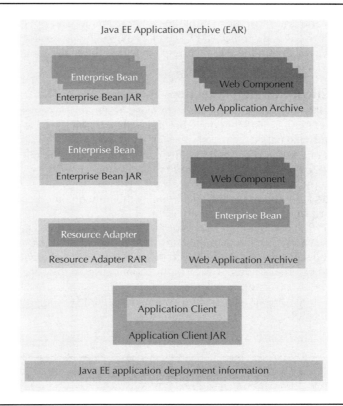

FIGURE 13-1. *A logical view of a Java EE application*

In Figure 13-1, we see a representation of the logical structure of a Java EE application.

Before we look at how this logical structure is reflected in the Enterprise Archive packaging format for Java EE applications, we will look a little more formally at Java EE application clients.

Application Clients

The Java EE platform includes a container for client-side applications, such as Java Swing or JavaFX GUI applications. This container, called the application client container, provides a number of the Java EE services that are available to Java EE components running in the web or Enterprise Bean container. Examples of these services include access to configured objects such as a JDBC data source in the JNDI namespace, and the abilities to inject references to Enterprise Beans running on the Java EE server and to call them.

An application client application always has a main class with a Java `main()` method. The application client container upon initialization calls the main class, and the application has a particularly simple lifecycle because the application container does not ever instantiate the main class; it runs the `main()` method until it finishes.

One of the main features of the Java EE platform that an application client may take advantage of is access to the JNDI namespace.

Java EE application clients have access to a subset of the Java EE services available in the server-side web and Enterprise Bean containers. For example, an application client may look up any of the Enterprise Beans on its Java EE server in the JNDI namespace. We will be exploring the Java EE services available in the JNDI namespace across the entire platform shortly, and we will identify this subset for application clients.

Application Client Resource Injection

Because the application container never instantiates the main class, resource injection into the fields of the main class is available only into the static variables, and is performed prior to the `main()` method being called.

Application clients are packaged in a file called the application client JAR file. This type of file is a regular JAR file containing all the classes and resources needed by the application client code, with a couple of additional features.

The `MANIFEST.MF` file of the JAR file contains the fully qualified classname of the application client's main class in the `Main-Class` attribute.

An optional XML deployment descriptor file is located in the `META-INF` directory and called `application-client.xml`, which contains descriptive information about the application such as a logical and display name, together with descriptions of the references to Enterprise Bean components and external resources used by the application, if they are not already declared using annotations in the source code.

Figure 13-2 shows the structure of the application client JAR, together with an example application client JAR.

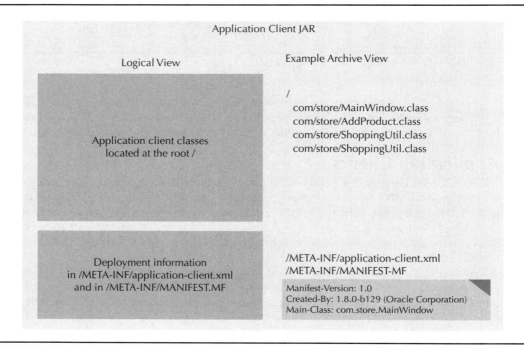

FIGURE 13-2. *The structure of an application client JAR*

Enterprise Archives: EAR Files

A Java EE Enterprise ARchive file, or EAR file for short, is the file format for distributing Java EE applications. It is a special kind of ZIP archive that may contain zero or more WAR files, Enterprise Bean JAR files, RAR files, and application client JAR files in its root entry. It may also contain a deployment descriptor in a file called `application.xml` in its `META-INF` directory, which may add further descriptions of the modules it contains (we will see examples later). It may also contain descriptions of references to Enterprise Bean components and external resources used by the application. It may also contain JAR files that contain libraries used by one or more of the Java EE modules in the application, under the `/lib` directory.

Java EE Application and Module Names

All modules within an EAR file have a logical name, called the module name. The module name of a Java EE module defaults to the archive entry name of its archive, minus the file extension. So, for example, in Figure 13-3, the default module name of the Java EE modules contained in the example EAR file are `ui/store`, `ui/catalog`, `adminsite`, `dataModelBeans`, and `admin-client`.

Java EE applications themselves have a logical name. The default logical name of a Java EE application is its filename, minus the `.ear` extension. So in Figure 13-3, the default logical name is `myShop`.

The default application and module name may be overridden in the optional `application.xml` deployment descriptor.

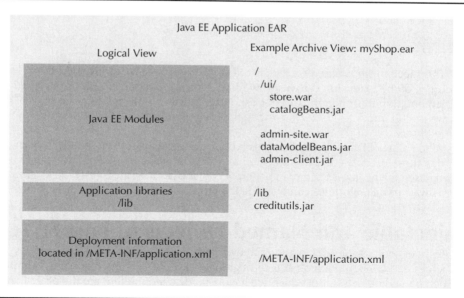

FIGURE 13-3. *The structure of a Java EE application*

Java EE Application External Libraries

The /lib directory of the EAR file provides a general-purpose means by which multiple Java EE modules in the same Java EE application can use common code. What about code that is shared across multiple Java EE applications? In this kind of situation, the Java EE archives, whether they be EARs, WARs, RARs, or application client JARs, use the JAR extension mechanism to declare a dependency on an external JAR file.

In order for a Java EE archive myApplication.ear to declare a dependency on a library called mybookutils, it adds a declaration of the dependency to its MANIFEST.MF file.

Listing: *Expressing an external dependency*

```
META-INF/MANIFEST.MF
Manifest-Version: 1.0
Extension-List: mydependency
mydependency-Extension-Name: mybookutils
mydependency-Specification-Version: 4.8
```

When deployed, the Java EE server looks for a JAR file satisfying the requirements of the EAR file. It will look for a JAR file, installed previously, that declares that it supports the mybookutils library, by expressing this in its MANIFEST.MF file.

Listing: *Satisfying an external dependency*

```
META-INF/MANIFEST.MF
Manifest-Version: 1.0
Extension-Name: mybookutils
Specification-Vendor: Library code LLC
Specification-Version: 4.8.1
```

This mechanism is based on the Java SE applet mechanism for installed extensions. Additional attributes of the extension syntax allow libraries to declare more vendor information, and also implementation information, and correspondingly, the additional Extension-List syntax allows Java EE modules to declare a dependency on a particular vendor and/or implementation of the library.

When a Java EE application bundles a library used by one or more of its modules, and one or more of those modules declares an external dependency on the same library, the bundled library will be used by the Java EE server in preference to any libraries that satisfy the external dependency. In this way, Java EE modules can override the installed libraries on the server if they need to.

Injectable and Named Objects of Java EE

As we have seen, the Java EE platform allows Java EE applications to access various available resources and configuration objects through named objects. Some of the most common examples of such named objects, all of which we have already encountered, are the other Enterprise Beans deployed in the Java EE server, configured JDBC DataSources and EntityManagers. In this section, we look at all the named objects available in the Java EE platform.

Named objects are available to Java EE components in one of two ways. First, they can be looked up in the Java Naming and Directory Interface (JNDI) namespace using the name under which the object is registered. Second, named objects can be injected into the Java EE component using one of the annotations @EJB, @Resource, @PersistenceContext, or @PersistenceUnit depending on the type of the object.

A Java EE component expresses its dependency on named objects either through the use of the annotations listed earlier, or through the deployment descriptor of the module that contains it. The deployment descriptor elements such as <env-entry>, <ejb-ref>, <resource-ref>, and <resource-env-ref>, are common to all the Java EE deployment descriptors and define the syntax defining a component's dependency on the different types of named objects. The annotations listed earlier, and the deployment descriptor syntax for dependencies on named objects that we explore in this section, apply equally to all Java EE component types, from web components through Enterprise Beans to application clients.

The power of this scheme, whether it be used for configuring Enterprise Bean references, general-purpose configuration objects, or JavaMail sessions, is that Java EE components can locate and use these named objects without having to understand any of the details concerning how the object has been configured into the Java EE server by the person who deploys the application, or by the person who administers the Java EE server. Equally, the deployer, or server administrator, can ascertain, through the use of annotations and deployment descriptors in a Java EE application, on which named objects a Java EE component depends, and so set up the correct named objects in the Java EE server that the Java EE application needs.

We can see an illustration of the named object scheme in Figure 13-4.

JNDI Namespaces

In the Java EE server, the namespace JNDI uses is divided up into different logical areas: for objects local to a particular component, for objects shared by all components within a particular Java EE module, for objects shared by all components within any Java EE module within a particular Java EE application, and finally, a logical area where objects can be put that are shared across any Java EE application deployed on the Java EE server. These scopes apply equally to all Java EE components with the exception of web components: web components do not have individual java:comp namespaces; they share the java:comp namespace with all the web components within the same WAR.

Namespace Name	Scope
java:comp	Local to a particular component (except web components)
java:module	Local to a particular Java EE module
java:app	Local to a Java EE application
java:global	Shared across all Java EE applications on the Java EE server

We have already encountered some of the named objects in these namespaces. All Enterprise Beans in a given application appear in the java:module, java:app, java:global namespaces, as we shall see.

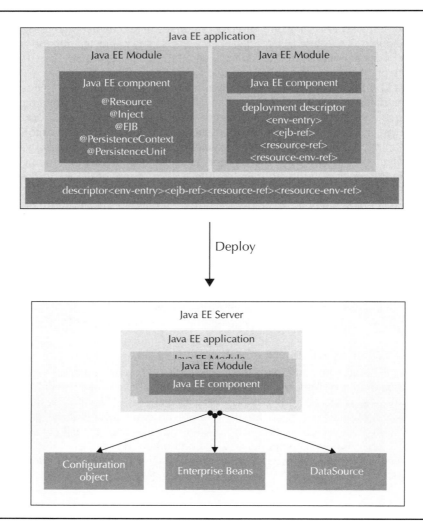

FIGURE 13-4. *Injected and named objects in Java EE*

In addition, all web applications are given names in the shared namespaces to which the Java EE server maps the `java.net.URL` to the web application's context root. In the `java:app` namespace, a web application has the JNDI name

```
java:app/<module-name>!ROOT
```

where `<module-name>` is the logical name of the web application.

In the `java:global` namespace, a web application has the JNDI name

```
java:global<app-name>/<module-name>!ROOT
```

The JNDI namespace of the Java EE server also contains the logical names of the applications and the modules that have been deployed on it. A Java EE component can access its application name, a `String` object, under the JNDI name `java:app/AppName`, and the name of its containing module, a `String` object, under the JNDI name `java:module/ModuleName`.

You can also tell whether you are running within an application client container or a server-side Java EE container such as the web or Enterprise Bean containers. A Java EE component's local `java:comp` namespace contains a `Boolean` object registered under the name `java:comp/InAppClientContainer`, which returns `true` if the component is within the Java EE application client container, and `false` otherwise.

We now explore some of the other named objects in the JNDI namespace.

Simple Environment Entries

Most applications have some kind of application-specific parameters that are useful to tune without having to recompile the source code. Filenames, user messages, and port numbers are all common examples. Environment entries give Java EE applications a general-purpose way to declare such properties in the deployment descriptor, and to use their (configurable) values from Java EE application code.

The simplest way to declare an environment entry is to create an `<env-entry>` element containing the name and value and add it to the application or Java EE module deployment descriptor, depending on where in the application you wish to access it. You can either inject the value into an instance variable using the `@Resource` annotation, or look it up on the JNDI `InitialContext` class.

To see this syntax, let's look at a familiar example. Recall the Async Enterprise Bean example from Chapter 9, consisting of an Enterprise Bean that calculates the largest prime number under a given limit, with a Java EE application client front end allowing the user to initiate calculations setting the upper limit. We see its GUI in Figure 13-5.

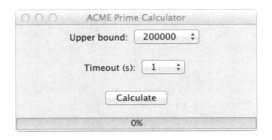

FIGURE 13-5. *The Asyc Enterprise Bean, main window*

A careful examination of the application client JAR reveals the addition of an environment entry with name `window-title` in the `application-client.xml` deployment descriptor.

Listing: *The Async application client deployment descriptor*

```xml
<application-client version="7"
    xmlns="http://xmlns.jcp.org/xml/ns/javaee"
    xmlns:xsi="http://www.w3.org/2001/XMLSchema-instance"
    xsi:schemaLocation="http://xmlns.jcp.org/xml/ns/javaee
    http://xmlns.jcp.org/xml/ns/javaee/application-client_7.xsd">
  <display-name>Async-client</display-name>
  <env-entry>
          <description>Title of window</description>
          <env-entry-name>window-title</env-entry-name>
          <env-entry-type>java.lang.String</env-entry-type>
          <env-entry-value>ACME Prime Calculator</env-entry-value>
      </env-entry>
</application-client>
```

This is used in the `PrimesWindow` class (which renders the window you see in Figure 13-5).

Listing: *Excerpt from the `PrimesWindow`*

```java
 public PrimesWindow() {
        try {
            String title = (String) InitialContext.doLookup(
                                    "java:comp/env/window-title");
            this.setTitle(title);
        } catch (NamingException r) {
            // the entry was not found, or was incorrectly specified
            // in the deployment descriptor
            this.setTitle("Find the largest prime under a limit");
        }
        ...
    }
 ...
}
```

Note the use of the `java:comp` scope because this environment entry is declared in a Java EE module. Also notice the use of `/env` in the naming: this is the Java EE convention for naming environment entries.

Similarly, if you try to invoke the `PrimeCalculator` bean with the maximum upper limit allowed in the UI, you will see the `PrimesWindow` display the violation, shown in Figure 13-6.

You will notice that the `PrimeCalculator` is now applying an upper limit to the calculations it will make. It injects this as an environment entry into an instance variable.

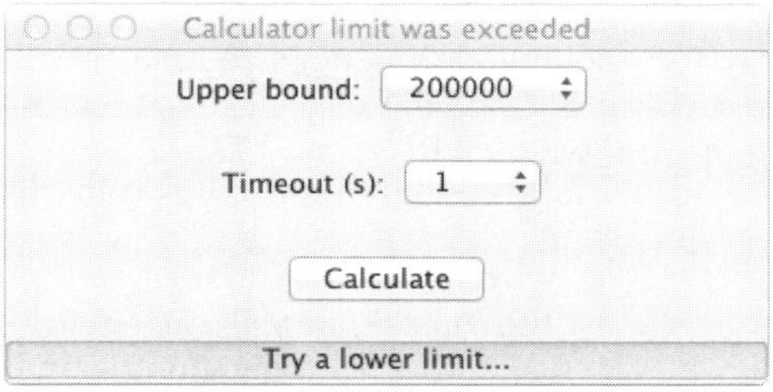

FIGURE 13-6. *The Primes Window, limit exceeded*

Listing: *Injecting an environment entry*

```
@Stateless
public class PrimeCalculator implements PrimeCalculatorRemote {
    @Resource
    SessionContext context;
    @Resource(lookup="java:comp/env/max-uppper-bound")
    int maximumBound;
    ...
}
```

Then it declares the value of the environment entry, called max-upper-bound, in its deployment descriptor.

Listing: *Listing an environment entry in an Enterprise Bean deployment descriptor*

```
<ejb-jar xmlns="http://xmlns.jcp.org/xml/ns/javaee"
        version="3.2"
        xmlns:xsi="http://www.w3.org/2001/XMLSchema-instance"
        xsi:schemaLocation="http://xmlns.jcp.org/xml/ns/javaee
                http://xmlns.jcp.org/xml/ns/javaee/ejb-jar_3_2.xsd">
    <enterprise-beans>
    <session>
        <ejb-name>PrimeCalculator</ejb-name>
        <env-entry>
            <description>Maximum Limit on Primes</description>
            <env-entry-name>max-uppper-bound</env-entry-name>
            <env-entry-type>java.lang.Integer</env-entry-type>
            <env-entry-value>150000</env-entry-value>
        </env-entry>
    </session>
</enterprise-beans>
</ejb-jar>
```

Notice how easy it would be to give this application to someone else and have them choose their own window title and upper bound on the prime calculations. It would simply be a matter of editing the deployment descriptors: no need to understand or touch the code.

Environment entries can be any of the following types: `String`, `Character`, `Byte`, `Short`, `Integer`, `Long`, `Boolean`, `Double`, `Float`, `Class`, and any Java `enum`. These types are usually enough to cover most of the configuration options you may need in a Java EE application.

We summarize the `env-entry` element with its subelements that are used to define environment entries in the following table.

`env-entry` Subelement	Purpose
`env-entry-name`	The logical name of the environment entry, used to map the value to /env/(logical name) in the JNDI namespace
`env-entry-type`	The Java type of the environment entry value
`env-entry-value`	The string value of the environment entry
`env-entry-description`	A text description of the environment entry

Enterprise Bean References

When a session bean is deployed, either just within an Enterprise Bean JAR or within an Enterprise Bean JAR contained in an EAR file, the Java EE server makes it available for lookup in the JNDI namespace, either by looking it up directly in the JNDI `InitialContext`, or by injection using the `@EJB` annotation with the lookup attribute.

The Enterprise Bean is available for lookup in the global, application, and module namespaces. An Enterprise Bean, you will remember, has a logical name, its bean name, which defaults to the short class name of its implementation class. This name may be overridden using the name attributes of the `@Stateful`, `@Stateless`, or `@Singleton`. The Enterprise Bean may have a no-interface view, in which case the methods on its implementation class can be called directly, or expose one or more remote (sometimes called business) interfaces. A combination of the bean name and, in the case that the client wishes to call the bean through one of its remote interfaces, the fully qualified class name of the desired remote interface, forms the basis of the JNDI names under which the Enterprise Bean is published.

If the Enterprise Bean is packaged in an Enterprise Bean JAR with module name `ejb-module` and packaged in an Enterprise Archive with logical name `enterprise-archive`, then the following table gives the JNDI names of the Enterprise Bean:

Scope	JNDI Name

Global	If deployed in an EAR:
	`java:global/enterprise-archive/`
	`            ejb-module/bean-name[!fq remote classname]`
	
	or, if deployed just in its Enterprise Bean JAR:
	`java:global/ejb-module/bean-name[!fq remote classname]`

Application	`java:app/ejb-module/bean-name[!fq remote classname]`
Module	`java:module/bean-name[!fq remote classname]`

A simpler alternative to using the `@EJB(lookup=jndi-name)` syntax for locating a reference to an Enterprise Bean is to use the name attribute of the `@EJB` annotation instead.

For example, for the Enterprise Bean described in the JNDI namespace in the table, the syntax `@EJB(name="bean-name")` locates the Enterprise Bean with the given `bean-name` in the closest scope.

You can in fact omit the name attribute altogether, and the container will use the Java type of the field you annotate as the name of the bean to locate in this case. This is a common style to use, particularly in smaller applications where there are fewer Enterprise Beans.

Enterprise Bean Named Objects

Now let's look at some named objects that are available to Enterprise Beans.

EJBContext   The `javax.ejb.EJBContext` is a very useful named object that can be accessed by all Enterprise Beans. It can be used, for example, to access security information about a call to a bean, like the Java Principal associated with the call. You will recall from Chapter 10 that it has the subinterfaces `MessageDrivenContext` and `SessionContext` for message-driven beans and session beans. The `EJBContext` may be injected into a field of the Enterprise Bean instance using the `@Resource` annotation:

```
@Stateful
public class MySessionBean {
    @Resource
    private SessionContext myContext;
...
}
```

The `EJBContext` instance associated with an Enterprise Bean is available in the JNDI namespace, and so can be explicitly found in the bean's component scope namespace using the JNDI naming context.

Listing: *Looking up the `EJBContext`*

```
@Stateful
public class MySessionBean {
    private SessionContext myContext;
     public void init() {
         try {

         SessionContext myContext =
           InitialContext.lookup("java:comp/EJBContext");
          ...

         } catch (NamingException ex) {
             // something is wrong in the environment
         }

...
}
```

TimerService

The TimerService is a useful named object that can be used by any Enterprise Bean except for stateful session beans. Like the EJBContext, it may be injected into a field on an Enterprise Bean using the @Resource annotation:

```
@Resource
private TimeServer myTimer;
```

or it can be found in the bean's component scope namespace under the name java:comp/Timerservice and looked up explicitly:

```
TimerService myTimeService =
    InitialContext.lookup("java:comp/Timerservice");
```

DataSource

When a Java EE application that needs a JDBC DataSource to access a relational database is deployed on a Java EE server, then its dependency on a DataSource must be resolved. How this dependency is resolved depends on the particular application server, but the outcome of that process, however it is achieved, will be a configured DataSource on the server under a given JNDI name. For the GlassFish application server, the configuration information about the DataSource is held in a supplemental deployment descriptor called glassfish-resources.xml.

Listing: *GlassFish configuration of a JDBC DataSource*

```
<?xml version="1.0" encoding="UTF-8"?>
<!DOCTYPE resources PUBLIC "-//GlassFish.org//DTD GlassFish
                 Application Server 3.1 Resource Definitions//EN"
                 "http://glassfish.org/dtds/glassfish-resources_1_5.dtd">
<resources>
  <jdbc-resource
      enabled="true"
      jndi-name="jdbc/myDatasource"
      object-type="user"
      pool-name="myConnectionPool">
    <description/>
  </jdbc-resource>
  <jdbc-connection-pool allow-non-component-callers="false"
                 associate-with-thread="false"
                 connection-creation-retry-attempts="0"
                 connection-creation-retry-interval-in-seconds="10"
                 connection-leak-reclaim="false"
                 connection-leak-timeout-in-seconds="0"
                 connection-validation-method="auto-commit"
                 datasource-classname=
                             "org.apache.derby.jdbc.ClientDataSource"
                 fail-all-connections="false"
                 idle-timeout-in-seconds="300"
```

```
                        is-connection-validation-required="false"
                        is-isolation-level-guaranteed="true"
                        lazy-connection-association="false"
                        lazy-connection-enlistment="false"
                        match-connections="false"
                        max-connection-usage-count="0"
                        max-pool-size="32"
                        max-wait-time-in-millis="60000"
                        name="myConnectionPool"
                        non-transactional-connections="false"
                        pool-resize-quantity="2"
                        res-type="javax.sql.DataSource"
                        statement-timeout-in-seconds="-1"
                        steady-pool-size="8"
                        validate-atmost-once-period-in-seconds="0"
                        wrap-jdbc-objects="false">
      <property name="URL"
                value="jdbc:derby://localhost:1527/databaseForHelloJDBC"/>
      <property name="serverName" value="localhost"/>
      <property name="PortNumber" value="1527"/>
      <property name="DatabaseName" value="databaseForHelloJDBC"/>
      <property name="User" value="hello"/>
      <property name="Password" value="hello1"/>
    </jdbc-connection-pool>
</resources>
```

Any Java EE component in the application can access the DataSource by injecting it into a field using the @Resource annotation. The least error-prone way to perform the injection is to use the lookup attribute to specify the JNDI name of the DataSource:

```
import javax.annotation.Resource;

public class MyDataBean {
    @Resource(lookup="jdbc/helloJDBCDatasource")
    DataSource ds;
    ...
}
```

Alternatively, if there is only one configured DataSource for the application, the dependency injection framework can infer the location of the DataSource, and the lookup attribute may be omitted.

```
import javax.annotation.Resource;

public class MyDataBean {
    @Resource
    DataSource ds;
    ...
}
```

Finally, the DataSource may be looked up explicitly using the JNDI InitialContext.

Listing: *Looking up a DataSource*

```
import javax.naming.InitialContext;
import javax.naming.NamingException;
@Stateless
public class MyDataBean {
    DataSource ds;
    ...
    public MyDataBean {
        try {
            this.ds = InitialContext.doLookup("jdbc/helloJDBCDatasource");
        } catch (NamingException e) {
            // the data source was not found at that name....
        }
    }
...
}
```

Java Persistence Objects: EntityManager, EntityManagerFactory

A Java EE application may depend on the Java Persistence API, in which case it will need one or more persistence units to be configured for the application. In order to configure a persistence unit for an application, the Java EE module that will utilize it must contain a persistence.xml file in the META-INF directory where the scope of the persistence unit will apply. In the case of Enterprise Bean JAR files, this is the META-INF directory of the JAR file, and although somewhat counterintuitive, for a WAR file, the WEB-INF/classes/META-INF directory.

The persistence.xml contains, at a minimum, the logical name of the persistence unit and may optionally include the logical name of a DataSource that the application would like the persistence implementation to use. For example, here is a persistence.xml file that defines a persistence unit of name myPersistenceUnit and that uses the DataSource named jdbc/myDataSource.

Listing: *Configuring a persistence unit in a persistence.xml file*

```
<?xml version="1.0" encoding="UTF-8"?>
<persistence version="2.1"
             xmlns="http://xmlns.jcp.org/xml/ns/persistence"
             xmlns:xsi="http://www.w3.org/2001/XMLSchema-instance"
             xsi:schemaLocation="http://xmlns.jcp.org/xml/ns/persistence
             http://xmlns.jcp.org/xml/ns/persistence/persistence_2_1.xsd">
  <persistence-unit name="myPersistenceUnit" transaction-type="JTA">
    <jta-data-source>jdbc/myDataSource</jta-data-source>
    <exclude-unlisted-classes>false</exclude-unlisted-classes>
  </persistence-unit>
</persistence>
```

You will recall from Chapter 12 that there are two ways to access the persistence unit in a JPA application. The most convenient way is to use a container-managed `EntityManager` injected into a field of the Java EE component that will use it. It is easiest because in this case the Java EE server manages the lifecycle of the `EntityManager` instance for the application. It is injected using the `@PersistenceContext` annotation and the name of the persistence unit:

```
@PersistenceContext(unitName="myPersistenceUnit")
private EntityManager entityManager;
```

If the Java EE module has only one configured persistence unit, then the `unitName` may be omitted:

```
@PersistenceContext
private EntityManager entityManager;
```

Unlike `DataSources`, however, the `EntityManager` instance is not registered by default in the component namespaces of components within a Java EE module. If you do wish to look up the `EntityManager` instance for a component in the JNDI namespace, you must put it there yourself. Fortunately, this is relatively easy: all you need to do is pick a memorable JNDI name for the `EntityManager`, and now use the `@PersistenceContext` annotation at the class level to make the registration, as in the following example:

```
@PersistenceContext(
    name="myPersistenceUnit-jndi-name",
    unitName="myPersistenceUnit"
)
@Singleton
public class MyBeanImpl implements MyBean {

    ...


}
```

This registers the persistence unit called `myPersistenceUnit` under the JNDI name `myPersistenceUnit-jndi-name` in the component's `java:comp/env` namespace. Then, from any instance method in the component, the `EntityManager` can be found as follows:

```
EntityManager em = InitialContext.doLookup("java:comp/env/
myPersistenceUnit-jndi-name");
```

If you wish to manage your own instances of the `EntityManager`, you can inject instead the `EntityManagerFactory`, which can be used to instantiate them. The annotation `@PersistenceUnit` is used to inject the `EntityManagerFactory`, specifying the name of the persistence unit:

```
@PersistenceUnit(unitName="myPersistenceUnit")
private EntityManagerFactory entityManagerFactory;
```

or, like the `@PersistenceContext` injection for the `EntityManager`, omitting the unit name if there is only one in the module.

The `@PersistenceUnit` annotation may also be used at the class level to register the `EntityManagerFactory` in the component's `java:comp` namespace, exactly as for the `@PersistenceContext` case.

Other Named and Injectable Objects

The named and injectable objects that we have looked at: application and module names, web application context roots, environment entries, Enterprise Beans, data sources, and persistence unit objects are not the only named and injectable objects in the platform. You can also inject and look up configured objects such as JMS connection factories, JavaMail sessions, and the current transaction in scope.

Here is a summary of the most commonly used named and injectable objects in the Java EE platform.

- Application and module names
- Environment entries
- Enterprise Beans
- JDBC data sources

   `javax.jdbc.DataSource`
- Java Persistence objects

   `javax.persistence.EntityManager, javax.persistence.EntityManagerFactory`
- Current transaction

   `javax.transaction.UserTransaction`
- Message destinations

   `javax.jms.Queue`

Where Does Injection Work?

In our discussion of the injectable objects in the Java EE platform, we started out by stating that the injection works in any Java EE component: web, application client, or Enterprise Bean. This is true, except that it is also available in other components in the Java EE platform, such as Java servlet filters or in JavaServer Faces managed beans. Here is a listing of all the sites in a Java EE application in which injectable objects may be utilized.

- Java servlets
   Servlet filters
   Web listeners
   Event listeners
- JSP tag library and event listeners
- JavaServer Faces managed beans
- JAX-RS resources
- WebSocket endpoints

- Enterprise Beans
  Interceptors

- CDI managed beans (see Chapter 14)

Summary

In this chapter, we looked at the packaging and deployment formats for Java EE applications, the EAR file format, and the JAR packaging and deployment format for application clients. We looked at the different ways in which a Java EE application can co-bundle library files and express dependencies on external libraries. We explored the most commonly used injectable named objects in the platform.

In our exploration of named objects, we implicitly touched on the topic of objects that Java EE applications use, but whose lifecycle they do not manage. We have already seen how the Java EE containers manage the lifecycle of application components. This means that it is high time to look at the topic of Contexts and Dependency Injection (CDI): the Java EE platform's general-purpose lifecycle management framework.

CHAPTER
14

Deconstructing
Components:
Java EE Contexts and
Dependency Injection

The Java EE dependency injection service is like the ultimate delivery service for programming: whenever you need an instance of something, you can rely on Java EE dependency injection to get you the right one.

Properly entitled Contexts and Dependency Injection, or CDI for short, this is the state of the art for modularizing applications. Integrated with the Java EE platform, CDI provides many ways to decouple implementations of the elements of a Java EE application. It grew from a desire to make it easier to bring together web components with Enterprise Bean components, and it shares and generalizes aspects from both tiers of the Java EE platform.

In this chapter, we will examine the CDI framework, its mechanisms, and APIs, while also looking at where CDI can be used in conjunction with the Java EE components and APIs that we already know.

Introduction to CDI

The fundamental concept of CDI is the consumer-producer relationship that it supports. Typically, the consumer side is an application component, a Java class, or Java EE component that needs another object to perform a specific task by calling its methods. The task may be encoding some data, performing an algorithmic step on a collection of numbers, sending a message, or storing data in a database. The producer side of the relationship is a Java object that can perform the task on behalf of the consumer. In ordinary Java programming, the consumer could be a Java class that creates an instance of another Java class that is the producer when it needs it. Or the consumer could be a Java class that requires an instance of the producer class to be passed into its constructor, where it stores it in an instance variable. One aspect of this kind of consumer-producer relationship is that it is tightly coupled: the consumer class is concerned not only with the type of the producer, but it also has to worry about the lifecycle of the producer instance. The producer class could hide itself behind an interface, but someone would still be responsible for instantiating an implementation of the interface.

What CDI does is decouple the consumer-producer relationship in a way that is typesafe. When a consumer needs an instance of a producer, the CDI runtime selects a suitable instance of the producer under its management and gives it to the consumer. Let's see this in diagram form in Figure 14-1.

On the Consumer side of Figure 14-1 at the right, the Java class needs a particular kind of object. In order to declare its need to the CDI framework, it defines an *injection point*. An injection point may be located at a field, method, or constructor, and is where the CDI runtime will inject the object that the consumer class needs. In order to do this, the CDI runtime analyzes the injection point declared by the consumer class, looking in its store of available CDI beans, on the producer side of Figure 14-1. Depending on whether there is a suitable instance of the CDI bean already being managed by the CDI runtime that will be suitable for the consumer class's injection point or whether the CDI runtime needs to create a new instance, the CDI runtime injects the instance it has selected into the injection site.

The CDI APIs include annotations that allow the consumer to define qualifying information that the CDI runtime will use to select the appropriate CDI bean to make the injection. It also includes the notion of a CDI bean producer: a class that gives an instance of a CDI bean when

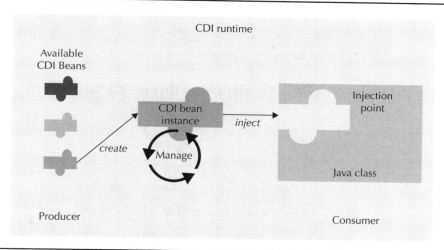

FIGURE 14-1. *The consumer-producer relationship in CDI*

the CDI runtime needs to inject one, but without being injected itself. It includes lifecycle annotations that give each CDI bean instance the ability to intercept the key stages in its lifecycle. It includes an interceptor model that allows applications to add Java classes that intercept CDI bean lifecycle and method invocations, and includes an event model, which allows CDI beans to notify each other of changes.

We have already encountered many examples of the CDI framework in Java EE at work: for example, the injection of references to Enterprise Beans into web components and JDBC `DataSources` and `EntityManagers` into Enterprise Beans.

CDI also includes the notion of Java EE scopes, which define how many instances of a CDI bean the CDI runtime will instantiate and how long each instance will live.

We will look at how these CDI concepts are formulated in the CDI APIs and how to use them in Java EE applications, but first, we will start with a simple example.

Goldilocks and the Three Bears

In this example, we retell the traditional children's story in which the little girl Goldilocks finds a house that belongs to three bears and tries various things in it, including the beds.

Before we look at any code, let's look at the general composition of this application.

The `GoldilocksServlet` has three injection points that are asking the CDI runtime to inject three instances of a CDI bean of type Bed. Bed is an interface that defines the API implemented by all of the CDI beans in the application. The `GoldilocksServlet` declares its injection points slightly differently from each other: one requests no special qualifying properties; the other two do. There are three CDI beans that implement the `Bed` interface, which declare different injection properties. You can see the result of calling the `GoldilocksServlet` in Figure 14-2.

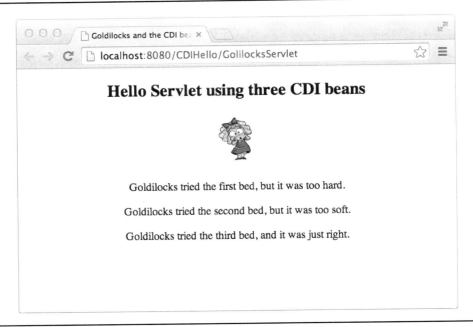

FIGURE 14-2.   *The Goldilocks application home page*

Let's look first at the CDI beans: DaddyBearBed, MommyBearBed, and BabyBearBed and the Bed interface they all implement.

Listing: *The bears' beds*

```
public interface Bed {
    public String tryIt();
}

@Comfort("firm")
public class DaddyBearBed implements Bed {
    @Override
    public String tryIt() {
        return "too hard";
    }
}

@Comfort("yielding")
public class MommyBearBed implements Bed {
    @Override
    public String tryIt() {
        return "too soft";
    }
}
```

```
public class BabyBearBed implements Bed {
    @Override
    public String tryIt() {
        return "just right";
    }
}
```

What we see is three classes implementing the single method Bed interface. But notice also that the DaddyBearBed and MommyBearBed have a class-level @Comfort annotation, while the BabyBearBed has none. The @Comfort annotation is an example of how a Java EE application can define an annotation that qualifies an injection point and qualifies a CDI bean that the CDI runtime can match and inject into that injection point.

Listing: *The @Comfort qualifier*

```
import static java.lang.annotation.ElementType.FIELD;
import static java.lang.annotation.ElementType.METHOD;
import static java.lang.annotation.ElementType.PARAMETER;
import static java.lang.annotation.ElementType.TYPE;

import static java.lang.annotation.RetentionPolicy.RUNTIME;
import java.lang.annotation.Retention;
import java.lang.annotation.Target;
import javax.inject.Qualifier;

@Qualifier
@Retention(RUNTIME)
@Target({TYPE, METHOD, FIELD, PARAMETER})
public @interface Comfort {
    String value();
}
```

What makes the @Comfort annotation a qualifier is that it is itself annotated with the @Qualfier annotation from the CDI APIs. We can see it has one attribute: value, which the CDI beans in this application use to declare a string describing their comfort level.
Now we turn to the GoldilocksServlet.

Listing: *The GoldilocksServlet class*

```
import java.io.*;
import javax.servlet.*;
import javax.servlet.annotation.WebServlet;
import javax.servlet.http.*;
import javax.inject.Inject;

@WebServlet(name = "GoldilocksServlet", urlPatterns = {"/GoldilocksServlet"})
public class GoldilocksServlet extends HttpServlet {
    @Inject
    private Bed bed3;
```

```java
@Inject
@Comfort("firm")
private Bed bed1;

private Bed bed2;

@Inject
public void initializeBed(@Comfort("yielding") Bed bean) {
    this.bed2 = bean;
}

protected void doGet(HttpServletRequest request,
                     HttpServletResponse response)
                       throws ServletException, IOException {
    response.setContentType("text/html;charset=UTF-8");
    try (PrintWriter out = response.getWriter()) {
        out.println("<!DOCTYPE html>");
        out.println("<html>");
        out.println("<head>");
        out.println("<title>Goldilocks and the CDI beans</title>");
        out.println("</head>");
        out.println("<body>");
        out.println("<div align='center'>");
        out.println("<h2>Hello Servlet using three CDI beans</h2>");
        out.println("<img width = '80' height='80'
                        src='Goldilocks.jpg'></img>");
        out.println("<p>");
        out.println("Goldilocks tried the first bed, but it was  "
                                    + bed1.tryIt() + ".<br><br>");
        out.println("Goldilocks tried the second bed, but it was  "
                                    + bed2.tryIt() + ".<br><br>");
        out.println("Goldilocks tried the third bed, and it was  "
                                    + bed3.tryIt() + ".<br><br>");
        out.println("</p>");
        out.println("</div>");
        out.println("</body>");
        out.println("</html>");
    }
  }
}
```

The first thing to notice about the GoldilocksServlet is that it has three instance variables: bed1, bed2, and bed3. Each is of type Bed, which means the GoldilocksServlet has no notion of the implementation classes that will fill out its instance variables. The bed3 variable is decorated with the @Inject annotation, which means that it is asking the CDI runtime to inject a suitable instance of the type Bed into this variable when the servlet class is first instantiated. There is no other information associated at this injection point, so this is a request to the CDI runtime to select the default CDI bean implementation, which since it declares no other annotations is the `BabyBearBed` bean. The `bed1` instance variable is annotated with the `@Inject` and `@Comfort("firm")` annotations, which means that it is asking the CDI runtime to inject a suitable instance of the type `Bed` when the servlet is first instantiated, and that the instance injected must be qualified with the `@Comfort("firm")` annotation. Among the CDI beans in this application, only the `DaddyBearBean` satisfies these requirements. Finally, the `bed2` instance variable has no `@Inject` annotation. So how is the value assigned at runtime? Notice the `initializeBed()` method, marked with the `@Inject` annotation, which assigns the value of `bed2`. This means that the CDI runtime will call this method after the servlet is instantiated, injecting the values of the method parameters. Notice that the Bed method parameter is marked `@Comfort("yielding")`, which is a request to the CDI runtime to inject a CDI bean of type `Bed`, which is marked with the `@Comfort("yielding")` annotation. In this application, this request is satisfied by the `MommyBearBed` bean. Now that we have understood how these instance variables are initialized, when the servlet is called, its `doGet()` method calls each of the three beans to create the page we see in Figure 14-3.

The main thing to notice in this application is that the `GoldilocksServlet` on the consumer side of the relationship not only has no knowledge of the implementation classes, it has no knowledge of how they are instantiated and passed to its fields and methods. How a suitable instance of a bean is injected into the `GoldilocksServlet` is governed by its use of `@Qualifier` annotations, and the injection points it uses are both into its instance variables (usually called fields in the CDI API documentation) and into a method.

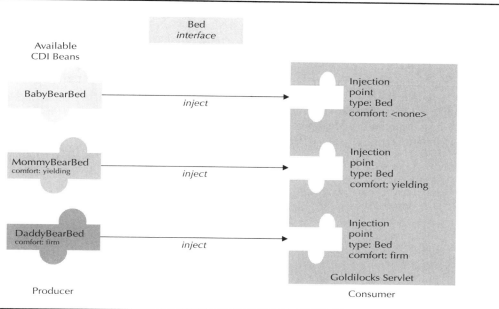

FIGURE 14-3. *Logical structure of the Goldilocks application*

With this simple example under our belt, we have already seen some of the primary aspects of the CDI framework in action. So we are in a good position to look a little more formally at how it works.

CDI Beans

A CDI bean is a source of instances of Java objects, called bean instances. A CDI bean may be a class, or a special kind of Java method called a producer method, or a special kind of field called a producer field. CDI beans that are Java methods or fields are marked with the `@javax.enterprise.inject.Produces` annotation.

A CDI bean has the following properties:

- **A set of bean types**   A bean type is a Java type that a consumer of the bean may use to access its functionality or data. Java interfaces, classes with or without generic type parameters, arrays thereof, raw, and primitive types may all be bean types.

- **A set of qualifiers**   A qualifier is a special kind of annotation, marked with the `@javax.inject.Qualifier` annotation, that adds metatdata to a bean that the CDI runtime uses to match it with an injection point.

- **A scope**   A bean's scope is something that defines when new instances of the bean are to be created.

- **An optional name**   A bean may be given a logical name using the `@javax.inject.Named` annotation, which can be used to refer to it. JavaServer Faces Expression Language can refer to CDI beans only if they are named.

- **A set of interceptor bindings**   This set defines all the interceptor classes that will be applied to this CDI bean.

Examples

All the CDI beans we saw in the Goldilocks example are CDI beans in the form of a Java class. For example, the `MommyBearBed` class is a CDI bean, with bean types of `Object`, `MommyBearBed`, and `Bed`. It has one qualifier `@Comfort("yielding")`, the default CDI scope of which is such that it is instantiated every time it is injected, with no logical name and no interceptor bindings.

Here are two examples of CDI beans that are methods:

```
public class ProducerMethodClass {
    @Produces
    public Integer getAnswerToUltimateQuestionOfLifeTheUniverseAndEverything() {
        return 42;
    }


    @Produces
    public Bed getMyBed() {
        return new BabyBearBed();
    }
}
```

The first produces bean instances with bean types `Object` and `Integer`, and the second produces bean instances with bean types `Bed`, `BabyBearBed`, and `Object`.

And here's a CDI bean that is a field of a class:

```
public class ProducerFieldClass {
    @Produces
    private Bed bed = new DaddyBearBed();
}
```

This produces bean instances with bean types `Bed`, `DaddyBearBed`, and `Object`.

Qualifiers

Qualifiers are used to express a conditional relationship between an injection point and CDI beans that might be injected into it. A qualifier is a special kind of annotation whose targets are class, method, field, and type; whose retention policy keeps its information at runtime; and which is itself marked with the `@Qualifier` annotation from the CDI API. Qualifier annotations may have attributes. In our Goldilocks example, the application-defined `@Comfort` qualifier has a single `value` attribute.

A CDI bean may declare multiple qualifiers to define the kind of injection point into which the CDI runtime may inject it. Equally, an injection point may define multiple qualifiers to define the kind of CDI beans that the CDI runtime may inject into it. In order for the CDI runtime to make the injection, all the qualifiers must match, using the `equals()` test. This means all the qualifier's attribute values must match exactly.

Thus, applications can define qualifiers to refine how the CDI runtime matches CDI beans to consumers. The `@Default` qualifier is built into the Java EE APIs and has a special meaning.

@Default

When either a CDI bean or an injection site does not declare any qualifiers other than `@Named`, it is the same as it declaring the `@Default` qualifier. For example,

```
public class BabyBearBed implements Bed {...}
```

is equivalent to

```
@Default
public class BabyBearBed implements Bed {...}
```

and either CDI bean definition matches either of these equivalent field injection points:

```
@Default
private Bed bed;
```

or

```
@Default
private Bed bed
```

@Named

The @Named qualifier has a single optional value attribute allowing CDI applications to use this annotation to give CDI beans logical names. This is a must when using CDI beans from JavaServer Faces Expression Language: the only way to reference a CDI bean instance from EL is by its @Named name. If the value attribute is omitted, the logical name of the bean is the short class name.

Injection Points

A Java class can declare three different kinds of injection points. It may declare any of its instance variables to be an injection point by annotating it with @Inject and any qualifiers. This kind of injection is called field injection. The CDI runtime injects a suitable CDI bean into the instance variable as soon as it has created the instance of the Java class. For example,

```
public class Car {
    @Inject
    private Driver driver;
    ...
}
```

Second, a Java class may declare an injection point on a method by annotating it with @Inject. The CDI runtime looks through the method parameters of this method, which may be annotated with qualifiers, and for each one attempts to find a suitable CDI bean that matches and injects an instance of it. The Java method-as-injection-point is known as an initializer method, and a Java class may declare one or more of them.

```
public class Car {
    @Inject
    public void initDriver(@Fast Driver driver) {
        ...
    }
    ...
}
```

Finally, a Java class may declare a single constructor as an injection point. The @Inject annotation is used to annotate the constructor, and the CDI runtime will attempt to supply CDI-suitable bean instances for each of its constructor parameters.

```
public class Car {
    @Inject
    public Car(@Safe Driver driver) {
        ...
    }
    ...
}
```

We can summarize what we have learned about CDI beans, injection points, and qualifiers in Figure 14-4.

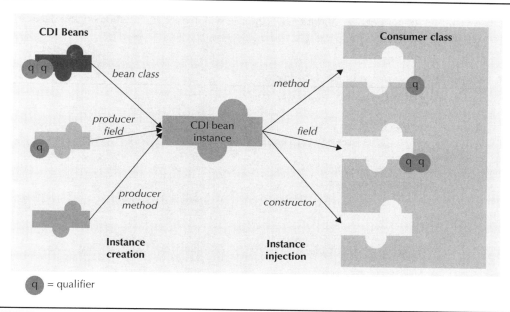

FIGURE 14-4. *Injection points, ways to produce CDI bean instances, and matching them up*

Lifecycle of a CDI Bean

So far we have not learned anything about the lifecycle of a CDI bean instance other than that it is instantiated and injected. CDI bean instances have a lifecycle, managed by the CDI runtime, for which the bean instance can receive callbacks.

@PostConstruct

A CDI bean may request that the CDI runtime call one of its methods after it has been instantiated and any injection it needs has completed. Any no-arg method on the CDI bean may be annotated with the `@javax.annotation.PostConstruct` annotation. The method may have any Java package access level. For example, in the Goldilocks example, if we need to know the moment after the `DaddyBearBed` instance is created and before it is injected into the servlet, we can define

```
@PostConstruct
private void doInit() {
    System.out.println("dad's bed got made");
}
```

@PreDestroy and @Disposes

Similarly, when the bean instance has been used and the CDI runtime is about to dereference it, the CDI bean instance may request a callback to be made immediately before this happens. The CDI bean annotates a suitable method with the `@javax.annotation.PreDestroy` annotation.

For example, after the `GoldilocksServlet` instance has fulfilled the client request, its injected beans are no longer needed, and the CDI runtime will invoke any methods marked `@PreDestroy` on them.

Listing: *Example usage of `@PreDestroy`*

```java
import javax.annotation.PreDestroy;

@Comfort("firm")
public class DaddyBearBed implements Bed {
    @Override
    public String tryIt() {
        return "too hard";
    }

    @PreDestroy
    public void doCleanup() {
        System.out.println("Bye: your bed was too hard in any case");
    }
}
```

The time at which a CDI bean instance is dereferenced clearly depends on the consumer class that is using it, in this example, the `GoldilocksServlet`. We shall shortly be exploring more about the lifetime of CDI bean instances, called the CDI bean scope, in relation to their consumers.

If a CDI bean uses producer methods or producer fields to create its bean instances, it may also declare a method on the class holding the producer fields or methods that the CDI runtime will call right before the bean instances are dereferenced. The class may have many methods marked `@Disposes`, each with a single parameter to hold the bean instance being dereferenced and marked `@Disposes`.

For example, here is a class called `BedFactory` that makes disposable `Bed` instances with a low comfort level. It has a producer method that creates instances of `Bed` objects that can be injected into any site expecting a bed of low comfort.

Listing: *Example usage for `@Disposes`*

```java
public class BedFactory {

    @Produces @Comfort("low")
    public Bed getDisposableBed() {
        return new DisposableBed();
    }

    void discardBedInstance(@Disposes @Comfort("low") Bed bed) {
        System.out.println("throwing out this bed -
                           maybe it wasn't very comfortable ?");
    }

}
```

Whenever the `Bed` instance the `BedFactory` class creates is about to be dereferenced, the `discardBedInstance()` method is called by the CDI runtime, passing in the instance to be dereferenced.

Though not specific to disposer methods, the `@Any` annotation is another CDI qualifier built into the Java EE APIs. This annotation basically means "matches anything." We can illustrate its uses here by adding a new producer method to the `BedFactory` that produces `FeatherBed` instances.

Listing: *Example usage for the `@Any` annotation*

```
public class BedFactory {

    @Produces @Comfort("low")
    public Bed getDisposableBed() {
        return new DisposableBed();
    }

    @Produces @Comfort("high")
    public Bed getAnotherBed() {
        return new FeatherBed();
    }

    void discardBedInstance(@Disposes @Any Bed bed) {
        System.out.println("throwing out this bed: " + bed +
                " was it too comfortable, or not comfortable enough ?");
    }

}
```

In this case, the `discardBedInstance()` is called for either of the Bed instances produced by either of the producer methods on the class.

CDI bean instances, once injected into their consumer, can define further stages in their lifecycle, defining their own API methods to transition between states. What lifecycle stages they define within the time they are injected is specific to their application and is not modeled within the CDI APIs. The CDI framework does, however, support such application-specific lifecycles with an event framework, which we shall explore. But first, we will look at the lifetime of a CDI bean instance.

Java EE Scopes

The scope of a CDI bean tells you how often a CDI bean instance is created. Some CDI beans are instantiated every time there is a consumer that needs to inject it. Other CDI beans are instantiated only once for the lifetime of their applications, and others still, like Goldilocks' taste in beds, fall in between those two extremes.

The Java EE platform contains a number of predefined scopes that a CDI bean may have. Advanced CDI developers create their own scopes, but this is not needed for most Java EE applications since the predefined ones usually work.

A CDI bean declares the scope to which it belongs with, at most, one scope per annotation. If a CDI makes no declaration of scope, then it belongs to the dependent scope. This scope is sometimes called a pseudo-scope because it simply says that the scope of the CDI bean instance is that of the consumer that injects it. Let's look at the predefined scopes in the Java EE platform.

Scope	Annotation	Meaning
Dependent	`@Dependent`	The CDI runtime instantiates a default scope CDI bean instance every time that it is injected into a consumer object. The bean instance inherits the scope of the consumer instance. If a CDI bean does not declare a scope, it defaults to having dependent scope.
Request	`@RequestScoped`	The CDI runtime instantiates a new request-scoped CDI bean instance for each HTTP request/response interaction encompassing the consumer instance.
Session	`@SessionScoped`	The CDI runtime instantiates a new session-scoped CDI bean instance for each HTTP session that encompasses the consumer instance. If the CDI bean is used by more than one injection point in the consumer instance within the same session, or by more than one consumer instance within the same session, they all share the same bean instance.
Application	`@ApplicationScoped`	The CDI runtime instantiates a new application-scoped CDI bean instance once for the lifetime of the application, which is shared by all consumer instances.
Conversation	`@ConversationScoped`	The CDI runtime instantiates one new conversation-scoped CDI bean instance for every developer-controller conversation scope, as discussed in Chapter 4.

In addition, CDI beans that are session-, application-, or conversation-scoped must be `Serializable`.

SleepScopes Example

Let's illustrate these scopes with a simple example. In this example, we have a web application containing three kinds of `Beds`: `DisposableBed`, `RegularBed`, and `BunkBed`.

Listing: *The SleepScopes beds*

```
import javax.enterprise.context.RequestScoped;
```

```
@RequestScoped
@Inexpensive
public class DisposableBed implements Bed {...}


import javax.enterprise.context.SessionScoped;

@SessionScoped
@Comfortable
public class RegularBed implements Bed, Serializable {...}


import javax.enterprise.context.ApplicationScoped;

@ApplicationScoped
public class BunkBed implements Bed, Serializable {...}
```

The three types of Bed have request, session, and application scope, respectively. The SleepScopesServlet injects instances of these beds and prints each bed object to the web page each time that the browser requests it.

Listing: *The SleepScopesServlet class*

```java
import java.io.IOException;
import java.io.PrintWriter;
import javax.servlet.ServletException;
import javax.servlet.annotation.WebServlet;
import javax.servlet.http.HttpServlet;
import javax.servlet.http.HttpServletRequest;
import javax.servlet.http.HttpServletResponse;
import javax.inject.*;

@WebServlet(urlPatterns = {"/SleepScopesServlet"})
public class SleepScopesServlet extends HttpServlet {
    @Inject
    @Inexpensive
    Bed bedA;
    @Inject
    @Comfortable
    Bed bedB;
    @Inject
    Bed bedC;

    protected void doGet(HttpServletRequest request,
                         HttpServletResponse response)
                            throws ServletException, IOException {
        response.setContentType("text/html;charset=UTF-8");
        try (PrintWriter out = response.getWriter()) {
            out.println("<!DOCTYPE html>");
            out.println("<html>");
            out.println("<head>");
            out.println("<title>Sleep test servlet</title>");
            out.println("</head>");
```

```
            out.println("<body>");
            out.println("<div align='center'>");
            out.println("<h2>Three beds to sleep in,
                         but which one has which scope ? </h2>");
            out.println("<h2>Request scope,
                         Session scope or Application scope ? </h2>");
            out.println("<p>");
            out.println("Bed A " + bedA + " <br><br>");
            out.println("Bed B " + bedB + " <br><br>");
            out.println("Bed C " + bedC + " <br><br>");
            out.println("</p>");
            out.println("</div>");
            out.println("</body>");
            out.println("</html>");
        }
    }

}
```

If you look at the qualifiers, you see that the CDI runtime will inject `DisposableBed` instances into bed A, `RegularBed` instances into bed B, and `BunkBed` instances into bed C. Now if you load the servlet page, you should see something like Figure 14-5.

So far, so good. Now in order to test which `Bed` is in which scope, by reloading the servlet page, you are creating a new HTTP request/response interaction. Therefore, any CDI bean used by

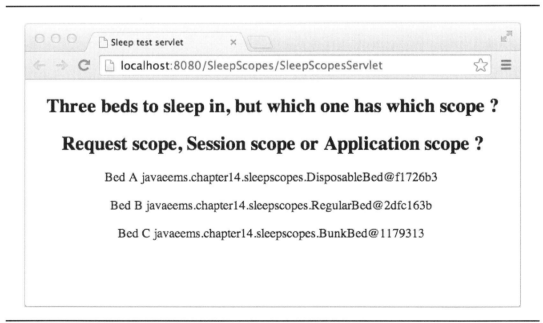

FIGURE 14-5. *The SleepScopes application home page*

this servlet that is in request scope will be reinstantiated and reinjected for each HTTP request/ response interaction. Since the `DisposableBed` is in request scope, because it uses the `@RequestScope` annotation, each time that you reload the page it will show a new instance of `Bed A`. Since each HTTP request is coming from the same browser client, all such requests are within the same HTTP session. Therefore, the CDI bean instance injected into `Bed B`, which is assigned to the `RegularBed` CDI bean, which is in session scope, remains the same instance: no new injection occurs since we are still within the same `HttpSession`. Similarly, for `Bed C`, the application-scoped `BunkBed`, the instance remains the same since only one instance of the `BunkBed` will be instantiated for the lifetime of the application and will be shared among all its injection points.

The reinstantiation and reinjection of `Bed B` can be triggered by opening up a separate browser and loading the servlet page. This creates a new `HttpSession` within the same application. So `Bed A` and `Bed B` will both be reinstantiated for the new `HttpSession`.

`Bed C` remains the same `BunkBed` instance, so your browser clients will have to fight over who gets which bunk of the shared instance.

Events

The CDI framework has an event mechanism. This allows applications to define events, provides the means for CDI beans to fire them using the CDI APIs, and allows them to selectively observe any or all of the events from other CDI beans.

The mechanism is relatively straightforward, and as you might expect from the CDI framework, has a high degree of separation between the sender and the observer of the events.

The event class is any Java class that contains the information that the event wishes to convey about when and why it was sent. The construction of the event is under the control of the application, so there are no restrictions on how this object is created.

A CDI bean fires the event by injecting an instance of the CDI API's `javax.enterprise` `.event.Event` class. With this Event instance, the CDI bean may fire instances of the event class it creates at will, using the Event method:

```
void fire(T event)
```

CDI beans that are interested in listening in on the broadcast of such events may register their interest by defining a method, which takes the event class as a parameter, annotated with the `@javax.enterprise.event.Observes` annotation.

Additionally, the application may annotate the event class it defines with one or more qualifiers. In turn, the CDI beans declaring an observer method may add qualifiers to the event class parameter of the observer method to refine which events it elects to receive from the CDI runtime.

Let's see the setup in picture form in Figure 14-6.

For a CDI bean that has elected to receive event notifications from the CDI runtime by declaring an observer method, there may not be an instance in existence when an event in which it is interested is fired. The CDI API allows for two possibilities in the case when there is no instance of the observing CDI bean: it either does not deliver the event because there is no instance to which to deliver it, or it will instantiate a new instance of the observing CDI bean and deliver it there.

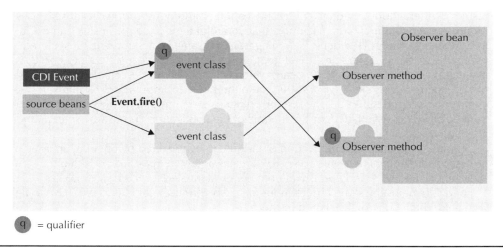

q = qualifier

FIGURE 14-6. *Creating, broadcasting, and observing events*

The observing CDI bean can control this behavior with the `notifyObserver` attribute of the `@Observes` annotation that it uses in its observer method. It has two options:

- `@Observes(notifyObserver=Reception.ALWAYS)`
- `@Observes(notifyObserver=Reception.IF_EXISTS)`

The former option instantiates the observing CDI bean if it needs to, which is the same behavior as though the attribute is omitted, and the latter option does not instantiate a new instance just to deliver the event.

We can see these two options in action, as well as an example of the overall CDI event mechanism, in the next example.

Goldilocks Observed

In the next example, we take a CDI twist on the Goldilocks story in which the grandmother and grandfather bears live next door and have a clear view into the bears' home from their window.

We can see now that in this Goldilocks Observed example, once Goldilocks makes her visits around the house, we can find out what the grandparents know.

Let's take a look at the code.

The event class in this application is the `SomeoneInBedEvent` class.

Listing: *The `SomeoneInBedEvent` class*

```
public class SomeoneInBedEvent {
    private final String name;
    private final Bed bed;
```

```
    public SomeoneInBedEvent(Bed bed, String name) {
        this.bed = bed;
        this.name = name;
    }

    public String getName() {
        return this.name;
    }

    public Bed getBed() {
        return this.bed;
    }
}
```

There is nothing special about this class: it is a plain old Java class, with no special annotations to mark it as an event class used by CDI.

There are again three `Bed` implementation classes: `BabyBearBed`, `MommyBearBed`, and `DaddyBearBed`, with a single method that is called by the `GoldilocksServlet` when it renders the first page in Figure 14-7. The three implementation classes are all very similar, so let's look at the `BabyBearBed` class.

FIGURE 14-7. *The Goldilocks Observer home page*

Listing: *The BabyBearBed fires an event*

```
import javax.enterprise.event.Event;
import javax.inject.Inject;

public class BabyBearBed implements Bed {
    @Inject
    Event<SomeoneInBedEvent> sibe;

    @Override
    public String tryIt(String name) {
        sibe.fire(new SomeoneInBedEvent(this, name));
        return "just right";
    }

    public String toString() {
        return "Baby's bed";
    }

}
```

Aside from its `tryIt()` method, this class injects an instance of the CDI API class `javax.enterprise.event.Event` parameterized with the defined event class that we just saw: `SomeoneInBedEvent`. The `tryIt()` method creates a new instance of the `SomeoneInBedEvent` class and uses the injected `Event` instance to broadcast it to its observers, using the `fire()` method. The `tryIt()` method of the `DaddyBearBed` and `MommyBearBed` classes follow the same pattern.

Now, let's look at the CDI beans that listen in to the broadcast of the events `GrandmotherBear` and `GrandfatherBear`.

Listing: *The grandparents' CDI bean classes*

```
import java.util.*;
import javax.enterprise.event.Observes;
import javax.enterprise.event.Reception;
import javax.enterprise.context.SessionScoped;
import java.io.Serializable;

public class RememberingBear {
    List<SomeoneInBedEvent> events = new ArrayList<>();

    public List<SomeoneInBedEvent> getEvents() {
        return events;
    }
}


@SessionScoped
public class GrandmotherBear extends RememberingBear
                                implements Serializable {
```

```
    public void listen(@Observes SomeoneInBedEvent whbimbe) {
        events.add(whbimbe);
    }
}


@SessionScoped
public class GrandfatherBear extends RememberingBear
                             implements Serializable {
    public void listen(@Observes(notifyObserver=Reception.IF_EXISTS) SomeoneInBedEvent whbimbe) {
        events.add(whbimbe);
    }
}
```

Both instances of these classes have, thanks to their common superclass `RememberingBear`, a list of events that its instances add to each time it receives an event. The observer method in each case is called `listen()`, with the single `SomeoneInBedEvent` parameter annotated with `@Observes`. Both grandparent CDI beans are session-scoped.

Now we can look at the `GrandparentsServlet`, which asks each grandparent to remember what they saw, if anything, as we see in Figure 14-8.

FIGURE 14-8. *What do the grandparents know?*

Listing: *The GrandparentsServlet class*

```java
import java.io.*;
import javax.servlet.*;
import javax.servlet.annotation.WebServlet;
import javax.servlet.http.*;
import javax.inject.Inject;
import java.util.List;


@WebServlet(urlPatterns = {"/GrandparentsServlet"})
public class GrandparentsServlet extends HttpServlet {
    @Inject
    GrandmotherBear grandmotherBear;
    @Inject
    GrandfatherBear grandfatherBear;

    @Override
    protected void doGet(HttpServletRequest request,
                         HttpServletResponse response)
                            throws ServletException, IOException {
        response.setContentType("text/html;charset=UTF-8");
        try (PrintWriter out = response.getWriter()) {
            request.getSession().invalidate();
            out.println("<!DOCTYPE html>");
            out.println("<html>");
            out.println("<head>");
            out.println("<title>Goldilocks and the CDI beans</title>");
            out.println("</head>");
            out.println("<body>");

            out.println("<div align='center'>");
            out.println("<h2>CDI beans with events</h2>");
            out.println("<img width = '80' height='80'
                                    src='bear-icon.png'></img>");
            out.println("<p>");

            out.println("Grandmother bear knows: <br><br>");
            this.printMemory(grandmotherBear.getEvents(), out);
            out.println("<br><br>");
            out.println("Grandfather bear knows ");
            this.printMemory(grandfatherBear.getEvents(), out);

            out.println("</p>");
            out.println("</div>");
            out.println("</body>");
            out.println("</html>");
        }
    }

    private void printMemory(List<SomeoneInBedEvent> events,
```

```
                                                PrintWriter out) {
    if (events.isEmpty()) {
        out.print("nothing, he was asleep !");
    }
    for (SomeoneInBedEvent e : events) {
        out.print(e.getName() + " tried " + e.getBed() + "<br>");
    }
  }
}
```

This servlet injects an instance of each grandparent bean into itself and prints out what events it has received. From Figure 14-8, we see that the `GrandmotherBear` receives events each time that the `GoldilocksServlet` tries out each `Bed`. But how is it that the `GrandmotherBear` gets the events from the different `Bed` instances and the `GrandfatherBear` does not? The key lies in the `@Observes` annotation used in the respective event observer methods. The `GrandmotherBear` uses `@Observes`, while the `GrandfatherBear` uses the `@Observes(notifyObserver=Reception.IF_EXISTS)` annotation. Since neither grandparent CDI bean has an instance in existence while the `GoldilocksServlet` is called, the events generated by that execution of that servlet cause a new `GrandmotherBear` instance to be created to which the events are delivered. But the `notifyObserver=Reception.IF_EXISTS` attribute on the `GrandfatherBear`'s `@Observes` annotation means the CDI runtime does not instantiate a new instance of that CDI bean in order to deliver the events. So the first time the `GrandfatherBear` bean is instantiated is when it is injected into the `GrandparentsServlet`. This instance never received any of the events.

Next door from the window, the grandmother bear saw Goldilocks try all the beds, while the grandfather must have been asleep and saw nothing.

Interceptors

Java EE interceptors, which we first encountered in Chapter 10 with Enterprise Beans, can also be attached to CDI beans. A range of use cases exists for interceptors just as for Enterprise Beans: from simple application auditing to custom authentication schemes and transformation of inputs and outputs to and from CDI beans.

The most common form of interceptor intercepts any method call to the CDI bean. The interceptor is a method on a class that takes a `javax.interceptor.InvocationContext` as its single method parameter, which is annotated with the `javax.interceptor.AroundInvoke` annotation. The `InvocationContext` gives an abstracted view of the CDI bean method instance that is to be invoked. For example, the best way for the Bear family to find out what goes on in their house while they are out, rather than relying on the grandparents next door, is to set up bugging devices in the house. Let's look at one of them.

Listing: *An interceptor as a BuggingDevice*

```
import javax.interceptor.AroundInvoke;
import javax.interceptor.InvocationContext;
import java.util.*;

public class BuggingDevice {
    @AroundInvoke
```

```
public Object intercept(InvocationContext context) throws Exception {
    Object result = null;
    Bed bed = (Bed) context.getTarget();

    String parameterString =
            Arrays.asList(context.getParameters()).toString();
    System.out.println("BedInterceptor: " + parameterString +
                            " is about to try " + bed + "...");
    try {
        result = context.proceed();
    } catch (Exception e) {
        System.out.println("BedInterceptor: ....which raised " + e);
        throw e;
    }
    System.out.println("BedInterceptor: ....and has found it to be " +
                                                        result);

    return result;
    }
}
```

AroundInvoke interceptors are wired to the Java method or methods on the CDI bean instance by annotating the `@javax.interceptor.Interceptors` annotation carrying the array of interceptor classes as its value attribute. For example, there is the code to add the `BuggingDevice` to the baby bear's bed.

Listing: *Attaching a `BuggingDevice` interceptor to the baby bear's bed*

```
import javax.interceptor.Interceptors;
import javax.enterprise.event.Event;
import javax.inject.Inject;

public class BabyBearBed implements Bed {
    @Inject
    Event<SomeoneInBedEvent> sibe;

    @Override
    @Interceptors(BuggingDevice.class)
    public String tryIt(String name) {
        sibe.fire(new SomeoneInBedEvent(this, name));
        return "just right";
    }

    public String toString() {
        return "Baby's bed";
    }
}
```

In contrast to the event mechanism, within the `InvocationContext` passed into the `AroundInvoke` interceptor is all the information associated with the Java method call; none of that needs to be re-created in an event class.

More advanced uses of interceptors for CDI beans include interceptors for the callbacks to the bean after construction, before disposal, before passivation, and after activation, the last two applying to session-scoped beans. These are declared in a similar way as the invocation interceptors, but by using the `@PostConstruct`, `@PreDestroy`, `@PrePassivate`, or `@PostActivate` annotations.

Packaging CDI Beans

When a Java EE application is deployed, the CDI runtime will look into each of the Java EE modules for CDI beans. It does this by using two techniques: it looks for Java classes that are annotated with a CDI scope annotation, and it looks in the Java EE archives for a file called `beans.xml`. In WAR files, the `beans.xml` home is in `WEB-INF/`, and in Enterprise Bean archives, its home is in `META-INF/`.

If there is no `beans.xml` file in a Java EE module, CDI can inject only Java classes that are explicitly marked with one of the scope annotations that we explored earlier. Therefore, in such modules, you may not assume that CDI will recognize Java classes that you intend to be injectable with an implicit dependent scope. When you do have Java classes you wish to inject that do not explicitly carry a scope annotation, you need to include a `beans.xml` file with its bean-discover-mode option set to all.

 Listing: *Example `beans.xml` file*

```
<?xml version="1.0" encoding="UTF-8"?>
<beans xmlns="http://xmlns.jcp.org/xml/ns/javaee"
       xmlns:xsi="http://www.w3.org/2001/XMLSchema-instance"
       xsi:schemaLocation="http://xmlns.jcp.org/xml/ns/javaee
           http://xmlns.jcp.org/xml/ns/javaee/beans_1_1.xsd"
       bean-discovery-mode="all">
</beans>
```

CDI Chat

Let us apply some of what we have learned to a familiar example: the WebSocket chat example from Chapter 4. You will recall that this example is a Java EE web application with an HTML front end using JavaScript to connect to a Java WebSocket, which implements a simple chat application. You can see the main Chat page in Figure 14-9.

The key application constructs in this application in Chapter 4 were the chat transcript, the list of active users of the application, and the user associated with the current WebSocket session. In Chapter 4, we used the WebSocket's `EndpointConfig` to store the global transcript and user list, and the Java WebSocket session object to store the current user. This is a perfectly valid approach and is a great way to understand the Java WebSocket APIs. But CDI offers an alternative approach, since it allows us to define CDI beans that live in the global scope and CDI beans that depend on the scope of the current WebSocket endpoint instance. So instead of hand-managing the relationships of the transcript end-user list to the global `EndpointConfig` object of the WebSocket endpoint and the current user to the WebSocket `Session` object, we can hand off some of that code and have CDI manage the objects for us. Most of the application is exactly the same when compared

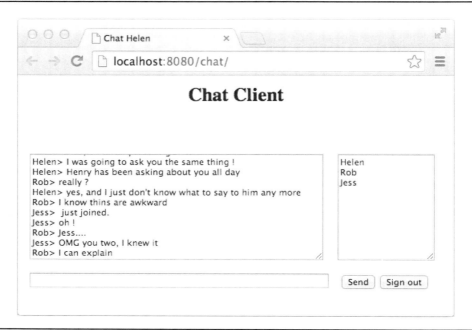

FIGURE 14-9. *The CDI chat client*

with the version from Chapter 4: the chat messages, the HTML, and JavaScript code. What has changed is the `ChatServer` endpoint and the `Transcript` object. Let's look first at the `Transcript`.

Listing: *The chat `Transcript` class*

```
import java.util.ArrayList;
import java.util.List;
import javax.enterprise.context.ApplicationScoped;

@ApplicationScoped
public class Transcript {
    private final List<String> messages = new ArrayList<>();
    private final List<String> usernames = new ArrayList<>();
    private final int maxLines;

    public Transcript() {
        maxLines = 20;
    }

    public String getLastUsername() {
        return usernames.get(usernames.size() -1);
```

```
        }

    public String getLastMessage() {
        return messages.get(messages.size() -1);
    }

    public void addEntry(String username, String message) {
        if (usernames.size() > maxLines) {
            usernames.remove(0);
            messages.remove(0);
        }
        usernames.add(username);
        messages.add(message);
    }
}
```

We can see now that the Transcript object has lost its connection with the WebSocket EndpointConfig: it used to have a static method that looked up the global instance of the Transcript on the EndpointConfig's user properties map. It has become a CDI bean with application scope instead. So when it is injected, there is always only one.

There is another application-scoped object now, the UserList, which holds the current list of users signed into the chat.

Listing: *The UserList class*

```
import java.util.*;
import javax.enterprise.context.*;
import javax.enterprise.inject.*;
import javaeems.chapter14.chat.event.*;
import javax.enterprise.event.Event;
import javax.inject.Inject;


@ApplicationScoped
public class UserList {
    private final List<User> users = new ArrayList<>();
    @Inject
    private Event<ChatEvent> eventSource;


    class UserImpl implements User {
        private String name;

        @Override
        public void setName(String name) {
            this.name = name;
            eventSource.fire(new UserJoinedEvent(this));
        }
```

```java
    @Override
    public String getName() {
        return this.name;
    }

    @Override
    public String toString() {
        return "User: " + name;
    }

}

@Default @Produces @Dependent
private User getUser() {
    User user = new UserImpl();
    this.users.add(user);
    return user;
}

public void deleteUser(User user) {
    this.users.remove(user);
    eventSource.fire(new UserLeftEvent(user));
}

public List<String> getUsernames() {
    List<String> usernames = new ArrayList<>();
    for (User u : this.users) {
        usernames.add(u.getName());
    }
    return usernames;
}

public String validateUsername(String newUsername) {
    if (this.getUsernames().contains(newUsername)) {
        return this.validateUsername(newUsername + "1");
    }
    return newUsername;
}

}
```

Notice that in addition to holding a list of User objects, this class acts as a producer of User beans thanks to its getUser() producer method. Notice also that it injects an Event into itself that it uses to fire events when its user list changes.

Now the User beans it produces are in @Dependent scope. So we should look next to see where the User beans are injected.

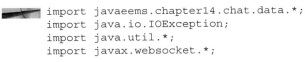

```java
import javaeems.chapter14.chat.data.*;
import java.io.IOException;
import java.util.*;
import javax.websocket.*;
```

```java
import javax.websocket.server.*;
import javax.inject.Inject;

@ServerEndpoint(value = "/chat-server",
        subprotocols={"chat"},
        decoders = {ChatDecoder.class},
        encoders = {ChatEncoder.class})
public class ChatServer {
    private Session session;
    @Inject
    private Transcript transcript;
    @Inject
    UserList userList;
    @Inject
    User currentUser;

    @OnOpen
    public void startChatChannel(Session session) {
        this.session = session;
    }

    @OnMessage
    public void handleChatMessage(ChatMessage message) {
        switch (message.getType()){
            case NewUserMessage.USERNAME_MESSAGE:
                this.processNewUser((NewUserMessage) message);
                break;
            case ChatMessage.CHAT_DATA_MESSAGE:
                 this.processChatUpdate((ChatUpdateMessage) message);
                 break;
            case ChatMessage.SIGNOFF_REQUEST:
                this.processSignoffRequest((UserSignoffMessage) message);
        }
    }

    @OnError
    public void myError(Throwable t) {
        System.out.println("Error: " + t.getMessage());
    }

    @OnClose
    public void endChatChannel() {
        if (this.currentUser.getName() != null) {
            this.addMessage(" just left...without even signing out !");
            this.broadcastUserListUpdate();
        }
    }

    void processNewUser(NewUserMessage message) {
        String newUsername =
            this.userList.validateUsername(message.getUsername());
        currentUser.setName(newUsername);
        NewUserMessage uMessage = new NewUserMessage(newUsername);
```

```
    try {
        session.getBasicRemote().sendObject(uMessage);
    } catch (IOException | EncodeException ioe) {
        System.out.println("Error signing " +
          message.getUsername() + " into chat : " + ioe.getMessage());
    }
    this.broadcastUserListUpdate();
    this.addMessage(" just joined.");
}

void processChatUpdate(ChatUpdateMessage message) {
    this.addMessage(message.getMessage());
}

void processSignoffRequest(UserSignoffMessage drm) {
    this.addMessage(" just left.");
    this.userList.deleteUser(this.currentUser);
    try {
        this.broadcastUserListUpdate();
        this.session.close(
            new CloseReason(CloseReason.CloseCodes.NORMAL_CLOSURE,
                                        "User logged off"));
    } catch (IOException e) {
        System.out.println("Error removing user");
    }
}

private List<String> getUserList() {
    return userList.getUsernames();
}

private void broadcastUserListUpdate() {
    UserListUpdateMessage ulum = new
        UserListUpdateMessage(this.getUserList());
    for (Session nextSession : session.getOpenSessions()) {
        try {
            nextSession.getBasicRemote().sendObject(ulum);
        } catch (IOException | EncodeException ex) {
            System.out.println("Error updating a client : " +
                                            ex.getMessage());
        }
    }
}

private void broadcastTranscriptUpdate() {
    for (Session nextSession : session.getOpenSessions()) {
        ChatUpdateMessage cdm =
            new ChatUpdateMessage(this.transcript.getLastUsername(),
                              this.transcript.getLastMessage());
```

```
        try {
            nextSession.getBasicRemote().sendObject(cdm);
        } catch (IOException | EncodeException ex) {
            System.out.println("Error updating a client : " +
                                                ex.getMessage());
        }
      }
    }
  }

  private void addMessage(String message) {
    this.transcript.addEntry(this.currentUser.getName(), message);
    this.broadcastTranscriptUpdate();
  }
}
```

We see quickly that the `User` beans are injected into each new instance of the `ChatServer` WebSocket endpoint. Remember from Chapter 4 that there is one instance of the `ChatServer` WebSocket endpoint per WebSocket connection with a browser client. So CDI injects exactly one distinct `User` instance into each `ChatServer` instance, into its `currentUser` field. Notice also that the CDI runtime injects the `Transcript` and `UserList` instances into the `ChatServer`'s other fields. All the lifecycle management of these three pivotal objects in the application are now under the control of CDI: there is no need for this endpoint to know about its `EndpointConfig` global or store anything in the `Session` object, and still less worry about maintaining the user list or current user. Finally, this CDI chat example adds a simple auditing bean to listen to the changes in the `UserList` bean.

Listing: *The `UserAudit` bean*

```
import java.text.SimpleDateFormat;
import javaeems.chapter14.chat.event.*;
import javax.enterprise.event.*;
import java.util.*;


public class UserAudit {

    void userJoined(@Observes UserJoinedEvent e) {
        System.out.println(e.getUser().getName() + " joined the chat at " +
                                    this.format(e.getTimestamp())));
    }

    void userLeft(@Observes UserLeftEvent e) {
        System.out.println(e.getUser().getName() + " left the chat at " +
                                    this.format(e.getTimestamp())));
    }

    String format(Date d) {
        SimpleDateFormat sdf = new SimpleDateFormat(
                                    "yyyy.MM.dd 'at' HH:mm:ss z");
```

```
        String formatted = sdf.format(d);
        return formatted;
    }

}
```

If you compare the CDI chat application with Chapter 4's version, you might try to determine which application has less code and which spends more of its code on the logic of chat, rather than on the lifecycle management of its data.

Summary

In this chapter, we explored the general-purpose paradigm of the CDI framework and APIs. We explored how to declare Java classes in such a way that they might be managed by the CDI runtime, instead of by the application, and the mechanism by which they can be injected into the consumer objects that need to use them. We explored the way in which CDI beans are matched to injection sites. We looked at the different places beans may be injected into a Java class. Using examples based around Goldilocks trying three different beds at the bears' house, we looked at how to declare events that are broadcast by the CDI runtime and how to listen in to them. We touched on CDI interceptors. We finished up the chapter by taking a familiar example, the WebSocket chat example from Chapter 4, and refactored its principal application data objects into CDI beans to illustrate how even the fundamental CDI mechanisms can simplify Java EE applications by taking on the work of managing the lifecycles of their objects.

CHAPTER
15

Java EE Security

lthough you may want the whole world to know about your Java EE application, you may not want the whole world to use it. And you will probably want to know something about who is using it.

In Chapter 7, we used the analogy of a castle with a guarded door that restricts entry only to known visitors. We explored the techniques available in the Java EE web container to secure web components within web applications deployed on a Java EE server. The HTTP and WebSocket protocols are not the only ways to get into the castle.

In this chapter, we look at the security mechanisms available in the Enterprise Bean container for securing Enterprise Beans in a Java EE application. The clients of Enterprise Beans can be other Enterprise Beans, Java EE application clients, or Java EE web components running in the Java EE web container. We look at how the security mechanisms in the Enterprise Beans container fit into the larger picture of other Java EE components making calls into it. We can see a visual representation of the Java EE platform and its access points in Figure 15-1.

Enterprise Bean Security

The Java EE platform assists developers in limiting access to Enterprise Beans in two basic ways: programmatically or declaratively. Using the programmatic approach, an Enterprise Bean elects to manage all access to its application logic itself. In this case, when the Enterprise Bean container receives an invocation for the Enterprise Bean, it in turn calls the Enterprise Bean, exposing the information about the caller that it has to the bean. The Enterprise Bean makes whatever checks about the caller's identity that it needs to in order to determine how and indeed whether to call the application logic. For example, is the caller allowed access at all, and if so, is the caller in a

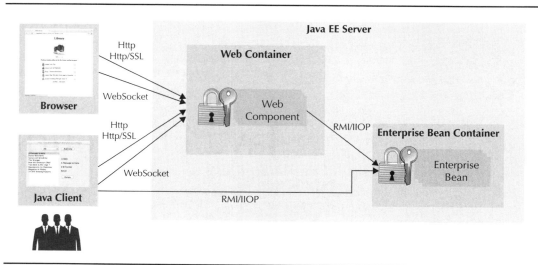

FIGURE 15-1. *Security of calls in the Java EE platform*

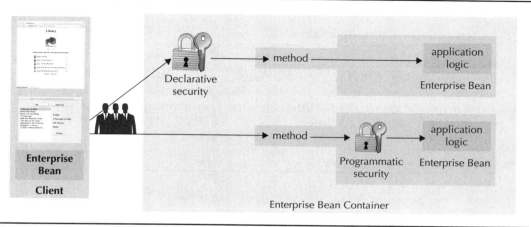

FIGURE 15-2. *Programmatic vs. declarative security of Enterprise Beans*

certain role that gives it a specific level of functionality? Using the declarative approach, the Enterprise Bean uses Java EE annotations and/or information it declares in its deployment descriptor to request that the Enterprise Bean container set up its security model. In this case, when the Enterprise Bean container receives a call for the Enterprise Bean, it requires the client to be authenticated and decides, based on the caller and the information declared by the Enterprise Bean, whether to allow the call to continue to the bean. In this case, the Enterprise Bean has the same access to the security information associated with the call as in the programmatic approach, but the container has already checked the caller's permissions to invoke the bean. We can see a visual representation of these two approaches, valid regardless of the client of the Enterprise Bean, in Figure 15-2.

Declarative Security

The declarative model is based on the abstraction of the caller as something called a security role. A security role has a name, and is used to provide a layer of abstraction between the application and how it understands the set of its callers and the actual authenticated names of the callers when the application is deployed. Just as for web applications, Enterprise Bean applications can declare access constraints in terms of security role names. For example: "only allow users that are part of the security role 'managers' to access my methods," or "allow 'administrator' users and 'paid-customer' users to access my methods." The person deploying the application makes the association between the database of known callers and the security roles to which they belong.

In the declarative security model, an Enterprise Bean uses one or more security annotations to define the security roles to which a caller must belong in order to have access to the bean. The annotations can be applied to the implementation class at the class level, in which case they apply either to all the methods of the bean or to individual methods of the implementation class, in which case the permission applies only to that method. In cases where an Enterprise Bean uses security annotations both at the method and class levels, the method-level annotation overrides the class-level annotation. If a client of the Enterprise Bean attempts to call one of its methods that is protected by a security annotation and the client does not have sufficient permissions to do so, the client receives an exception of type `javax.ejb.EJBAccessException`.

Let's take a look at the annotations, starting with the first and most widely useful.

@RolesAllowed

The `@javax.annotation.security.RolesAllowed` has the single value attribute, which takes an array of security role names. What it means is that only authenticated users that are part of one or more of the security roles that it lists may have access to the Enterprise Bean or Enterprise Bean method it annotates.

Listing: *An Enterprise Bean allowing only certain users*

```
import javax.ejb.Stateful;
import javax.annotation.security.RolesAllowed;

@Stateful
public class LibraryBean {
    @RolesAllowed({"customer", "backend"})
    public List<String> getBookTitles() {
        ...
    }
    ...
}
```

In this example, only users that are part of the customer and backend security roles are allowed access to the `getBookTitled()` method of the `LibraryBean`.

@PermitAll

The `@javax.annotation.security.PermitAll` annotation has no attributes. When it annotates an Enterprise Bean class or method, its meaning is that any authenticated users may access the class or method, whether they belong to one of the security roles defined by the application or not. This is a useful shorthand for allowing everyone access, but it is not the same as using `@RolesAllowed` with all the security roles listed for that application: `@PermitAll` allows users that don't belong to any security role to have access, as well as those who do belong to a security role.

@DenyAll

The `@javax.annotation.security.DenyAll` annotation has no attributes. When it annotates an Enterprise Bean class or method, its meaning is that no one can access the class or method.

You may not mix these annotations at the same level; for example:

```
@RolesAllowed({"customer", "backend"})
@PermitAll
public List<String> getBookTitles() {
    ...
}
```

is not permitted and would lead to a deployment error. However, you can use the annotations at both the class and method levels. As mentioned, the security annotations at the method level override the security annotations at the class level. This does not mean that the access allowed is additive when you have both; rather, it means that if there is a security annotation at the method level, that is the definitive amount of access control for that method. If there is no security annotation at the method level and there is a security annotation at the class level, the amount of access granted to the method is that defined in the class-level security annotation. Finally, of course, if there is no security annotation that applies to a method, any caller is allowed to call it, authenticated or not.

@DeclareRoles

The `@javax.annotation.security.DeclareRoles` has a single attribute, value, which takes a list of security role names, and it is used at the class level of an Enterprise Bean. Unlike the other security annotations, it does not allow access based on role names; rather, it tells the deployer of the application (or the tool that the deployer is using) which roles the bean is using, either in explicit declarations such as in the `@RolesAllowed` annotation, or in security roles used programmatically (examples of which we shall see later). This allows the deployer to map the users registered in the Java EE server to the roles that the bean uses.

Let's look at an example of some of these annotations in action and the override rules.

Declarative Security Example

This example takes the form of an Enterprise Bean, called `HelloBean`, with a Java EE application client that makes calls to it. The application client has a GUI, as we see in Figure 15-3.

The application client can ask the `HelloBean` to say hello, ask to say hello to a given name, and change the greeting the `HelloBean` uses to say hello. But only if they are authenticated and in the right security rule can they do all three. Let's look at the bean implementation class to see who is allowed to do what.

FIGURE 15-3. *The declarative security GUI*

Listing: *The HelloBeanImpl class*

```java
import javax.ejb.Stateful;
import java.io.Serializable;
import javax.annotation.security.PermitAll;
import javax.annotation.security.RolesAllowed;
import javax.annotation.security.DeclareRoles;

@Stateful
@PermitAll
@DeclareRoles({"registered-user", "administrator", "guest"})
public class HelloBeanImpl implements HelloBean, Serializable {
    private String greeting = "Hello";

    @Override
    public String sayHello() {
        return greeting;
    }

    @RolesAllowed({"administrator", "registered-user"})
    @Override
    public String sayHelloTo(String name) {
        return greeting + " " + name + " !";
    }

    @RolesAllowed("administrator")
    @Override
    public void setGreeting(String greeting) {
        this.greeting = greeting;
    }

}
```

We can see that `HelloBeanImpl` is a stateful session bean, which from its `@DeclareRoles` annotation we can tell uses the roles registered-user, administrator, and guest. It has a `@PermitAll` annotation at the class level, which means that, unless a bean method has its own security annotation, then all authenticated users will be allowed to call the method. This is the case, for example, for `sayHello()`. But the `sayHelloTo()` method uses the `@RolesAllowed` annotation to limit access to authenticated users who are in either the registered-user or administrator role. The `setGreeting()` method, similarly, may be called only by authenticated users in the administrator role.

Now, to check this, we need to set up some users. No matter what Java EE server you are using, this is a two-step process: first you need to add users to the application server, supplying a username and credential, and second, you need to decide which user to associate with which security role in the application.

This example was built and tested on the GlassFish application server. Adding users in GlassFish may be done by means of the GlassFish Admin console, adding usernames and passwords to the file realm. GlassFish uses a specific deployment descriptor packaged in the Enterprise Bean JAR called the `glassfish-ejb-jar.xml` file to associate usernames with security roles.

For this example, we have set up three users: `cecile`, `alex`, and `jared`. The following table shows the roles to which they are associated:

User	Roles
Cecile	guest
Alex	registered-user
Jared	administrator

And here's the corresponding `glassfish-ejb-jar.xml` file.

Listing: *The `glassfish-ejb-jar.xml` file defining role user associations*

```xml
<?xml version="1.0" encoding="UTF-8"?>
<!DOCTYPE glassfish-ejb-jar PUBLIC "-//GlassFish.org//DTD GlassFish Application Server
3.1 EJB 3.1//EN" "http://glassfish.org/dtds/glassfish-ejb-jar_3_1-1.dtd">
<glassfish-ejb-jar>
  <security-role-mapping>
    <role-name>administrator</role-name>
    <principal-name>jared</principal-name>
  </security-role-mapping>
  <security-role-mapping>
    <role-name>registered-user</role-name>
    <principal-name>alex</principal-name>
  </security-role-mapping>
  <security-role-mapping>
    <role-name>guest</role-name>
    <principal-name>cecile</principal-name>
  </security-role-mapping>
  <enterprise-beans/>
</glassfish-ejb-jar>
```

Now when `cecile` logs in, she can call `sayHello()`, since as a member of the `guest` role she is permitted. But when she tries to call either of the other methods, she is not allowed, as you can see in Figure 15-4.

FIGURE 15-4. *Cecile is not permitted to say hello to a given name*

FIGURE 15-5. *Alex may not change the greeting*

When `alex` logs in, he can call `sayHello()` and `sayHelloTo()` since he is in the `registered-user` role, but he cannot call the `setGreeting()` method, shown in Figure 15-5, because he is not in the `administrator` role,

Only `jared`, as a member of the `administrator` role, can call all three methods.

We will not look in detail at the client code, but we will look at the method that is called when the user tries to change the greeting in the client window.

Listing: *The `changeGreeting()` method of the client window*

```
public void changeGreeting() {
    try {
        helloBean.setGreeting(changeGreetingTf.getText());
    } catch (EJBAccessException ejbae) {
        JOptionPane.showMessageDialog(this,
            "You do not have permission to change the greeting !");
    }
}
```

Notice that the method explicitly handles the `EJBAccessException`, which is thrown if the user does not have the correct role membership to execute the method.

Programmatic Security

Every Enterprise Bean has access to the security information that its container holds about the current caller through the container-provided `javax.ejb.EJBContext` object. We first encountered this object in Chapter 10 when we were exploring the Enterprise Bean Timer Service. There are two methods that grant access to the security context of a call. The first one is:

`Principal getCallerPrincipal()`

which returns the `java.security.Principal` associated with the caller. If the caller is not authenticated, as can happen in the case of unauthenticated web components making a call to the Enterprise Bean, the `Principal` in this case is a reserved `UserPrincipal` that is supplied by the Java EE server to signify that the caller is unauthenticated. The name of the `Principal` depends on which Java EE server you are using. In the case of the GlassFish server, the `Principal` has the reserved name `ANONYMOUS`.

The second method that grants access to the security context of a call is

```
boolean isCallerInRole(String roleName)
```

which tests whether the caller is in the security role with the given `roleName`.

These methods are analogous to their companion methods for web components on `javax`
`.servlet.http.HttpServletRequest` for servlets, JSPs, and JavaServer Faces; `javax.ws.rs`
`.core.SecurityContext` for JAX-RS components; and on `javax.websocket.Session` for Java WebSocket components.

The `EJBContext` object may be injected into an Enterprise Bean; for example:

```
import javax.ejb.Stateful;
import javax.ejb.EJBContext;
import javax.annotation.Resource;

@Stateful
public class LibraryBean {
    @Resource
    EJBContext myContext;
    ...
}
```

With these methods, an Enterprise Bean may implement its own access control. It may do so by checking for specific users using `getCallerPrincipal()` before allowing a method invocation to proceed. It may use the security roles defined for the Enterprise Bean and gate method execution based on membership of a security role or roles by using `isCallerInRole()`.

Enterprise Beans may also use the declarative and programmatic security models together, using the declarative model to provide basic access control, and using the programmatic model to refine the tasks performed by the Enterprise Bean based on the caller identity and/or the caller's membership of certain security roles. We will see this in action later in the chapter.

Application Client Authentication

In the declarative security example, we did not explain how the user was authenticated to the application client of the application. The means by which an application client authenticated with the Enterprise Bean container is specific to the Java EE server implementation that you are using. Some provide a single sign-on capability, allowing application clients to authenticate once and access the Enterprise Beans of more than one application without having to reauthenticate. Some application clients may integrate with the operating system's certificate store and perform SSL certificate authentication. Some may provide a basic username-password scheme, akin to the HTTP basic authentication mechanism, and a default UI for gathering the credential for the user prior to obtaining a reference to an Enterprise Bean that declares some access restriction. This last model is the case for the GlassFish server.

All application clients, regardless of which Java EE server implementation they are part of, must provide support for the `javax.security.auth.callback.CallbackHandler` interface.

The purpose of this interface is to allow applications to define their own mechanisms for gathering a user credential. If an application client application implements this interface, it must implement the single method

```
void handle(Callback[] callbacks)
        throws IOException, UnsupportedCallbackException
```

which is called by the application client container when it needs to gather credential information, requiring the implementation to fill out the `Callback` objects it passes into the method to fulfill the credential interaction. In turn, the application client registers its callback handler class in an entry in its `application-client.xml` deployment descriptor. Let's take a look at this in action, together with the deployment descriptor syntax.

In the declarative security example, we relied on the GlassFish application client container's default login screen. But using our own customer `CallbackHandler`, we can customize this screen and supply the credentials ourselves. We will see how to do this with a simple GUI. First, we write the `CallbackHandler`.

Listing: *A custom `CallbackHandler`*

```
import javax.security.auth.callback.CallbackHandler;
import javax.security.auth.callback.PasswordCallback;
import javax.security.auth.callback.NameCallback;
import javax.security.auth.callback.UnsupportedCallbackException;
import javax.security.auth.callback.Callback;
import java.io.*;


public class MyCallbackHandler implements CallbackHandler  {

    @Override
    public void handle(Callback[] callbacks)
            throws IOException, UnsupportedCallbackException {
        MyLoginWindow mlw = MyLoginWindow.gatherCredential(
                                "Login to Declarative Security");
        if (mlw.isCanceled()) {
            return ;
        }
        for (Callback c : callbacks) {
            if (c instanceof NameCallback) {
                ((NameCallback) c).setName(mlw.getUsername());
            } else if (c instanceof PasswordCallback) {
                ((PasswordCallback) c).
                        setPassword(mlw.getPassword().toCharArray());
            }
        }
    }
}
```

This `CallbackHandler` uses another class, `MyLoginWindow`, to retrieve the credentials from the user. On GlassFish, the `CallbackHandler` is invoked with the simple basic authentication protocol, so we expect only to be passed a `PasswordCallback` and a `NameCallback` object to fill out in the `handle()` method. Once the username and password values have been filled out, the `handle()` method completes and the authentication commences against the supplied credential.

We will not look through the GUI code of the `MyLoginWindow` class; instead, shown in Figure 15-6 is the login screen the user will see.

While this is a simple GUI, you can easily imagine something more elaborate, something that integrates tightly with a larger GUI application, or something that connects to a systems-specific system to gather the credentials.

Declaring the `CallbackHandler` in the `application-client.xml` is simply a matter of adding an element `<callback-handler>` with the classname of the `CallbackHandler` implementation. For example, here is the `application-client.xml` needed to run this custom login process.

Listing: *An application client deployment descriptor declaring a* `CallbackHandler`

```xml
<?xml version="1.0" encoding="UTF-8"?>
<application-client version="7"
                    xmlns="http://xmlns.jcp.org/xml/ns/javaee"
                    xmlns:xsi="http://www.w3.org/2001/XMLSchema-instance"
                    xsi:schemaLocation="http://xmlns.jcp.org/xml/ns/javaee
                    http://xmlns.jcp.org/xml/ns/javaee/application-client_7.xsd">
  <display-name>DeclarativeEnterpriseBean-client</display-name>
  <callback-handler>javaeems.chapter15.hello.client.MyCallbackHandler
                                              </callback-handler>
</application-client>
```

FIGURE 15-6. *Custom application client login GUI*

Security Identity Propagation

Probably the most common scenario for Java EE security is the situation when the clients of a collection of Enterprise Beans are web components and other Enterprise Beans rather than application clients.

In the Java EE platform, you can choose whether you want a web component or an Enterprise Bean to use the identity with which it was called to be propagated to the Enterprise Bean it is calling, or whether you want the call to be made with some other identity.

It can be useful to use the latter mechanism to isolate the identities and roles set up in the web layer of an application from those in the Enterprise Bean layer. In such cases, using the second mechanism, you can ensure that all the calls into the Enterprise Bean layer occur under a single identity reserved for calls from the web layer. This mechanism is known as the Run-As mechanism.

Before we look at the syntax, Figure 15-7 illustrates the various permutations of a browser and application client calling web components that in turn call into the Enterprise Bean layer of an application. Each time that a web component or Enterprise Bean component is called, there is the possibility of that component passing on the identity of its caller to an Enterprise Bean it itself calls, or using the Run-As mechanism to pass on some other defined identity.

The way to read Figure 15-7 is to see that the browser has authenticated and makes calls to two web components under a given identity A. The first web component, when it calls its Enterprise Bean, elects to pass on the caller identity A, so the Enterprise Bean it calls knows that call as identity A. The second web component that the browser calls has chosen to use the Run-As mechanism to call its Enterprise Bean with a different identity, identity B, from that with which it was called.

When a web or Enterprise Bean component wants to call other Enterprise Beans with the same identity as its own caller, there is nothing to do: this is the default mode for these components.

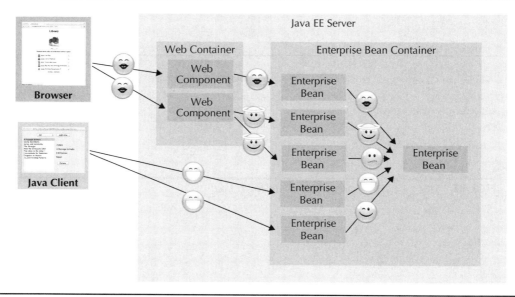

FIGURE 15-7. *Permutations of identity propagation in the Java EE platform*

To use the Run-As mechanism, the web or Enterprise Bean component declares a single role name, which the Java EE server will use to derive the identity that it would use to call any Enterprise Beans.

For Java servlets and Enterprise Beans, declaring this role name is easy: you simply annotate the servlet or Enterprise Bean implementation class with the `@javax.annotation.security.RunAs` annotation, specifying the security role name as the value of the single value attribute. For example:

```
import javax.annotation.security.RunAs;

@RunAs("auto")
@Stateless
public MyFacadeBean {
    @EJB
    CalculatorBean calculator;
    ...
}
```

In this example, no matter who the caller of the `MyFacadeBean` is, when any of its methods call the `CalculatorBean`, they will occur as an identity within the security role called `auto`. The question is which identity? The `auto` role may potentially have several users associated with it. How the Java EE server selects the specific user from within the `@RunAs` defined role is a configuration task that is specific to the Java EE server on which the application is deployed. In the special case when only one user has been associated with the security role, as we saw in the declarative security example for the GlassFish server, then that single user is the one that is selected as the RunAs identity. This can often prove an easy way to set up the `@RunAs` identity, and frequently applications that use this facility set up a special user and assign it and only it to a special role just for use with this mechanism.

Now that we have explored the concepts of identity propagation from between the tiers of a Java EE application, looked at some of the options for how it may be configured, and seen how to access security information programmatically, let's pull together some of these ideas into a familiar scenario: the Library example of Chapter 12.

The Library Example with End-to-End Security

When last we looked at the Library example, we had upgraded its data layer to use the Java Persistence API. In this chapter, we have learned enough to require authentication to use this application and apply the Java EE security model to it through the web and Enterprise Bean layers.

For this application, we have set up three users and associated them with three roles:

User	Role
cecile	adult
alex	child
jared	administrator

When we first try to access the application, we are asked to sign in, as shown in Figure 15-8.
If we sign in as Cecile, we will see a list of books, but they are books for adults, as we can see
in Figure 15-9. Whereas, if we log in as Alex, we will also see a list of books, but they are all
children's books as Figure 15-10 shows. Furthermore, if either Alex or Cecile try to add or delete
a book or add an author, they will see the page shown in Figure 15-11. Finally, if we log in as
Jared, we see all the titles in the library, both for adults and for children, and we can add authors
and add or delete books in the library, as shown in Figure 15-12.

Let's take a look at where the Java EE security model is being used in this application. First,
in the `web.xml` deployment descriptor of the web application piece, we have protected the
JavaServer Faces pages in the application using the form login mechanism and constrained
access to those JavaServer Faces pages only to authenticated users in one of the roles
administrator, adult, or child.

FIGURE 15-8.   *Signing into the Library application*

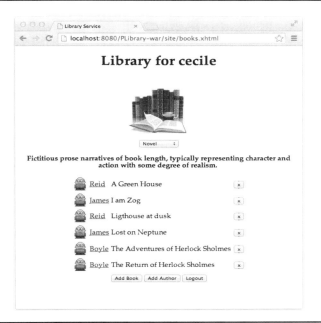

FIGURE 15-9. *Cecile's books for adults*

FIGURE 15-10. *Alex's books for children*

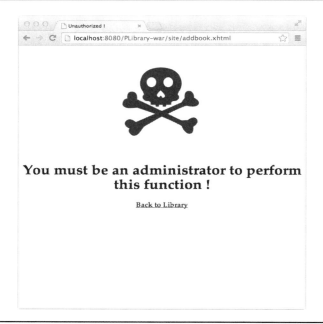

FIGURE 15-11. *Unauthorized access*

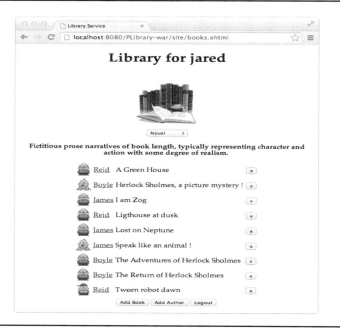

FIGURE 15-12. *Jared has all the books*

Listing: *The web deployment descriptor for the Library example*

```xml
<?xml version="1.0" encoding="UTF-8"?>
<web-app version="3.1"
        xmlns="http://xmlns.jcp.org/xml/ns/javaee"
        xmlns:xsi="http://www.w3.org/2001/XMLSchema-instance"
        xsi:schemaLocation="http://xmlns.jcp.org/xml/ns/javaee
        http://xmlns.jcp.org/xml/ns/javaee/web-app_3_1.xsd">
    <context-param>
        <param-name>javax.faces.PROJECT_STAGE</param-name>
        <param-value>Development</param-value>
    </context-param>
    <servlet>
        <servlet-name>Faces Servlet</servlet-name>
        <servlet-class>javax.faces.webapp.FacesServlet</servlet-class>
        <load-on-startup>1</load-on-startup>
    </servlet>
    <servlet-mapping>
        <servlet-name>Faces Servlet</servlet-name>
        <url-pattern>*.xhtml</url-pattern>
    </servlet-mapping>
    <session-config>
        <session-timeout>
            30
        </session-timeout>
    </session-config>
    <welcome-file-list>
        <welcome-file>site/books.xhtml</welcome-file>
    </welcome-file-list>
    <login-config>
        <auth-method>FORM</auth-method>
        <form-login-config>
            <form-login-page>/login.xhtml</form-login-page>
            <form-error-page>/error.xhtml</form-error-page>
        </form-login-config>
    </login-config>
    <error-page>
        <exception-type>
            javaeems.chapter15.library.
        </exception-type>
        <location>/site/accessdenied.xhtml</location>
    </error-page>
    <security-constraint>
        <display-name>ViewAndEdit</display-name>
        <web-resource-collection>
            <web-resource-name>ViewableAndEditable</web-resource-name>
            <description/>
            <url-pattern>/site/*</url-pattern>
        </web-resource-collection>
        <auth-constraint>
            <role-name>administrator</role-name>
```

```
              <role-name>adult</role-name>
              <role-name>child</role-name>
          </auth-constraint>
      </security-constraint>
      <security-role>
          <description/>
          <role-name>administrator</role-name>
      </security-role>
      <security-role>
          <description/>
          <role-name>adult</role-name>
      </security-role>
      <security-role>
          <description/>
          <role-name>child</role-name>
      </security-role>
</web-app>
```

Notice the `<error-page>` declaration in this deployment descriptor. What it says is that any unhandled exception of type `UnauthorizedAccessException` (that the Library application now defines) that is thrown by any of the managed beans takes the browser to the page /site/ accessdenied.xhtml: this is the page with the skull and crossbones that Alex and Cecile see when they try to add a new book or author.

Now let's look at an excerpt from the `LibraryBeanImpl` class.

Listing: *Excerpt from the `LibraryBeanImpl` class*

```java
import javax.annotation.security.PermitAll;
import javax.annotation.security.RolesAllowed;
import javax.annotation.security.DeclareRoles;
import javax.annotation.Resource;

@PermitAll
@Singleton
@DeclareRoles({"adult", "child", "adminstrator"})
public class LibraryBeanImpl implements LibraryBean {
    @PersistenceContext
    private EntityManager em;
    @Resource
    SessionContext sessionContext;

    @Override
    public List<Book> getBooksByGenre(String genreName) {
        Query query = em.createNamedQuery("findAllBooks");
        List<Book> books = query.getResultList();
        List<Book> genreBooks = new ArrayList<>();
        for (Book b : books) {
            if (b.isInGenre(genreName)) {
                if (sessionContext.isCallerInRole("child")) {
```

```
                        if (b instanceof ChildrensBook) {
                            genreBooks.add(b);
                        }
                    } else if (sessionContext.isCallerInRole("adult")) {
                        if (!(b instanceof ChildrensBook)) {
                            genreBooks.add(b);
                        }
                    } else {
                        genreBooks.add(b);
                    }
                }
            }
        }
        return genreBooks;
    }


    @RolesAllowed("administrator")
    @Override
    public void addBook(String title,
                        int authorId,
                        List<String> genreNames,
                        boolean isChildrens,
                        int age) {
        int id = this.generateNewBookId();
        Author author = this.getAuthorForId(authorId);
        if (author == null) {
            throw new RuntimeException("bad author");
        }
        List<Genre> genres = this.getGenres(genreNames);
        Book newBook;
        if (isChildrens) {
            newBook = new ChildrensBook(id, title, author, genres, age);
        } else {
            newBook = new Book(id, title, author, genres);
        }
        em.persist(newBook);

    }


    @RolesAllowed("administrator")
    @Override
    public void addAuthor(List<String> foreNames,
                        String lastName,
                        String description) {
        int id = this.generateNewAuthorId();
        Author a = new Author(id, foreNames, lastName, description);
        em.persist(a);
    }


    @RolesAllowed("administrator")
    @Override
    public void deleteBook(int id) {
```

```
        Book b = em.find(Book.class, id);
        em.remove(b);
    }
...
}
```

Notice first that in using the `@PermitAll` annotation at the class level, all authenticated users are allowed to call methods on this bean, unless the method has a security annotation that says otherwise. Which is indeed the case for the `addBook()`, `addAuthor()`, and `deleteBook()` methods, each of which uses the `@RolesAllowed` annotation to allow only users in the administrator role to call these methods. This explains why only Jared can edit the contents of the Library application, as he is the only user in the administrator role.

Second, notice that while the `getBooksByGenre()` method is accessible to all authenticated users, its implementation uses the `SessionContext` that has been injected into the `LibraryBeanImpl` class to determine to which role the current caller belongs, and so list only children's books to users in the child role, and books for adults for the callers in the adult role. This explains why Cecile and Alex see a different selection of books, because Cecile is in the adult role and Alex in the child role.

Finally, we look at an excerpt from the `AddBookJSFBean`, used by the JavaServer Faces `addbook.xhtml` page, which adds new books to the library.

Listing: *Excerpt from the `AddBookJSFBean`, handling an `EJBAccessException`*

```java
import javax.ejb.EJB;
import javax.ejb.EJBAccessException;

@Named("addBookBean")
@RequestScoped
public class AddBookJSFBean {
    @EJB
    LibraryBean librarybean;
    private String title;
    private String genreName1;
    private String genreName2;
    private Author author;
    private boolean childrensBook = false;
    private List<Integer> ages = new ArrayList<>();
    private int age;

    public void add() {
        List<String> genres = new ArrayList<>();
        this.addIfNotEmpty(genreName1, genres);
        this.addIfNotEmpty(genreName2, genres);
        try {
            librarybean.addBook(this.title,
                                this.author.getId(),
                                genres,
                                childrensBook,
```

```
                                  this.age);
        } catch (EJBAccessException e) {
            throw new UnauthorizedAccessException(
                            "Error adding a new book",
                            librarybean.getClass().getSimpleName(),
                            "addBook" );
        }
    }
...
}
```

The add() method catches the EJBAccessException thrown by the libraryBean, such as when Alex or Cecile try to add a book to the library, and throws an UnauthorizedAccessException, which, thanks to the <error-page> declaration in the web.xml deployment descriptor, takes them to the /site/accessdenied.xhtml page.

We could go further with this application: for example, using the web security APIs, which we covered in Chapter 7, to disable functions in the JavaServer Faces pages when they are not permissible to the current authenticated user. That is left as an exercise to the reader.

Summary

In this chapter, we started where Chapter 7, with its examination of the declarative and programmatic security features of the Java EE web container, left off. We explored both the declarative security model of the Enterprise Bean container, using an application client to Enterprise Bean example to show how Enterprise Beans may be annotated to limit access to their methods. We took an excursion into the world of application client authentication and looked at how the login process can be customized. We looked at the programmatic access Enterprise Beans have to their caller information and saw how Java EE server components can control the identity that is passed on to Enterprise Beans they call. Finally, we looked at how to take a familiar Library application and apply Java EE end-to-end security to both limit its exposure and differentiate its functionality based on who is using it.

CHAPTER
16

Many Hands Make
Light Work:
Java EE Concurrency

The Java EE concurrency API is to compute-intensive tasks what multilane freeways are to traffic management.

For many years, computation tasks could be performed more and more quickly because of improvements in one aspect of the underlying processing power of processors: the chip speed. However, as the chip architectures started to approach the physical limits of what could be manufactured, chip designers turned to another technique to increase the computing power of their architectures: parallel processing. In terms of managing traffic on roads, this is rather like the realization that increasing the speed limit can only be taken so far: if your concern is the overall throughput of vehicles, you have to start adding more lanes to the road. Whether a chip has multiple cores or an architecture is based on multiple chips operating in parallel, the concept is the same: if a computing task, such as running a complicated web site, analyzing very large datasets, or converting information from one format into another, can be broken down into a number of independent tasks, they can be executed in parallel instead of sequentially, take advantage of the parallel processing capabilities of a multiprocessor or multicore architecture, and so complete their work more quickly and efficiently. First becoming prevalent in the 1990s in large computer systems suited for running web servers, multicore and multiprocessor architectures have become prevalent on billions of platforms from server machines, to desktop systems, laptops, tablets, and smartphones.

For certain kinds of computing tasks such as running multiple applications on a desktop, it is relatively easy for the system to know how to separate tasks out from one another and decide which can be executed in parallel. For other kinds of tasks, such as analyzing demographic information across a database of census information, it is more difficult. So increasingly, programming languages and platforms are evolving ways to allow applications to introduce concurrent techniques themselves. Figure 16-1 shows the conceptual flow of executing a task concurrently versus in parallel.

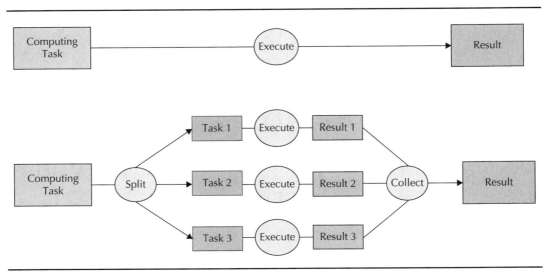

FIGURE 16-1. *Parallel execution of a large task*

The Java SE platform contained facilities for breaking computing tasks into subtasks that could be executed in parallel, starting with the humble Thread class. Difficult to use correctly due to its low-level nature and the ease with which race conditions, thread starvation, and locking conditions can arise, the Java SE platform has a collection of APIs called the concurrency APIs for a higher-level approach to concurrent programming. All the techniques at heart rely on the ability to create multiple threads to process a collection of tasks in parallel.

For Java EE programmers, the Java EE containers take on the job of thread management, and indeed, in the Enterprise Bean container, application-created threads are strongly discouraged because the container has no way to know of their existence and integrate them into the lifecycle and other services they provide. As we have seen, the Java EE platform itself allows applications to define components that can act in a concurrent manner, such as stateless session beans that are instantiated each time they are needed, or WebSocket endpoints that are instantiated once for every client that connects to them. Until recently, however, there has not been a way to execute work in a concurrent manner and wholly under the application's control. In this chapter, we will look at the Java EE Concurrency API.

Tasks and Executors

The core concepts of the Java EE Concurrency API are that of a task and an executor. A task is a piece of computing work that the application would like to complete. Tasks are created by Java EE applications and can be any kind of application work, from mathematical computations, to processes that affect large database tables, to conversions of data from one form into another. Tasks may or may not have a result when they are complete. An executor is a service provided by the Java EE platform. A Java EE concurrency executor service provides the means for applications to submit tasks. It maintains a pool of container-managed threads that execute the task and can inform the application of the progress of each task's execution.

Application tasks are classes that implement either the `java.lang.Runnable` or `java.util.concurrent.Callable<V>` interfaces. The `Runnable` interface is suited for application tasks that do not return a result, for example, a task that compresses a video file. It has one method that you probably already know:

```
void run()
```

which the application implements with the code that executes the task.

The `Callable<V>` interface is suited for modeling application tasks that produce some result object (of type `V`) at the end of their execution, for example, calculating the average age as a double of respondents in a sample from a country-wide census report. It has one method:

```
V call() throws Exception
```

which the application implements with the code that executes the task, returning the result of the task execution.

The Java EE platform provides the service by which application tasks, either `Runnable`s or `Callable<V>`s, are executed in the form of instances of the interface `javax.enterprise.concurrent.ManagedExecutorService`. For example, the `submit()` calls allow you to submit a single task for execution by the service

```
Future<V> submit(Callable<V> task)
```

which returns a `java.util.concurrent.Future` object, which gives you a reference to the task (and its result) as it is completed by the service, or

```
Future<?> submit(Runnable task)
```

that also returns a `Future` object, which gives you a reference to the task as it is completed by the service, and whose `get()` returns `null` upon the completed execution of the `Runnable`.

You can also submit collections of tasks in return for a corresponding collection of `Future` objects. You can do this, for example, with the method

```
List<Future<T>> invokeAll(Collection<? extends Callable<T>> tasks)
                                          throws InterruptedException
```

We can see the general idea behind using tasks and executors in Figure 16-2.

The executor service maintains a pool of threads that it uses to work on the tasks that have been submitted to it. How many threads are used at any one time is very dependent on the Java EE server implementation and the system on which it is deployed. All the application needs to concern itself with is formulating the correct tasks that model the operations in the application and processing the results.

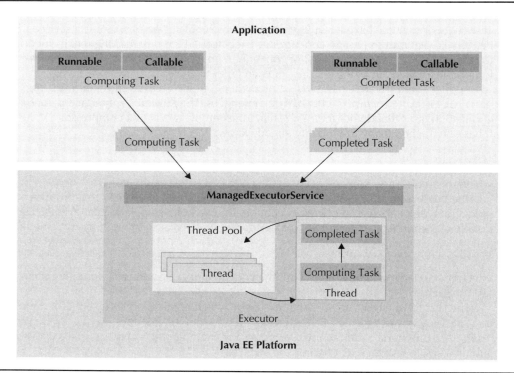

FIGURE 16-2. *Tasks and executors in the Java EE Concurrency API*

Before we look any more into the Java EE Concurrency API, let's look at a relatively simple example.

Concurrent Prime Calculator

We first encountered this algorithm for calculating the highest prime number less than a given upper bound in Chapter 10 when we explored asynchronous Enterprise Bean behavior. In this example, we take the same algorithm in terms of a task that can take a non-trivial amount of time to complete. We will compare the results of executing a number of these tasks sequentially, using traditional Java looping, or concurrently, using the Java EE Concurrency API.

Running the Concurrent Prime Calculator

When you run the application, you will see something like Figure 16-3.

The application takes a maximum upper bound and randomly creates a number of upper bounds less than the maximum. For each of these, the application calculates the largest prime

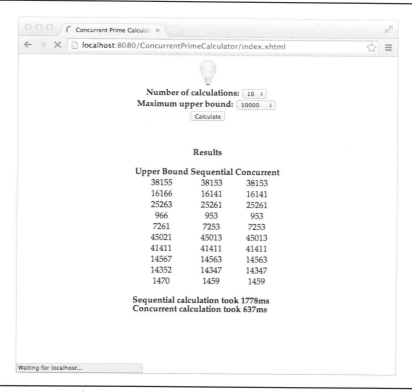

FIGURE 16-3. *Running the Concurrent Prime Calculator*

below it. When you press Submit, the application makes the calculations, first executing the calculations serially, and then concurrently. The page displays the results of the calculations (which will always be the same, regardless of the mode of calculation) and also the time taken to complete the calculations for each mode. From the web page, you can adjust the number of calculations, and you can adjust the maximum upper bound that will be applied. If you spend some time adjusting these variables, you should consistently see that the calculation completes much more quickly when the individual calculations are executed concurrently as compared to when the same individual calculations are executed sequentially. How much more quickly depends on the number of individual calculations; for example, if there is only one calculation, the time will be more or less the same! The difference in speed also depends on the type of Java EE server and system on which you are running the application.

Architecture of the Concurrent Prime Calculator Example

Since we are not going to take a look at all the code in the application, let's look at the overall architecture in Figure 16-4.

The web page is generated by the index.xhtml JavaServer Faces page. The page uses a request scoped-managed bean called ConcurrencyBean. The ConcurrencyBean creates PrimeCalculation objects, one for each of the individual calculations that the application makes by each mode. Each PrimeCalculation object uses a slightly modified version of the PrimeCalculator Enterprise Bean from Chapter 10 to make the calculation. The ConcurrencyBean assembles two lists of the PrimeCalculation objects, one that it iterates through a loop, and the other that it submits to a ManagedExecutorService instance to execute concurrently.

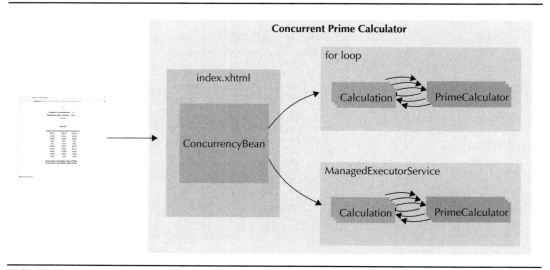

FIGURE 16-4. *Concurrent Prime Calculator architecture*

Code Analysis

First let's look at the `PrimeCalculation` class.

Listing: *The `PrimeCalculation` class*

```
import java.util.concurrent.Callable;
  import javaeems.chapter16.primes.beans.PrimeCalculatorRemote;
  import javax.naming.*;

  public class PrimeCalculation implements Callable<Long> {
      private long upperBound = 10;

      public void setUpperBound(long upperBound) {
          this.upperBound = upperBound;
      }

      @Override
      public Long call() {
          try {
              PrimeCalculatorRemote primeCalculator = InitialContext.doLookup(
                      "java:global/ConcurrentPrimeCalculator/PrimeCalculator");
              return primeCalculator.calculateMaxPrimeBelow(upperBound);
          } catch (NamingException ne) {
              System.out.println(ne.getMessage());
              return (long) -1;
          }
      }

  }
```

Notice that this class implements the `Callable` interface from the Java EE Concurrency API because it is an application task that returns a result, the largest prime lower than the given bound. Notice that within the `call()` method, this class looks up the instance of the `PrimeCalculator` Enterprise Bean to which it will delegate the actual computation.

Now let's look at the `ConcurrencyBean`.

Listing: *The `ConcurrencyBean` class*

```
import javax.enterprise.context.RequestScoped;
  import javax.inject.Named;
  import java.util.*;
  import javax.annotation.Resource;
  import java.util.concurrent.Future;
  import java.util.concurrent.ExecutionException;
  import javax.enterprise.concurrent.ManagedExecutorService;

  @Named("concurrencyBean")
  @RequestScoped
  public class ConcurrencyBean {
      @Resource
      ManagedExecutorService executor;
      private int numberCalculations = 5;
      private long lastParallelTime;
```

```java
    private long lastSequentialTime;

    private List<Long> sequentialResults = null;
    private List<Long> parallelResults = null;
    private List<Long> upperBounds = null;
    private int maxUpperBound = 1000;


    public void reset() {
        this.lastParallelTime = 0;
        this.lastSequentialTime = 0;
        this.sequentialResults = null;
        this.parallelResults = null;
        this.upperBounds = null;
    }

    public int getMaxUpperBound() {
        return this.maxUpperBound;
    }

    public void setMaxUpperBound(int maxUpperBound) {
        this.maxUpperBound = maxUpperBound;
    }

    public int getNumberCalculations() {
        return this.numberCalculations;
    }

    public void setNumberCalculations(int numberCalculations) {
        this.numberCalculations = numberCalculations;
        this.reset();
    }

    public void doCalculate() {
        this.getSequentialResults();
        this.getParallelResults();
    }

    public List<Long> getSequentialResults() {
        if (this.sequentialResults != null) {
            return this.sequentialResults;
        }
        this.sequentialResults = new ArrayList<>();
        long then = System.currentTimeMillis();
        for (Long upperBound : this.getUpperBounds()) {
            PrimeCalculation c = new PrimeCalculation();
            c.setUpperBound(upperBound);
            this.sequentialResults.add(c.call());
        }
        this.lastSequentialTime = System.currentTimeMillis() - then;
        return this.sequentialResults;
    }

    public List<Long> getUpperBounds() {
        if (this.upperBounds == null) {
            this.upperBounds = new ArrayList<>();
            for (int i = 0; i < this.numberCalculations; i++) {
```

```
                    double d = Math.random();
                    long nextUpperBound =
                            (long) (2 + (d * (this.maxUpperBound - 2)));
                    this.upperBounds.add(nextUpperBound);
                }
            }
            return this.upperBounds;
        }

    public Long getLastParallelTime() {
        return this.lastParallelTime;
    }

    public List<Long> getParallelResults() {
        if (this.parallelResults != null) {
            return this.parallelResults;
        }
        this.parallelResults = new ArrayList<>();
        long then = System.currentTimeMillis();
        List<PrimeCalculation> calculations = new ArrayList<>();
        for (Long upperBound : this.getUpperBounds()) {
            PrimeCalculation c = new PrimeCalculation();
            c.setUpperBound(upperBound);
            calculations.add(c);
        }
        try {
            List<Future<Long>> resultList = executor.invokeAll(calculations);
            for (Future<Long> next : resultList) {
                this.parallelResults.add(next.get());
            }
            this.lastParallelTime = System.currentTimeMillis() - then;
            return this.parallelResults;
        } catch (InterruptedException e) {
            System.out.println("The executor encountered an error
                            making the calculation: " + e.getMessage());
        } catch (ExecutionException ee) {
            System.out.println("The calculation threw
                                an error: " + ee.getMessage());
        }
        return new ArrayList<>();
    }

    public Long getLastSequentialTime() {
        return this.lastSequentialTime;
    }

}
```

Notice that this request-scoped bean holds the JavaServer Faces properties that govern the number of calculations it will perform, numberCalculations, and also the variable maxUpperBound controlling the maximum upper bound for the calculations. When the doCalculate() method is called, the ConcurrencyBean creates a single list of randomly generated upper bounds for all the calculations that will be made in the method getUpperBounds().

Next look at the implementation of the getSequentialResults() method. This method uses the list of upper bounds to create PrimeCalculation objects, one with each upper bound, and iterates in a traditional Java `for` loop, calling the `call()` method on each `PrimeCalculation` object that it creates. In this way, the single calling thread of the `getSequentialResults()` method performs each prime number calculation, the next one starting only after the previous one has completed, like a line of single-file traffic on a single-lane country road.

In contrast, the implementation of the `getParallelResults()` creates a list of `PrimeCalculation` objects with the same upper bounds as in the sequential version. Notice that the `ConcurrencyBean` injects an instance of the `ManagedExecutorService` into itself, to which the `getParallelResults()` method submits the list of `PrimeCalculation` objects for execution using the method call `invokeAll()`. It loops through the `Future` object that that this `invokeAll()` method returns, calling `get()` on each one to assemble the results. Notice that since the `get()` method call on the `Future` object blocks until the calculation has completed, this iteration loop waiting on the future objects completes only when all the calculations have been made, though it does know what order the calculations have completed.

You can see that there is slightly more overhead in using the `ManagedExecutorService`, but there is an easy payoff in terms of performance.

The Java EE Concurrency API

We already looked at the `Runnable` and `Callable<V>` interfaces that a concurrent application task must implement to use the executor service. In our example, the class we used for modeling the calculation, other than implementing `Callable`, was just a plain Java class. Such application tasks can in fact be other Java EE components such as the CDI beans we looked at in Chapter 14, though care must be taken when using such objects: the lifecycle of a concurrent task can be unpredictable. The completion of a concurrent task depends on a number of factors outside the nature of the task itself, such as how many other tasks are executing in the executor service, or the resource constraints of the underlying system running the Java EE server. The results are unpredictable if the lifecycle of a concurrent task is ended before the task has been completed. It is better to stick to `@Application` or `@Dependent` scope objects if you choose to implement concurrent tasks as managed objects.

Concurrent task objects do, however, retain all the privileges of the Java EE environment once they have been submitted to an executor service. This is important because the Java EE environment in place when a concurrent task is submitted to the executor may not even exist at the time when the concurrent task is actually executed. This can easily happen, for example, if a request-scoped bean submits the task and does not wait for the result to be computed. The request scope, and all associated information such as the JNDI context and security information about the call, may have been destroyed before the task is executed. This allows concurrent task objects to reliably use services like resource injection and JNDI lookup, such as the lookup of the Enterprise Bean in the Concurrent Prime Calculator example.

ManagedExecutorService and ManagedScheduledExecutorService

The `ManagedExecutorService` interface holds the methods required for submission of concurrent tasks to the service. Additionally, it has methods, which allows the application using the service to shut the service down. The method

```
void shutdown()
```

prevents any new tasks from being submitted to the executor service and puts the service into the shutdown state. Any tasks currently being executed continue to be executed until the last one has completed when the executor enters the terminated state. You can await the terminated state with the blocking call

```
boolean awaitTermination(long timeout,
                         TimeUnit unit)
                         throws InterruptedException
```

If you cannot wait for such a civilized winding down of the service, you can call the method

```
List<Runnable> shutdownNow()
```

which prevents any new tasks from being submitted to the executor service and returns any incomplete tasks without executing them any further.

Under normal circumstances, the ManagedExecutorService instances provided by the Java EE platform are shut down by the Java EE container, in which case any unexecuted tasks are canceled and any in-process tasks are interrupted.

In addition to the ManagedExecutorService, its specialization, the ManagedScheduledExecutorService, offers additional facilities for scheduling the start of execution of application tasks, both at specified times and at specified time intervals.

For example,

```
AlarmCallable myAlarm = new AlarmCallable("ring ring");
myScheduledExecutor.schedule(myAlarm, 8, TimeUnit.HOURS);
```

schedules the given alarm callable to have its call() method in 8 hours' time and

```
BackupTask backup = new BackupTask(BackupTask.LOG_FILES);
Future backup = myScheduledExecutor..scheduleAtFixedRate(
                                      backup, 30, TimeUnit.MINUTES);
```

schedules all the log files to be backed up every 30 minutes.

Obtaining a ManagedExecutorService Instance

The Java EE platform provides two service instances of the ManagedExecutorService for use by Java EE applications, one instance of the ManagedExecutorService, and one of the ManagedScheduledExecutorService. They may either be injected using the @Resource annotation, such as

```
import javax.annotation.Resource;

  public class MyComponent {
     @Resource
       ManagedExecutorService executor;
  ...
  }

  or
```

```
public class MyComponent {
    @Resource
      ManagedScheduledExecutorService scheduledExecutor;
  ...
  }
```

or these instances are available in the JNDI namespace for lookup under the names
`java:comp/DefaultManagedExecutorService` and
`java:comp/DefaultManagedScheduledExecutorService`.

Identifying and Monitoring Concurrent Tasks

It is often useful to be able to add information to a task you have created for later identification and also monitor the progress of a task that you have submitted to the executor service. In order to do this, two additional interfaces are relevant. First, the `ManagedTask` interface gives a standard way to add arbitrary properties to a concurrent task, as well as defining some commonly used identifying properties. Implementing this interface requires a task to implement the method

`Map<String,String> getExecutionProperties()`

while the interface defines static Strings to use as standard keys in the Map, such as `ManagedTask`
`.IDENTITY_NAME`, `ManagedTask.LONGRUNNING_HINT`. These standard keys allow you to give the task a identifying name, and to set a boolean value to indicate whether the task is expected to take a long time to complete or not, respectively.

The other method that implementing `ManagedTask` requires a concurrent task to implement is

`ManagedTaskListener getManagedTaskListener()`

allowing the concurrent task to supply an instance of the `ManagedTaskListener` to the executor service. If the concurrent task does this, the executor service will call the listener back at specific times during the submission and execution of the task.

ManagedTaskListener	Time Called

`void taskSubmitted(Future<?> future,`
`        ManagedExecutorService executor,`
`        Object task)`
	Called after the task has been submitted and before the task has started.

`void taskStarting(Future<?> future,`
`         ManagedExecutorService executor,`
`         Object task)`
	Called when the executor is about to start executing the task.

`void taskAborted(Future<?> future,`
`        ManagedExecutorService executor,`
`        Object task,`
`        Throwable exception)`
	Called whenever the executor has to cancel the task, for example, if the Java EE server is shutting down.

`void taskDone(Future<?> future,`
`        ManagedExecutorService executor,`
`        Object task,`
`        Throwable exception)`
	Called after the task has been executed.

We can see the different states of a `ManagedTask` as it is processed in by an executor service in Figure 16-5.

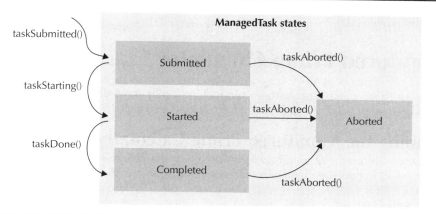

FIGURE 16-5.   *The states of a* ManagedTask

The ManagedThreadFactory

When more complicated execution patterns are required than the submission methods of the executor service allow for, then the Java EE Concurrency API provides the means for Java EE applications to spawn new threads of their own. In the traditional Java SE approach, the application would create a new thread by creating a Runnable and instantiating it, or creating a subclass of Thread and instantiating it by hand. All such threads are outside the control of the Java EE containers and lack the contextual properties Java EE applications need, such as the current transaction and the JNDI naming context. So the Java EE Concurrency API provides an instance of a ManagedThreadFactory, from which new threads can be created. Like the managed tasks of the executor service, threads created from the ManagedThreadFactory carry the entire Java EE context, and so services such as looking up managed objects through JNDI or injecting resources work in such threads.

The instance of the ManagedThreadFactory provided by the Java EE server to a Java EE application is available either to be injected using the @Resource annotation

```
import javax.annotation.Resource;

public class MyComponent {
   @Resource
    ManagedThreadFactory myManagedThreadFactory;
...
}
```

or may be looked up in the JNDI namespace under the reserved name java:comp/ DefaultManagedThreadFactory.

The single method on the ManagedThreadFactory is

```
Thread newThread(Runnable r)
```

which allows you to pass a `Runnable` object, a task of some sort, and receive back a Java EE container-managed thread that you can use to execute it.

Monitored Prime Calculator Example

We will continue our study of concurrent task execution using the Java EE Concurrency API by taking our Prime Calculator example and looking a little more deeply into the task execution, applying some of what we have learned about managed tasks.

Running the Monitored Prime Calculator

When we open up the Monitored Prime Calculator example, we see that we have the same ability to kick off and configure a number of calculations, as shown in Figure 16-6.

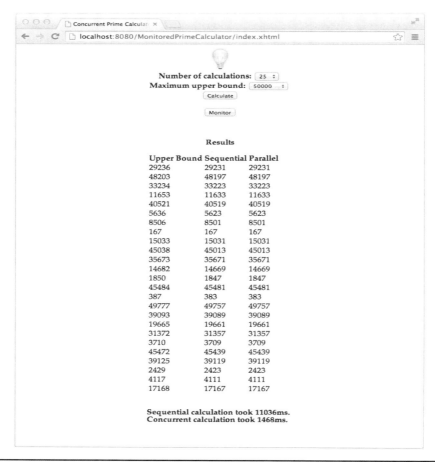

FIGURE 16-6. *A monitored prime calculation*

By clicking the Monitor button, we can bring up another page that monitors each individual calculation as it is executed, shown in Figure 16-7.

As you play with this example, you might notice that while the order of execution of the sequential tasks is entirely predictable (as it should be: they are executing in order within each loop), the order of execution of the concurrent tasks is not.

Architecture of the Monitored Prime Calculator

Let's look at an overall picture of this updated application, shown in Figure 16-8.

In this update, we have added `CalculatorListener` classes that track the progress of each prime calculation. All the `CalculatorListener` instances pass updates to a singleton Enterprise Bean called `MonitorBean`. This in turn notifies a WebSocket endpoint called `MonitorBroadcaster` to which the `monitor.html` web page connects when it first loads. In this way, the `monitor.html` page receives information about every prime calculation task as it completes. Let's take a look at the code.

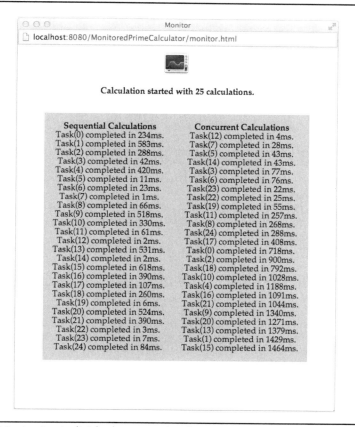

FIGURE 16-7.   *Monitoring individual managed tasks*

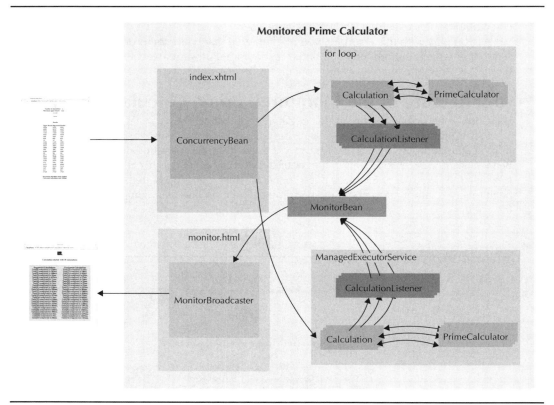

FIGURE 16-8.   *Architecture of the monitored Prime Calculator*

First, the `ConcurrencyBean` managed bean and `PrimeCalculator` Enterprise Beans are largely unchanged, so we will jump straight to the `Calculation` class, which you will recall from earlier manages the prime calculation.

Listing: *The* `Calculation` *class*

```
import javaeems.chapter16.monitoredprimes.beans.MonitorBean;
import java.util.concurrent.Callable;
import javaeems.chapter16.monitoredprimes.beans.PrimeCalculatorRemote;
import javax.enterprise.concurrent.ManagedTask;
import javax.enterprise.concurrent.ManagedTaskListener;
import javax.naming.InitialContext;
import javax.naming.NamingException;
import java.util.*;

  public class Calculation implements Callable<Long>, ManagedTask {
      public static String SUBMIT_TIME_KEY = "SUBMIT_TIME_KEY";
```

```
public static String START_TIME_KEY = "START_TIME_KEY";
public static String END_TIME_KEY = "END_TIME_KEY";
public static String EXECUTION_TYPE = "EXECUTION_TYPE";
public static String SEQUENTIAL = "sequential";
public static String CONCURRENT = "concurrent";

private final long upperBound;
private final MonitorBean mb;
private final Map<String,String> executionProperties = new HashMap<>();

public Calculation(MonitorBean mb, int id, long upperBound, String type) {
    this.mb = mb;
    this.upperBound = upperBound;
    this.executionProperties.put(EXECUTION_TYPE, type);
    this.executionProperties.put(
            ManagedTask.IDENTITY_NAME, Integer.toString(id));
}

@Override
public Long call() {
    try {
        PrimeCalculatorRemote primeCalculator = InitialContext.doLookup(
                "java:global/MonitoredPrimeCalculator/PrimeCalculator");
        return primeCalculator.calculateMaxPrimeBelow(upperBound);
    } catch (NamingException ne) {
        System.out.println(ne.getMessage());
        return (long) -1;
    }
}

@Override
public ManagedTaskListener getManagedTaskListener() {
    return new CalculationListener(this.mb);
}

@Override
public Map<String,String> getExecutionProperties() {
    return this.executionProperties;
}
}
```

Notice that the `Calculation` class now implements the `ManagedTask` interface from the Java EE Concurrency API. This requires it to expose a `Map` of execution properties and produce an instance of a `ManagedTaskListener`. The `Calculation` class is evolved to use the execution properties to store its execution type: sequential or concurrent, and the upper bound of the prime calculation. It also defines keys for its execution properties to store the submission, start, and end time of its execution, but does not set the values. Notice also that the `Calculation` class looks up a reference to the singleton `MonitorBean` Enterprise Bean that it uses to construct the instances of `CalculatorListener` it produces.

The `CalculatorListener` class has an instance variable to refer to the `MonitorBean`, as we can see from its code.

```java
import javaeems.chapter16.monitoredprimes.beans.MonitorBean;
import javax.enterprise.concurrent.ManagedTaskListener;
import javax.enterprise.concurrent.ManagedExecutorService;
import javax.enterprise.concurrent.ManagedTask;
import java.util.concurrent.Future;

public class CalculationListener implements ManagedTaskListener {
    private final MonitorBean mb;

    public CalculationListener(MonitorBean mb) {
        this.mb = mb;
    }

    @Override
    public void taskSubmitted(Future<?> future,
                              ManagedExecutorService executor,
                              Object task) {
        ((ManagedTask) task).getExecutionProperties().put(
                              Calculation.SUBMIT_TIME_KEY,
                              Long.toString(System.currentTimeMillis()));
    }

    @Override
    public void taskAborted(Future<?> future,
                              ManagedExecutorService executor,
                              Object task,
                              Throwable exception) {
        System.out.println("Task Aborted: " + task);
    }

    @Override
    public void taskDone(Future<?> future,
                              ManagedExecutorService executor,
                              Object task,
                              Throwable exception) {
        ((ManagedTask) task).getExecutionProperties().put(
                    Calculation.END_TIME_KEY,
                    Long.toString(System.currentTimeMillis()));
        mb.taskCompleted(task);
    }

    @Override
    public void taskStarting(Future<?> future,
                          ManagedExecutorService executor,
                          Object task) {
        ((ManagedTask) task).getExecutionProperties().put(
                          Calculation.START_TIME_KEY,
                          Long.toString(System.currentTimeMillis()));
    }

}
```

You can also see from its code that in implementing the `ManagedTaskListener` interface, it sets the submission, start, and end time as execution properties of the task, the `Calculation` object, to which it listens. Additionally, when the task is complete, it notifies the `MonitorBean`.

The `CalculationListener` interface is called only during the concurrent calculation, at some point after the submission of the corresponding `Calculation` instance to the `ManagedExecutorService`. Let's look briefly at the sequential calculation in the `ConcurrencyBean` class.

Listing: *Excerpt from the `ConcurrencyBean` class*

```
public List<Long> getSequentialResults() {

if (this.sequentialResults != null) {
return this.sequentialResults;
}
this.sequentialResults = new ArrayList<>();
long then = System.currentTimeMillis();
int id = 0;
for (Long upperBound : this.getUpperBounds()) {
Calculation c = new Calculation(mb,
id++,
upperBound,
Calculation.SEQUENTIAL);
c.getExecutionProperties().put(
Calculation.SUBMIT_TIME_KEY,
Long.toString(System.currentTimeMillis()));
c.getExecutionProperties().put(
Calculation.START_TIME_KEY,
Long.toString(System.currentTimeMillis()));
long l = c.call();
c.getExecutionProperties().put(
Calculation.END_TIME_KEY,
Long.toString(System.currentTimeMillis()));
this.mb.taskCompleted(c);
this.sequentialResults.add(c.call());
}
this.lastSequentialTime = System.currentTimeMillis() - then;
return this.sequentialResults;
}
```

We can see that the execution properties to do with timing are set "by hand" by the application code, as is the notification of completion to the `MonitorBean`.

You may be wondering why the `CalculationListener` does not look up the `MonitorBean` itself, rather than relying on a reference to be passed in to its constructor. The answer is that while a managed task inherits the Java EE calling context of its caller, the `ManagedTaskListener` instance that they produce does not necessarily do the same. So it is good practice not to depend on the full Java EE calling context being available from within a `ManagedTaskListener`.

Whether sequential or concurrent, the `MonitorBean` is notified as each calculation completes, and each `Calculation` object carries with it in its execution properties the timing information for its execution.

Listing: *The MonitorBean class*

```
import javaeems.chapter16.monitoredprimes.web.Calculation;
import javaeems.chapter16.monitoredprimes.web.MonitorBroadcaster;
import javax.ejb.Singleton;
import javax.ejb.LocalBean;
import java.util.*;
import javax.enterprise.concurrent.ManagedTask;


@Singleton
@LocalBean
public class MonitorBean {
    private final List<MonitorBroadcaster> listeners = new ArrayList<>();

    public void add(MonitorBroadcaster pbe) {
        this.listeners.add(pbe);
    }

    public void remove(MonitorBroadcaster pbe) {
        this.listeners.remove(pbe);
    }

    public void calculationStarted(int numberCalculations) {
        for (MonitorBroadcaster pbe : this.listeners) {
            pbe.sendUpdate("xx");
            pbe.sendUpdate("iCalculation started with " +
                        numberCalculations + " calculations.");
        }
    }

    public void taskAborted(Object task) {
        Calculation calculation = (Calculation) task;
        for (MonitorBroadcaster pbe : this.listeners) {
            pbe.sendUpdate("iError in Task: " + calculation.
                getExecutionProperties().get(ManagedTask.IDENTITY_NAME));
        }
    }

    public void taskCompleted(Object task) {
        for (MonitorBroadcaster pbe : this.listeners) {
            if (task instanceof Calculation) {
                Calculation c = (Calculation) task;
                String prefix;
                if (c.getExecutionProperties()
                  .get(Calculation.EXECUTION_TYPE)
                  .equals(Calculation.CONCURRENT)) {
                    prefix = "c";
                } else {
                    prefix = "s";
```

```
            }
            long submitTime = Long.parseLong(c.getExecutionProperties()
                                   .get(Calculation.SUBMIT_TIME_KEY));
            long startTime = Long.parseLong(c.getExecutionProperties()
                                   .get(Calculation.START_TIME_KEY));
            long endTime = Long.parseLong(c.getExecutionProperties()
                                   .get(Calculation.END_TIME_KEY));
            int id = Integer.parseInt(c.getExecutionProperties()
                                   .get(ManagedTask.IDENTITY_NAME));
            pbe.sendUpdate(prefix + "Task(" + id +
                    ") completed in " + (endTime-startTime) + "ms.");
        } else {
            pbe.sendUpdate(task.toString());
        }
    }
}
```

Looking at the `MonitorBean`, we can see that it allows instances of the `MonitorBroadcaster` WebSocket endpoint to be registered for updates and removed when done. When the `MonitorBean` receives a task completion notification, it notifies its list of `MonitorBroadcaster` endpoints. In turn, the `MonitorBroadcaster` endpoints update the client WebSocket, residing in the `monitor.html` page, with a simple format of a text message that allows the results to be tabulated as they are sent.

In this way, the `monitor.html` page can show the completion of each individual computation as it happens, whether in the sequential or concurrent calculation.

Summary

Many hands make light work!

In this chapter, we looked at the general principles of concurrent programming in the context of multicore and multiprocessor system architectures. We explored the concepts of a Java EE concurrent task and an executor, the main elements of the Java EE Concurrency API. We looked at the two kinds of executor service available to Java EE applications for use in creating concurrent applications, and by means of an example based on time-consuming mathematical calculations, we compared traditional sequential execution of a task with managed task execution based on the Java EE Concurrency API. We looked at the facilities available in the APIs to track task execution, and possibly convinced ourselves that there are a large number of compute-intensive tasks that can benefit from being processed in parallel.

Index

Join the Largest Tech Community in the World

 Download the latest software, tools, and developer templates

 Get exclusive access to hands-on trainings and workshops

 Grow your professional network through the Oracle ACE Program

 Publish your technical articles – and get paid to share your expertise

Join the Oracle Technology Network
Membership is free. Visit oracle.com/technetwork

@OracleOTN   facebook.com/OracleTechnologyNetwork

Reach More than 700,000 Oracle Customers with Oracle Publishing Group

Connect with the Audience that Matters Most to Your Business

Oracle Magazine
The Largest IT Publication in the World
Circulation: 550,000
Audience: IT Managers, DBAs, Programmers, and Developers

Profit
Business Insight for Enterprise-Class Business Leaders to
Help Them Build a Better Business Using Oracle Technology
Circulation: 100,000
Audience: Top Executives and Line of Business Managers

Java Magazine
The Essential Source on Java Technology, the Java
Programming Language, and Java-Based Applications
Circulation: 125,000 and Growing Steady
Audience: Corporate and Independent Java Developers,
Programmers, and Architects

For more information
or to sign up for a FREE
subscription:
Scan the QR code to visit
Oracle Publishing online.